Good Listener

Meditations on Music and Pauline Oliveros

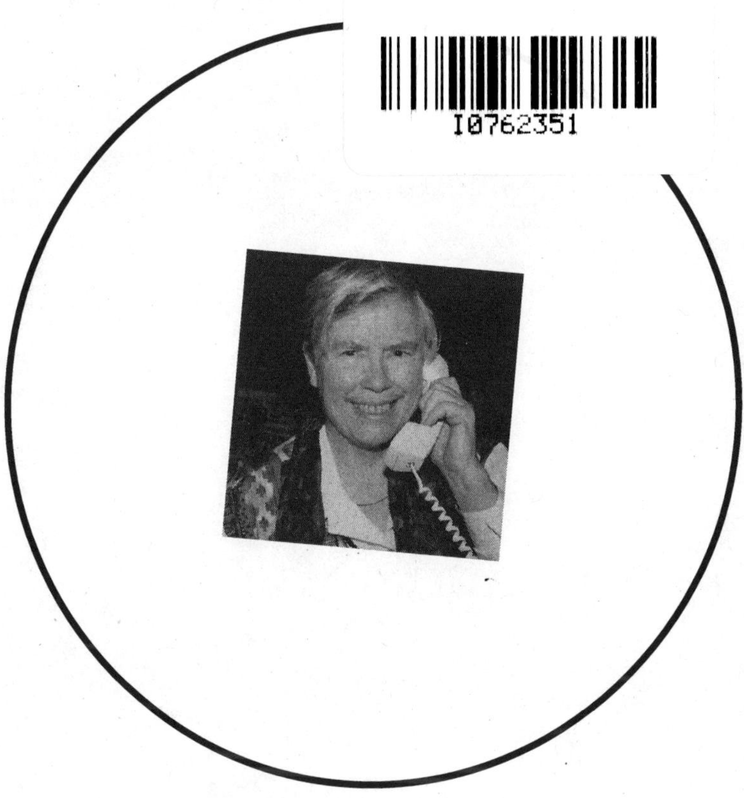

Michael Ned Holte

Sming Sming Books

Good Listener

Meditations on Music and Pauline Oliveros

Michael Ned Holte

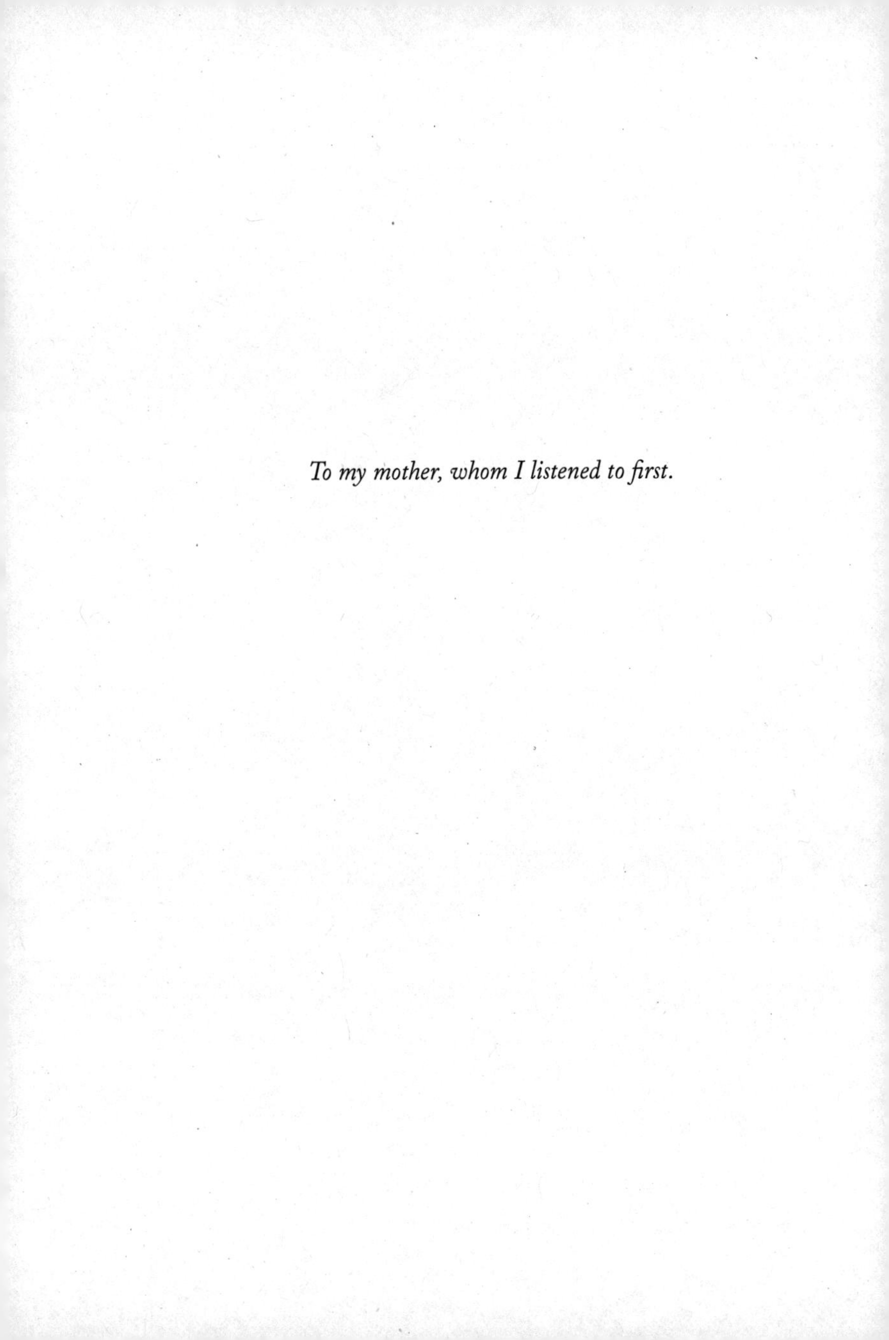

To my mother, whom I listened to first.

1

What constitutes your musical universe?

These five words, in the form of a question, constitute *Sonic Meditation XXI*, the shortest of the language-based series of twenty-five meditations initiated by Pauline Oliveros in the early 1970s. Written while Oliveros was teaching at University of California San Diego, these meditations are both explicitly pedagogical (they teach us how to listen) and implicitly functional as, or like, text scores (they are music). They are accessible, intended for practicing musicians and non-specialists alike. This is how Oliveros introduces them in her *Sonic Meditations* (1974):

> Sonic Meditations are intended for group work over a long period of time with regular meetings. No special skills are necessary. Any persons who are willing to commit themselves can participate. The ♀ Ensemble to whom these meditations are dedicated has found that non-verbal meetings intensify the results of these meditations and help provide an atmosphere which is conducive to such activity. With continuous work some of the following becomes possible with Sonic Meditations: Heightened states of awareness or expanded consciousness, changes in physiology and psychology from known and unknown tensions to relaxations which gradually become permanent. These changes may represent a tuning of mind and body. The group may develop positive energy which can influence others who are less experienced. Members of the Group may achieve greater awareness and sensitivity to each other. Music is a welcome by-product of this activity.

Most of the *Sonic Meditations* are directional and generate a specific, yet open-ended activity. One (*XII*) asks participants to "Choose a word. Listen to it mentally. Slowly and gradually begin to voice this word by allowing each tiny part of it to sound extremely prolonged. Repeat for a long time." Another rather sublime example (*V*) instructs, "Take a walk at night. Walk so silently that the bottoms of your feet become ears." But *Sonic Mediation XXI* is different.

What constitutes your musical universe?

It doesn't ask for activity, besides pondering. What constitutes *my* musical universe? The question is concise, but the answer is potentially as vast as the last of those five words implies. In a group context, one can assume there is an expectation that a participant might share their answer. In 2019, I taught a class at CalArts called Pauline Oliveros for Artists. *Sonic Meditation XXI* was among the scores and meditations we considered. I was amazed at how earnestly my students attended to the question, and how (seemingly) easily, concisely they had each mapped out their musical universe, some content to describe their sound environment in the given moment of reflection. Others simply named some bands they were into! We had a productive conversation about the proximity of "sound" and "music," and how those terms are and are not related. "Music is a welcome by-product of this activity," Oliveros noted at the outset of her meditations. As I imagine it, a musical universe is vast, but not nearly as vast as the whole universe of sound.

By comparison to my students, my own confrontation with *Sonic Meditation XXI* was bewildering, overwhelming, too vast. In 2020, I made a first attempt to describe my musical universe by considering the past, detailing every more or less crystalline memory of my relationship to music. This started with a trip with my family to the Grand Ole Opry in Nashville at the tender age of four, when I had little awareness, let alone agency, about what music I would consume. There was a lot of country music, at home, on vinyl, on 8-track, on the radio, on *Hee Haw*, at the 4-H Fair: Patsy Cline, Mac Wiseman, Charley Pride, Ronnie Milsap, George Jones. Waylon, Willie, and the Boys.

The narrative gradually revealed a sense of taste, so to speak, with desire for specific songs, like Debby Boone's "You Light Up My Life," which I listened to repeatedly on a 45 record. Debby Boone on repeat would gradually be replaced by Michael Jackson, then Prince, then the Beastie Boys, then Metallica, then Public Enemy and Sonic Youth. Format is inevitably connected to these music memories, which included radio (*"Chantilly Lace" on AM radio while my dad gets ready for work.*), the arrival of MTV (*Watching the world premiere of Michael Jackson's "Thriller," all fourteen minutes of it, in my grandma's family room.*), cassettes (*Iron Maiden's "Stranger in a Strange Land" on cassette for my fourteenth birthday, with Eddie, their skeletal mascot, in sci-fi drag, and the agreeably toxic plastic smell of the cassette packaging still lingering in my nostrils.*), and even my own decidedly failed efforts to learn how to play the guitar (*Black Kramer guitar and Marshall microstack. Guitar lessons from Mike Kalember of local heavy metal favorite Raven Bitch. Learning the chords for "Iron Man" and not much else. It wasn't the teacher's fault.*).

This may or may not be what Oliveros had in mind when she described the *Sonic Meditations* producing "heightened states of awareness or expanded consciousness, changes in physiology and psychology from known and unknown tensions to relaxations which gradually become permanent." The effort to resurface these musical memories was a fun exercise, if sometimes embarrassing. (Joe Brainard's brilliant *I Remember* was an obvious precedent.) I petered out around the end of high school, with an awareness that my first year of college was in some sense a "big bang" in the expansion of my musical universe which hopefully continues some thirty years later. But this focus on the past seemed like a limited way to approach Oliveros's prompt. I was left wanting and envious of my students' ability to so succinctly describe the immediate *present* of their musical universe. And I also considered that the universe has a future, however uncertain.

Speaking of which, I have not yet listened to anything today, at least not intentionally.

2

All of these Sonic Meditations are intended to begin with observation of the breath cycle.

Perhaps I don't think about breathing enough. Involuntary, unconscious, ongoing: It never goes on my to-do list. But perhaps it should.

From March 1, 2006 until December 31, 2021, I maintained a daily log. It began as a way to keep track of my activities, particularly those related to my work as a critic and a curator. I would note every exhibition I saw, every studio visit, every lecture, every lunch meeting. It also included things I was reading and occasional life events, both significant and banal. And every year, on January 1, I would begin a new log by opening a new Word document. More recently, it took the form of a Google Doc. Either way, it was searchable, and therefore became a useful tool whenever I needed to remember when something specific had taken place.

The log expanded year by year, accounting for more things: travel, long walks, my weight, cooking, email correspondence. I have sometimes considered that this gradual accumulation of minutiae is the most important thing I've ever written, even if I was the only one who would ever read it. But it was always intended as a self-reporting of data, never a diary meant for consumption. I grew to understand the project as a kind of daily accounting for *work*, however loosely defined. Simultaneously, I have come to realize that one who teaches at an art school, writes criticism, and curates exhibitions will inevitably carry a loose, but expansive definition of work.

In 2020, I regularized an occasional tic of my logging by preserving one headline (almost) every day from the *New York*

Times, which I read every day. "Pope Francis Apologizes After Slapping Away a Clinging Pilgrim" was the first headline I noted to start the year. There was no specific criteria for what kind of headline I would choose. They came from articles about world events, politics, art and culture, technology, and astrophysics. Sometimes I was simply drawn to the use of language by the *Times* editors, which also marked a constantly shifting moment in time. I understood the project as a way to account for my considerable time spent with the "newspaper," by which I mean the online version. But I also thought of it as a modest homage to the *Today* series by On Kawara, in which the artist made a fastidious painting of the day's date along with a storage box that included a section of the day's newspaper (most often the *New York Times*) from whatever city he happened to be in at the time. On February 2, 2020, the headline I selected was, "Coronavirus Looks Increasingly Like a Pandemic, Experts Say." Suddenly, a new vocabulary consumed the news: alien (to me) terms like "COVID-19" and "coronavirus," and previously unknown (to me) phrases such as "social distancing," "flattening the curve," and "contactless delivery." All of this was "unprecedented" and, suddenly, "the new normal."

During the long haul of the pandemic, I spent considerably more time at home, and among other changes, I listened to more music than I had ever listened to before in my life—and I have always listened to a lot of music. I began to keep track of most everything I listened to with intentionality in my daily log. This primarily consisted of albums, which most often were files streamed from Spotify, but sometimes took the form of compact discs played in my car (which I've had since March 20, 2006, according to my daily log), or actual vinyl records. Some days I listened to eight, nine, ten, eleven albums, especially on days that weren't consumed by teaching and meetings on Zoom. I would listen while making elaborate salads, reading for class, or just watching the shadows move around the inside of the house over the course of the day. Occasionally I would escape to the park for exercise and fresh air and a change of scenery, invariably with music playing through my earphones. And I would dutifully document everything I listened to, as if attempting to draw a map of my musical universe while also observing a continued, if gradual, expansion of that map.

I have not yet listened to anything today, at least not music. I did listen to the news on the radio while driving to and from the farmer's market. Currently, I can hear the traffic whizzing by on Arlington, and a little kid squealing a house or two away. I can also hear the by-now familiar oscillations of the refrigerator and the click-clack of my fingers on the keyboard as I write this.

3

Sitting in a parking lot on my third day of article writing. I could listen to the stereophony of car starter gagglings, motor wigglings, door squeals, and "bllaps" forever. It's almost like Debussy, compared to Saturday's Wagnerian bulldozer.

In 1968, Oliveros shared "Some Sound Observations" with the readers of the third issue of *Source: Music of the Avant-Garde*. As the punning title suggests, the diaristic article is shot through with the composer's characteristic humor, along with a few admonishments. In brief paragraphs, it describes sounds occurring in the immediate present: the "deep drone" of a bulldozer "eating away at the hillside," off and on for several days; the rustle of trees which reminds her of tape hiss; a performance of Robert Ashley's *The Wolfman* (1964), which continues to reverberate indefinitely: "I attended dinner at a Syrian restaurant and ate a concert with my Wolfman ears."

Some of these sound observations attempt to jostle the stubborn foundations of classical music: "Why shouldn't a music department in a university devote itself entirely to music composed since 1950? Without a substantial body of new literature and instrumentation, the symphony and opera will become defunct—dead horses in the twenty-first century. Who Cares." Some address the limitations of concert halls and recording studios to adapt to the emerging needs of electronic music and its composers who will gallop into the twenty-first century.

Some of these sound observations are memories, transporting her from the present of her desk in the suburbs of San Diego to elsewhere in time and space: "When I was sixteen, my accordion teacher taught me to hear combination tones. The accordion is particularly able to produce them if you squeeze hard enough."

Or: "In New York, Terry Riley led me fifteen blocks out of our way to hear a building ventilator." This memory is immediately followed by a question that transports her (and us) inward, or perhaps everywhere at once: "I wonder what microbes hear?"

Here and throughout these observations, memories, questions, factoids, and speculations, Oliveros evokes the hallucinatory and prods gently at the sublime, nimbly transforming auditory sensation into words. In this, one of her earliest published texts, she plants the seeds for her *Sonic Mediations* a few years later, and what she would synthesize, some two decades later, as Deep Listening. But for the moment, her ears are fully open ("MY EARS FEEL LIKE CAVES," she blares, in the reverberating wake of Ashley's *Wolfman*) to the past, present, and future.

4

I first encountered the music of Pauline Oliveros in 1999, on Sonic Youth's mind-bending, millennium-ending, double-length album *SYR4: Goodbye 20th Century*. In some sense, it is an album of covers of works by significant avant-garde composers. These included some familiar names: John Cage, Steve Reich, Christian Wolff, Yoko Ono. It also included composers whose names and music were unknown to me at the time, including Takehisa Kosugi (who is a guest on the album), Cornelius Cardew, George Maciunas, James Tenney, and Pauline Oliveros. Like so many things about Y2K, it was both hello and goodbye, celebration and funeral.

Oliveros's composition, *Six for New Time (For Sonic Youth)*, was commissioned by Sonic Youth for the occasion. Just over eight minutes in length, it plays to the group's ability to summon a thick cacophony of electric guitars that is just barely hammered into place with insistent percussion. Here, the squall builds up slowly, with the four usual members of SY (Kim Gordon, Thurston Moore, Lee Ranaldo, drummer Steve Shelley) augmented with occasional member Jim O'Rourke and virtuoso percussionist William Winant: six performers for *New Time*.

I was always intrigued by its lyrics, solemnly incanted like prayers by Moore.

This one
And
This one
And
This one . . .

Which "one"?, I wondered. And what was that about "Hell's Angels in a pink van"?

I didn't know anything about Oliveros at the time, so I didn't have context for understanding the work on her terms, but nevertheless it seemed to fit the band like an old glove. Like their version of Wolff's *Burdocks* (1970–1971) or Tenney's *Having Never Written a Note for Percussion* (1971), they made it their own. (*Six for New Time* is the only newly commissioned work on the album.) Only later would I realize its strangeness—Oliveros rarely worked with guitar, before or since; and the fragmentary lyrics were a poem written by Oliveros's partner IONE, a commission inside a commission. But it also points to her eagerness to work with others, in diverse contexts, to push her own boundaries, to keep moving and not become a "dead horse" upon arrival in the twenty-first century. Only today would I consider it was a missed opportunity for her to not play on the album, as Kosugi and Wolff do. I am left to imagine her accordion, swelling through the circuits of her Expanded Instrument System, alongside the dense thicket of Sonic Youth feedback.

I encountered the original score for *Six for New Time*, built around a lopsided hexagon (or cube in perspective), in Oliveros's papers held by the Olin Library at Mills College in October 2015, just a few weeks after meeting the composer. What sequence of serendipities led to this moment? Or was it a slow pursuit that had built up gradually but determinedly, just like Oliveros's composition?

Good fortune . . .
No time . . .
Time . . .
Being . . .

5

Today I am looking at and listening to some of James Tenney's *Postal Pieces*. As the title suggests, these are pieces—scores—printed on postcards and intended for mail delivery. In this sense they echo the earlier scores of George Brecht and other artists who were part of the Fluxus movement, as well as the mail art of Ray Johnson. Most are written instructions, though a few, including *Having Never Written a Note for Percussion* (1971), make inventive use of Western notation. Each of these pieces is dedicated to fellow composers, including John Bergamo, Alison Knowles, La Monte Young, Harold Budd, Philip Corner, Susan Allen, Max Neuhaus, and Pauline Oliveros. It's easy to see each of these scores as a sure sign of admiration and affection, delivered by the postal service.

The *Postal Pieces* were composed between 1954 and 1971, and therefore coincide with the earliest of Oliveros's *Sonic Meditations*. Several call for a small ensemble, including *Swell Piece No. 2* (March 1971), the work Tenney dedicated to Oliveros. (Two other *Swell* pieces were dedicated to Alison Knowles and La Monte Young, respectively.)

SWELL PIECE NO. 2 (for any five or more different sustaining instruments):

for Pauline Oliveros

Each performer plays A-440, beginning as softly as possible, building up to a maximum intensity, then fading away again into (individual) silence. This process is repeated by each performer in a way that is rhythmically independent of any other performer, until a previously agreed-upon length of time has elapsed. Within each tone, as little change of pitch or timbre as possible.

The gradually swelling form recalls several of Oliveros's *Sonic Meditations*. Most of the *Sonic Meditations* are built around an idea of individuals gaining awareness of their own bodies before gradually finding a group identity. *Teach Yourself to Fly*, the first of the *Sonic Meditations*, initiates this motif:

> Any number of persons sit in a circle facing the center. Illuminate the space with dim blue light. Begin by simply observing your own breathing. Always be an observer. Gradually allow your breathing to become audible. Then gradually introduce your voice. Allow your vocal cords to vibrate in any mode which occurs naturally. Allow the intensity to increase very slowly. Continue as long as possible naturally, and until all others are quiet, always observing your own breath cycle.
>
> Variation: Translate voice to an instrument.

Tenney's *Swell Piece No. 2* is likely an homage to the *Sonic Meditations*, but I consider that its title might also refer to the accordion, Oliveros's longtime instrument of choice, with its swelling bellows that double the lungs as they process the air and pump blood through the body. ("Begin by simply observing your own breathing.") And given her appreciation of puns, one might also consider another meaning of the title and imagine her replying to his postcard with one of her own: "Dear Jim, that was a swell piece you sent me. Here's one for you. Pauline"

6

The swell of the accordion, with its bellows constantly expanding and contracting, also calls to mind the mandala Oliveros introduced in the early 1970s as both a pedagogical and compositional tool. In its earliest and most basic form, her mandala is a circle with a dot in the center, with the circle representing awareness and the dot representing attention. Later, she revised the terms to global attention and focal attention. Clearly borrowing from Eastern spiritual practices, which Oliveros discusses at length in her text "MMM: Meditation/Mandala/Music" (first delivered as a lecture at the Walker Art Center in 1980), the mandala also represented a break from the burdens of Western classical tradition, a rebuke of the determined linearity of that tradition's musical notation (reading left to right) and understanding of time. Oliveros's subsequent mandala-like scores developed in graphic and musical complexity, but active listening is always (and often literally) at the center of their interpretation.

For Oliveros, awareness and attention are not fixed states, but constantly in flux, a listening continuum between passive hearing and active listening. One can learn to train their attention, and Oliveros's *Sonic Meditations* and much of the work that followed attended to that practice and its implications. These compositions depend on the active engagement of performers responding to one another and/or the larger sound environment. Her later theory and practice of Deep Listening emerges out of this same relationship:

> *Deep Listening* for me is learning to expand the perception of sounds to include the whole space/time continuum of sound–encountering the vastness and complexities as much as possible. Simultaneously one ought to be able to target a sound or sequence of sounds as a focus within the space/time continuum and to perceive the detail or trajectory of the sound or sequence of sounds.

This morning I am listening to a hip-hop mix, delivered via Spotify according to the algorithms that somehow define me as a listening subject. My starting place was J Dilla's *Donuts* (2006), but after that I have been in the hands of an artificial intelligence. I oscillate between attraction to many of the songs Spotify chooses for me and the queasy repulsion I feel at the notion of a machine thinking it knows what I want to listen to (and the fact that it is sometimes correct). I'm also attending to too many emails and preparing for a long day of Zoom meetings, while also writing this. Admittedly, my listening is hardly deep or focused right now, but there is nevertheless a need for music, even as a distant soundtrack for my cluttered head, drawing an outer ring around my day.

7

When I taught my seminar Pauline Oliveros for Artists, I made a mandala diagram with a circle and a picture of Oliveros in the middle. The picture was cropped from a color snapshot of Oliveros, holding a telephone handset up to ear and smiling broadly: always listening. I shared it with the class. I envisioned the course as one that took Oliveros—meaning her music but also her writing and teaching—as a focal point for our collective attention, for the three hours that we gathered together every week. By design, we also frequently expanded outward, into a variety of subjects and texts, while always inevitably returning to Oliveros as our center.

We read and considered Valerie Solanas's *SCUM Manifesto* (self-published in 1967), alongside our listening to Oliveros's *To Valerie Solanas and Marilyn Monroe, in Recognition of their Desperation* (composed in 1970), and even looked at Alice Neel's intimate, life-size painting of Andy Warhol, shirtless and corseted two years after being shot in the abdomen by Solanas. We read Karen Barad's essay "Nature's Queer Performativity" (2011) in conjunction with our listening to Oliveros's *Primordial/Lift* (1998), a composition inspired by a predicted tilting of the Earth's axis. We contemplated Oliveros's pioneering work in electronic music and her book of collected writing, provocatively titled *Software for People* (1984), as premonitions of Donna Haraway's *Cyborg Manifesto*, the first version of which was published in 1985.

We escaped our classroom to visit other parts of CalArts that remained mysterious and unknown to many of my art students, including the gamelan studio, with its extraordinary collection of percussion instruments from Bali and Indonesia, and the synth studio, with its vintage Serge modular synthesizers. We also went outside, to perform some of the *Sonic Meditations*, "enhanc[ing] or paraphras[ing] the auditory environment so perfectly that a listener cannot distinguish between the real sounds of the environment and the performed sounds" while also "becom[ing] performers by not performing" (*Ear Ly* or *Sonic Meditation XVI*). The outer rim of our awareness gradually expanded to include the campus environment—birds, the rustle of trees, the distant chatter of ambulating students, the rattling fan of an old HVAC system—and well beyond the edge of campus, to the almost rhythmic rumble of big trucks on the nearby freeway and the whistle of a jet flying overhead. And we seemed to draw closer to Oliveros every time we stretched the limits of our attention.

8

Yesterday I revisited the exhibition *Witch Hunt* (2021–2022) at the Hammer Museum. One of the works included is a video installation by the artist duo Pauline Boudry / Renate Lorenz, titled *Telepathic Improvisation* (2017). The work is an interpretation of a score by Pauline Oliveros of the same name, which is also the second part of *Sonic Meditation III*:

Telepathic Improvisation

To the musicians with varied or like instruments:

Tuning—each musician in turn sits or stands in front of the audience for a few minutes. The audience is asked to observe the musician carefully and try to imagine the sound of his or her instrument. The audience is instructed to close eyes and attempt to visualize the musician, then send a sound to the musician by hearing it mentally. The musician waits until he or she receives an impression of a sound mentally, then he or she produces the sound. Members of the audience who have successfully "hit the target" raise their hands as feedback to the musician.

In the interpretation, the audience is invited to communicate telepathically with the four performers in the video, a tableau set on a spare black stage. The performers are stylized (and stylish) in red and white garments that recall jumpsuits and pajamas. There is stage lighting in the background, a guitar which is eventually used, and blocky white platforms—an homage, I'm guessing, to similar kinetic objects made by the artist Robert Breer, who was involved with Experiments in Art and Technology (E.A.T.)—that move around the space, occasionally carrying a performer strumming the guitar, a camera, and a fog machine. There is a giant pair of handcuffs that dangle ominously above the stage. I am thinking about this set, in relationship to the pictures I've seen of Oliveros and the ♀ Ensemble, consisting mostly of her students from UC San Diego, performing the *Sonic Meditations* on a large blanket on the grass. Both conjure a sense of openness, experimentation, and (studious) play. The numerous blank, nearly empty moments in the video remind me of the blank, nearly empty moments at the beginning of a performance of any of Oliveros's *Sonic Meditations*. ("Begin by simply observing your own breathing.") This space/time can be decidedly awkward for the uninitiated, but there is something generous and powerful in letting something be/come.

Boudry / Lorenz have explicitly defined their projects as queer and "trans-chronic." In the case of *Telepathic Improvisation* they "explore the ways in which others (including other objects) might become part of our striving for alternative political and sexual imaginations," and collide Oliveros into a revolutionary speech by Ulrike Meinhof, which she had adapted from Black Panther Fred Hampton: "Protest is when I say I don't like this. Resistance is when I put an end to what I don't like." Their version of *Telepathic Improvisation* confirms for me that Oliveros, the *Sonic Meditations*, and the ♀ Ensemble who performed them in the early 1970s, were always already queer, trans-chronic, and political.

"Protest is when I say I don't like this. Resistance is when I put an end to what I don't like." Revolution is pushing forward: creating a new understanding of space/time and the unfolding set of possibilities in its becoming.

9

"I wonder what an androgynous musical form would be?," Oliveros asks in her "Rags and Patches," a delightful, delirious text from 1974 that patches together epistolary exchanges (with poet and Oliveros-lover Lynn Lonidier, with the Feminist Art Program at CalArts); madcap adventures in the Land of Oz (or is it Alice's Wonderland?); considerations of Jill Johnston, Charlotte Moorman, and Sappho; and manifesto-like moments, like this incredulous passage:

> Browsing in a psychology text, I came across the notion that music is a phallic phenomenon because it penetrates the ear! What a physiological displacement! Did someone lose his body? Come now, Freudians, one can *receive* music but also actively penetrate it, not to mention all the other finer variations. Maybe we need banana shaped ears. Maybe the psychologist assumed that only men (probably dead men) write music. According to a certain social paradigm, it follows then, that maybe only women should listen to it! or eat it! Of course that paradigm leaves out a large assortment of very fine variations in relationships. How many of you out there think you are in the minority? If everyone came out of the closet the world would change overnight—Rattle them bones! Rattle them cages!

"Rags and Patches" was initially written as the fifth article in a series, starting in 1972, for the publication *Numus West*. For whatever reason, the fifth of these was not published until a decade later, in the anthology *Software for People*. In her retrospective introduction to the series, Oliveros notes that "Rags and Patches" was, "too long to be included and perhaps too outrageous for the direction *Numus West* wished to represent." Too outrageous or too outraged? One wonders. Or perhaps too androgynous? (Had anyone previously wondered what an *androgynous musical form* would be?)

“Divisions Underground,” the fourth article in this series, begins to set the scene that would follow, introducing us to its protagonist the Patchwork Girl of Oz, whose ears are made of gold and is known to her friends as Scraps. The adventure includes a Crooked Magician, who brings Scraps to life, and an animated phonograph that tags along with Scraps and her friends, consigned to its life playing a classical music record. “You're supposed to like it, whether you do or not,” cautions the phonograph, “and if you don't, the proper thing is to look as if you did. Understand?”

This is only the tip of the proverbial iceberg. Oliveros follows the Patchwork Girl's origins story with an account of a dream in which she plunged to the depths of the ocean in a Siren-like turn and “vengefully” twanged the bones of an old sea captain like a “human guitar.” It is worth considering that Oliveros deemed “Rags and Patches” (perhaps) more outrageous than this.

I also learned in “Divisions Underground” that Mozart, when asked what music he liked best, supposedly replied, “No music.”

What constitutes your musical universe?

10

Yesterday I was invited to attend an event called Pauline in the Garden, hosted by the artist David Horvitz and his friends Lucia and Emmett. The invitation requested me to "please bring an offering for the garden for the ghost of Pauline Oliveros. Rocks, shells, bells, whistles, tea, leaves, etc." I brought a bag of shishito peppers from my own garden, that were out of season but still perfectly edible if a little tough, and of course carried seeds that could be planted. (I didn't bring anything for the ghost of Oliveros, because I don't really believe in ghosts, even though sometimes I wish I did.)

David's garden sits on an abandoned lot in West Adams. The building that had been there had been razed, and whoever owns the property seems to accept its new life as a garden, which is remarkable given the rising real estate prices in the neighborhood. The garden is charmingly eclectic with a variety of flora, whether intentionally planted or volunteered. There are many shells, leftover from oyster dinners, gently delineating pathways and points (plants) of interest and heavy wooden benches by the local design firm Terremoto. There is also a vertical sculpture made of two-by-fours that serves as a perch for local crows. Or maybe it's a perch that looks like a sculpture. David sets peanuts there, which are quickly spotted and enjoyed. A drawing of a peanut, looking a little like a squashed globe, graced the invitation; I took it as an auspicious sign.

I had last visited the garden in October during the long stretch of drought, and I was happy to see the garden looking lush and green after the recent deluge. About forty or more people had gathered for this tribute. Despite the pandemic and the surging case numbers, the garden provided a congenial and hopefully safe setting. Printed scores (taken from Oliveros's *Anthology of*

Text Scores) were distributed and a variety of instruments were offered: metal chimes, wooden flutes, maracas, a small zither. I decided upon a sturdy metal sheet pan, which afforded a number of percussive possibilities.

We began with *Breathe In/Breathe Out* (1982), which is an easy and inviting introduction to Oliveros and her scores, focused primarily on (yes) breathing and listening. We then performed *Sounds from Childhood* (1992), which encourages participants to make three to five sounds one loved making as a child, "especially the ones that adults admonished you for making." Everybody seemed to love this score, judging by the resulting cacophony. It allowed for release and reduced inhibitions. There were several children in attendance, who took part effortlessly. For my part, I made a loud sputtering motorboat sound with my lips, slapped the wall of the adjacent building, and dropped my sheet pan onto an open expanse of the garden, making a loud, short metallic splash. I doubt I was this noisy as a baby, but it was fun to pretend. As the afternoon gradually gave way to darkness, we shifted into *Response Ability* (1978) which, despite the name, allowed for a continuation of our collective playfulness.

Listen for a call. When the call comes, answer with your own call.

Call until you receive an answering call. Echo that call.

Across the street from the garden, a car had double-parked (a favorite Los Angeles pastime) and its car alarm started bleating endlessly. We immediately began echoing the call in cheerful unison.

11

One of the strangest challenges of writing these daily meditations on Oliveros is that there is simply not enough time in the day to write all of the things I am thinking about or observing or reacting to. Right now, I am thinking once again of the *Today* series by On Kawara, in which the tightly focused act of painting of the day's date might suffice to represent all of the other stuff of the day, including its clutter and excess. ("A landscape of time," as Alejandro Cesarco put it, referring to the horizontal orientation of Kawara's date paintings.) My daily log was a useful way to account for the clutter, rhythms, and demands of the day without having to describe those things. It was, as the word "log" suggests, a kind of running tally of data sets. When the day ended, the next tally began. For his part, Kawara would destroy a painting if he didn't finish it by midnight. We know that he completed over three thousand of these paintings between January 1966 and his death in 2014. But I wonder how many got destroyed along the way. (There were also many days in which no art*work* was made at all.) Is there any accounting for the waste product, the *frass* of his termite-like project?

Another precedent for these texts is the book *20 Lines a Day* by Harry Mathews, in which the writer and OULIPO member would knock out twenty lines a day on the typewriter—following Stendhal's mantra of "twenty lines a day, genius or not!"—as a kind of warm-up for the other writing he needed to do. Like Mathews, I have other things to do. And, like Mathews, I have tended to write these meditations early in the day, before committing to life's other pesky demands, including other writing projects. Unlike Mathews, I am often writing more than twenty lines a day, and (so far) I've been writing every day. Even so, I am often left with the realization that I have not yet gotten to the thing I really wanted to write or think about. But then, thinking and meditating are not necessarily the same thing. "All of these Sonic Meditations are intended to begin with observation of the breath cycle." There is (one imagines) always tomorrow.

12

This morning, I am sitting in my home office and listening to *Horse Sings from Cloud*. When I taught my Pauline Oliveros for Artists seminar, I started by having the class listen to this composition, a solo work for accordion and voice, from the album *Accordion & Voice*. The album also includes *Rattlesnake Mountain*, which is a solo accordion work, without voice. It was first issued by Lovely Music, Ltd. in 1982, and later reissued on CD by Important Records. It is also available on Spotify. I often recommend it as a starting place for those who express curiosity about Oliveros and her music, but seem unsure of where to dig in. With Oliveros, it is the center I often return to.

It's always interesting to know what version of Oliveros people know or begin with. Most seem to know her as the Deep Listening person, which of course she is, though the phrase "deep listening" came relatively late in her development. Some know her as a pioneer of electronic music, especially since the late 1990s when much of that material began to get released. And more recently, with the release of Lisa Rovner's documentary *Sisters with Transistors* (2020), which arrived as a balm during the pandemic. Others know her as the lady with the accordion. There are relatively few accordion players of note in contemporary music, and even fewer radical feminist lesbians who are. The accordion stands out in a crowd. In Oliveros's papers at Mills, I found a *Far Side* comic, with new inductees in Heaven receiving their harps and new inductees in Hell receiving their accordions. She was an avant-garde accordionist with a sense of humor. In other words, she's in a league of her own.

In *Horse Sings from Cloud*, Oliveros seems to perform a duet between her voice and her accordion. This version begins with a sustained tone played on the accordion, which is followed by the voice. But at a certain point, it is hard to tell which one is in the lead. And perhaps leading is not the point anyway. This goes on for over twenty minutes, but time becomes nebulous, suspended but ever-so-gradually evolving. Occasionally—not often or regularly—the notes change, but it's never clear exactly why. Until one reads the score:

Sustain one or more tones or sounds until any desire to change the tone(s) or sound(s) subsides. When there is no desire to change the tone(s) or sound(s), then change.

13

I cannot think of another musical composition structured around a relationship between change and desire, and certainly not before *Horse Sings from Cloud*. As the primary organizing principle, this dynamic relationship quickly distinguishes the composition from the indeterminacy of Cage—which is also to say that in Oliveros's composition, the performer's desire and their agency (to change or not change) are not mediated through chance operations, such as the use of the *I Ching*.

The first published version of Oliveros's score for *Horse Sings from Cloud*, dated 1975, is concise and instructional, following quite directly from *Sonic Meditations*; the second version, written nearly a decade later, is longer and decidedly more poetic, "to reflect Oliveros's growing understanding" of the work. Both texts are meditative and interpretative, emphasizing the performer as an active, embodied agent in determining the outcome of the work. There is also a personal and political dimension to building a work around change and desire, and the development of *Horse Sings from Cloud* closely mirrors Oliveros's own emergence as a significant feminist and queer voice in contemporary music.

The work has most often manifested as a solo performance, for voice and accordion, performed by Oliveros. There is at least one group realization of it, with a quartet of women negotiating change and desire with various bellowed instruments—Heloise Gold on harmonium, Julia Haines on accordion, Linda Montano on concertina, and Oliveros on bandoneon. It was performed at the Marymount Manhattan Theatre on January 27, 1983.

Horse Sings from Cloud was one of several titles Oliveros gave the work, which began as *Rose Mountain Slow Runner* and became *The Pathways of the Grandmothers*. The former was performed for Robert Ashley's *Music with Roots in the Aether* (1975–1976), a fourteen-hour "opera for television." The latter was performed for KPFK Close Radio on January 5, 1978. At nearly ninety minutes, it is by far the longest continuous performance by Oliveros that I am aware of. There may have also been an even earlier iteration titled *Gravity is the Fourth Dimension*. Each instance of the work represents a shifting set of relations to change in desire, in art and life. As Oliveros has stated, "the title itself is a meditation."

14

I think it's worth stating what is probably obvious: My experience of listening to Oliveros's performance of *Horse Sings from Cloud* is different from her experience of performing it. This is presumably true for most works of performance, especially those in which the body of the performer is a vessel or vehicle that carries meaning or feeling. And particularly for a musical work that is so intricately tied to the performer, their being and their agency, as they enter into a pitched tussle with their own desire. (Pun intended.) I am a receiver for that meaning and feeling. But I also like to imagine that I am not just a receiver for it. I like to imagine myself with banana-shaped ears, so that I can penetrate the music in return—"not to mention all the other finer variations."

15

Sustain one or more tones or sounds until any desire to change the tone(s) or sound(s) subsides. When there is no desire to change the tone(s) or sound(s), then change.

At a certain point I had imagined I would continue keeping a daily log indefinitely, and after fifteen years, I had no doubt in my ability to do so. My decision to stop writing it came as a surprise to me. Yet, my decision to write a daily meditation on Oliveros is more of a continuation than a negation of that project. Or that's how I understand it (already? only?) fifteen days into it. It could evolve into something else. I may only realize what it is, once it becomes that.

16

Any attempt to define or describe my musical universe must include a consideration of Steve Roden, an artist and composer who is also a friend and has sometimes been a collaborator. I met Steve in 2004, shortly after writing a short review of his work for *Artforum*, but I first became aware of him in the late 1990s, and I'm sure that I read about his work before ever hearing or seeing it in the world. Among the first things I knew about was a series of musical pieces performed on canonical objects of modernist design—a Knoll chair by Harry Bertoia, a George Nelson "bubble" lamp, an Eames plywood leg splint. One could imagine this as a send-up or a critique of modernist optimism, but the works are incredibly reverent. And subtle. The eccentric percussive sounds were all processed and looped, and one would never be able to guess their original source, but the knowledge of the source object seems important to the work. Steve is a serious collector, a flea market devotee, and an early eBay explorer, and so much of his work refers to artifacts of art and design. I was designing furniture around the time I first heard about these compositions, so I was immediately intrigued. But it would be years before I'd actually hear these pieces; Steve eventually gave me a set of the three mini-CDs.

I suspect I first encountered the name Steve Roden in the *LA Weekly*—it was a time before most people were regularly using the internet, and everyone in big cities would pick up free alternative weekly newspapers to learn about what was happening in local culture. This was also years before I would start my daily log, so I can only try to piece together my earliest encounters with Steve's work by looking at his exhibition history and his discography. It seems likely that the first thing I saw (or heard) in person was in 2000, titled *reading without reading/within (further)* and installed at the Guardshack, a tiny ad hoc space at the entrance of Bergamot Station, an art gallery complex in Santa Monica. I don't remember anything else about it.

In 2002, I visited an exhibition of Steve's work in Santa Barbara, titled *some reconstructions of wandering & inner space*. Steve likes to use very poetic titles, though the poetry is often borrowed (or "found" in art speak) or subtly altered. I still remember a lot of things about the exhibition, including a series of drawings made with a variety of thin, green marker lines on lined notebook paper. I recall that these were somehow related to a book by Hermann Hesse, but I don't remember which one, and I also don't remember the system Steve used to produce the drawings. (The book, I discover after some digging, was *Wandering*. Perfect.) Steve's work often results from a generative, if convoluted, system that is often only known to him. Sometimes he explains it, but even when he does one could never "reverse engineer" the system to get back to the original referent, whether Hesse or Eames or Jacques Cousteau or whoever.

I also remember that the Santa Barbara exhibition included a painting, which I recall as being a square covered with a gentle, brushy grid and quite a bit of pink. It was titled *listen (4'33")* (2002) in obvious homage to John Cage's influential modernist composition. I don't know what, if any, system Steve used to make the painting. I assume it took more than four minutes and thirty-three seconds to paint it. Maybe he was listening to a performance of Cage's work as he painted? Further research (i.e. pulling the small catalog off my bookshelf and re-reading the essay by Christoph Cox) reveals that the painting:

> translates a verbal description from the score of John Cage's famous "silent composition" *4'33"* (in which, for four minutes and thirty-three seconds, the performer makes no intentional sound).

In Roden's translation, Cage's 93-word text determines not only the length of each line... but also its color (a different hue for each word). The result is a polychrome lattice of 434 wayward lines, the arrangement of which is largely intuitive, but the constitution of each component is determined in silence.

In 2001, I encountered three sound installations by Steve at the MAK Center for Art and Architecture at the Schindler House. The innovative concrete and redwood house, which was designed by Austrian immigrant Rudolf Michael Schindler and built in 1921–1922, was designed for two couples and served as an important social hub in West Hollywood, where actors mingled with the avant-garde. It's my favorite work of architecture in Los Angeles, a defining and decidedly utopian example of California modernism, and a reliably strange and specific place to see (or hear) contemporary art. It was an empathic pairing, and like Steve's work, the Schindler House would continue to be an important presence in my life ever since.

Steve had made three compositions using sounds from the house—he essentially used it as an instrument, much like he had done with the Bertoia chair and Nelson lamp. But he also made field recordings and included his own voice, singing a line from Schindler's manifesto on "space architecture":

it will be a quiet, flexible background for a harmonious life

These works were presented on speakers located in different parts of the house, including the thicket of bamboo in the garden behind the house. John Cage (who was born and raised in Los Angeles) briefly lived at the Schindler House with his first male lover. He also had romantic feelings for Pauline Schindler, the architect's wife. One of the works, *pathway. ('it was a lovely sight, against the sky')* (2001), includes a performance of Cage's

4'33" (1952), which Steve did privately, alone in the house in the middle of the night.

In 2011, Steve performed Cage's *4'33"* every day for the entire year. Most of these performances were also private and took place wherever he happened to be on a given day: at home, in the airport, in Carsten's loft, in the Walter Benjamin archives, and so on. As Steve remarked, retrospectively:

> It was an exercise in both writing and listening, but also an activity to see how the score could be opened up to offer activities beyond listening. By performing it daily, I explored how the piece may transform through repetition, and investigated what kind of experiences it might suggest over time. In this sense, Cage was on my mind every day.

The following year, Steve compiled accounts of these 365 performances in the form of a book (*365 x 433*), and in 2016, I included the book in an exhibition I organized at the Schindler House, titled *Routine Pleasures*. I placed Steve's thick book on a bench in the glazed corner of R.M. Schindler's studio, where Steve had first performed Cage's composition. One could read the book while looking out at (or listening into) the garden, where I had installed a recording of a performance of Pauline Oliveros's *The Tuning Meditation* (1979) with the speakers hiding in the bushes.

17

John Cage's *4'33"* transformed what music could be, and it also opened up new possibilities for what a score might look like (or not look like). The original score is lost. The version of the score that I know best was written several years after the fact by Cage and primarily consists of a written description. It describes that the work was first performed by David Tudor on August 29, 1952 at the Maverick Concert Hall in Woodstock, New York. It was performed on the piano, or at the piano, with Tudor closing and opening the lid of the keyboard to indicate the three distinct, measured parts, which added up to four minutes and thirty-three seconds. Famously, the virtuosic pianist did not sound a single note on the instrument. "However," Cage notes in the text score, "the work may be performed by an [any?] instrumentalist or any combination of instrumentalists and last any length of time."

Of course, when Cage's so-called "silent" work was first performed, in 1952, it was highly controversial. Many in the audience assumed it was a Dadaist prank; some got up and left, unaware (or unimpressed) that they were witnessing music history. "They missed the point," Cage later observed to Richard Kostelanetz.

> There's no such thing as silence. What they thought was silence, because they didn't know how to listen, was full of accidental sounds. You could hear the wind stirring outside during the first movement. During the second, raindrops began pattering the roof, and during the third the people themselves made all kinds of interesting sounds as they talked or walked out.

I love how Steve Roden's performance of the work takes absolute liberty with Cage's last sentence: "the work may be performed by an instrumentalist or any combination of instrumentalists, and last any length of time." Yet, it steadfastly uses the score as a pretext for the daily exercise of active listening, and then as a way to induce "activities beyond listening." Quite radically in its own way, it also abandons the idea of an audience, which Cage's work always depended on. (Hence the composer's disappointment in the work's initial reception.) I should say Steve was always performing the score for a knowing audience of one: himself.

Today I have been listening to Steve's music—*winter couplet* (2002) and *view* (1999), so far—as a "quiet, flexible background" while I tidy my desk and write this text. I am also listening to a recording of Cage's *4'33"* performed by James Tenney at the Schindler House on June 28, 2002, one year or so after Steve's private performance there. Tenney's performance marked "the coincidence of several Cage anniversaries: the fiftieth anniversary of the seminal work *4'33"* performed in 1952, the ninetieth anniversary of Cage's birth, and the tenth anniversary of his death."

Tenney, who was a professor at CalArts and elsewhere, provides some historical context for Cage's work to the audience. Then the performance begins. As I listen, I hear a beep from what I assume is a digital timer that indicates the start of the performance, followed by the fuzzy spaciousness of the recording as it more fully describes the tone of Pauline Schindler's studio and the garden beyond, which is where the audience was situated. (How many microphones were used? Was there only one, aimed at the piano?) Eventually other sounds enter the fold, circa 2002: birds in the garden, a plane flying overhead. (Coincidentally, one can also hear a plane flying overhead in Steve's version.) While listening to the performance, twenty years later, I become aware of my own immediate environment, circa 2022: The chatter of my neighbors beyond my closed window and the sound of one of them sweeping the driveway; my partner Leslie several rooms away, talking to her mother on the phone; the whoosh of water filling the washing machine. All of this commingles with the percussive plinking and plunking of the prepared piano as Tenney launches into Cage's *Sonatas and Interludes* (1946–1948), one of two interpretations of it by Tenney that I have heard. Cage would soon abandon such works, which he deemed overly expressive in comparison to the indeterminate works that would follow, all largely determined by use of the *I Ching* and other chance operations set in motion by the composer. But Tenney's performance of *Sonatas and Interludes* reminds one (me at least) how bright and bristling Cage's music could be, here exploring the sonic possibilities of adding hardware and little objects to alter the tone and timbre of the piano's wires before he turned to the nuts and bolts of listening itself.

18

Today's object of attention: Two versions of *Duo for Accordion and Bandoneon* (1964), performed by Pauline Oliveros on accordion and David Tudor on bandoneon. I listened to the second performance first, a live recording from the concert "Lovely Music Live," which took place at the Marymount Manhattan Theatre on January 27, 1983. I listen to this while racing north on the 110 freeway to Pasadena, where I am installing an exhibition. The duet is relatively frenetic, with passages of inactivity when I focus on the drone of my tires on the road. This duet—and maybe any duet—suggests a conversation, and in some ways, I suppose it is: Tudor and Oliveros were old friends when they performed this in 1983.

I am immediately reminded that the accordion and bandoneon are, among other things, reed instruments. The bellows are like lungs blasting out air through raspy throats with every squeeze; their instruments are two voices, talking to each other, sometimes excitedly and perhaps even drunkenly. Toward the end of the performance, the duet becomes harmonious and Oliveros's voice joins in, singing long, sustained tones.

I am also reminded that the bandoneon, which is smaller than an accordion and square in profile, is the instrument most closely associated with tango music, which developed in Argentina, Uruguay, Cuba, and elsewhere, following European trade routes through Africa and into Latin America. It is impossible for me to listen to this duet and not think of a tango, even if the arrhythmia of this music seems far removed from the popular genre. I believe this is due to the expressive timbre of the instruments and the bandoneon in particular. If there is a score for this, I have not seen it, nor can I imagine what it might look like.

But I am suddenly remembering a wonderful lime green cover for sheet music with a bandoneon on it, found in Oliveros's papers at Mills. It reads:

GUARDIA VIEJA
TANGO – MILONGA
MUSICA DE
JULIO DE CARO
LETRA DE
J. DE GRANDIS
ARREGLO PARA BANDONEÓN

I had intended to spend time with the first version of *Duo for Accordion and Bandoneon* when I got home, but instead I am now listening to Julio De Caro (1899–1980) and his *orquestra típica*, acquainting myself with the *guardia vieja* of the Buenos Aires tango.

19

This morning, still considering the tango entanglement and the populism of the bandoneon and accordion, which one can easily forget in the hands of David Tudor and Oliveros. "Just over one hundred years old, the accordion is a survivor," Willard Palmer observes in the liner notes to Oliveros's 1984 album *The Wanderer*. "It is the only surviving portable, acoustic instrument capable of playing melody, harmony, and rhythm without accompaniment. Its progress and its survival are due greatly to its rich fold and ethnic heritage, as well as to its classical history."

The first version of their duet was performed at the San Francisco Tape Music Center in 1964, in a concert called *The Tudorfest*, which was organized by Oliveros and her colleagues at the center. Tudor was spending time in the Bay Area when not touring with the Merce Cunningham Dance Company, for which he was the musical director. The concert included six works by John Cage, which makes sense given that Tudor was the primary and most important interpreter of his piano music, as well as more frankly experimental pieces like *Cartridge Music*, which was also on the bill. There were also two works by Toshi Ichiyanagi, and Oliveros's *Duo*. Tudor plays on all the compositions. Oliveros plays French horn or tuba on several of the works by Cage. She was well versed on the French horn, though there are only a few early recordings of her playing the instrument.

In its first instance, Oliveros and Tudor performed their duet on a seesaw that swiveled 360 degrees, designed by Elizabeth Harris. The lighting was designed by Anthony Martin. Both Martin and Harris were frequent collaborators with Oliveros in the 1960s and contributed to many of her more theatrical projects. Apparently Oliveros had written a score, but abandoned it because it was too difficult to use on the swiveling, tilting seesaw.

Dangling overhead in a cage was a mynah bird named Ahmed that belonged to Oliveros's housemate Laurel Johnson. The original title of the piece was *Duo for Accordion and Bandoneon with Possible Mynah Bird Obligato, Seesaw Version*. According to Oliveros's account, the bird had refused to keep quiet when she and Tudor had first practiced the work, imitating sounds from the bellowed instruments: The duo became a trio. But then in the first public performance of the work, Ahmed stayed silent, due to the low light level (according to Oliveros) or perhaps stage fright (my guess) and refused his *obligato*. Birds will be birds.

20

It's late, and I'm sitting in relative silence in my office, listening to the blood race around my head, after a long day of plotting points around the city, drawing a large triangle over the hours.

After a few minutes the sound reminds me of crickets, far in the distance. I am recalling a very specific experience of listening to crickets in a canyon at Red Rock National Park in Oklahoma, in August 1995. It sounded like thousands of crickets, and maybe there were thousands. I am also remembering Aram Saroyan saying "crickets" over and over again, in his gently croaky voice. But I'm not really hearing crickets, just imagining them.

Is the sound—I mean the real sound of my blood circulating—hitting against my eardrums from the inside, forgoing the lobed receptors on either side of my head? Lately I've been lying awake for long stretches, with too much on my mind. The world is finally quiet, maybe too quiet, and I can hear the two frequencies my body makes, high and low. Sometimes I have observed these tones harmonizing with the refrigerator several rooms away.

21

One indicator of my musical universe is the iPod in my 2006 Scion TC. It's been full for at least a decade with CDs that I've tediously downloaded and imported via iTunes, which is also to say it hasn't changed for over a decade. The iPod interface was exciting and new when I bought the car; sixteen years and 190,000 miles later it is a relic of another technological era. Nevertheless, it is stuffed with amazing music, including many things you'd never find on Spotify.

Today I turned to Alice Coltrane, as I often have for many years, during long freeway commutes. Especially in moments of tremendous stress, which describes the first half of the day. Like Oliveros, Alice Coltrane reminds me to breathe. Today I decided upon the album *Transcendence*, recorded in 1977 for Warner Bros., which seems amazing and surprising in retrospect because this music sounds more cosmic than corporate. It represents a transitional moment in her development, from inheritor of the lineage of avant-garde jazz in which she emerged, playing piano with John Coltrane's final quintet, into more frankly devotional music that is inspired by Vedic traditions but is also completely her own. The first half of the album features her signature harp playing, alongside a string quartet; the second half of the album focuses her vocals, accompanied by her organ and a chorus of voices, handclaps, tambourine, and other instruments.

I prefer the second half of the album, and especially the song "Sivaya," which is the first song on the second side of the album. It's incredibly catchy and gets stuck in my head anytime I hear it. Her voice is deep (I want to say husky), and almost embarrassingly forthright. I don't pray, but I do listen to Alice Coltrane, and sometimes I am compelled to sing along, despite not fully knowing or understanding the words.

22

I keep thinking about the duet of Oliveros and David Tudor. Were Oliveros and Elizabeth Harris, who designed the swiveling seesaw, aware of Simone Forti's *See-Saw* from 1960? It seems likely, but the history is also fuzzy. Oliveros and Harris would have been in the same circle as Forti, who had lived in San Francisco from 1955 until 1960 or '61, when she and Robert Morris moved to New York. Forti had been part of the Anna Halprin Dancers' Workshop, which eventually moved into the same building as the Tape Music Center, at 321 Divisadero. But that happened a few years after Forti had moved to New York. Still, it seems like that word of Forti's *Dance Constructions* had reached the Bay Area. I will try to remember to ask Simone about this when I next see her, but I don't imagine anyone else is too worried about these two dueling seesaw performances some sixty years later.

For the record, I am less interested in establishing precedent or potential borrowing (mynah birding?) and am more interested in the proximity of these two works by artists who were both at the center of everything yet remain somewhat elusive if not marginalized in the larger or "major" historical narratives around post-war art, music, and performance. (Oliveros was born in 1932, Forti in 1935.) In both cases this might be due to their varied output and the circumscribed expectations of any given field or discipline. Forti is best known in dance, and it's taken longer for the (visual) art world to recognize her contributions. Sound is also central to so much of her work, and she's had some belated releases of her musical work. In the case of Oliveros, I believe her contributions to contemporary and experimental music have been recognized, but her contributions to the field of experimental performance and site-based practices (among other areas of exploration) are relatively unknown.

For now, I consult Forti's *Handbook in Motion*, first published in 1974 by the Press of the Nova Scotia College of Art and Design, Halifax, and read her account of *See-Saw*. It was first performed at Reuben Gallery in New York, as part of a "Christmas Program of Happenings" over the course of four nights, in December 1960. The program also included a work by Jim Dine, and two short pieces by Claes Oldenburg. Forti is billed as Simone Morris, because she was at that time married to Robert Morris who performs in the work with Yvonne Rainer. In real life, the two performers would become lovers and Simone would marry Robert Whitman in 1962.

The seesaw is a familiar object, most closely associated with the playground and children. It's also called a teeter-totter, and both phrases have a pleasing sing-song quality that echoes the action of the object they name. The seesaw also provides an easy metaphoric device and instant drama: it requires two (or more) people to function; it demands interdependence in order to achieve balance.

Both performances in question (Forti's and Oliveros's) are for a man and a woman. "The piece, performed by a man and a woman, is about twenty minutes long," Forti's description begins. In the original version, Morris and Rainer walk out in black trench coats and remove them to reveal matching red sweaters and shorts. Both performances are playful and humorous, and both incorporate an additional sounding object. In Oliveros's *Duo*, it's Ahmed the mynah bird; in Forti's *See-Saw*, it's a found noisemaker that makes a "moo" sound whenever it's tilted. Forti's version also included a song (an obligato?), which she sang from the edge of the performance. She describes it as something she remembers hearing. It begins like this:

Way out on a sun-baked desert
Where nature favors no man
A buffalo met his brother
At rest on the sun-baked sand . . .

Forti has a wonderful voice, and briefly trained with Pandit Pran Nath. I don't have a recording of her singing it, but I can still imagine hearing her singing it.

23

This morning I listened to Simone Forti's *Al Di Là* as I drove to the market and back. The CD, released by Tashi Wada on his Saltern label in 2018, features songs that were part of artworks or performances exhibited at The Box, a gallery in Los Angeles, in 2012. The show was called *Sounding* and remains memorable because I knew so little of this aspect of Simone's work prior to the show. It was a revelation. The works spanned from the early 1960s to 1984. I recall how the eclectic installations—including projections, photographs, objects found or built, wonderfully spare but ebullient drawings—dotted around the voluminous gallery, with Simone's voice and various other sounds connecting the dots and filling the space. One of my favorite works on the CD is *Censor*, which is for two performers. One shakes a pan full of nails; the other sings a song.

Censor was inspired by an experience in the New York subway. A train on my habitual route would always make a terribly loud screeching while careening around a particular curve. One day I spontaneously sang as loud as I could as we turned that corner. None of the other passengers gave any indication of having heard me.

Censor was first performed in 1961, as part of the *Five Dance Constructions and Other Things*, which took place at Yoko Ono's loft. Today, *Censor* takes place in my car, on the freeway of Los Angeles.

24

Tonight I am listening to Golden Offence Orchestra's performance of Oliveros's *To Valerie Solanas and Marilyn Monroe in Honor of Their Desperation* (1970), which was released on cassette in an edition of 150 by the cultish Stockholm-based label XKatedral in 2017. I don't have the energy to write about it, so in honor of my desperation I am content to listen and look at the candy-red cassette.

25

Golden Offence Orchestra was active in Stockholm from 2012–2014. We met monthly and were solely devoted to playing Pauline Oliveros's *To Valerie Solanas and Marilyn Monroe in Honor of Their Desperation*. After about six months of playing this music, Oliveros's compositional tactics began to infiltrate the social behaviours and exchanges within the ensemble. The interpretational complexities of the score musically and socially manifested tensions between individual will, group mentality and hierarchy structures. The Golden Offence Orchestra gradually dissolved just as the piece does. Oliveros's music has the ability to brutally transform the senses, and by doing so, to transform and crack perceptions of sensorial and social constructs. We express our sincere gratitude for her profound insights and contributions to music.

Last night, after *To Valerie Solanas and Marilyn Monroe*, I listened to Ellen Arkbro's recent album *Sounds while waiting* (2021). Arkbro was a member of Golden Offence Orchestra and played concertina on the Oliveros piece; her 2017 album *For Organ and Brass* was among the music I discovered during the early months of the pandemic and played repeatedly in the yawning stretches of the day, going nowhere. *Sounds while waiting*—how perfectly the title describes how her music has functioned for me—is remarkably sustained, to use an Oliveros term of endearment. Sustained but definitely not static. There is a cluster of tones (I guess those are chords) being played that vibrate intensely against one another. I read the description on Bandcamp and learn that she is playing multiple organs at the same time in large resonant spaces. In each song, we can hear the whole space shimmering on a molecular level. Or so I imagine. The result, even at a relatively low volume on my mediocre desktop speakers, is hypnotic, enveloping, and lingering, brutally transforming my senses. My ears continue to vibrate for a few moments when each of the songs end. And in the brief gap between songs, I become acoustically aware of the surrounding world again. "MY EARS FEEL LIKE CAVES," to quote Oliveros—or LIKE LITTLE CATHEDRALS.

26

Walk so silently that the bottoms of your feet become ears.

I go to Kenneth Hahn State Recreation Center for some exercise, and without really trying, I perform a version of Oliveros's *Sonic Meditation V*, which is also titled *Native*. It's a cool, but sunny morning that offers glorious views of the city from the ocean to downtown and beyond. The first instruction is to "take a walk at night," so my performance immediately diverges from the tidy score. But soon my feet become ear-like, as I become acutely aware of the crunch underfoot as I walk—of asphalt, then grass, then gravel, then sand, then concrete. My pace is relatively steady, but the sound changes when the ground changes.

Meanwhile, my other ears—the ones on either side of my head—become aware of a wild array of sounds as I climb and circumnavigate: the squawk and flutter of geese and ducks around the artificial pond, the chatter and chirp of dozens of other birds, the conversation of other visitors to the park and my own voice as I engage in conversation, the disconcerting choking of a little dog that gets worked up by an encounter with a bigger dog, the distant whoosh of traffic in the canyon between oil fields, the rumble of a large portable generator used by a landscape crew, the surprising clang of branches being thrown into the back of a truck, funk music playing from a small speaker, the spinning wheels of the bicycle that circles the track clockwise, passing me five times as I circle in the opposite direction . . .

27

At night, completing another Thursday triangle connecting home in South Los Angeles to Pasadena to Valencia to home again, I listen to the CD of Milford Graves/Don Pullen, *Live at Yale University* (1966). It was already in my CD player. The last time I tried to listen to it, it didn't fit the mood. It's intense and uncompromising, it demands attention and doesn't recede politely into the background. I want to call their sprawling duets "controlled chaos," but that sounds like a jazz cliché. (Like "Alone Together.") How about a meticulous frenzy of empathic improvisation? Pullen reminds me that the piano is a percussion instrument; Graves reminds me of the sonority of drums, gongs, bells. Dead tired, I let their thunder and blister overtake me and carry me home.

28

Did Tehching Hsieh ever want a day off?

I have said almost nothing of my month so far, which has largely been consumed by the installation of an exhibition at the Armory Center in Pasadena that has been in the works since late 2018 and finally opens today, and the relentless demands of CalArts. It has, in a nutshell, been exhausting. But I have not wanted to make this an exercise in journaling. I have wanted to make this a meditation on Oliveros and, more specifically, an attempt to perform her *Sonic Meditation XXI* and answer the question it poses: What constitutes [my] musical universe? Perhaps I have moved a little closer to an answer, gradually drawing a circle around that universe, day by day, over the course of the past four weeks. But there is still so much more I want and need to say about Oliveros and about that universe.

29

The longer this text gets, the less possible it is to reread it or maintain a sense of it as a totality. Is coherence even a goal? Am writing it for an audience, or for myself?

I've been thinking a lot about the idea of private performance—for an audience of one. For example, Steve Roden doing *4'33"* every day, or Tehching Hsieh's year-long endurance pieces, or Allan Kaprow's notion of "performing life." Barbara T. Smith, who has been a presence in my life for most of January, has described her performances as "works that have engaged me on a deeply felt level, often excruciating, sometimes ecstatic." Acts of embodiment, they are focused on her "own inner growth rather than works intended to entertain an audience. Indeed, the role of the so-called audience is often that of witness, participant, or indirect observer. What I have wanted for the audience was a shared sense of immediate effect."

I titled my exhibition *how we are in time and space* after a phrase I heard Barbara say when we first met. What is compelling to me about her work is its steadfastness, a commitment to seeing something through, even if the work changes or if she changes in the process of the work's fulfillment.

When there is no desire to change the tone(s) or sound(s), then change.

There is time for critical reflection later. Perspective comes from distance. Today is about focusing on today.

30

At dinner with Nancy Buchanan and Barbara T. Smith last night after the opening of my exhibition, I was asked what I'm working on next. Such a cruel question. I wanted to say "nothing," but I mentioned that I've been writing about Pauline Oliveros. This was received with instant, collective enthusiasm. And lots of questions. Nancy told a funny story about an interaction with Oliveros at a performance event at UC San Diego. (I suspect it was one of the *What's Cooking?* series organized there in the late 1970s and early 80s.) Nancy was there participating in an Allan Kaprow happening, and at some point found a purple crystal bead. Oliveros was doing a silent (non-speaking) performance, and Nancy wanted to interact with her, so she gave her the bead. Later, at a panel talk, Kaprow called upon Oliveros, at which point she extracted the purple bead from her mouth and stuck it in his hand.

We also discussed *Three Day Blindfold*, a performance by Linda Mary Montano at the Woman's Building in Los Angeles in March 1975, which Nancy and Barbara both witnessed. As the title suggests, Montano was blindfolded for the duration of the three-day performance, and Oliveros became her guide. She did not speak during the event. It was the beginning of a seven-year relationship.

31

Nancy Buchanan follows up with an email regarding Oliveros's *The Pathway of the Grandmothers*, which she performed live on January 5, 1978 for Close Radio, a half-hour weekly radio program on KPFK Los Angeles that ran from 1976 to 1978. (The work is listed as *Pathways to Grandmothers* in Close Radio documentation, but elsewhere listed as *The Pathway of the Grandmothers*.) Nancy programmed Close Radio with Paul McCarthy, John Duncan, Linda Frye Burnham, and others, with some ninety artists and groups participating, including Chris Burden, Barbara T. Smith, Allison Knowles, Carolee Schneemann, Linda Mary Montano, the Los Angeles Free Music Society, Mike Kelley, and Tony Oursler's The Poetics—it's a remarkable list of people working at the intersection of performance, conceptual art, and experimental music.

Paul, John & I invited her to do a live performance. She & Linda [Montano] came to my house, where to my amazement, Pauline drank a large glass of whole milk. Then we drove to the station.

I don't know if you've ever seen it, but KPFK has a large performance space (I think called "Studio Z") that is extremely resonant. It's the top floor of the building.

We all lay on the floor in the warm sunlight streaming in the windows & my son Page, who was then twelve, told me he felt transported. Pauline played her concertina & sang for almost an hour and a half. What a gift! But the engineer didn't get it, and without turning off his mic to the upstairs, said, "Thank God THAT'S over!" We were mortified, of course. Pauline seemed to shrug it off. I think it's truly a gem in the entire Close collection. Paul may remember more about it.

Coincidentally, I had talked to Paul McCarthy about Close Radio and Oliveros on Saturday night. I'll make a mental note to visit KPFK and Studio Z.

32

Sustain one or more tones or sounds until any desire to change the tone(s) or sound(s) subsides. When there is no desire to change the tone(s) or sound(s), then change.

I want to begin the new month by sustaining my meditation on *Horse Sings from Cloud*. Rather than writing, I will re-read (and share) excerpts from "The Title Itself is a Meditation," a lecture on Oliveros I delivered last April:

> Like *Horse Sings from Cloud* and *Rose Mountain Slow Runner*, the title *The Pathway of the Grandmothers* is an aspect of the work itself and follows the logic of the score: It is shaped by the composer's desire for change as well as her willingness to suspend that desire, hold it in reserve, sustain it.
>
> The first recorded performance of the work that I'm aware of takes place in the context of a fourteen-hour "opera for television" by composer Robert Ashley, titled *Music with Roots in the Aether*, realized in 1975–1976. Ashley's opera devotes two hours each to seven different composers—Ashley himself and six of his peers: David Behrman, Philip Glass, Alvin Lucier, Gordon Mumma, Terry Riley, and Pauline Oliveros. Each two hours typically consists of a one-hour conversation between Ashley and the other composer, which is referred to as a "Landscape"; this often includes a performance of some kind. The second hour focuses on the performance of one or more works by the composer, without Ashley's presence.
>
> As Ashley describes it in "All Music Can Be Understood,"
>
> *Music with Roots in the Aether* is the realization of an idea I had worked out in various ways for about ten years—to make an opera of personalities and to illustrate those personalities with

actual quotations, for example, to quote the music of David Behrman by having David Berhman perform his music.

... Because so much of my work has had to do with "speech" and its relationship to music, I conceived of *Music with Roots in the Aether* as a series of "duets"—another composer and myself—alternating with "solos" by the composer. In each of those seven portraits the theater of the music is established in the landscape we inhabit and in the uninterrupted ("performed") camera style of the video recording.

Oliveros's "solo" in this context is *Rose Mountain Slow Runner*, and is perhaps the first recorded version of it in any medium, as well as the only visual document of its performance that I am aware of. It is preceded by the "duet" with Oliveros and Ashley, who are situated in lounge chairs, with a massive floral arrangement between them and a crackling fireplace off to the side. Ashley, slouching, takes frequent sips from a Budweiser tall boy. Oliveros's Budweiser is badly hidden but ignored, partially tucked behind her chair.

[I am imagining her drinking a large glass of whole milk instead.]

Provocatively, and against all expectations set in motion by the sedate but decidedly awkward conversation we are witnessing, Oliveros's duet with Ashley is titled *Unnatural Acts Between Consenting Adults*. Their conversation—this *Landscape with Pauline Oliveros*—is more elliptical than straightforward. Both composer-performers are comfortable with long pauses in the space/time continuum ...

33

Against all semantic expectations of pure dialogue implied by the word "duet," there are two additional figures who participate in these "unnatural acts": Carol Vencius, who appears as "The Masked Woman," and Linda Montano, as "Huckleberry Linda." A few minutes after the title sequence, The Masked Woman enters the frame, and initiates a process to gradually transform Oliveros from a butch lesbian in sandals and a Greek fisherman's hat to a festive femme in a leopard-skin blouse and blonde wig. The drag transformation begins with the application of press-on fingernails.

"How do those feel?" inquires The Masked Woman.

"Terrible," replies Oliveros.

"They feel terrible, huh?" Then, teasing gently: "Get used to it. They're not hurting you?"

"No, it isn't hurting. At least not physically."

Consent has been given, if reluctantly, and the unnatural act of transformation continues. ("When there is no desire to change . . . then change.") Ashley looks on, bemused, trying to keep the duet going long after it's turned into a trio. Or quartet: Every few minutes, seemingly unprompted by the conversation, the camera pulls back to reveal a grand piano. Improbably, a supine figure is situated under its lid and atop the soundboard, resting on cushions apparently scavenged from a nearby couch. This—we can only surmise from the credits and by process of elimination—is Huckleberry Linda. She is adorned and partially disguised with lilacs. Another Budweiser sits on the edge of the piano, close at hand. We might also assume she is lying in state, if not for her occasional movements. This too, perhaps, is an unnatural act? (The title promises unnatural *acts*—plural.) But unnatural for whom—the viewer? Ashley? The piano's mysterious occupant? Or for *what*—the piano?

Surely a human body draped across the sound board represents an unlikely approach to the piano, albeit one that obliquely recalls John Cage's *4'33"*, first performed by the pianist David Tudor in 1952, who opened and closed the lid of the piano, according to the timing indicated by the score, but never played a note—or one that recalls the many subsequent degradations of the instrument by artists associated with Fluxus (including several students of Cage): for example, Philip Corner's *Piano Activities* (1962), in which a team of artists in formal attire brutalizes the instrument, or George Maciunas's *Piano Compositions for Nam June Paik* (also 1962), some of which direct the performer to care for the piano (tuning it, polishing it), with many others sullying its formal attire (stretching its strings with a tuning key until they burst, placing a cat or dog inside while playing Chopin, and so on). New Zealand-born composer Annea Lockwood's *Piano Burning* (1968) and *Piano Drowning* (1972) also come to mind . . .

These examples are all musical, in the way Cage implied with *4'33"*: There is sound; it is given some sense of order; it exists in the interpretative context of the field of music. And in all of these cases the piano is a reminder of the classical music conservatory—an immediately recognizable metonym of its history, structures, and values. In the same breath, we might also consider these acts "extramusical": Our understanding of them relies to a large extent on more than the resulting sounds—or lack thereof—initiated by the score. In many cases these extramusical acts are visual, or at least partially so, reprioritizing a viewer's sight along with their hearing. Perhaps it bears remembering that these *Unnatural Acts between Consenting Adults* take place within the decidedly extramusical context of Ashley's "opera for television." Opera, whether for stage or television, is an inherently synthetic medium explicitly intended for acoustic and visual reception—and for those modes in combination.

Add Huckleberry Linda's unnatural act to the list of indignities suffered by the poor piano since Cage, or perhaps his teacher Henry Cowell before him, or perhaps the entire long history of the piano as the central sign of Western classical music. The establishment of every *doxa* is inevitably [followed] by a countervailing spasm of unorthodoxy. Even Beethoven was considered a brute in his day.

Exactly once, off-camera, we hear the sounding of a piano key, muffled by the otherwise silent occupant. At another moment, we see Huckleberry Linda holding up two folded sheets of paper. A score? If there is a reading in progress, it too is silent. While Ashley eventually prompts Oliveros to comment on her drag performance, not once in the conversation does either refer to the prone figure laying in the piano. Perhaps some unnatural acts are best left unmentioned? . . .

35

Then again, Huckleberry Linda is hiding in plain sight, revealed by the camera's occasional choreography, but disguised by the use of this odd persona, escaping in the slipperiness of language and identity: Huckleberry Linda is one of many names adopted by Linda Montano; others include Rose, Mary Montano, Mummie, Linda Mary Montano, Linda Montano, Linda M. Montano. In her performance/video, *Learning to Talk/ Living in Mandeville*, realized in 1977, Montano would inhabit a sequence of characters from Lamar Breton to Sister Rose Augustine to Kay Pryor to Linda Lee to Dr. Jane Gooding to Nadia Grozmolov to Hilda Mahler to La Padma. The threshold between persona and character is often a tenuous one, and some among these *dramatis personae* were clearly based on real life. For example, Sister Rose Augustine follows directly from Montano's two years of training in the Catholic Order.

Sometimes a persona remains elusive, accessible only to the person who inhabits the role. What can we possibly know about Huckleberry Linda, shrouded in darkness under the lid of a grand piano, seen (fleetingly) but not heard (beside a single off-screen plunk of the piano) and unannounced beyond the title cards of this "opera for television"?

Huckleberry Linda is Linda Montano. That we know, but there is no hint provided to the viewer to indicate that Linda Montano is also Rose Mountain.

"Rose Mountain is the name of a friend," Oliveros eventually admits, "and Slow Runner is me. But that's only part of it."

Indeed.

She continues: "Rose Mountain, of course, is a beautiful image; Slow Runner is ambiguous because there are runner roses. So the image then can build and it will depend on your own reaction to it. But the title itself is a meditation. The image for me is the mountain which is a spiral of roses, slowly spiraling."

"The name of a friend" is putting it mildly, or perhaps carefully in the context of Ashley's landscaping. With the notable exception of this Slow Runner and her mysterious friends, *Music with Roots in the Aether* is decidedly a men's club, suggesting that New American Music, whatever else that might be, is also mostly a continuation of a deeply patriarchal past. (Ashley's "Landscape with Alvin Lucier" features the latter composer in the guise of a fly fisherman, and "Landscape with Gordon Mumma" is staged in an athletic stadium with the composer, who enters on his bicycle, wearing ridiculously short shorts.) Oliveros's acceptance as woman—and particularly as a lesbian—in this club was, by the mid-70s, long-standing but rarely discussed out in the open.

Such negotiations—perhaps a polite word for indignities—were often managed quietly if not completely sublimated. But with the development of her *Sonic Meditations* in the early 1970s, Oliveros emerged as one of the foremost feminist and queer voices in new music . . .

36

Oliveros's *To Valerie Solanas and Marilyn Monroe in Recognition of Their Desperation*, first performed in 1970 and then again seven years later, was among the most profound realizations of feminist themes composed for classical orchestra in that or any decade. But Ashley's fourteen-hour opera for television presented a rare opportunity for a different kind of performance—less abstract or hypothetical, more fully embodied and visual, with the composer at the center of that transformation. Ashley is a willing dupe—his costume changes too, when the camera's attention is trained elsewhere. But, Oliveros's "unnatural act" is a Trojan horse that disrupts the masculine order of Ashley's opera, with The Masked Woman and Huckleberry Linda along for the ride.

Awkward and unruly, the drag transformation overruns the clock—that is, the tidy one-hour parcel of video real estate—forcing Ashley and his crew to improvise while Oliveros's toenail polish dries. From the context of the sexual politics of the present, Oliveros's gender bender seems tentative and archaic. [See, for example, Pauline Boudry and Renate Lorenz's performances based on Oliveros's scores. Or *RuPaul's Drag Race*.] But it also inaugurates or at least centralizes a new mode of performance for her—one that encompasses music, but is closer to the more holistic "living art" practice of her new partner (in art and life), Linda Montano.

Oliveros's performance in *Music with Roots in the Aether* also offers an example of what the theorist Elizabeth Freeman would years later, in her book *Time Binds: Queer Temporalities, Queer Histories*, define as "temporal drag":

What happens if we... reconsider "drag," so central to theorizing the mobility of gender identification and the visible excess that calls the gender binary into question, as a temporal phenomenon? As an excess, that is, of the signifier "history" rather than of "woman" or "man"? These questions might reenvision the meaning of drag for queer theory, asking: what is the time of queer performativity?

Oliveros's solo performance of *Rose Mountain Slow Runner* provides a proleptic answer to Freeman's question. It also provides another transformation: In the previous sequence, Oliveros transforms from one woman-presenting persona to another—from dyke to femme; by the solo performance, Oliveros is "herself" again, or perhaps some new synthesis of her previous identities. Here she is wearing a sleeveless jumpsuit dyed with a spectral pattern—willfully exploring or even exploiting the "visible excess that calls the gender binary into question"—barefoot, with her shaggy, silvering bowl cut, and otherwise unadorned with the notable exception of her accordion. She is seated on a small stage covered with a patterned rug, situated between two microphones—one for her voice, one for her accordion. The ostentatious floral arrangement remains in the background, connecting this performance and the space it occupies to the opera's previous episode. Her eyes stay closed, oblivious to the camera as it moves continuously, allowing us to get close, emphasizing the oneness of Oliveros and her instrument. She is clearly more comfortable in this setting than she was during the makeover. If the "duet" with Ashley was an unnatural act, this is an intimation of Oliveros in her "natural" or liberated state.

It is worth considering Oliveros's own description of the work, *Rose Mountain Slow Runner*, which she conveyed in her conversation with Ashley:

The song is non-verbal. That's very important as far as this particular work is concerned; somehow words are too specific, but sounds are more direct. Again, sounds simply don't have the associations that words would set up. So if I'm successful in my task of giving up intentions, whatever emotional states I might be experiencing will come through in those sounds. The song may change. It may change during the course of the song, and something may arise, or it may change from time to time. The song came as a result of various experiences that I needed to work with, and it was a way of channeling feeling, and channeling it directly.

The performance she describes unfolds over some forty-five minutes, charting a course for "queer temporality," both within and against the grain of Ashley's opera, responsive to her own emotional states—her desire and her desire for change—"channeling feeling and channeling it directly." . . .

37

Slow Runner first converged with Rose Mountain on March 22, 1975, as Linda Montano commenced a performance called *Three Day Blindfold/How to Become a Guru*. It occurred at the Woman's Building in Los Angeles, the vibrant hub of feminist art activity on the West Coast. Montano had arrived there from San Francisco, Oliveros from La Jolla. By Montano's account, which appears in her book *Art in Everyday Life*, the performance was a life-altering event.

ART For three days I lived blindfolded in a gallery at the Woman's Building. Pauline Oliveros became my guide and didn't speak during the event.

LIFE . . . Pauline Oliveros became my guide for that time and we moved without guilt for those three days. I keep repeating similar experiments in other ways in order to become familiar with expanded body feelings.

This piece was a vacation.

It changed my life.

The performance would also change the life and trajectory of her surreptitious but willing guide, Pauline Oliveros. Change is the dominant force and a recurring motif for both Montano and Oliveros upon their merger. While the performance at the Woman's Building ended after three days, Oliveros and Montano quickly became inseparable, two circles in a closely overlapping Venn diagram, as partners in art and life for the next seven years, with those categories—"art" and "life"—losing distinction and giving way to continuum.

In 1981, Montano published *Art in Everyday Life*, a chronological account of her "life vita" to that point, beginning with her birth in Saugerties, New York in 1942, and her "art vita" since 1964. As the title of the book signals, the imbrication of these categories is central to the narrative. Also central to the narrative is Montano's relationship with Oliveros, which coincides with the dissolution of her marriage to the photographer Mitchell Payne. Following their initial encounter at the Woman's Building in March 1975, Oliveros appears consistently throughout the book—as a guide, as a deliberate collaborator, as a casual accomplice, as a muse, as a lover, and as life partner. There are moments of pure, expansive joy that mark the onset of this exciting new relationship, overlapping a sense of mourning, as her relationship with Payne faltered.

For a three-day performance titled *Listening to My Heart . . . A Congenital Murmur* (1975) at Camerawork Gallery in Marin County, Montano spent three days listening and reflecting: "All of my life I have had a congenital heart murmur which has always fascinated me. I took this time to hear what it was murmuring. I was also preparing myself to live alone after five years of marriage." And then, in a sudden mood shift, she notes that "Pauline Oliveros came to the opening disguised as a suburban woman and was recognized by Minette Lehmann just as she was leaving. Minette knows the rest of this story." If Oliveros's appearance at the opening was unexpected, her drag performance as a "suburban woman" was even less likely. It's unclear if Oliveros considered her undercover act as life or art (perhaps Minette Lehmann knows the answer), but it points to a new set of extramusical possibilities for her. Was Montano's predilection for adopting personae already rubbing off? In any event, the surprise appearance in drag, done with the assistance of Carol Vencius, apparently served as a rehearsal for *Unnatural Acts Between Consenting Adults* shortly after.

Given Montano's inclusion of this detail focusing on Oliveros's surprise appearance in costume at the opening, it is perhaps curious that Montano neglects to mention her own participation in Oliveros's contribution to Ashley's opera in her "art vita." Based on a conversation I had with Montano [in January 2021], her memory of the performance for *Music with Roots in the Aether* is faint at best; she indicated that she generally felt unseen by Oliveros's peers in contemporary music. In this sense, her performance as Huckleberry Linda, silently draped over the piano but unremarked upon, mostly out of the camera's framing, is intended as a rather literal sign of her marginalization in this aspect of Oliveros's life. Montano would increasingly have a larger role in Oliveros's work in subsequent years, even following their break up in 1982, from art direction on stage productions to photo credits to playing the concertina on the quartet version of *Horse Sings from Cloud*. Some of Montano's contributions are attributed to her various personae . . .

38

In December 1975, the couple drove to the Mojave Desert in Oliveros's VW bus, and enacted an extended art/life performance, which Montano titled *Living Art: A Complex Theory Which States That Life Can Be Art (Living with Pauline Oliveros in the Desert for Ten Days)*:

ART Pauline Oliveros and I lived in the desert for ten days and agreed that everything we did would be considered art. We documented the event.

LIFE Living art was incredibly exhilarating . . . I thought that the life/art transference was finally made because I began interacting more truthfully and spontaneously. I called each day art and not life.

I was happy and making art at the same time.

Montano's account suggests two circles of a Venn diagram perfectly overlapped, and besides the textual documentation and a few photographs, the performance described primarily existed for a tidy, private audience of two. If, by the end of 1975, Montano had achieved her exhilarating ideal of "life/art transference," the following years spent with Oliveros would bring many challenges, too. Montano relocated from the Bay Area to join Oliveros in the suburbs of San Diego, and on November 1, 1976, she conducted a three-hour performance titled *Astral Travel . . . While Staying Physically in Leucadia I Will Travel Astrally to Bud's Ice Cream in San Francisco*, in which she attempted to overcome her sense of isolation and missing her friends: "During the event I visualized myself there and retained the image for three hours. Two friends went to Bud's and no one saw me." . . .

[When I was writing this last year, I had not considered the connection of this astral travel performance to the second half of Oliveros's *Sonic Meditation III*:

Telepathic Improvisation

To the musicians with varied or like instruments:

Tuning—each musician in turn sits or stands in front of the audience for a few minutes. The audience is asked to observe the musician carefully and try to imagine the sound of his or her instrument. The audience is instructed to close eyes and attempt to visualize the musician, then send a sound to the musician by hearing it mentally. The musician waits until he or she receives an impression of a sound mentally, then he or she produces the sound. Members of the audience who have successfully "hit the target" raise their hands as feedback to the musician.

It strikes me now, as it did then, that so much of what Montano describes as an "art/life transference" was a call and response with Oliveros, a constant reverberation, even when the telepathic communication was delayed in months or years. One can fully sense their deep entanglement when paging through Montano's book *Art in Everyday Life*, which was published shortly before the couple broke up.]

39

On August 19, 1977, Montano received tragic news of her estranged husband's accidental death. The event would become the subject of several performances by Montano as well as a video titled *Mitchell's Death* (1977), by now a classic example of early performance video. The set up for the single-channel, black-and-white video is seemingly simple: The camera tightly frames Montano's face, which practically glows with a ghostly pallor in the high contrast lighting. Her face, a death mask, is pierced with acupuncture needles. Her eyes are closed, or perhaps looking downward—they never meet the camera. She is reciting (or perhaps reading) a text. Her tone is measured, undramatic, monotonous, but her voice is also filtered through a heavy delay. Its echoes stretch and spatialize time, collapsing past into present.

Friday a.m., August 19, I wake at 7 or so. Look at the clock. I wish that chicken would stop crowing. Preacher Man running around the yard, echoing himself into the adjacent meadow. Pauline goes out to find him, comes back. I tell her my dream. A new one. Instead of being bothered by the baby, I throw sand at it when it throws sand at me. Pauline says something about her dream . . . a dead fetus and bloody clothes. She then goes outside and tries to catch the chicken.

At 10:30 I ask Pauline's advice about selling a tape recorder, which belonged to Mitchell and me. Things from my past. Then the phone rings. It's 11 a.m. It's J from Kansas.

Hello Linda, this is J from Kansas. I have some very shocking news for you. Mitchell is dead. From a gun accident. I scream, start to faint, call Pauline. Pauline, Mitchell is dead!

The narrative continues at length and through the stages of grieving, with Montano traveling to Kansas to visit Payne's dead body in the mortuary and to attend his funeral. Referencing *The Tibetan Book of the Dead*, she gently gives him permission to pass through the bardo: "Don't be afraid Mitchell. It's okay. Go on. Don't be scared. Surrender. Whatever fears you are experiencing are only illusions. Go on. Don't fear. Don't worry. No more worry."

("When there is no desire to change . . . then change.")

Pauline's presence in the narrative is significant: caretaking, making tuna sandwiches, administering foot massages. What is less obvious, or at least uncredited, is her presence in the extraordinary sound design of the video—a resonant delay that recalls Oliveros's own tape delay experiments from the previous decade, and anticipate her development of the Expanded Instrument System (EIS) a decade later. The video version of *Mitchell's Death* follows several live performances, detailed in *Art in Everyday Life*. The first of these took place at Artist's Coalition at 424 F Street in San Diego, September 21, 1977. Montano wore the same clothes she had worn to Payne's funeral, a patterned tunic, with the addition of "a man's moustache and eyebrows glued on." In this guise, Montano taped down the keys of a chord organ to produce a thirty-three-minute drone—one minute for each year of Payne's life. The following March, Montano repeated this thirty-three-minute drone at a tribute to Payne at LAICA (the Los Angeles Institute of Contemporary Art), with Minette Lehmann showing slides and discussing Payne's photographic work.

The first live performance of *Mitchell's Death* occurred the following month at UC San Diego's Center for Music Experiment, a programming space at the university directed by Oliveros. For this performance, Montano showed a video of her applying white makeup and then acupuncture needles to her face, and was accompanied by Oliveros, playing a bowl gong, and Al Rossi, playing a shruti box. As Montano describes it:

> I entered the space after Al and Pauline. Al began playing the sruti [*sic*] box and I turned on the monitor and the light on the lecturn. [*sic*] Both Al and Pauline chanted and I sang on one note the story of Mitchell's death from the moment I heard about it to the time I saw him in the mortuary.
>
> When the text was completed I turned off the light and monitor and left the space.

In the context of *Art in Everyday Life*, Montano's description represents the category "Art." She leaves the category "Life" notably empty. However, in discussing this performance four decades later, Montano completely reversed her understanding of the categories, describing *Mitchell's Death* as "a funeral"—"life, not art." . . .

40

What remains remarkable, even now, is how little this merger between Oliveros and Montano has been considered in the critical assessment of either artist's work from this period, which continued until their circles separated in 1982. On July 4, 1983, Montano would embark on her most demanding and perhaps best-known work to date—another merger, in which she would become literally tied to the artist Tehching Hsieh, for a complete calendar year. Titled *Art / Life: One Year Performance 1983–1984 (Rope Piece),* the conditions of the work demanded that the artists remained connected with an eight-foot rope but were not allowed to touch. Another variation on the idea of "unnatural acts for consenting adults," the artists were practically strangers when they entered into this arrangement, initiated by a signed contract. While the one-year structure, accompanied by a formal agreement, closely follows the logic of three previous one-year works by Hsieh, the work's sense of entanglement recalls an earlier collaborative performance, *Handcuff* (1973) by Montano, in which she was handcuffed to the artist Tom Marioni for three days.

A few months after severing her umbilical connection to Hsieh, in a work that exacted a heavy emotional toll on both artists, Montano embarked on a solo performance of substantially longer duration, titled *Seven Years of Living Art* (1984–1991).
As Montano described it (on a now, seemingly-defunct website):

SEVEN YEARS OF LIVING ART is a time-based, endurance/ performance which focuses the mind in a directed way so that art becomes a vehicle for meditation. Wearing one color of clothing each year that corresponds to the color of a specific Chakra (Hindu energy system), I was able to stay attentive to my intention. That is, to train the mind not to wander, shop around, or buy into the millions of distractions that impinge minute-to-minute.

Remarkably, this endurance performance was immediately followed by *Another Seven Years of Living Art*, extending to December 8, 1998. Montano repeated the sequence of seven colors while eliminating some of the conditions of the first iteration. “At first I performed very strict disciplines but later allowed the natural flow of the Chakras to become an internal discipline.” Her ability to sustain this long-term embodiment of “living art,” training attention while allowing for subtle changes over time, inevitably recalls the composition by Oliveros that was named for her and represents their merger:

Sustain one or more tones or sounds until any desire to change the tone(s) or sound(s) subsides. When there is no desire to change the tone(s) or sound(s), then change.

41

This morning I am listening to a recording of a 1992 concert of Pharoah Sanders and Sonny Sharrock from Frankfurt, which I found on YouTube yesterday. I'm still in awe of the things that get unearthed there. There is no video of the eighty-three-minute concert, just a black-and-white photograph of the two musicians, with Sanders in a dashiki and Sharrock in a suit. In the concert they are joined by Charnett Moffett on bass and Pheeroan akLaff on drums. The concert follows closely from Sharrock's 1991 *Ask the Ages*, which features Sanders and Moffett, with Elvin Jones on drums. It remains one of my favorite albums of all time, and I return to it often; it's among the gems encrusted in the ancient iPod in my car. I bought that CD in my first year of college, at B-Side Records and Tapes in Madison, Wisconsin, where I spent more time and money than I would want to admit. But, it was certainly part of my education.

Jazz was a new field of interest once I got to college, at least partially influenced by Dennis Strelow, who lived two doors down in the dorms. I was quickly drawn to more "out" versions of jazz, like John Coltrane and his diaspora, including those who played on his last group, including Alice Coltrane and Pharoah Sanders, and many who played on his larger ensemble work *Ascension* (1966), including Archie Shepp and Marion Brown. Like John Coltrane, many of them made records for Impulse. *Tauhid*, Sanders's first record for Impulse, recorded in 1966 and released in 1967, was an immediate favorite when I found it. It happens to be the first occasion where Sharrock appeared on a recording, and his utterly unique guitar playing is a highlight of the album. I don't remember the exact order of things, but I also remember finding Wayne Shorter's *Super Nova* (1969) around that time, which features both Sharrock and John McLaughlin on guitar.

Electric guitar was not exactly new or alien to jazz, but Sharrock's playing was highly unusual if you place it in relation to Wes Montgomery or Grant Green. Though it should also be said it's impossible to imagine Sharrock without these forebears. I want to say Sharrock is less tasteful—especially if one considers his "out there" record *Monkey-Pockie-Boo* (1970) or his work with Last Exit in the 1980s—though he can be extremely tasteful when he wants to be. At some point I remember Sharrock noting that he wanted to play the guitar like John Coltrane played the saxophone, which is to say BIG—in a word I might not use to describe Montgomery or Green—though one might also add dense, relentless, and ferocious. Ferocious but melodic. An electric guitar can also do things a saxophone cannot, and Sharrock's guitar creates an extraordinary, sometimes otherworldly sense of texture, that also seems to parallel or anticipate Jimi Hendrix. It's on *Tauhid*—which, coincidentally, was released the same year as *Are You Experienced?* (1967)—as things gradually build to a crescendo or a cacophony. I don't really hear the cacophony as "cacophony" anymore, but I understand that as something I was initially drawn to: the noise and sheer intensity of it. I become aware of it when listening to this music around others who don't know it by heart. This is true of Sanders's saxophone playing, too, in which he overblows the reed to produce an incredibly distorted, vibratory squall. Almost like hollering or crying, and sometimes he is actually hollering rather than doing it with the saxophone.

The interplay between Sanders and Sharrock is incredible, which makes *Ask the Ages* seem like it picks up right where *Tauhid* leaves off, albeit twenty-five years later. But what's so memorable, now, another thirty years later, are the melodies on *Ask the Ages*. The songs are flat out beautiful (see, for example, "Who Does She Hope to Be?"), even when they veer off the road and fly into outer space. They always get back on the road as if nothing happened.

The YouTube concert features a mix of songs from *Ask the Ages* ("Little Rock" and "Many Mansions") and *Tauhid* ("Japan," "Upper and Lower Egypt," and "Venus"), with the added bonus of John Coltrane's "Mr. P.C.," (1960) named after the bass player Paul Chambers—another part of the lineage. It's strange to hear these live versions of songs I've been listening to for so many years—familiar and totally fresh at the same time.

42

Today I was listening to two albums by Pharoah Sanders while driving to and from Chinatown: *Village of the Pharoahs* and *Wisdom Through Music*. Both of these incredible albums were released on Impulse in 1973, the year of my birth. In 2011, Impulse (which is now owned by Universal Music Group) sandwiched both albums together on a CD as part of their 2-on-1 series. Rather delightfully, the booklet accompanying the CD includes reproductions of both of the original LP sleeves, inside and outside, without further embellishment. At the centerfold of the CD booklet, one finds the back cover of *Village of the Pharoahs*, with a great picture of Sanders sitting cross-legged on the grass, next to the front cover of *Wisdom Through Music*, with a close-up of his face, eyes closed in concentration. There are album credits, but no "liner notes," such as an essay expounding upon the music. Sadly. I am a fan of liner notes and consider them an essential supplement to most jazz albums released in the 1950s on important labels like Blue Note and Columbia. (Perhaps Impulse ditched liner notes? Something for future research.) Reading the earnest and sometimes urgent essays by poet-critics LeRoi Jones/Amiri Baraka and A.B. Spellman, among others, offered valuable insights into the music when I first started listening to it, translating its turbulent affect and exploratory—*liberatory*—ambition into words, making rhetorical cases for the significance of this music in the lineage of the field and in the culture at large. It's important to remember that this liberatory music, and Black music in general, was (is?) considered threatening to many (white) listeners. And certainly demanding, if not threatening. In any case, Sanders or Impulse must have decided this music, circa 1973, could speak for itself, and perhaps it does. The 2-on-1 CD in its cheap plastic jewel case is by now a relic, of course, but you won't find the wonderful accompanying images or a list of the musicians or the pictures of Sanders and his bands if you listen to these on Spotify.

43

What constitutes your musical universe?

In September 1991, I met Mark Markin, and my musical universe expanded exponentially. Mark was the roommate of Dennis Strelow, who lived two doors down in the dorms. Dennis became my roommate the following year, and Mark fell in love with my friend and then-current roommate Salomon, who had covered his half of our dorm room with images of Madonna (the pop star, not the mother of Christ). But before all of that, Mark was an eccentric guy who lived at the end of the hall and often played music with his door open at an extreme volume when Dennis wasn't around. The music was not only EXTREMELY LOUD, but it was also strange. Meaning, I didn't even know what it was. But I was curious about it, and soon enough Mark and I became friends and he began introducing me to new music, art, and film. We also had the same astronomy class, which became a pretext for our friendship. His influence was enormous; I can't overstate it. He was a year older and already studying film, which at UW-Madison was a concentration in the School of Communication Arts called Film, Television, Radio. Mark is the primary reason I decided to pursue a degree in film. We spent many hours watching films, talking about films, and making films. (I'm in one of Mark's films.) But more than anything, I think he blew my mind with the music he was listening to, most of which became part of my world. The first time I heard Philip Glass was when Mark played *Einstein on the Beach* (1976) VERY LOUDLY with the door open. I remember the scary, violent high-pitched strings of George Crumb's *Black Angels* (1970) performed by Kronos Quartet, which Mark played VERY LOUDLY with the door open. (Crumb died last week at the age of ninety-two. I immediately thought of this first encounter with his music in the dorms. And then I remembered that, four years later, I bought a Crumb/Cage record at a Goodwill in Oklahoma while moving to Los Angeles.) Mark also introduced this captive audience (usually willing) to Brian Eno, Harold Budd, King Crimson, Arvo Pärt, Steve Reich, Terry Riley—all immediately shaped my musical universe, even if I didn't actually like some of it upon my first listen. Perhaps it's fairer to say I was unprepared for what I was hearing, though my enthusiasm for noisy experimental rock music and Sonic Youth in particular, at least laid some foundation for embracing the challenges of this music. He was also into things like Roy Orbison (who my mom was also into), Annie Lennox, and K.D. Lang. Pop stuff, which is where he connected musically with Sal. He was very avant-garde, but also well-rounded. Mark also made music, usually low-fi experiments with keyboard or found sounds recorded on cheap cassette tapes: bedroom ambient. This was all incredibly inspiring.

Last night I found an archival radio program with Harold Budd from September 10, 1984, from a late-night radio show called *SNAP!*, which was hosted by Deirdre O'Donoghue on KCRW radio from 1982 to 1991. I texted the episode to Mark, who now lives in New York. We both conspired to listen to it today. I am listening to it now.

44

Amid so much bad news in the world (continued COVID deaths and stupidity, vaccine protests in Canada, Russia's seemingly inevitable invasion of Ukraine . . .), one headline caught my attention as I scrolled through the *New York Times* on my phone this morning:

Curling's Scottish Soundtrack, Delivered by Bagpipers from Beijing

I will admit that I have a soft spot for curling and tend to get absorbed in it every four years when the Winter Olympics are on television. And I also have a soft spot for a sport that has its own soundtrack.

The musicians are self-described amateurs mostly from Beijing. None of them have ever been to Scotland. But they were dressed as though they had just arrived from the Highlands: red plaid kilts adorned with the little pouches with long tufts of horsehair known as sporrans, all part of the uniform they had ordered from abroad.

The steady squeal of "Scotland the Brave" held its own against the din of the arena—the selection a nod, no doubt, to curling's Scottish roots. But the anthem is also sort of a default tune for the instrument; tutorial videos on how to play it were easy to find online. And the band needed that help since their teacher, the only one they could find in China, had recently left the country.

"We just like bagpipes," the leader of the pipers, Zhang A Li, said after one of their pregame performances—a staple of curling tournaments whether in China or Chicago, "and we all just came together."

The story inspired me to listen to Yoshi Wada's album *Off the Wall* (1985) featuring the composer and Wayne Hankin on bagpipes, accompanied by Marilyn Bogerd on "adapted organ" and Andreas

Schmidt Neri on percussion. There is something transportive about the bagpipes. Tashi Wada told me his father traveled to Scotland to learn the bagpipes at the source. His use of them extends their lineage, but also intersects with the lineage of American minimalist music, and in the case of this album, Terry Riley in particular. Tom Johnson, longtime critic for the *Village Voice*, who had a front row seat for the development of American minimalism (and adjacencies) and is one of its most important interpreters, wrote the astute liner notes for *Off the Wall*. Here's an excerpt:

> It may be more accurate to think of Wada as a sculptor than as a composer because his music seems to be a physical reality, like wood or stone, and also because of the way he treats this material. Most composers work with ideas. Their basic interest is in melodies, harmonies, thematic relationships, tone rows, tonal centers, emotional qualities, and other rather abstract things, all of which can then be conveyed in sound, but none of which really are sound. Wada, on the other hand, works directly with the sound itself. His music would sound silly arranged for church organ for example. And if he prefers to preserve some improvisatory freedom rather than to notate specific musical ideas, this is at least partly because he is not so interested in the kinds of musical ideas that can be written down on paper. He wants to maintain direct contact with the physical reality of the sound.

45

It's taken me a few days to get back to the Harold Budd radio show from 1984. It's a wonderful mix of his own recordings and an eclectic sample of things he liked, from Brian Eno ("Spider and I"—"spine-tingling" by Budd's description) to Pink Floyd ("Obscured By Clouds") to Popol Vuh ("Wehe Khorazin" from the *Fitzcarraldo* soundtrack) to The Cure, erroneously called The Call by Deirdre O'Donoghue ("All Cats are Grey"), to Waylon Jennings ("Precious Memories," a traditional Protestant song that Budd and his brother used to sing in church) to the traditional mariachi song "Son De La Negra" by Nuevo Tecalitlán ("bought in Guadalajara, Mexico in 1971"). Budd refers to himself as the "world's greatest living fan of Waylon Jennings." He admits to not being influenced by Erik Satie ("at all") or even liking his music when asked. He confesses to a surface interest in most music, despite revealing a broad range of enthusiasms, but also talks about how he connects to music through emotion and memory. In nearly two hours of examples and low-key conversation, he sketches his musical universe.

46

This morning I am listening to a recording of Harold Budd's 2004 concert at REDCAT, which I attended, courtesy of SoundCloud. The concert was organized by SASSAS—the Society for the Activation of Social Space through Art and Sound—an organization I joined twelve years later. I remember it was billed as Budd's retirement concert, though that proved to be untrue. Or perhaps he retired and then unretired. Apparently, it happened before in the 1970s, before a collaboration with Brian Eno changed his trajectory. The concert featured Budd on piano, accompanied by Jon Gibson on soprano saxophone (if memory serves), Clive Wright on guitar, and Alex Cline on gong, and others. The concert started with Cline playing *Lirio* (1971), a composition for solo gong. I've never seen the score, which apparently consists of the instruction "under a blue light, roll very lightly on a large gong for a long duration." It's an early work and coincides with Budd's time teaching at CalArts in the early 1970s and his friendship with James Tenney. It's interesting to think about Budd's blue light alongside Oliveros's blue light from her first *Sonic Meditation* composed the same year, *Teach Yourself to Fly*. Elsewhere I've read *Lirio* is intended as a twenty-four-hour performance for solo gong, but that always seemed preposterous. Even in 1971 the drugs didn't last that long. But I like the open-endedness and lack of pressure in "a long duration." The version performed by Cline was relatively short, meaning short relative to my expectations. I could have listened to it for a much longer duration. A little internet searching reveals some writing on this work by Gavin Bryars who also mentions an earlier Budd work, *Magnus Colorado* (1969), several gongs accompanied by a "very soft colored light," and a later work called *Blue Room with Flowers and Gong* (1985). Bryars notes that these works with colored light were likely influenced by Budd's friendship with Mark Rothko, who was working on the paintings for Rothko Chapel when they eventually met. I think it's also important to remember Budd, best known for his piano performance, was once a drummer who played in an army band with Albert Ayler. As I write this, my desk lamp spotlights my hands on the keyboard of my laptop like a little theater, while Cline's performance of *Lirio*, rolling very lightly on the gong, rattles my desk speakers.

47

Thinking about "Bismillahi 'Rrahmani' Rrahim"—a playlist:

Marion Brown
"Bismillahi 'Rrahmani' Rrahim"
Vista
ABC Impulse!, 1975

Harold Budd
"Bismillahi 'Rrahmani' Rrahim"
The Pavilion of Dreams
Obscure, 1978

Pharoah Sanders
"Let Us Go Into the House of the Lord"
Summun Bukmun Umyun - Deaf Dumb Blind
ABC Impulse!, 1970

Lonnie Liston Smith and the Cosmic Echoes
"Let Us Go Into the House of the Lord"
Astral Traveling
Flying Dutchman, 1973

Harold Budd
"Let Us Go Into the House of the Lord/Butterfly Sunday"
The Pavilion of Dreams
Obscure, 1978

John Coltrane
"After the Rain"
Impressions
Impulse!, 1963

Lonnie Liston Smith and the Cosmic Echoes
"Aspirations"
Astral Traveling
Flying Dutchman, 1973

His Name is Alive
"Bismillahi 'Rrahmani' Rrahim"
Sweet Earth Flower: A Tribute to Marion Brown
High Two, 2007

48

Amid CalArts Zoom duties and sifting through a seemingly bottomless pile of email, I'm listening to *Improvised Music New York 1981*, a free improvisation set with Derek Bailey, Fred Frith, Sonny Sharrock, John Zorn, Bill Laswell, and Charles K. Noyes. It takes me back to my undergraduate years when most of these musicians entered my universe—a full decade after this recording was made. (I actually didn't hear it until 2010, when Hadi Tabatabai shared the files with me during my residency at Headlands.)

While I can't overstate the influence of friends like Mark Markin who opened my musical universe exponentially, I also shouldn't underestimate my own instincts and impulses for finding music on my own. One's musical universe is inevitably shaped by a combination of external forces (friends, radio, MTV, Spotify suggestions based on algorithms, what's on display at the record store, one's cultural context, and so on) and internal forces (taste, curiosity). Perhaps Oliveros's mandala provides a useful way of thinking about it: The outer ring of my universe is all the music I am aware of, but the dot in the center is what I am most attentive to, in the present or over a long period of time. Some musical obsessions fall away (gone, but not forgotten) while others linger or grow over the course of time.

49

I remember hearing that one's musical tastes stop developing at age twenty. Like bones, I guess. Somehow this idea immediately frightened me, and I took a silent vow to never stop seeking out or listening to new music. Which isn't to say I don't still listen to many things I listened to when I was twenty. In fact, it is startling to think of how long some of that music, which was a new discovery twenty-eight years ago, continues to be part of my world. I was also around twenty when I took a cosmology class and learned about different models for the universe and its evolution following from the Big Bang. The two that seemed to be the most likely were completely opposite concepts. One, referred to as "cold death," theorized a universe that keep expanding outward toward absolute inertia; the other prophesized a universe that would reach some unknown outer limit, at which point it would contract, like a rubber band, snapping back to an infinitely small, infinitely dense point which would apparently precede another Big Bang. The joy of cosmology was accepting that we would never know the answer but could attempt to picture each of these models, stretching the imagination like a rubber band. This is one version of the sublime.

50

Last night I made my second trip to REDCAT this week, to attend a concert by two CalArts grads: Anna Luisa Petrisko (who used to perform as Jeepneys) and Elisa Harkins. It was my first indoor (or outdoor) concert of this scale, meaning an audience of about a hundred or so people, all politely seated, since the pandemic arrived almost two full years ago.

Anna Luisa was accompanied by two other musicians, Julius Smack and Adee Roberson, all barefoot and wearing hand-dyed gowns. The set was electric with a large video projection and the same image multiplied on stacks of monitors stacked around the stage, with idyllic images of nature juxtaposed with moving shapes and primitive video effects. This was designed by Anna Luisa in collaboration with Chloe Scallion, who created several versions of a transfuturist opera while at CalArts. Anna Luisa played a keyboard and a small tabletop xylophone, and sometimes raked her hand across a hanging row of xylophone chimes. Julius Smack played a small electric drum set, and danced, and Adee Roberson played a lone snare drum. Everybody sang at times. The mix was retrofuturistic, nodding heavily in the direction of new age, but with bouts of tension or at least intensity, including the final song, which was built around three percussion instruments. It was New Age music for a newer New Age.

Elisa Harkins performed on a stark stage, with a chair and a microphone stand, wearing a ceremonial Muscogee (Creek) dress. She was also barefoot. She danced rather athletically while singing along to music she had pre-recorded, all with a clear sense of preparation and purpose. The lighting scheme was straightforward but effective. She sang in a mix of Muscogee (Creek), Cherokee, Algonquin, and English, and her songs veered into very contemporary takes on First Nation themes, with a pulsing dance beat and autotuned vocals. Other songs were more stripped down, with Elisa playing a hand drum, which she had made using elk and borrowed from tradition. Her performance of the intertribal AIM (American Indian Movement) Song was particularly moving. She ended each song with "Mvto! Thank you!" and even gave an encore which was demanded by the cheering audience. It was a brilliant combination of pop stagecraft, folk knowledge, and political expression—and a perfect example of performance as embodied research and scholarship. Mvto! Thank you, Elisa!

51

Twice this week at REDCAT, I also saw the exhibition by Black Quantum Futurism (a collaborative project by Camae Ayewa and Rasheedah Phillips), titled *CPT Reversal* (2021–2022). CPT stands for "Colored People's Time," which has historically been used in a racist, derogatory sense, but in physics the acronym stands for "change, parity, time reversal." The exhibition deliriously conflates these ideas, with an installation that often mixes craft fair and science fair. There is a fountain titled *River of Time* (2021), a wall of viewing portals, and profusion of videos on monitors, but my favorite part of the exhibition is *Dismantling the Master's Clocks* (2015–2021), a series of vintage clocks altered using collage and other crafty approaches. There is also a lot of information graphics throughout the show, and one graphic in particular gets my attention. It's a mandala, with a smaller circle inside a larger circle. The larger circle is labeled with eight events, "Event A" to "Event H," and each of these events has an arrow, like spokes of a wheel, pointing to the small, inner circle labeled "NOW."

This reminds me of a mandala diagram by Oliveros that proposes a similarly nonlinear model of time, but differently. The circle is labeled "TIME," with arrows pointing in both directions, clockwise and counterclockwise. Inside the circle are two more arrows, forming a cross. The vertical arrow points up to the present, and down to the future; the horizontal arrow points right to the past and left to "PAST/PRESENT/FUTURE." Just outside the circle, is the provocative phrase "NO TIME." I am always arrested by this juxtaposition of all time—conflated as PAST/PRESENT/FUTURE—and NO TIME. Found in Oliveros's papers at Mills, this mandala was undated, adding to its own apparent timelessness. It is also scaleless: Time is posed as a concept, and a direction, not a measure. But timelessness—NO TIME—doesn't really exist, does it? As a concept it stretches the imagination beyond the threshold of the explicable, tantalizing but indefinitely out of reach.

52

Each mandala is unique in its elaboration whether as art, process, or construction even though its basic properties include 1) a center, 2) symmetry, 3) cardinal points. Only the center is constant. Symmetry can be varied and diverse, bilateral, dynamic, rigid and well defined (as our circle with the dot) or absolutely fluid like the earth. The cardinal points may be precise in number, odd or even, many or few (the amount depending on the mandala), or the points may be infinite or non-existent as in a circle. There is always more room for more in a circle as in the unlimited capacity for our expanding global attention. But in any case, and in all uses, the mandala is a plan for action of some kind or else it is not a mandala.

—Pauline Oliveros, "MMM: Meditation/Mandala/Music," presented on April 14, 1980 at the Walker Art Center

53

We can be in tune with time
We can be a slave to time
Or we can be in total aspiration
Trying to catch time
There must be a fourth way
To flow with time
This is the organic way

This is the way of the Organic Society
To flow with time

—Don Cherry, "Relativity Suite," on *Organic Music Society* (1972)

54

Sometimes there is too much happening in the Eternal Now of the musical universe I am trying to account for in this daily writing project. My awareness contracts into intense attention, and then I get distracted or my mind wanders and my ears shift into another direction. Sometimes all of these points of concentration overload and collide into some gooey conflation of past/present/future.

For example, yesterday I was considering the influence of Dan Graham, who died last weekend. Among his many contributions to culture, he made an important and idiosyncratic video-essay called *Rock My Religion* (1983–1984), which wove together American music, culminating in punk and no wave (Black Flag, Patti Smith, and Sonic Youth all feature), and American religious traditions, including the Shakers. I tried to briefly outline Graham's work and importance to my students at CalArts, recalling seeing him lecture there in room A211H at least a decade earlier. I showed them video documentation of his *Don't Trust Anyone Over 30*, a 2004 multimedia marionette play made in collaboration with Rodney Graham, Tony Oursler, and the band Japanther—ironically aware that most of my students are eighteen or nineteen, and their teacher showing them this work is long past thirty. Also, not without irony, Dan Graham turned sixty-two in 2004.

Meanwhile, more or less, I am listening to an album of bagpipe compositions and improvisations by David Watson and Matthew Welch, a day or two after learning my friends' teenage son Joseph is swapping out his electric bass for the pipes. The Bandcamp page describes Watson and Welch's *Woven* (2021) as "a result of fleshing out a sonic-architectural outline through which we can fluently improvise and respond to each other's playing within certain confines of the musical score, whose structure is clear and austere, amidst the often torrential down-pouring of skirls. The sounds of pipes tuning in a space move seamlessly to blissful drones and scintillating shredding displaying our dual search for both the beautiful, and the rebellious." This reminds me to re-listen to another album by Watson and Tony Buck, *Ask the Axes* (2019), one of four beautiful records released on the Besom Presse label. I'm also compelled to look up "skirl," which I discover is "a shrill, wailing sound, especially that of bagpipes."

Meanwhile, more or less, I am considering the return of New Age aesthetics, prompted in large part by Anna Luisa Petrisko's concert at REDCAT, and a subsequent listen to her album *Green* (2018), as well as a meeting with Elizabeth Herring, a current CalArts student who is preparing an exhibition based on a real or hallucinated cappuccino cafe in the desert, with an assortment of rattan and wicker furniture, plastic flowers, and windchimes. She shows me a vintage copy of Shakti Gawain's *The Creative Visualization Workbook* (1982), in a visually arresting combination of yellow, blue, and purple, with a dense, floral mandala on the cover. We ended the meeting discussing why and how (the) New Age has been renewed, how capitalism has participated in that renewal, and if the movement or aesthetic (or, likely, both) is ripe for critique or somehow beyond its grasp. A day or two earlier, I happened upon—or my algorithms led me to—Alice Damon's *Windsong*, an album recorded in 1981, first released in 1990, and re-released four months ago by a label called Morning Trip/Yoga Records. It too features a mandala, in pale blue on its white cover.

Meanwhile, more or less, I note several archival Steve Roden recordings which have been recently (re-)released on vinyl and I listen to them anew on Spotify. *Oionos*, a 2006 sound installation Steve made in Athens, is a delight. The hour-long recording was initially installed in a tree near the Church of St. Dimitris Loumbardiardis, designed by architect Dimitris Pikionis. Steve's work often leads me to further research, and I am drawn to looking up Pikionis and the church. As soon as I finish listening to *Oionos* I conspire to listen to it again.

Meanwhile, more or less, I'm having a Don Cherry moment, or perhaps a Don Cherry week, and find myself listening to a selection of his recordings from the 1970s while driving to and from CalArts, and between Zoom meetings at home. These include *Organic Music Theatre: Festival de jazz de Chateauvallon* (1972), *Organic Music Society* (1973), *Blue Lake* (1973), *Eternal Now* (1974), and *The Codona Trilogy* (1979/1981/1983). I am always reminded of the continuity from one album to another, but also the way in which collaboration—unfurling an expansive tapestry of musical traditions, techniques, and instrumentation—defines each Don Cherry project. Strangely, Cherry can be repetitive and restless at the same time. The music keeps moving, even when his own voice remains consistent, and he resorts to familiar melodies and motifs. But the admixture and interplay are always compelling, at least for me, and has been since I first encountered his pocket trumpet on Ornette Coleman's *The Shape of Jazz to Come* (1959) in my college years.

Meanwhile, more or less, I am revising my syllabus for my seminar Routine Pleasures, which I am planning to teach in the fall, exactly ten years after I last taught it, and I'm enjoying the prospect of covering Cherry's Organic Music Society and Oliveros's Deep Listening Band in the same class, among other hot topics.

55

When I first saw the small church it totally took my breath away, and I immediately began to think about a work that could exist in resonance with it–but not distract from it. The church itself is still in use, and I wanted the work to be gentle and out of the way of the people who worship there. I decided to use the large tree in the front of the church for a hanging work that would [have] a little bit of visual presence as well as sound which could blend with all of the insect noises and the overall quiet of the area.

The audio was built from field recordings and small "poor" objects such as tin whistles, toy harmonicas, and the like. These "instruments" suggested by the museum of musical instruments in Athens, where the proper instruments take up most of the museum, but there is a wonderful display case in the basement with musical toys, religious objects, and other sounding devices not considered musical instruments. I felt that these simple things related to Pikionis's ideas about architecture and craft, and his interests in indigenous culture in conjunction with intellectual and modern culture. I felt there could be a relationship.

–Steve Roden, notes from *Oionos* (2022)

Steve's "poor instruments" remind me of the "little instruments" used by the Art Ensemble of Chicago. I remember seeing Roscoe Mitchell's mind-boggling rig of these musical and extra-musical instruments—bells, chimes, drums, squeaky toys, novelty noise makers—which was included in the exhibition of *The Freedom Principle: Experiments in Art and Music, 1965 to Now* at MCA Chicago. It was one of my favorite things I saw in any museum in 2015 (or any other year). I am also reminded of a video by Steve, titled *everything she left behind that fits in my hand* (2012), which I included in my 2016 exhibition *Routine Pleasures* at the Schindler House. The silent video features a series of tightly framed shots of his hand opening and closing to momentarily reveal a sequence of tiny objects—both familiar and unrecognizable—that had once belonged to the choreographer Martha Graham. Steve had purchased a box of these objects on eBay. His tender relation to these objects rendered their unlikely acquisition incredibly tender and surprisingly poignant, immediately elevating their presumed value (or lack thereof). This tenderness and transvaluation recalls Steve's email signature, borrowed from the artist Joseph Albers:

easy - to know
that diamonds - are precious

good - to learn
that rubies - have depth

but more - to know
that pebbles - are miraculous

56

What constitutes your musical universe?

By now, it is probably clear that my musical universe is intensely visual—contained in and spilling out of objects, almost always connected to images, sometimes mental but more often physical. Amidst the terrible news about war in Eastern Europe, I woke up to a relatable article in the *New York Times*, "Shelf Life: Our Collections and the Passage of Time," by film critic A.O. Scott, about the stuff we—critics are the specific focus of the article—tend to accumulate: books, records, CDs, DVDs, band T-shirts. All of which speaks to a specific generation (X) and also to the gradual obsolescence of that generation and all its physical clutter. Indeed, all those Criterion Collection DVDs are gathering dust, and when I finally buy a new car (an inevitability) I will rarely listen to CDs, if ever. So, yes, I'm a dinosaur, and there is nostalgia in the collections and piles, but I believe there is also stubborn if futile resistance to the endless streaming services and the obvious priorities of corporate media. (Also, Spotify is missing a lot of music, especially the kind I listen to.) Who or what are these collections for, the article asks. For me. I've never been obsessive about vinyl, and only bought a record player (again) because I had accumulated records, including those by friends and students. Same goes for cassettes. Some things are only available in one format. I prefer to hold a record in my hands, or a tape, or even a CD, and look at and/or read the accompanying information when I listen to it. Thumbnails on my laptop or phone don't do the same thing. Likewise, I'd rather see images of artwork printed in books using photolithography than as JPEGs found on Google. Of course, I listen to music on Spotify and search images on Google all of the time. But not exclusively, and not without a sense of loss. Discovering new music in a record store carries a different sense of risk—music used to cost money—and reward than having Spotify conjure an algorithmic stream of likely interest. A resolute "90s guy," as A.O. Scott puts it, I will likely die a dinosaur, gathering dust along with my books and CDs. Marie Kondo can wait.

57

What constitutes your musical universe?

By now, it is probably clear that my musical universe is that of a listener, not a maker. I am not trained in music beyond some guitar lessons with Mike Kalember, the bass player for Raven Bitch, in my teenage years. (You can look him up on the Encyclopaedia Metallum.) For a year or two I subscribed to the magazine *Guitar for the Practicing Musician* and tried to learn to play a few things using tablature notation. I can't read staff notation, though at various points I have almost had a handle on it. In fifth grade, my teacher Mr. Perry taught us how to play the autoharp and had us write rudimentary compositions. Mine was called "Carnival," and as the name insinuates it sounded a little like carnival music from a horror film. At some point after I had moved to California, I let my mom sell my black Kramer guitar and amplifier. I don't remember the details, but I clearly wasn't using them. In college I took a class called Black Music in America, which remains one of the classes that influenced me the most. It fulfilled my ethnic studies requirement. It was taught by an enthusiastic white guy named Eric Schumacher-Rasmussen. (Some Googling yields: "He has an MA in Afro-American Studies from the University of Wisconsin-Madison, where he wrote his master's thesis on 'The Blues and Gospel Impulses in the Rock Dialogic: Bruce Springsteen and Guns 'n' Roses.' He is a voting member of the Rock and Roll Hall of Fame.") I still have all the books from his class, which include LeRoi Jones's *Blues People*, Greil Marcus's *Mystery Train*, Peter Guralnick's *Sweet Soul Music*, and Charles Shaar Murray's *Crosstown Traffic*. I usually sold my books back to the university bookstore at the end of the semester to generate a little bit of spending money, but this was a rare case where I kept the books. (From other influential classes, I also kept and still have Petronious's *Satyricon*, Plato's *Symposium*, Nietzsche's *Beyond Good and Evil*, Duras's *The Malady of Death* . . .) I lent and lost my copy of *Blues People* at some point and bought a new copy, though I preferred the original cover design. I also took a class called Physics in the Arts, in which we learned about light and sound waves among other things. I was never very good at physics or math, but as with astronomy, the concepts appealed to me. I think about that class whenever I try to make sense of just intonation or see an oscillator in action. I am a collector, a connoisseur, a critic, a curator. Like many of my interests, music has been an area of autodidactic research. What I know about music, I primarily know from reading about it, watching musicians perform, talking to composer friends and colleagues, and, mostly, from listening. I currently own two musical instruments: a shruti box, which I bought online while teaching my Oliveros class, and a small Tibetan bell that I bought at a New Age shop in Solvang. The bell hangs over my desk, and I sometimes clang it with a pencil to sharpen my attention.

58

What constitutes your musical universe?

By now, it is probably clear that my musical universe contains plenty of black holes: pop music, for example, which is of little interest, at least since I was a teenager; but also (lest one accuse me of snobbery) most classical music, which rarely captures my attention, with some notable exceptions from the twentieth century (but is that classical or modern?); not to mention dance music (a broad category—I listened to a lot of so-called intelligent dance music, a.k.a. IDM, circa Y2K, but rarely danced to it); most rap music since the late 90s, with the notable exceptions of Kendrick Lamar and Nipsey Hussle; most R&B and soul, though I have fondness for Nina Simone, Stevie Wonder, Funkadelic, among others; most country music after the 1970s; and most rock music (a sprawling category that includes metal, grunge, "alternative") since the early 1990s. There is no shortage of other dark matter, much of which remains outside of my immediate awareness. There is music I hear but don't really listen to. The center of my musical universe is undoubtedly American, though I have enthusiasm for a scattered collection of "world music." Invariably, I prefer Feldman to Bartók, Perry (as in Lee "Scratch") to Beyoncé, No Neck Blues Band to Fleetwood Mac, Cat Power to Björk. I'm not sure I could justify these purely hypothetical choices; thankfully no one is asking me to do so. My musical universe is idiosyncratic, utterly my own.

59

Hiking in Kenneth Hahn today, I'm listening (again) to Don Cherry's *Organic Music Theatre: Festival de jazz de Chateauvallon* (1972), which was issued by the non-profit label Blank Forms last year, along with *Summer Sessions* (1968) and a fat four-hundred-ninety-six-page volume of Blank Forms journal, titled *Organic Music Societies*. All feature cover art by Moki Cherry, Don's invaluable partner in life and art. Both records are beautiful objects—especially *Chateauvallon*—but thankfully they are also on Spotify, which makes it easier to listen to while hiking. In my car, I've been listening to Don Cherry's *Om Shanti Om* (recorded in 1976 and released on CD in 2020) repeatedly; like *Chateauvallon* it features the amazing Brazilian percussionist Naná Vasconcelos, master of the one-stringed berimbau, with Moki on tanpura. I love it when such a remarkable trove of material (whether music or paintings or writing) by a longtime favorite gets unearthed, adding to what's already known, reshaping my understanding of the whole body of work. Or, rather, what I temporarily assume is whole. There is always more to be uncovered, isn't there?

My musical universe might be deeper than it is wide, or quite possibly it's very wide but clotted with dark matter and rife with rabbit holes.

60

Not on Spotify: The New York Jazz Collective's 1997 album *I Don't Know This World Without Don Cherry*, featuring a swinging number of the same time written by clarinetist Marty Erhlich. I find it on YouTube and suffer through the five seconds of pop-up advertising before the song begins. On Discogs, the online marketplace for music, twenty-eight copies of the CD are available starting at $2.10. I visit Discogs often, not so much to buy and sell (though I have purchased records and CDs from vendors found there), but to get information. (It's the musical cousin of eBay and Craigslist and shares their more-is-less aesthetic.) It's a great way to find out how many Pauline Oliveros albums exist, or who plays on what Don Cherry recording, or what multiple variations of the cover art looks like. It's exceedingly rare when I have an album that doesn't show up on the site. I consider that my musical universe is actually a small galaxy contained in the universe named Discogs.

61

Witchi-tai-to, gimee rah
Whoa rah neeko, whoa rah neeko
Hey ney, hey ney, no way

Witchi-tai-to, gimee rah
Whoa rah neeko, whoa rah neeko
Hey ney, hey ney, no way

Water spirit feelin'
Springin' round my head
Makes me feel glad
That I'm not dead

Today Elisa Harkins texted me with Jim Pepper's version of "Witchi Tai To," a traditional peyote song that became a crossover psychedelic/pop/jazz/folk hit at the end of the 1960s. I had sent Elisa a link to Don Cherry's *Organic Music Theatre: Festival de jazz de Chateauvallon*, a 1972 concert which includes a cover of "Witchi Tai To," and in return she responded with Pepper's "original," and a brief education on the song, which has subsequently been performed by her friend and poet laureate Joy Harjo, among many others. Pepper, who was Kaw and Muscogee Creek, first recorded the song with the band Everything is Everything in 1968; the song appeared again as the first song on his solo debut from 1971, *Pepper's Pow Wow*. Further research—Discogs—reveals yet another version of "Witchi Tai To" on Pepper's album *Comin' and Goin'* which was recorded in 1983 and released in 1987. Coincidentally, or probably not, Don Cherry plays on the album, as do Naná Vasconcelos and Colin Wallcott—the three, as Codona, had recorded their third and final album together in 1982. Pepper and Cherry also appear together on Charlie Haden and Carla Bley's exceptional ensemble album *Ballad of the Fallen*, recorded in 1982 and released in 1983. My attention shifts from interpretations of traditional peyote songs to interpretations of protest songs, just as my divided attention shifts between my laptop to the television screen and the real-time atrocity of Russia's invasion of Ukraine.

62

My graduate assistant Rodrigo Arruda's current exhibition at CalArts is a story of cannibalism and colonization, especially pertaining to the history of Brazil, and includes a number of folk tales retold. My favorite is "How a Tortoise Killed a Jaguar and Made a Harmonica of Its Bones," which Rodrigo describes as being "freely adapted" from *Amazonian Tortoise Myths* (1875) published by Charles Frederick Hartt. Hartt was a Canadian-American geologist member of the crew of Swiss-American scientist and creationist Louis Agassiz, who traveled to different regions of South America to search for proof of Agassiz's theory of the "superiority of the Caucasian race." It goes like this:

The Tortoise was taking a stroll deep within the Amazon Forest when it noticed the Monkey eating fruits on top of the Palm Tree. "Throw me some fruits, Monkey!"

"Sure, my dear Tortoise," says the Monkey.

The Monkey then carries the Tortoise to the top of the Palm Tree. "I'll be right back to pick you up," says the Monkey.

The Tortoise eats more fruits while waiting for the Monkey.

The Monkey, however, does not come back.

After hours of waiting, the Tortoise is hopeless.

Suddenly, the Tortoise sees the Jaguar walking by and the Jaguar quickly spots the Tortoise stuck at the Palm Tree. Planning to devour the Tortoise, the Jaguar gets closer, and in its deep, seductive voice, it says:

"My dear Tortoise, would you like my help getting down?"

Aware of the Jaguar's plan, the Tortoise cunningly agrees:

"Yes, dear Jaguar. Please catch me as I jump!"

The Jaguar then approaches the Palm Tree and opens its arms. The Tortoise jumps but flips itself mid-way through the fall, landing its shell directly onto the Jaguar's head.

The Jaguar dies instantly and the Tortoise goes away freely.

A few days later, while walking near the same Palm Tree, the Tortoise sees the Jaguar's bones lying on the ground.

It then carves one of the bones into a little harmonica which it uses to sing:

"How I killed a Jaguar and made a harmonica of its bones."

I enjoy imagining this tortoise jamming on its jaguar harmonica in a duet with the Patchwork Girl from Oliveros's "Rags and Patches," who plunges to the bottom of the ocean and vengefully picks the bones of an old sea captain like a human guitar.

63

Yesterday, some sound observations arrived via text message from Ruoyi Shi, my former graduate assistant, who is currently in residence in an isolated forest in Georgia. (During a previous residency, Ruoyi made some incredible drawings for my forthcoming pamphlet on Oliveros's tape and synth music.)

It's quite noisy during the daytime here as there is construction going on, but the sound in the forest after sunset is very fascinating.

I feel like I should not do any "deep listening" at night as the sound includes everything, and it can be a little scary.

I pressed for further details which arrived this morning.

There is the water, wind, creatures from the woods, and the sound from the cabin itself. And it is so quiet that I sometimes think the sound of my breath belongs to another person.

64

At times I feel very far from where I started with this meditation. My Don Cherry moment has stretched into the second week (not for the first time!), and I find myself locating unexpected connections. For example, the eponymous 1978 album by Mandingo Griot Society, which features Cherry alongside Foday Musa Suso, the extraordinary Gambian kora player—and, yes, griot. I only learned about the album in the past few days, exploring Cherry's connections.

Suso's debut solo album, *Kora Music from the Gambia* (also 1978) is highly recommended. The kora is a twenty-one-stringed instrument native to West Africa. I first encountered Suso and his kora on Kronos Quartet's *Pieces of Africa*, which I bought at or around the time of its release in 1992. It was among my first introductions to the category of world music and remains a favorite of mine. (I saw Kronos Quartet perform at the Madison Civic Center around that time, or perhaps the following year.)

As it turns out, Suso spent time in Chicago, where the *Mandingo Griot Society* album was recorded at Curtis Mayfield's studio. Among the other members of Mandingo Griot Society was drummer Hamid (Hank) Drake, associated with the that city's Association for the Advancement of Creative Musicians and a frequent collaborator with Fred Anderson, William Parker, and Peter Brötzmann; more recently, he appears on Natural Information Society's exceptional double album *Mandatory Reality* (2019), which has been in heavy rotation in my car since last summer. That album, and Joshua Abrams's guembri (a three-stringed lute of the Gnawa people of West Africa, also called a sintir), brought my attention back to Codona (the name stands for Collin-Don-Naná), without fully realizing Drake as a direct connection. Anyway, I am always excited by these connections and circles—or, perhaps, elliptical digressions is a more accurate description. I am imagining a complex, conspiratorial weblike mapping of these networks of personal interest and obsession.

I am (often) thinking about collaboration and how the group informs my understanding of an individual member, but of course also what the individual brings to the group. This is not just true in music, but it is perhaps easiest to identify in music. Don Cherry, for example, played in so many different groups and contexts, many of which he initiated. By the 1970s he had seemingly transitioned from the jazz idiom in which he had started in the late 1950s (famously, as part of Ornette Coleman's revolutionary quartet) toward what is generically called world music, though he never exactly left jazz behind, even when he traded pocket trumpet for harmonium and incorporated folk tunes from many different cultures into his "collage music." He also proclaimed, "It's not my music," meaning he was borrowing but not taking, and giving back in return. His musical universe was modular but accumulative, open and generous.

I've been eager to dig into thinking about Oliveros as a collaborator, who was also open and generous, in a way that provides a compelling (if unlikely) parallel with Deep Listening Band and other group endeavors. I will get there eventually.

65

Yesterday my musical universe contracted to the corner of Hollywood and Argyle, the location of Amoeba Records. Amoeba was, for many years, on the corner of Sunset and Cahuenga, and a compulsory stop anytime I was in its vicinity (very generously defined), but I dislike its new location: It's a smaller store (it's still huge but feels cramped) on an even busier corner in Hollywood with even worse parking options. Its temporary closure preceding its relocation, coupled with the risks and challenges of going anywhere during the pandemic, has made it a rare destination. It's also true that I have used Spotify and Bandcamp to "discover" new music more and more, but I also purchase LPs and CDs I want directly from the record labels. Despite so many streaming options, Amoeba was incredibly busy on this Saturday afternoon, and they probably haven't missed my more regular purchases. (Surely there are plenty of other people who sift the oddball used CDs in the Experimental section looking for treasure.) Still, I rarely fail to find something I desire when I'm there; I inevitably left with a handful of goodies, including Oliveros's *Accordion & Voice* on vinyl (which I already have on CD), re-pressed by Important Records last year, and *Organic Music Theatre: Festival de jazz de Chateauvallon* on CD (which I already have on vinyl), so I can listen to it in my Scion. (Both of these are readily available on Spotify, for the record.) I also bought a copy of *Pepper's Pow Wow*, because "Witchi-Tai-To" has been on my mind (or stuck in my head) so much in the past week or two. I also picked up Sun Ra and His Arkestra's *Omniverse*, released on CD last year; it was recorded in 1979, a year after his *Lanquidity* album, which remains my favorite of his recordings. (Remarkable that it's taken me this long to even mention Sun Ra; my musical universe often overlaps his musical omniverse.) Coincidentally (or not), the cover art of *Omniverse* and *Festival de jazz de Chateauvallon* both feature spirals and the color purple. I also picked up Mary Halvorson's album *The Maid with the Flaxen Hair*, a suite of guitar duets with Bill Frisell, released on John Zorn's Tzadik label in 2018. Frisell has been a favorite guitarist since I first encountered him on Zorn's first *Naked City* album, which I bought in that magical music year of 1991. Halvorson has been a recent favorite, especially the 2020 album *Artlessly Falling* by her Code Girl ensemble, which I've listened to on repeat during several stretches of the pandemic. Last but not least, a live recording from 1986 by The Group and first issued in 2012, which I found under Marion Brown in the Jazz CD section. The Group also features Ahmed Abdullah on trumpet, Andrew Cyrille on drums, Billy Bang on violin, and Fred Hopkins on bass, replacing the original bassist Sirone (Norris Jones). For whatever reason, this is the one I pop into the CD player as soon as I get back to my car and head toward my next destination. Later, at home, I read the extensive and endearing liner notes written by Abdullah on how The Group became a group and how they picked their name. Further research revealed that this The Group is not the only group called The Group.

66

A very abbreviated playlist for a long, round-trip commute:

Sun Ra
"Over the Rainbow"
Omniverse
El Saturn Records, 1979 (reissued by Modern Harmonic, 2021)
Composed by Harold Arlen with lyrics by Yip Harburg for the film *The Wizard of Oz* (1939).

Mary Halvorson with Bill Frisell
"The Nearness of You"
The Maid with the Flaxen Hair
Tzadik, 2018
Composed by Hoagy Carmichael with lyrics by Ned Washington for the film *Romance in the Dark* (1938).

67

(Improvisation for Duos and Trios)

Today, an all-too-rare trip to the CalArts library. Formally a frequent destination anytime I was at school, the library became a COVID casualty, not unlike Amoeba. I went over a pandemic year without setting foot on campus, and even longer without visiting the library. It was a loss, not that I lacked for books or other media in my immediate quarantine surroundings. Since returning to campus in September, a visit to the library seems like a decadent diversion. (As does reading, sadly.) In my early years of teaching, before I was an administrator, I had more unstructured time to spend, and I often invested it in the library. The ostensible purpose of today's visit: Derek Bailey's *Improvisation: Its Nature and Practice in Music*, a thin treatise originally published in 1980 that is an essential take on the form. I've been thinking about the connective tissue between Deep Listening Band and Organic Music Theatre, among other subjects of interest, and Bailey's book seemed like a key to thinking through their proximity.

Bailey was already on my mind after listening to Halvorson and Frisell's album of guitar duets, rife with idiosyncratic versions of so-called "standards," which called to mind Bailey's own *Ballads* (2002), and his subsequent *Standards* (2007), both on the Tzadik label. (Calling all Hoagy Carmichael fans!) As far as I know, Frisell and Bailey never played together, but both played guitar in trios with John Zorn on alto sax and George Lewis on trombone—Bailey on *Yankees* (1982); Frisell on *News for Lulu* (1988) and its follow-up *More News for Lulu* (1992).

Halvorson, for her part, has played in numerous ensembles led by Anthony Braxton, who played in a trio with Bailey and Lewis, released as *Trio (Pisa) 1982* in 2012. Bailey and Braxton also recorded several duo sets, of which I have two on CD—*First Duo Concert (London 1974)* and *Moment Précieux* (1987). In this context, it should also be mentioned that Bailey and Braxton played on a trio date, *Company 2* (1977), with saxophonist Evan Parker, and later Bailey and Zorn played on a trio date, *Harras* (1995), with William Parker (no relation) on bass.

I couldn't find Bailey's *Improvisation*, which wasn't where it was supposed to be on the shelf, so I left the library with a trio of other books instead.

68

Three books, checked out from the CalArts library, to add to a hypothetical bibliography in progress—such a bibliography would be one way of describing my musical universe:

Harold Budd with Vincent Plush, May 3, 1983, Los Angeles, CA
Yale University Oral History of American Music, 1990

Julia Eckhardt, ed.
Éliane Radigue: Intermediate Spaces
umland editions, 2019

Peter Garland, ed.
Soundings 13: *The Music of James Tenney*
Soundings Press, 1984

I find all of these things while scanning the shelves. None are sought intentionally; nevertheless, I am drawn to them and check them out from the library. I had previously encountered two of the volumes (Budd and Tenney) on the shelves, and I had seen the volume on Radigue online but didn't order it for some reason. Perhaps it was already out of print. Books on contemporary composers have a very small audience, even smaller than the audience for their music. Needless to say, I am among that very small audience, at least during this trip to the library.

Next question: Will I actually read them, and if so, when?

69

In this text, which began on January 1, I have not yet mentioned a previous project (challenge? experiment? performance?) in which I did not buy any books for an entire calendar year, 2013. I ended 2012 with a flurry of book purchases, hitting up Book Soup on Sunset and placing several orders on Amazon. This was the last time I (intentionally) purchased something on Amazon. In many ways, I came to understand the experiment as a way to rethink my relationship to consumption, which I certainly did. I have an intense relationship to books and own more than I need and acquire more than I could ever hope to read. Libraries are aspirational, once said some enabler.

Perversely, I was given one-hundred-eighty-seven books in 2013—on average, roughly one book every other day. (Yes, I kept track.) I was curating a biennial and visiting a lot of artists in their studios, which accounts for many of the books I was given. Some people also took pity on me when they learned of my self-imposed deprivation and made a point of giving me books. Most of the books I acquired were not books I would have purchased. Nevertheless, I was touched by the generosity. I had also made a book, *Proper Names*, and gave away several hundred copies.

In the end, I came to the conclusion that books were less of a problem than Amazon, which made it far too easy to acquire books and music. My decision to not use Amazon is inevitably political or ethical, given my awareness of their shitty labor practices and their gross capitalist priorities, but it really started for personal reasons (i.e., addiction). When I started buying books again in January 2014, I did so with more discrimination and greater intentionality. I buy books from independent bookstores or directly from publishers, which tend to be small, independent publishers. (I occasionally use the library, though not often enough.) My music purchases follow the same pattern.

I have attempted to gradually apply the lessons from that year (2013) of self-imposed deprivation toward consuming other things with greater intentionality, extending toward the food I eat and the music I listen to. This year (2022) is a year of listening with more purposeful awareness and attention.

I wrote this while listening to Éliane Radigue's *Occam Ocean, Vol. 4* (2021).

70

Some Sound Propositions

Today, my attention narrows on Éliane Radigue, as I begin reading *Intermediary Spaces*, which begins with an incredibly poetic text by the composer, written in 2008. Could (her) writing ever be as near to the sublime as (her) music? This introductory text begs the question. ("Everything I knew about contemporary music basically came from reading," she notes at one point.) This intro is followed by a long-form interview by Julia Eckhardt, the book's editor, who, importantly, has also played viola on Radigue's compositions of the past decade or so. Incredibly, Radigue only began composing for acoustic instruments in 2008, at the age of seventy-six, when the cellist Charles Curtis performed her composition *Naldjorak*. All of her work prior to this is electronic, and occasionally with voice, and absolutely singular. I've had several long bouts of engagement with Radigue's music—it's exceptionally demanding, in terms of the attention required to experience and appreciate its subtlety—and I've also considered her in parallel to Oliveros. Both composers are among the pioneering women featured in the recent documentary *Sisters with Transistors* (2020); both experienced (and overcame) explicit or implicit chauvinism, especially when working in electronic music studios; both invented new ways of making music in this context; both preferred using a synthesizer without a keyboard and its associations with traditional (Western) tonality: Oliveros was one of the first people to see and use a Buchla 100 series; Radigue favored the ARP 2500. There is also a close generational parallel: Both composers were born in 1932—Radigue on January 24, Oliveros on May 30. Both are air signs. Both were close with James Tenney. Most of this I already knew, but one connection I learn from the book is that Oliveros (along with Maggi Payne) provided valuable assistance in the realization of Radigue's *Labyrinthe Sonore* (*Sound Labyrinth*), which was composed in 1970 but first realized during a residency at Mills College in 1998. I am still in the midst of the book, but this intersection warrants further investigation and elaboration: the merger of Radigue's labyrinth and Oliveros's mandala.

71

En route to Pasadena today, heading northbound on the 110 freeway, I observed a silver BMW sedan with a California vanity license plate that read:

FERMATA

A fermata is a musical notation that looks like this:

𝄐

In classical staff music, the notation indicates an indefinite pause. I know this because it is also the title of a novel by Nicholson Baker published in 1994, in which the male protagonist can pause time. The protagonist generally uses this for sexual purposes, inducing pleasure without consent, and the book was controversial when it came out. Among the details I remember about the book are the name of the protagonist, Arno Strine, and the musical meaning of its title. When I see the license plate, I assume the driver is either a composer, a musician, or possibly a conductor. A less likely possibility is that they are a fan of Baker's novel, or, still less likely, his literary agent.

I consider taking the written cue as a prompt, but there is no safe way to pause when traffic on the freeway is moving. The music I am listening to while driving is Éliane Radigue's *Triptych*, three electronic compositions from 1978 commissioned by the choreographer Douglas Dunn. Radigue composed the works, all created with the ARP 2500 synthesizer, after a three-year break from making music, in which she studied or practiced Tibetan Buddhism. One could consider this her fermata, or one of several indefinite pauses. The music develops slowly and gradually, with enormous subtlety. I give it as much attention as I can devote without crashing my car. At times I drive with one window open, then two (it is warm today, and gas prices are high); my aging car creaks and groans, and at times the electric hum of Radigue's music synthesizes with the rest of my sonic environment.

72

73

I am still processing two encounters with the music of Florian Hecker on Saturday, both organized by Equitable Vitrines. The first was an exhibition, the second was a concert, yet both situations ("events"?) complicate the way such familiar terminology frames experience.

The concert, titled *FAVN*, took place at REDCAT. The composer was nowhere to be seen; rather, the stage was occupied with a rippled screen, resembling the one designed by Charles and Ray Eames, set at angle, and a tall, thin black speaker, touching ground but suspended from above by cable. Positioned behind these was a pale blue fabric backdrop. In total, and all spot-lit, the three elements recalled a constructivist composition. It became the visual focus for an audio composition that activated speakers all around the hall and audience. I wondered about the frontality of the experience: Was a concert hall, built around a proscenium and frontality, the ideal space to encounter this work? It struck me as a critique, or perhaps even a parody of the concert experience, while undermining those expectations. Its content, alluded to in its title, was a reconsideration of Claude Debussy's *Prélude à l'après-midi d'un faune* (*Prelude to the Afternoon of a Fawn*), an orchestral work from 1894, based on Stéphane Mallarmé's symbolist poem "L'après-midi d'un faune" ("The Afternoon of a Faun") from 1865–1876. Both works are considered significant examples of early modernism in their respective fields. Hecker seemingly had modernism on his mind; while his revision had little of the melodic charm of Debussy, one is reminded that the complex orchestral structure of Debussy's work (not to mention its charm) was difficult to apprehend in its time; likewise, Hecker's sound montage (if that's the right word) eludes ready description or explanation. All of the sounds were processed and seemingly several generations removed from their origin. It was often aggressive, pummeling the body as much as the eardrums. (Ear plugs were offered at the entrance—usually a clue that you're not in for an easy ride—but they would have done little to prevent the music from jostling my intestines and other body parts. This is not intended as a complaint.) A libretto by poet Robin Mackay, recorded and processed to some degree, lent a sense of order to what might have seemed chaotic, or at least *stochastic* (meaning random—a word that specifically recalls Iannis Xenakis, the architect-mathematician-composer who seemed to be another likely precursor here.) Mackay's poem hewed closer to its point of origin—Mallarmé—and my favorite part of it was hearing the little gasps of the libretto's reader, filtered and clipped, but insistently human. The lineage of modernism is, among other possibilities, a questioning of the place of the human in relation to an increasingly indifferent world, coinciding with new technological paradigms. Or at least that's a working definition. I enjoyed the "performance" more in retrospect than in real time.

Earlier in the day, I visited Hecker's exhibition *Resynthesizers* (2021–2022) at the MAK Center for Art and Architecture at the Fitzpatrick-Leland House, an incredible example of R.M. Schindler's "Space Architecture," built in 1938. Over the three stories of the house, the exhibition pitted three compositions by Hecker, each a dense thicket of algorithmically-generated electronic sound playing through stacked speaker cabinets, against three different fragrances (or "olfactory accords," as the press release poetically calls them) designed for the exhibition by the firm Symrise, coded to refer to "three milestones of fragrance chemistry dating from 1874, 1966, and 2021 respectively," and another libretto by Mackay, which unfolded over three micro-encapsulated electrophoretic ("E-link") displays casually leaning against walls or windows. The house framed this trio of trios, while also allowing moments of visual perforation and escape, with vantages of the surrounding landscape and the Saturday afternoon traffic on Laurel Canyon below. The sun's relationship to the house was also a beautiful, unscripted counterpoint. The aural and the olfactory senses both resisted the snare of language—Mackay's allusive, but slippery libretto hardly nailed things in place. The effect of all of this was at times overwhelming, but unlike my seated experience at REDCAT, I always had the agency of movement, and I took pleasure in my body's relationship to the forces (sound waves, smells) in the space. This, despite the music's inhuman quality. (Which, again, is not a complaint; I take its utter indifference to me—to humans in general—as part of the gambit.) The stairways were particularly rich, as the sound and scents from one trio overlapped with another. There were several other people in the house when I was there, and at one point I noticed another body (it was actually the composer) moving between the speaker and me, inhibiting the sound, just barely. I knew I could also leave whenever I wanted, and that sense of liberty actually prolonged my desire to stay in the house. But I knew the music would outlast me, and I had a concert to get to that evening. And my tongue tickled from the strange perfumes.

74

Thinking about *Prelude to the Afternoon of a Faun*—a playlist:

Claude Debussy
Prélude à l'après-midi d'un faune, 1894

Florian Hecker
FAVN, 2022

Marion Brown
Afternoon of a Georgia Faun
ECM, 1970

75

Online, I find an interview from 2008 of Éliane Radigue by Stephen O'Malley of Sunn O))) on his *Ideologic* blog: "Some of your music has been qualified as 'environmental music.' Could you tell us about the genesis of your work?"

We could talk about environmental music concerning my early sound pieces. They were mostly played in exhibitions, galleries, and used by other artists. My first environmental piece was made for the artist Marc Halpern, during the "Salon des artistes décorateurs." He had made a sculpture out of a glass block with moving elements inside. Inside the base, there were loudspeakers that diffused three tracks with different durations—each was about nine minutes long—that played endlessly and that desynchronized from each other progressively. The music was thus evolving on its own. Then I made a more complex piece based upon the same principles for Tania Mouraud entitled *One More Night* at the Galerie Rive Droite. Tania Mouraud's scenery was totally white and the walls were covered with double boarded panels inside which Rolen Star—a type of loud speakers that diffuse sound through walls—were screwed. The sounds weren't very nice, almost inaudible, but it had a certain character. More recently, I made a piece called *Labyrinthe Sonore* (*Sound Labyrinth*). The concept emerged in the 1960s but could only be realized in 1998 at Mills College, where I was invited to teach a seminar for graduate students. This seminar was based upon continuous tracks that we used in the *Labyrinthe*, but those tracks had already been made decades earlier. The piece played with the temporal evolution of seven soundtracks without an end that were slightly different from one another and that were diffused through loudspeakers all along the musical score. We also worked on the localization of the sound by including different interventions by Maggi Payne and Pauline Oliveros, with some piano and wind instruments. We worked on an entire composition outside of the music school. It was fantastically interesting work. That was in October. The evening before the concert, there was a torrential weather, which prevented us from using the music as initially planned. As an indication, the key words were "the map is the score," which meant that the composition itself would define the partition. That's why I had to go all over the partition again. And everything went very well. Beside the students, people like Pauline Oliveros or J.D. Parran gave me a hand. If I had to make another environmental piece, it would be something of the same sort—open and not fixed once and for all.

I am suddenly reminded of a sandwich board I saw and happened to photograph while visiting Oliveros's papers at the Mills College library in 2015: It featured a chalk drawing of a labyrinth with an invitation to "Walk the L for reflection & renewal." I can't quite believe this campus labyrinth had any relation to Radigue's composition, some seventeen years later.

76

I am also reminded of seeing Sunn O))) in concert at the Regent Theater, Los Angeles, in May 2016. I recall the date because I was in the midst of trying to buy my house, and eighty text messages from my real estate agent accumulated unattended on my phone during the concert. (I also remember the theater threatening to take away any phone that was used during the concert. An extreme measure, and possibly illegal, but in this case I appreciated the lack of distraction from my phone or anyone else's.) The concert was, appropriately, more aural than visual—a fog machine engulfed the stage and the performers who wore druid-like robes. The sheer theatricality of the concert—including the contorted operatics of the singer, Attila Csihar—recalled (knowingly?) Spinal Tap's infamous performance of their Ur-metal classic "Stonehenge," in which a tiny replica of the ancient monument, as designed by guitarist Nigel Tufnel, was at risk of being trampled by a dwarf. Rather than a replica of Stonehenge, there was a wall of Sunn amplifiers that served as an intermittently visible backdrop that also provided a literal wall of sound. My friend Justin and I took in the concert from the balcony, standing roughly above the soundboard. I *felt* the slowly evolving din as much as I heard it; I distinctly remember the sensation of sound waves coursing through my body and wiggling the very tip of my nose. I'd never felt sound do *that* before.

77

Today, a long overdue trip to Kenneth Hahn, listening to the Sunn O))) album *Monoliths and Dimensions* (2009). Its fifty-three-minute span coincides perfectly with my three-mile hike. I've listened to it before, but never in this context, and sometimes (if not always) context is everything. Sunn O))) is one of those bands (if that's even the right word—project? concept?) that I would seemingly like, but have never fully warmed up to. I should say, for the record, I do *like* them, but I've never been obsessed with them or even bought their music. Perhaps the concert, which I thoroughly enjoyed, nevertheless confirmed some of my suspicions: They are utterly serious about sound but cloak that seriousness in something decidedly silly or at least distractingly arch. That they remind me of Spinal Tap either means I'm in on the joke, or that they (like Spinal Tap) are not. Neither reality is entirely satisfying. Maybe what makes me suspicious is that Sunn O))) so clearly aspires to be art (including its embrace of irony), but for me its pretensions actually get in the way of the art.

I should also note, for context, that I was a huge fan of heavy metal in my adolescence, with Black Sabbath, Iron Maiden, and Metallica in heavy rotation (or whatever you call the version with cassettes playing in a boombox) along with their posters adorning my walls. Shortly after getting my driver's license in 1989, I drove to the Alpine Valley Music Theater with my friend Nick to see Metallica in concert, during their . . . *And Justice for All* tour, which will remain one of my most significant music memories. Metal was my gateway drug for lots of other music that would help shape my own identity and, on occasion, annoy others. (All of the aforementioned bands had their own pretensions to seriousness in their own context; maybe that is what has defined my musical universe for as long as I've consciously chosen one.) I still have long hair but have long moved on from having any steadfast identification with the genre. Still, I have maintained an interest in a number of bands—Earth, Om, Sleep—that have expanded the category in various directions. I was curious to see Sunn O))) perform and would do so again. When I saw (heard) them at the Regent Theater I knew that no home experience would be a suitable equivalent to the live experience—listening to them on my home speakers or on headphones would never make my nose wiggle.

Regardless of my equivocations, *Monoliths and Dimensions* is a great album: It checks so many boxes it almost seems designed for me. Its song titles reference two of my favorite composers: Miles Davis on the opening track, "Agharta," which is also the name of his double album from 1975; and Alice Coltrane, on the closing track "Alice." There are guest performances by Stuart Dempster, longtime collaborator of Pauline Oliveros and founding member of Deep Listening Band; Julian Priester, who played on John Coltrane's *Africa/Brass* (1961), was a regular in Sun Ra's Arkestra (including on *Lanquidity* [1979]) and part of Herbie Hancock's incredible Mwandishi band, among many other great ensembles; and Eyvind Kang, who is a colleague at CalArts. (The title *Monoliths and Dimensions* presumably recalls Sam Rivers's 1967 Blue Note album *Dimensions & Extensions*, on which Priester appears.) There is even a drawing by Richard Serra on the cover, intimating both "art" and "heaviness." For me, the best track is "Alice," which alludes to her expansive, transcendent post-jazz compositions. "Alice" begins with a slow build up, typical for Sunn O))), but eventually brings more lushness, delicacy, and movement to the signature bottom-heavy stew the group is clearly capable of; the trombone interplay between Dempster and Priester is particularly intricate and rich and speaks to the intersection of so much musical history. It's a fitting tribute to its namesake, though by the end, one might also forget it's a Sunn O))) record.

78

Desert Trip: Arrival—a playlist:

Alice Coltrane
Kirtan: Turiya Sings
Impulse!, 2021

Sunn O)))
Monoliths and Dimensions
Southern Lord, 2009

Deep Listening Band
The Ready Made Boomerang
New Albion, 1991

79

Desert Trip: Departure—a playlist:

Stuart Dempster
In the Great Abbey of Clement VI
New Albion, 1987

Herbie Hancock
Mwandishi
Warner Bros. Records, 1971

Miles Davis
Agharta
CBS, 1975

80

Agharta (1975) is the first Miles Davis album (CD) I ever purchased. I bought it from the Exclusive Company record store on State Street in Madison, during my freshman year of college. I had been going to the Exclusive Company since I could drive a car, which allowed me to venture to Madison in my last year or two of high school. State Street, which connects the university to the state capitol building, was usually my destination. Only later, when I was living in Madison, would I discover and eventually come to prefer B-Side Records, also on State Street, which was relatively tiny and far more discerning: B-Side covered most every genre you could think of, but tended to focus on the cream of the crop and, inverting the usual expectations, carried more experimental music than pop. The store was an index of the passions of its highly knowledgeable staff. But for a few years at least, the vast expanse of the Exclusive Company had a lot of appeal. My first encounters there were limited to the ground floor, where rock music was located—I bought Nirvana's *Nevermind* (1991) there the day it was released—but soon after I became increasingly drawn to the cramped basement where the jazz and classical sections were located. The people who worked in the basement were highly opinionated. Charles was the name of the older gentleman who oversaw the classical section. I remember seeing him wearing a black cowl walking on State Street. He always seemed wholly unimpressed with my purchases—especially jazz, which he clearly held in contempt, but also contemporary classical music like Philip Glass, Morton Feldman, and John Zorn, which were among the first new music CDs that I bought there. Unimpressed, but largely indifferent. A younger guy ("the jazz guy"?) also worked there, and he was not only unimpressed by my decision to purchase Miles Davis's *Agharta*, but *actually tried to dissuade me from buying it*. I think he knew it was my first

Miles Davis CD, maybe I even told him so (and maybe I was wearing a dumb Red Hot Chili Peppers T-shirt, or another band T-shirt purchased down the street at the Cat's Meow), and he probably thought *Kind of Blue* (1959) or *Birth of the Cool* (1957) or even *Bitches Brew* (1970) would be a better place to start. Davis's mid-70s electric stuff was in fact *demanding* and totally divisive in its own time, and by the early 90s its reputation had not fully recovered. In fact, *Agharta*—which documents the first of two concerts Davis and his septet played in Osaka on February 1, 1975 (*Pangaea* completes the marathon)—was first issued in the US in 1991. In other words, I was unwittingly on the cutting edge of its rediscovery. I think I was attracted to the psychedelic cover representing the mythical city of the album's title—much later I would learn that the cover of the US version was designed by John Berg, replacing the (equally psychedelic) cover art by Takaaki Amano that Davis had commissioned. (In truth, I like Berg's cover just as much, but don't really understand why a replacement was needed. Neither seem likely to woo the large youth audience Davis was imagining at that time.) Anyway, the guy from the basement might have had my best interests in mind when he tried to keep me from buying *Agharta*—maybe he had just heard it and hated it, or *he* wasn't quite ready for its treasures?—but his stubbornness inspired my own in return. Of course, he eventually accepted my money, and I left the store with what would prove to be a monumental purchase. I would come to love *Bitches Brew* and *Kind of Blue* and *Birth of the Cool* (probably in that order, reverse chronologically—*E.S.P.* [1965] might actually be my favorite of his albums), but my point of entry was *Agharta*, with its longform modular jams awash in cascading wah-wah guitar waves courtesy of Pete Cosey and Reggie Lucas, which summoned the ghost of Jimi Hendrix, for me and possibly for Miles Davis. (Hendrix's live-in-the-studio *Radio One* was the first CD I ever bought, when it was first released in 1988.) *Agharta* was a gateway drug, leading to more Miles, to more jazz in every direction, to "world" music, and mostly to more music that is nearly possible to describe or categorize. In retrospect, it was an unlikely place to begin, but over thirty years later, *Agharta* continues to reveal itself with every listen.

81

"Willie Nelson" is a song by Miles Davis.

82

September 28, 1991. I remember crying when I learned that Miles Davis had died. Not uncontrollable sobbing, but more an insistent welling up of tears. I didn't cry much then (and still don't), so this was very unusual. More unusual is the fact that I don't recall having ever listened to Miles Davis before his death. Also unusual: I learned Miles Davis had died from Chuck D, who made a dedication to him or perhaps it was a moment of silence when Public Enemy performed on *Saturday Night Live*. One of my favorite groups at the time, I was beyond excited to see PE on *SNL*. There was always so much energy in and around their music—the dense, aggressive tracks produced by the Bomb Squad, Chuck D's distinct, authoritative voice dropping political bombs in rhyme form, the unhinged jestering of Flavor Flav—and in their highly crafted, militant imagery. Public Enemy irritated a lot of (white) people, and they seemed eager to embrace their controversy, working what we now call the attention economy. I was a (white) fan, who reviewed *Fear of a Black Planet* (1990) for his (mostly white) high school newspaper, named after the Norse god Odin. And I still have a *Fear of a Black Planet* T-shirt from the era, now holey and faded to a beautifully antiqued gray. I can't say exactly why tears welled up when Chuck D announced that Miles Davis had died. The death notice was, like Public Enemy's music, blunt and sincere. Perhaps I sensed a musical lineage that I hadn't been aware of, sensed for just a moment the expanse of a universe of which I had only glimpsed a tiny fragment.

83

Miles Davis died four days after I bought Nirvana's *Nevermind* at the Exclusive Company in Madison. I didn't connect those two events at the time, and I'm still not sure how to connect them now.

84

What constitutes your musical universe?

In a word, memory. (But also what I'm listening to this minute—e.g., Sonic Youth's *In/Out/In* [2021], a newly released album of pre-breakup material spanning the 00s, which happens to bring its own flood of memories as I listen with nostalgic curiosity—and everything I will listen to in the future. And, I should probably add, everything I've listened to but have forgotten.)

85

Public Enemy's *Fear of a Black Planet* was recorded at several studios including Greene Street Recording Studio at 112 Greene Street, Lower Manhattan, and released on April 10, 1990. "Fight the Power" was among the songs they recorded there and was used by Spike Lee in the propulsive opening credit sequence of *Do the Right Thing* (1989), which instantly became one of my favorite movies when I first saw it on VHS (it wasn't shown in theaters in my hometown).

Sonic Youth's *Goo* was recorded at two studios, including Greene Street Recording Studio, and released on June 26, 1990. Chuck D makes a guest appearance on the song "Kool Thing" (a song about LL Kool J), which I first heard when the video debuted on MTV's Sunday night alternative showcase *120 Minutes*, which I was watching with friends in Heather Bray's basement.

86

This morning, I skipped the farmer's market to indulge another pleasure which has become less routine, and finished reading the long Radigue interview, which spans her entire career as she shifts from feedback experiments to composing for the ARP 2500 synthesizer to her involvement with Buddhism to her eventual compositions for acoustic instruments, beginning with *Naldjorlak* (2008) for cellist Charles Curtis. I'm listening to Radigue's *Jetsun Mila* (1986) as I write this.

A few sound observations:

Radigue's shift to acoustic instruments is not as dramatic as her shift away from the synthesizer, which largely defined her singular body work from 1971, when she acquired the ARP 2500 in New York, to 2006 when she got rid of it. Her earliest works—*Asymptote Versatile* in 1963; *Chess Game* in 1964—were scored for classical instruments. *Geelriandre* (1972) incorporates prepared piano, played by Gerárd Frémy, "who must remain the only performer. His piano playing should intentionally emphasize—or fight—or disappear into what is proposed," which was proposed by Radigue's synthesizer and magnetic tape. There is also the human voice, which appears on *Les Chants de Milarepa* (*Songs of Milarepa*) (1983), provided by Lama Kunga Rinpoche and Robert Ashley.

Related to this is the incredibly long gestation period of Radigue's research, which often results in one composition a year. Her productivity has seemingly swelled exponentially since beginning her series of *Occam* compositions in 2011, but it is possible to see this as the manifestation of a lifetime of research into sound and harmonics. Each composition is created in dialogue with the performer(s), based on their deep, somatic knowledge of their chosen instrument, and set in motion with an image of water's movement. These compositions are not notated but created through oral transmission.

Third, the title of the book, *Intermediary Spaces*, might define this dynamic relationship between composer and performer; it is also the definition of the Buddhist concept of bardo.

I had more thoughts, but they started to disintegrate before I could sit down to write them.

87

A colleague recently shared images of the CalArts admissions bulletin from the early years of the school, perhaps 1971. The design, in orange, ochre, and purple, with white handwritten text, recalls Sister Mary Corita (but was perhaps done by Marshall Henrichs, who had designed *Blueprint for a Counter Education* in 1970—further investigation is needed). The description for the School of Music is particularly sweet and provocative:

An instrument is something more than a source of sound; it is an image in a composition; it has a personality and a historical role. The playing space required by a gamelan is a small universe.

CalArts has one of the longest-running gamelan departments in the United States—technically it's an MFA Balinese and Javanese Music and Dance Specialization. When I taught my seminar Pauline Oliveros for Artists, some of my students (most of whom were art students, not music students) had no idea what gamelan was, or that it is offered at CalArts. So, I immediately took the class to visit the gamelan room, with its extraordinary and relatively rare collection of instruments. I Nyoman Wenten, longtime gamelan instructor at CalArts, very graciously allowed us to interrupt his conversation with several music students and gave us a quick introduction to the instruments and their parallel traditions (Balinese and Javanese). For three years I had a tiny office near the gamelan studio, and certain percussive tones generated by the mallet instruments in that room would penetrate across the hallway and through two layers of concrete block walls, surging through my body. When I first arrived at CalArts, I didn't really know much about gamelan music but was struck by its potency, quite literally. I renamed my class on artists' writings Gamelan by Osmosis in honor of this small but resonant universe.

88

Today I listened to a podcast with Stuart Dempster, called *Tones and Drones*, while walking at Kenneth Hahn. There were numerous gems, including his imitation of the sounds made by garbage trucks on his street. (It's Tuesday; I can relate.) He also displayed his predilection for puns, which he shares with Oliveros. There was a lot of useful background information about Deep Listening Band, and the cistern in Fort Worden Historical State Park, where the first two albums by Deep Listening Band were recorded. One perfect sound bite for the occasion: "Music is where you listen to it."

89

Thinking about the origins of Deep Listening Band, or: "Music is where you listen to it"—a playlist:

Stuart Dempster
"Standing Waves" (1976), "Didjeridervish" (1976), and "Standing Waves" (1978/1987)
In the Great Abbey of Clement VI
New Albion, 1987

Pauline Oliveros
"Watertank Software"
Vor der Flut (Hommage an einen Wasserspeicher)
Eigelstein Musikproduktion, 1985

Pauline Oliveros
"The Receptive," "A Love Song," and "The Gentle"
The Well and the Gentle
hatART, 1985

90

Yesterday I was trying to get to the bottom of Deep Listening Band and was excited to find Pauline Oliveros's contribution to *Vor der Flut (Hommage an einen Wasserspeicher)* (1985), a recording made in the enormous underground water cistern in Cologne, Germany, which had been emptied for a few weeks in 1984. The title translates to "before the flood." I had seen passing references to it in the Oliveros literature (e.g., her later collection of essays, *Sounding the Margins: Collected Writings 1992–2009*) but had never encountered the album or her *Watertank Software* (1984), which appears on it. Searching on YouTube yesterday, I found the audio and video document of Oliveros's performance. The album and video were conceived by Hinnerick Bröskamp; the production value is extremely high and quite theatrical in its staging and costumes (which could just be fashionable 80s attire worn by European musicians). I don't know most of the musicians, and perhaps I should, but they and their instruments were seemingly chosen (by Bröskamp) for their range of resonant possibilities. Oliveros's Titano accordion, accompanied by her voice, stands out in this crowd which tends toward *Dune*-ish neoprimitivism ("old wave"?). You can find the whole video (in parts) by searching "vor der flut" on YouTube. The liner notes from the album, which I found on Discogs, reveal:

In December 1984 musicians from different countries and the "Tanzforum der Oper/Köln" met in the almost one-hundred-year-old drinkingwatertank [*sic*] (Wasserspeicher) SEVERIN (which had been emptied for refurbishment) located on the southside of Cologne for an exceptional music and dance project. The recordings of this double-LP testify for the unique acoustics of the subterraneous colonnade. All takes have only been recorded with microphones distributed throughout the tank, without using any additional studio-effect equipment before it was finally flooded again.

Oliveros's performance in the cistern is obviously an important precursor to the album *Deep Listening* (1989), with Oliveros, Stuart Dempster, and Panaiotis, who recorded it in the Fort Worden cistern in Washington State in 1988. Dempster's own performances, including his astonishing *In the Great Abbey of Clement VI*, which first appeared in 1979, set a precedent for such a use of intensely reverberant spaces. Another thing I discovered yesterday, is that three of the six tracks on Oliveros's double album *The Well and the Gentle* (1985), were also recorded in the SEVERIN drinking water tank at the time of *Vor der Flut*. I've never had a copy of *The Well and the Gentle*, which was only released on vinyl (I should have it, but it's pricey. I saw it once, in my friend Lorenzo's apartment in Venice, Italy), and I've only listened to it on YouTube. Not carefully enough.

It was Dempster who hipped Oliveros to the Fort Worden cistern in the wake of her participation on *Vor der Flut*. The reverberation in both spaces is immense—the Fort Worden cistern clocks fourty-five seconds and the SEVERIN water tank twenty-five seconds. What's perhaps most important to acknowledge is that the idea of playing music in a vast, empty cistern did not start with Oliveros, Dempster, or Deep Listening Band. (It should also be noted that this band didn't become a Band until after the album *Deep Listening* [1989].) Many of the impulses of recording music in a complexly resonant space like a cistern were already apparent on *Vor der Flut*. However, the specific language of improvisation developed by Deep Listening Band, playing together in complexly resonant spaces, is quite unique and develops (as most good things do) over time. As Dempster has noted (on *Tones and Drones*), "The cistern is an instrument that you learn to play."

91

Deep Listening Band: A Complete Discography?

Pauline Oliveros, Stuart Dempster, Panaiotis
Deep Listening
New Albion, 1989

Deep Listening Band
Trogdolyte's Delight
¿What Next? Recordings, 1990

Deep Listening Band
The Readymade Boomerang
New Albion, 1991

Deep Listening Band
Sanctuary
Mode, 1995

Deep Listening Band
Tosca Salad
Deep Listening, 1995

Deep Listening Band and the Long String Instrument
Suspended Music
Periplum, 1997

Deep Listening Band
Non Stop Flight
Music & Arts, 1998

Deep Listening Band / Joe McPhee Quartet
Unquenchable Fire
Deep Listening, 2003

Deep Listening Band
Then & Now Now & Then: Celebrating 20 Years
Taiga Records, 2008

Deep Listening Band
Needle Drop Jungle
Taiga Records, 2012

Deep Listening Band
Octagonal Polyphony
Important Records, 2012

Deep Listening Band
Great Howl at Town Haul
Important Records, 2012

Deep Listening Band with Joe McPhee and Randy Raine-Reusch
Looking Back
ZA Discs, 2013

Deep Listening Band
Dunrobin Sonic Gems
Deep Listening, 2014

92

The mission of the Deep Listening Band is to seek out, listen to, and interact with unusual spaces in order to make music. Space is an integral part of sound. One cannot exist without the other. We explore natural, constructed, imaginary, and virtual spaces to savor and enjoy their salient acoustical characteristics. This work is done with ears, voices, instruments, technology, shared experiences, and perceptions. Performance space is ordinarily held as a stationary paradigm in performance practice, but qualitative changes occur with our instruments and voices throughout the exploration process.

Listening to space changes space and changing space changes listening . . .

Deep Listening Band has performed in caves, cisterns, cathedrals, concert halls, and a great variety of unusual spaces including virtual cyberspaces. We always begin with a listening meditation before we sound the spaces. Listening creates new shapes and feelings . . .

> —Pauline Oliveros, "Space for Listening and Listening to Space: A Musician's Way of 'Looking'" (2006)

93

Yesterday, while traversing the city, I listened to Joe McPhee Quintet's *Common Threads* CD, which was released by Oliveros's Deep Listening label in 1996. McPhee is a frequent member of Deep Listening Band, appearing (by my count) on five of their albums. Stuart Dempster performs on *Common Threads*, playing trombone, didjeridu, and "little instruments"; his son Loren Dempster plays cello. The quintet also includes Eyvind Kang on violin and erhu, which is a two-string spike fiddle native to China; Michael Bisio plays bass. (Bonus: The CD packaging was designed by Dick Higgins, Fluxus artist, poet, and occasional musician who had studied with John Cage at the New School for Social Research; Higgins was also a faculty member at CalArts in its earliest years.)

McPhee plays tenor and soprano saxophone, as well as pocket trumpet, an instrument first brought into advanced jazz territory by Don Cherry. *Common Threads* was recorded live at the Tractor Tavern in Seattle on October 19, 1995, which, coincidentally, is the day Don Cherry died. The first track is titled "Spirit Traveler (for Don Cherry)." At fourty-seven minutes, it's an epic tribute, recalling some of Cherry's long-form suites or sides, such as "Symphony for Improvisers" (1967) and "Complete Communion" (1967). Either of those titles would be an apt description of McPhee's album, too, though *Common Threads* says it just as beautifully. The performance ebbs and flows, gathers and explodes, intimating an expansive musical network that connects Deep Listening Band to Don Cherry and the deep lineage of ("jazz") improvisation and beyond.

94

When I put "jazz" in scare quotes it's a way of saying "yes" and "no" at the same time: Yes, there is a deep lineage of jazz improvisation, and both Don Cherry and Joe McPhee are important participants in that lineage; and no, jazz does not adequately define the full range of musical improvisation and its histories, nor does it fully describe the musical activities of Cherry or McPhee, who have both engaged in improvisation with musicians working in many other cultural (and improvisatory) idioms. The latter approach is better described as free improvisation: Rather than working around a prescribed theme, with individual musicians taking solos, there is a sense of working toward a common result through improvisation. One could describe it as a kind of communication through music. As a process, it can be messy or ecstatic or both. It stresses some people out, and I generally assume (as someone who listens to a fair amount of free improvisation but does not make music) that it's most fun for the participating musician(s) to listen to. In any event, "bad" or "good" is usually in the ear of the beholder.

95

Recto/Verso, or two sides to every story: Today, I devoted some of my trip on the way to CalArts and on the return home, to *Unquenchable Fire* (2003) by Deep Listening Band and Joe McPhee Quartet. It's my first listen to the whole thing. (The CD, purchased through Discogs, arrived yesterday.) Intertwined, the trio and quartet form a septet of endless possibilities, and often a dense thicket punctuated by the writer Rachel Pollack reading excerpts from her novel which shares its title with the album. The book, published in 1988, was awarded the Arthur C. Clarke Award for Science Fiction the following year. Really, with Pollack's voice, it's an octet, though surely an unusual one. All participants seem to have some relation to the Hudson Valley: McPhee was raised in Poughkeepsie; Pollack taught at the Omega Institute in Rhinebeck for over thirty years; Oliveros lived across the river in Kingston, which is the home of the Deep Listening Institute and where this album was recorded. Carrying over from *Common Threads* (1996), I am primarily trained on the interplay between McPhee, who plays soprano sax, alto clarinet, and a Casio digital horn here, and Stuart Dempster, who plays trombone and didjeridu. David Gamper of DLB and Joe Giardullo of JMQ both play "flutes"—plural—among other things. The number of woodwinds involved stretches my understanding of the Deep Listening Band concept, as does the addition of drums by Karen Jurgens of JMQ. Oliveros's accordion seems to take a backseat on the album, as does the cello of Monica Wilson, but that's on first listen. Pollack's texts are brief but evocative interjections of magic realism. McPhee might be quoting Ornette Coleman's "Broken Shadows" on the fifth track. I don't know what to make of it all, really, but that's okay. I will (of course) keep listening.

96

Faculty Development Fund Application
April 6, 2022

Project Description

I am requesting $1,250.00 in order to travel to Mills College in Oakland to study the Pauline Oliveros Papers at the F. W. Olin Library. In October 2015, I met Oliveros (1932–2016), and with her encouragement visited Mills and spent two days with the papers, with the generous assistance of Janice E. Braun, Director of the Library and Special Collections. I was preparing for the exhibition *Routine Pleasures* (2016) at the MAK Center for Art and Architecture, in which I included work by Oliveros on loan from the Olin Library.

That brief research trip, and my many discoveries in the archive, led to a much larger research project which continues today. In fall 2019, I taught a seminar called Pauline Oliveros for Artists at CalArts that was driven by this research. I have also written and presented two substantial papers on Oliveros, one of which will be published as a pamphlet later this year. (Its title is *Bog Time*, after the pond at Mills College which inspired a number of her tape and synthesizer works in 1967, when she was director of the Tape Music Center there.) Some of this work has already been supported by the Faculty Development Fund, for which I am grateful.

My continued research is aimed at a book-length study, which I hope to complete during my creative leave in the spring 2023 semester. I hope to do this work at Mills in the summer, but the timing of the trip will depend upon the availability of the papers and the library staff. I am also aware of the increased precarity of Mills and the Olin Library in the wake of its merger with

Northeastern University. The requested funding would support four days of research, travel, and accommodations. I appreciate your consideration.

97

What constitutes your musical universe?

Yesterday I made a quick detour into the CalArts library to check out Stuart Dempster's *The Modern Trombone: A Definition of Its Idioms*, published in 1979 by University of California Press. The library has three copies, and I found two on the shelf. Unlike many books I borrow from the library, Dempster's book is seemingly popular and has been checked out consistently over the years, presumably by students who are studying the trombone. I checked it out as part of my effort to get to the bottom of Deep Listening Band. I haven't gotten much deeper than the table of contents (already intriguing!) and the foreword, in which Dempster argues that, "The trombone is not an instrument in the usual sense, since it has no reed to make the sound; rather it is a *resonator* of whatever sound is introduced into the mouthpiece."

This "non-instrument" is similar to a megaphone; its real function is to focus the sound rather than to amplify it. That is to say, the trombone primarily controls the quality of tone produced and, secondarily, increases the loudness. It is this quality of tone that produces the sound of a trombone rather than the sound of, say, a baritone horn. That the trombone can be simulated by a garden hose fitted with a mouthpiece and a funnel (for a bell) only clarifies the point that the garden hose is a nonadjustable-length trombone, just as the trombone is an adjustable-length garden hose.

98

Today Dave Muller gave me two records when I visited his house. One is a double album by Dick Slessig (a.k.a. Dick Slessig Combo), which is a long-form cover of George McCrae's soul hit "Rock Your Baby" (1974). It was the second release on Dave's very occasional label 75 Records. He also gave me a 7-inch single by my colleague Sam Durant, titled *Behind the Center*, a solo guitar performance from 1994. To be played at 33 ⅓ RPM, the record was released by Lucky Garage Record Company.

Dave and I discussed a long and nebulous minor history of mostly obscure bands that originated in or included students in the School of Art at CalArts. Both Durant and Slessig are examples, coinciding with Dave's time at CalArts when he founded his occasional and itinerant exhibition/event program *Three Day Weekend*. At the moment my record player is not set up, so I am watching (and listening to) a Slessig performance from 2012 on YouTube. It was part of a *Three Day Weekend* at Public Fiction, an occasional and itinerant exhibition/event space started by my curator-designer friend Lauren Mackler. Public Fiction used to be headquartered in a storefront on Avenue 50 in Highland Park. I drove past it last week, though it hasn't been Public Fiction in a long time. In the video, Dick Slessig Combo is slowly constructing a nearly unrecognizable rendition of "Jive Talkin'" (1975) by the Bee Gees with guitar, bass, drums. A table top occludes the bottom third of the frame; the fixed camera reveals fragments of the three band members and, mostly, their instruments. The drummer plays the drums with brushes, and for some time, plays a guitar with brushes. In the background, one can watch people come in and out of the space. I recognize some of them—people now or still in my life almost exactly ten years later (including Dave, who I met twenty years ago). Little kids run in and out;

some of them are probably in college now, starting bands of their own. There is often more activity at the threshold than in the band's studious movements.

99

That kind of a Saturday—a playlist:

Acetone
1992–2001
Light in the Attic, 2017

Dirty Three
Ocean Songs
Touch and Go Records, 1998

Susan Alcorn
The Heart Sutra
Ideologic Organ, 2020

Eugene Chadbourne
To Doug
Rectangle, 2011

Mary Halvorson Octet
Away with You
Firehouse 12 Records, 2016

Brian Thummler
Ghost Birds
Cassauna, 2021

100

After the farmer's market, I listened to some of Deep Listening Band's *Tosca Salad* (1995) on the drive home, appropriately enough given the smell of fresh vegetables wafting up from my market bounty in the back seat. The title of the album is, of course, a corny play on "tossed salad"—the album is a tasty mélange assembled from a variety of different recording sessions, with a handful of guest musicians including Ellen Fullman and Joe McPhee. It's actually more of a composed salad than a tossed salad, to follow the metaphor, with recordings presented in chronological order. A note on the CD insert informs me that the Tosca Salad is on the menu at Mary P's restaurant in Kingston, New York, where Oliveros and David Gamper lived and where many of these improvisations were recorded. Of course, the album's title—and presumably the salad, too—is a punning reference to Giacomo Puccini's opera, *Tosca*, from 1900. This is not Oliveros's first run-in with the Italian composer: Her tape piece *Bye Bye Butterfly* from 1967, widely considered a significant early example of electronic music, incorporates a recording of Puccini's opera *Madama Butterfly*, which he composed in 1904.

Among the tracks on *Tosca Salad* are a trio of duets, comprising a round robin with the three core members of DLB: "Dempster Oliveros Duet," "Gamper Dempster Duet," and "Oliveros Gamper Duet," recorded at the Trinity United Methodist Church in Kingston. Gamper joined the band in 1990, replacing Panaiotis after the initial *Deep Listening* record, and became a mainstay with Oliveros and Dempster until his death in 2011. It is particularly satisfying to hear Oliveros and Dempster play together, even if it's a brief duet; longtime friends, the two were part of the incredible Bay Area contemporary music scene that emerged in the late 1950s and 60s. In 1966 (or 1965, according to contradictory evidence), Dempster commissioned Oliveros to compose a solo work for him, for which she created *Theater Piece from Trombone*, staged by Elizabeth Harris and performed live at the Tape Music Center at 321 Divisadero Street with a simultaneous audience on KPFA. According to notes on the website *radiOM*, the narrator "Charles Boone describes the action and setting preceding the very theatrical performance involving candles, hose, funnels and other unusual props. For this performance KPFA had telephone lines installed into the San Francisco Tape Music Center so that concerts before a live audience could also be heard live by the radio listening public." (I found a recording of this today, so more on this soon.)

Oliveros and Dempster both took part in the premiere performance of Terry Riley's *In C* in November 1964, along with Steve Reich, Jon Gibson, and Morton Subotnick, among others—an extraordinary confluence. (It's a pity a recording of it doesn't exist.) Earlier that year, Dempster and Oliveros both participated in *Tudorfest*, a tribute to David Tudor that Oliveros organized at the Tape Music Center. Oliveros and Dempster joined Tudor and an impressive ensemble (including Subotnick again, Linn Subotnick, Loren Rush, John Chowning, and Warner Jepson, among other notables) that performed three compositions by John Cage—*Music Walk* (1958); *Atlas Eclipticalis with Winter Music, Electronic Version* (1961); *Concert for Piano and Orchestra* (1958)—with Dempster on trombone and Oliveros on French horn. (Thankfully a recording of this exists.) Thirty years later, Oliveros rather unexpectedly picks up the French horn again for the song "Coming Together" on *Tosca Salad*, in which the DLB trio mingles with the duo of Fritz Hauser (percussion) and Urs Leimgruber (on soprano and alto saxophones), eventually coming together as a quintet.

101

Listening to the archival description of Oliveros's *Theater Piece* (1966) for Dempster *before* the madcap performance begins is quite amusing, suggesting the likely influence of Spike Jones and Rube Goldberg. One has to remember the description and then pair that memory with the sounds; we're taken back to the era of radio plays and the need for visual imagination when listening. Surely visual imagination (and/or sight) is at the root of all listening. There is a similar prefatory description of a work by Terry Riley and La Monte Young, *Concerto for Two Pianists and Five Tape Recorders* (referred to as "Concert for Two Pianos and Tape Recorders" by the interlocutor, Glenn Glasow); it appears on Riley's *Music for the Gift* (2000). The *Concerto* was recorded live 1960 Hertz Hall, University of California Berkeley. At one point Glasow calmly notes, "La Monte Young is under the piano, and I'm not sure why." In Oliveros's *Theater Piece*, Dempster gets *in* the piano, or so we're told—a premonition of Linda Mary Montano doing the same during Oliveros's segment of Robert Ashley's *Music with Roots in the Aether* (1975–1976). I am also reminded of John Cage's *Water Walk* (1959), which he performed on the television show *I've Got a Secret* in 1960. In all of these examples, the piano is used as an instrument but also serves as a sign of "serious music."

Dempster also provides insight into *Theater Piece* (including its correct title and date: 1966) in his book *The Modern Trombone*. In chapter eleven, "Theatrical Innovations," he observes that, "Musical site-sound relationship is probably nowhere more obvious than in the trombone glissando: everyone knows this visual cliché," by way of introduction to his use of the garden hose.

Various references have been made throughout this book to garden hose instruments. As stated before, a garden hose fitted with a trombone mouthpiece is really a trombone of *nonadjustable* length, just as a trombone may be considered an *adjustable*-length garden hose. The first composition that ever considered this idea was Pauline Oliveros's *Theater Piece for Trombone Player and Tape* (note use of the word "player"). No trombone per se is used in this work but rather the acoustical and visual abstractions of it; however, this does not make it any *less* a trombone piece. If the piece were to be for a player of another brass instrument, it would be necessary to use different size hoses and mouthpieces, which would make it an entirely different venture. The hoses are simply resonators and, as such, are no different from any brass of similar length and bore.

Beyond this, Dempster reveals another set of unusual details that doesn't appear in the archival recording of the performance:

These hoses in the Oliveros work were originally "woven" into two sculptures by the choreographer Elizabeth Harris. One, a "candle trumpet," has funnel bells on the end where candles are placed. An extremely tight interrelationship between sight and sound is achieved because the breath of the performer can control the amount and type of light that the candle gives. The other sculpture, a "sprinkler horn," allows for lawn sprinklers to rotate, spewing forth baby powder, smoke, or whatever else might have been loaded in them. Many vocal sounds imitating animals are used.

Without accompanying images, I am once again left to my imagination.

102

Last night, Leslie treated me to seeing Bill Frisell play at Zebulon for my birthday. It was the first time I've seen him play live despite being a fan of his music for thirty years. He came to my attention by way of John Zorn's *Naked City* (1990), which I bought from the basement of the Exclusive Company in Madison during my freshman year of college. It's an album (well, CD) that changed my life, in no small part because of the virtuoso guitarist who could twist and turn through Zorn's elaborate, breakneck miniatures, switching from thrash to surf to tasty jazz licks on a dime. Frisell is as restrained as Zorn is indulgent. His own work, much of it likewise released by the Elektra Nonesuch label, is similarly capacious, if far less severe in its approach. In my late teens and early 20s, I highly valued indulgence. Now as I climb over that big hill, I appreciate the restraint. Last night, playing with bassist Thomas Morgan and drummer Rudy Royston, the group was in a happy place with smiles all around. Frisell only let it rip a few times, and just barely. Although, he loved working his tidy array of pedals for a variety of looping and splicing effects, which frequently served as a discombobulating bridge between tunes. Like Zorn, Frisell is a brilliant interpreter, and in addition to his own compositions, his extension catalog includes innumerable cover versions, from Monk to Madonna, Dylan to Ives. The show included several covers, including an utterly captivating version of Burt Bacharach's "What the World Needs Now is Love." It's never been truer than it is right now.

103

This evening in a meeting with my student Razan AlSarraf, she told me she learned the accordion in the fourth grade, among the many instruments she played while growing up in Kuwait.

104

Yesterday, on my commute to and from school, I listened to Bill Frisell's *Have a Little Faith* (1992), which was released just around the time I was discovering his music. The whole album consists of cover versions of songs that are loosely connected as American songs, spanning a diverse set of composers and genres. The album starts with Aaron Copland's *Billy the Kid*, a ballet suite composed in 1938, and continues with tunes by Charles Ives, Bob Dylan, Muddy Waters, John Hiatt, Stephen Foster, Sonny Rollins, and John Philip Sousa. Notably, Frisell also covered Ives with Naked City on their album *Grand Guignol*, also released in 1992, although that album strikes a very different, decidedly ominous, tone. *Have a Little Faith*, as the title suggests, is not exactly light fare but is contemplative, spacious, and playful. Its climax, and probably its biggest surprise, is Madonna's "Live to Tell" (1986), which also happens to feature Frisell's most spectacular guitar heroics. It's also often rendered unrecognizable in the process. Like Naked City, there is something deconstructive in the approach to these found songs as "texts" to be worked with, through, and against. The instrumentation on the album is also unusual: it's a quintet for guitar, bass (Kermit Driscoll), drums (Joey Baron, a Frisell regular and Naked City mainstay), clarinets, and accordion. It actually sounds like a much bigger band at times. Don Byron's presence on clarinet is particularly bright; Guy Klucevsek's accordion brings an immediate "folk" quality to the proceedings, though he is known for his avant-garde approach to the instrument, which is also in evidence here at times. Really, Klucevsek is the first accordionist I knew by name and paid attention to. Growing up in Wisconsin, I only knew the accordion from the polka bands that would play at weddings and other occasions. Klucevsek's approach to the instrument in this context (American Studies 101) is both that and not-that. I also bought his CD *Manhattan Cascade* (1985) around the same time, featuring solo works for accordion by Zorn ("Road Runner"), Anthony Coleman, Lois V Vierk, and other new music composers in New York, including the accordionist of record.

105

Today, a trip to Kenneth Hahn for some much-needed exercise, which actually took me across La Cienega Boulevard via the pedestrian bridge to the Stoneview Nature Center, with its Tree of Life labyrinth, learning garden, and tidy display of compost bins, and then to the Baldwin Hills Scenic Overlook, before looping back to Kenneth Hahn, drawing a snaking ouroboros in the process. Along the way I listened to *Sounding / Way*, an album by Pauline Oliveros / Guy Klucevsek. I love the insistent "/," rather than, say, an "&," as if to suggest a duel as much as a duet. The no-nonsense, black-and-white picture of the pair on the cover (taken by Linda Montano) maintains a poker (polka?) face. But, in any event, these are the two titans of avant-garde accordion, finally brought together for this summit, which took place at the Yellow Springs Institute in Chester Springs, Pennsylvania, circa 1986. Oliveros self-released it as a cassette in 1986, and Important Records re-released it on vinyl in 2019. (I have the clear vinyl copy, for whatever it's worth). The two-sided format of cassette or LP makes perfect sense for this recording, which consists of one accordion duet from each performer with Klucevsek's *Tremolo No. 6 (Nucleic Chains)* on Side A, and Oliveros's *Tuning Meditation* on Side B. Both compositions make a strong case for the instrument's harmonic capabilities. Klucevsek's *Tremolo* does this with speed and intensity, and Oliveros's *Meditation* replies with long, unhurried drones. The works clock in at eighteen minutes and seventeen minutes, respectively. Both seem like extremely demanding works to perform, at least to my untrained ears. I was surprised by this performance of *Tuning Meditation*, because I had never heard a duet version or an instrumental version. In fact, the score, from 1979, follows quite directly from the example of the *Sonic Meditations* (*XVI* in particular) and explicitly indicates the voice:

Using any vowel sound, sing a tone that you hear in your imagination. After contributing your tone, listen for someone else's tone and tune to its pitch as exactly as possible. Continue by alternating between singing a tone of your own and tuning to the tone of another voice. Introduce new tones at will and tune to as many different voices as are present. Sing warmly.

Of course, the accordion, in ways I've already discussed, is a reed instrument that recalls the voice, with the bellows doubling the lungs. It's not a stretch to think of an accordion as a voice. *Horse Sings from Cloud* (1975) is a demonstration of this doubling. The version of *Tuning Meditation* I know best is a performance led by Oliveros at The Kitchen in 1979. One gets a sense of the participants sitting in a circle, replicating the composer's awareness/attention mandala, and one also senses the presence of both trained and untrained singers. This horizontality is one of the most radical aspects of Oliveros's meditations—the group begins to articulate itself as a group with its individuals producing tones and then matching another person's tone. In sum, this process oscillates between dissonance and consonance, suggesting a model of democracy in the swell and commingling of voices. It's often awkward, even as it collectively reaches for the sublime. The version by Oliveros / Klucevsek feels wholly different, with two voices calling and responding to one another in more intimate dialogue. It's hard to tell who is who, given the constant attempt to match tones. It develops slowly, and changes occasionally, but never dramatically. It's measured and controlled, even if improvised in response to the score's prompt. I am left wondering if Oliveros / Klucevsek closed their eyes while performing it, listening (rather than watching) in order to tune to the tone of the other's voice. In any event, their accordions sing warmly, together.

106

I was totally incorrect two days ago when I observed that Guy Klucevsek was "the first accordionist I knew by name and paid attention to." Some mental block prevented me from remembering (or admitting to myself?) that I was a big fan of "Weird Al" Yankovic in my formative years, and I owned a copy of his hit album *In 3-D* (1984), which was in heavy rotation along with Michael Jackson's *Thriller* (1982), Prince's *Purple Rain* (1984), and Van Halen's *1984* (1984). All of these artists were in heavy rotation on MTV, and the parodies of "Weird Al" provided a refreshing note of critical self-awareness to the repetitive churn. It's almost easy to forget that the accordion was an important part of the schtick, along with the wacky patterned shirts, nerdy glasses, and the frizzy helmet of hair. The cover illustration on his eponymous debut from a year earlier features him playing the accordion, as does the photograph on the cover of *Polka Party!* from 1986. But let me also admit that (until now) I never gave too much thought to Al's contribution to the field of accordion playing. I was too busy enjoying—groaningly—his lyrical send-ups of high-value targets, including many of my childhood favorites.

In recent days I've not only been listening to a fair amount of Guy Klucevsek, and exploring his catalog (mostly thanks to Spotify) and his eclectic range (playing with everyone from Oliveros to Laurie Anderson to Anthony Braxton to Tom Waits), but also his irreverent humor and his penchant for parody. Look no further than his own take on the populist polka genre with *Who Stole the Polka?* (a reference to Public Enemy's "Who Stole the Soul," perhaps?) from 1991, or *Polka Dots & Laser Beams* a year after. I also appreciate playful album titles such as *Free Range Accordion* (2000) and *Teetering on the Verge of Normalcy* (2016). I am currently listening to his *Well-Tampered Accordion* (2016). LOL.

Does the accordion come with a license to pun? Oliveros, while not prone to interpretations of other songs or polka, nevertheless shares a similar knack for punning titles. *Deep Listening* (1989) is an obvious example, given its origins in a cistern (and Stuart Dempster is an eager co-conspirator); *Crone*—rhymes with drone—*Music* (1989–1990) is another. (There are many, going back to the 1960s, and often in her writing too, "Some Sound Observations" included.) I wonder if the pun, and its reliance on idiomatic speech, follows the accordion's immigrant journey, and its self-aware and self-deprecating sense of folk(sy) humor. Or perhaps it's the other way around, with jokers, pranksters, and class clowns naturally finding their way to the bellows? I am again reminded of the *Far Side* in which the devil greets new arrivals to Hell and hands them each an accordion.

I am also reminded of another find in the Oliveros papers at Mills: a Xerox copy of a paste-up for what appears to be a postcard, dated 1981, promoting The Big Jewish Band of San Diego. The Big Jewish Band of San Diego consists of exactly two members: Jay Welder on mandolin and Dr. Pinchus Olinsky on accordion. Olinksy is actually Oliveros in drag, with moustache and beard, suit and tie, glasses and hat—like Weird Al's favorite uncle—and it says it's her in parenthesis. As far as I know Oliveros was not Jewish. But, following her appearance in Robert Ashley's *Music with Roots in the Aether* (1975–1976), it's not her first drag performance. It's hard to guess what the occasion was for this (it lists Ron Robboy as director); perhaps it's part of another performance. I've never seen any other reference to it in the Oliveros literature. The target of its humor seems to be San Diego, not Jews, and I certainly hope that's the case. A quick Google search reveals, courtesy of the *Chicago Jewish News*, that, "There is one thing San Diego has never had: a large Jewish population," and the city once had housing covenants (redlining) that prohibited sales to non-whites and non-Christians. In 1981, Oliveros gave up her teaching post and left San Diego for upstate New York, and just like that, The Big Jewish Band of San Diego folded as quickly as it was formed, barely leaving a trace.

107

Yesterday, I attended the afternoon opening of Simone Forti's new exhibition at The Box. I tend to dislike openings because I can't actually spend time with the work, or give it quality attention, although I did get to spend time with Simone and talk to Barbara T. Smith and Tashi Wada, among others. I've seen all of Simone's shows at The Box—this is the fourth or perhaps fifth—and each one has been quite different, although all or most have foregrounded sound. This show was titled *An Other Pretty Autumn* (2022), named after a long poem by Simone, a recording of which was read by three readers and filled the space. But it was hard to hear over the various conversations. I knew I needed to come back as soon as I entered the show. One thing I immediately became aware of was how much I needed to pay attention to my body in the space. This should not be a surprise, given Simone's relation to dance and movement. I am in awe of how she uses objects to choreograph my own (awkward) movements. (Rarely do I feel more clumsy than when I'm in the company of dancers. I've been aware of this fact since 2008 when I first met Simone when we performed together in a reconsideration of Allan Kaprow's *18 Happenings in Six Parts* [1959] at Los Angeles Contemporary Exhibitions or LACE.) In the current show, there are a lot of objects (obstacles) and materials to negotiate: three big video projections of Simone weeding; framed drawings or paintings on Trader Joe's bags; a three-panel poem suspended in space; *See Saw* (1961) rendered nearly unfamiliar, its fulcrum hanging from the ceiling and its plank leaning against the opposite wall; a block of wood nearby on the ground—a likely tripping hazard for anyone not paying attention—titled *That Block* (2022); and a gong suspended from the ceiling and hanging at face height. I didn't find the title of the gong and wondered about its function. It was still, silent, although I gave it the slightest of taps with my knuckle, gently forcing the issue to coax its warm tone. It reminded me of a gong similarly suspended in Milford Graves's show at Artist's Space in New York last fall. Outfitted with an Arduino that induced a vibration, Graves's gong was perpetually resonating during the show. I guess it's still resonating in my head.

108

Today, driving home from CalArts, I listened to Oliveros's *St. George and the Dragon* (1994). At forty-seven minutes, it's one of her longer solo works for accordion, and fills most of my return trip. I haven't listened to it in a long time. Years? Perhaps. It was probably among the first Oliveros recordings I purchased, most likely found in the contemporary classical bins at Amoeba. The CD also includes *In Memoriam Mr. Whitney* (1994), a collaboration with the eclectic choral group American Voices, with Oliveros contributing her voice along with her accordion. The album never clicked as much as many others, and I had largely let it slip my attention. Today, I gave it as much focus as I could while driving. *St. George and the Dragon* is an intense piece, likewise fitting for the drive, as I traversed three freeways at the onset of rush "hour." I had the volume turned up quite loud. The harmonics produced by the accordion are wild. I'm reminded of the duet with Klucevsek on *Tremolo No. 6 (Nucleic Chains)* (2019) given the speed with which she pushes and pulls the bellows. It's a relatively frenetic performance, especially in comparison to the slower development of *Horse Sings from Cloud*, and without her voice accompanying the accordion, the tone is not as warm. Given its rather cool, even harsh affect, it recalls Oliveros's early Buchla works from 1966–1967: It takes some (listening) work to find the human being at the core of the thing. As with *In Memoriam*, *St. George* was recorded in the Clark Chapel at the Pomfret School in Pomfret, Connecticut. Oliveros arrived at the chapel early and improvised with the space. The title of the work refers to a statue of the saint and the dragon in the chapel. One could also imagine it as a metaphor for Oliveros and her instrument dueling with the space:

Made of rough stone, the acoustics of the space are reverberant and challenging for the performer. I like to perform by listening to the space as a musical instrument. I include all that I hear from the space and within it. This time a noisy squirrel joined me. Thus, the work becomes a kind of interactive duet taking the surroundings as metaphor and as an acoustic reality to be integrated into the performance and composition. The microphones for this recording were arranged to pick up the sound of the accordion and the sound of the reflections from the chapel about equally.

Recorded in 1991, *St. George and the Dragon* recalls and coincides with the improvisatory and recording methodologies being developed by Deep Listening Band, in which the site is another instrument and an unwitting collaborator, performing and being performed.

109

Yesterday's delivery, today's listen:

Fritz Hauser with David Gamper, Urs Leimgruber,
Pauline Oliveros
Deep Time
Deep Listening, 2005

According to the liner notes:

Deep Time is a tape composition commissioned in 1991 by the Pauline Oliveros Foundation for Deep Listening Band with funds from the New York State Arts Council of the Arts.

Fritz Hauser's tape features recordings of sounding stones (manufactured by Arthur Schneiter) and various watches and clocks (thanks to the Bucher family in Switzerland for permission to record that family clock!) The performers improvise with the tape. Recordings in April 1991 were engineered by Hans Ulrich. Editing and mixing was done by Hans Ulrich and Fritz Hauser at Mo Studio in Basel, Switzerland.

On October 26, 1994, Pauline Oliveros, David Gamper, Urs Leimgruber, and Fritz Hauser recorded two versions of *Deep Time* in Gamper's basement studio on Abeel Street in Kingston, NY. These tapes were edited and mastered four years later—October 16–18, 1998—at Gamper's current studio in New York.

110

Yesterday I listened to each version of *Deep Time* (2005, composed and recorded in 1991), on my way to and on my way home from CalArts—loudly, to overcome the acoustic competition with traffic. There is a lot of subtlety here, some of it lost in context. I am immediately struck by how percussive its focus is, which makes sense given Fritz Hauser's leading role, with his recordings of sounding stones and clocks. And Hauser plays live on top of the recording, too. The use of "field" recording is also unusual, but I appreciate how it creates a consistent backdrop for two rather different group improvisations, both around thirty-two minutes each. My first listen to anything is necessarily provisional: I can only take in so much information at once. Despite the outside presence of clocks, I didn't focus on time too much. But I did observe that both versions seemed to really kick in around twenty minutes, and there's something on the backing track that must have propelled that. The most jarring moment comes later when the grandfather clock rings out. While the work was commissioned for Deep Listening Band, I am not sure if the recording is, without the presence of Stuart Dempster, actually a Deep Listening Band album. (Which would cause me to adjust my DLB discography). But, much like Joe McPhee's *Common Threads* (1996), which does include Dempster, it expands my understanding of Deep Listening Band.

111

It's surprising how certain musical memories can resurface even without hearing a note. Yesterday, I was meeting with a student who is researching Lil' Kim, and it led to a conversation about my first job in Los Angeles, which was working as an assistant to the director Peter Spirer on the documentary *Rhyme & Reason*. *Rhyme & Reason* is a surprisingly intimate, anthropological documentary on rap music and culture. It took several years to make. I worked on it in fall 1995 into spring 1996, and it made its debut in 1997. I have written on it and lectured on it elsewhere, but for the sake of concision, I like to argue it's a film that marks the transition of rap from subculture to culture. I arrived in Los Angeles in August 1995. It was the summer of the O.J. Simpson murder trial, a year after the Northridge earthquake, three years after the acquittal of the cops who beat Rodney King and the subsequent uprising that erupted at Florence and Normandie. It was a volatile time in the city, and the rap world was part of it. Biggie Smalls, who is featured in *Rhyme & Reason*, was murdered outside the Peterson Automotive Museum on Fairfax and Wilshire while the film was in postproduction. (This followed shortly after the murder of Tupac Shakur in Las Vegas.) This site was on the bus route I took to get to Peter's house, which was on Crescent Heights, just north of Sunset Blvd. I was a naive young white person from Wisconsin, barely aware of the implications of my being. My experience of working on *Rhyme & Reason* was a wild and eye-opening introduction to the city. I talked to Dr. Dre on the phone my first day on the job; I also met many other rap stars, from Kurtis Blow (a producer on the film) to Ice-T (in his Hollywood Hills studio, memorably featuring tanks with baby sharks) to Sen Dog of Cypress Hill (at a mall in Lynwood). I saw parts of the city I may never see again. I provided a version of this narrative to my student.

This morning, listening to NPR on the way to CalArts, there was an interview with B-Real of Cypress Hill, discussing their eponymous debut, noting that it was released in August 1991, one month before Nirvana's *Nevermind*. Both were in constant rotation in Madison, Wisconsin, that fall, enjoyed by an overlapping demographic, despite genre differences. At parties, one could hear "Smells Like Teen Spirit" immediately followed by "How I Could Just Kill a Man," with revelers enthusiastically singing along to both. Cypress Hill immediately defined a new, West Coast style of hip-hop, featuring an infectious combination of Spanglish and marijuana. The latter was more immediately relevant to my experience; otherwise, the world described in their lyrics seemed far removed, and it was. In the ecstatic bloom of 1991, I could not have imagined moving to Los Angeles, nor meeting Sen Dog, just a few years later. I came home today, after another delirious drive home in the city that's been my home for twenty-six years and counting, and listened to *Cypress Hill*.

112

Among its many super powers, music has the ability to conjure memory from thin air. In Chris Marker's *La Jetée* (1962), the protagonist is able to travel through time because of a particularly intense memory of a face. For me, certain songs can instantly transport me to a specific time and place, a mood, an occasion. One memory usually leads to another, and sometimes a recollection of a time and a place, a mood, an occasion leads to a memory of the music that accompanied it. I haven't listened to them in ages, but at the moment I am thinking about a show by bass-drum duo godheadSilo at Spaceland, with Leslie and Justin, still my two most faithful musical companions, exactly twenty-five years ago today.

113

Yesterday was the hundredth birthday of Charles Mingus, and the *New York Times* profiled an intergenerational group of musicians who continue to be inspired by his legacy as a composer, band leader, and bass player. I was particularly struck by the commentary by bassist, singer, and composer Miles Mosley:

> One of my favorite ideas of Mingus's is that rhythm is felt in a circle. Each of us feels time in a slightly different place. When I refer to "time" in music, it's the rhythm, the beat, the tempo. And Mingus would put his band together depending on who felt the rhythm where in this concept of a circle: ahead of it, on top of it, behind it. And he would make it so that the entire band equaled a group of musicians that created a full circle of time.
>
> What Mingus embraced in his music, what you're hearing, is someone embracing the idea that you want to cultivate a collection of humans because they are different from one another, not because they are the same. You're not hearing a bunch of people in unity. You are hearing a bunch of people sharing a concept and expressing it uniquely to themselves, all at once ... The small things that separate us on a common goal is what makes us more powerful.

It's the first time I considered Mingus in relation to Oliveros, brought together by the platonic ideal of the circle and its potential relation to time travel.

This morning I'm listening to *Money Jungle* (1962), with Mingus, Max Roach, and Duke Ellington, chopping it up in a heated intergenerational session that remains one of my favorite trio performances and one of my favorite albums in any genre.

114

Some four months into this writing, I am aware of how the daily structure I've assigned myself accommodates both focused listening and expansive digression, following the basic shape of Oliveros's attention/awareness mandala. This is also a tug-of-war between past and present—between (having) time and (having) no time. I am also aware there is so much I have yet to touch upon regarding my musical universe, generally, and Oliveros, specifically. That will be the future.

115

Tashi Wada: *Duets*
Performed by Charles Curtis and Peter Ko, cello
Followed by a conversation with Wada, Curtis, and Michael Ned Holte

May 14, 2022, 5:30 p.m.
Arlington Garden (Olive Allee)
275 Arlington Drive
Pasadena, CA 91105

Tashi Wada is a Los Angeles-based composer and performer. In his work, he uses precise tuning and gradual changes in pitch to explore harmonic overtones, resonance, and dissonance. Wada grounds his compositions in the belief that "music should be as direct as possible," and uses seemingly simple structures to generate rich and unanticipated perceptual effects. Wada positions his work in relation to American experimental music, microtonal music, and so-called drone music. His practice is also informed by interdisciplinary performance and Fluxus-affiliated artists. Wada studied composition at CalArts with James Tenney and has performed with Charles Curtis, Corey Fogel, Simone Forti, Julia Holter, and his father, the composer Yoshi Wada.

For his contribution to *how we are in time and space*, Wada will present *Duets*, a composition for two cellos, performed here by Charles Curtis and Peter Ko. The *Duets* were composed between 2006 and 2008, and four of these were performed by Curtis and Judith Hamann for the 2014 album *Duets*, on Wada's Saltern label. Marcia Hafif was close to both Wada and Curtis, and her painting *85. June 1965* was selected as the cover artwork.

Duets will be performed in the Olive Allee at Arlington Garden, and the performance will be followed by a conversation about the composition and Marcia Hafif with Tashi Wada, Charles Curtis, and Michael Ned Holte, curator of *how we are in time and space: Nancy Buchanan, Marcia Hafif, Barbara T. Smith*.

The score for each duet consists of a diagonal line drawn across music staff, indicating a glissando—a gradual and perceptible movement across two octaves. This is accompanied by a verbal instruction: "The players descend in unison very slowly . . . " Given the rigorous framework of the score, an exact doubling is difficult to achieve, producing a very tenuous unison. The subtle differences between the players and their movement through the glissandi generates much of the drama of the work, as well as its harmonic play.

"The drawing of a bow across a string is in a sense a materialization of elapsing time," observes Curtis in his liner notes for *Duets*. "How far can we enter into a single moment, such that for that brief speck of time, for an instant, unison is registered? This would suggest a different sense of unison, as a state of complete integration hidden behind the disparity and change caused by the passing of time."

116

Yesterday, Warren Olds sent me the revised design of my "Bog Time" pamphlet on Oliveros's tape and electronic music, with an emphasis on the "bog"-titled compositions she made using the Buchla in 1966 and 67. The timing is quite perfect, considering the way in which my interest in time travel has bubbled to the surface recently. ("I think about using all of these delays as a time machine," Oliveros remarked to Tara Rodgers in the 2010 book *Pink Noises: Women on Electronic Music and Sound*. "Because when I play something in the present, then it's delayed and comes back in the future. But when it comes back in the future, I'm dealing with the past, and also playing again in the present, anticipating the future. So that's expanding time.") Oliveros's use of tape delay and the later development of her Expanded Instrument System (EIS) are among my considerations in the pamphlet.

Given how little attention I've given to her electronic and tape music in the present writing (and given how much attention I need to devote to other fires burning at school and in my inbox and elsewhere in the coming days), I will begin to re-read (and share) excerpts from the pamphlet prior to its publication. And I'll save most of the footnotes and the exquisite drawings by Ruoyi Shi for those who get the pamphlet.

117

NEWLY-FOUND POWERS

Beginning on July 22, 1967, Pauline Oliveros presented a twelve-hour concert of tape and electronic music at Ronald Chase's loft at 136 Embarcadero in San Francisco. Titled "Tape-athon," the concert included thirty radically experimental works created within the previous six years. As a concert of tape music, most of the compositions were prerecorded, but were being presented to a live audience for the first time. Many were accompanied in this context by a diverse array of extra-compositional material: films by Chase and Jack Foss, slide projections and other visuals by Lynn Lonidier, choreography by Elizabeth Harris, a performance by the San Francisco Mime Troupe, and more, emphasizing the significance of multimedia innovation and collaboration in the overlapping circles of new music, electronics, experimental theater, and proto-psychedelic stagecraft that marked the Bay Area milieu in which Oliveros was operating. The concert began at 6 p.m. with a work emphatically titled *Another Big Mother* from 1966, and ended, presumably at or around 6 a.m. with *Bog Road*, a recent work from 1967. One can only imagine the audience that persevered for a full trip around the clock was treated to a mind-boggling program of auditory and visual overload.

The Tape-athon was also an ending of sorts: an elaborate send off, thrown by Oliveros to herself and a willing audience before she relocated to San Diego. The concert marked a moment of transition following a formative and decidedly profuse fifteen years of development, a period that spans her arrival in the city in 1952, with college studies at the San Francisco State College (now San Francisco State University), to her leading role in a generative community of like-minded composers and performers working at the frontier of new music in the Bay Area.

Central to this development was the San Francisco Tape Music Center, which developed out of two concerts organized by Oliveros and Ramon Sender under the name *Sonics*. The first *Sonics* concert took place on December 18, 1961, and included Sender's composition *Traversals* (1961), Terry Riley's *M . . . Mix*, later known as *Mescalin Mix* (1960–1961), and Oliveros's *Time Perspectives* (1961), among other works. All three works were evidence of a shared sensibility emerging from profound technical opportunities availed by new electronic equipment. This included quality tape recorders, which had only become commercially available in the 1950s and were crucial to this group of composers exploring and pioneering new tape-delay techniques using multiple recorders in the early 1960s. Riley would dub his version the Time Lag Accumulator.

Following a second *Sonics* concert, Sender and Subotnick founded the San Francisco Tape Music Center in 1962. Oliveros had received the prestigious Gaudeamus Award and was traveling in Europe at the time, but she joined Sender and Morton Subotnick in their new endeavor on her return. The Tape Music Center at 1537 Jones Street served as a recording studio, performance space, and social hub that quickly became the most significant locus of electronic music on the West Coast. A fire the following year brought a temporary setback, but by 1963 the Tape Music Center had relocated to 321 Divisadero Street with new equipment—professional Ampex tape machines, a patch bay, ring modulators, amplifiers, mics, and an array of tape recorders and loop machines—and with new momentum. It also found kinship and collaborative opportunities in the context of new neighbors, including the Anna Halprin Dancers' Workshop, Canyon Cinema, and listener-sponsored radio station KPFA, which frequently showcased new music and local composers . . .

Even before the Tape Music Center came into being, Oliveros had gamely produced *Time Perspectives* in her "home studio," employing a Sears Silvertone tape recorder and microphones, while improvising sounds using her own voice and common household materials such as cardboard tubes, which were used for filtering sound, and the bathtub, which was used for reverberation—defamiliarizing familiar sources. The Silvertone tape recorder had two built-in speeds (7 ½ and 3 ¼ inches-per-second), so recorded material could be raised or lowered a precise octave. In addition, Oliveros varied the speed by hand-winding the tape while in recording mode. In a concert setting, she played *Time Perspectives* simultaneously on two tape players to achieve quadraphonic sound.

The composition immediately established a number of key values that would recur throughout Oliveros's long and varied career: first, an investment in temporal flux, which she achieved through acoustic reverberation as well as novel techniques such as tape delay, often using these in combination; second, a desire to improvise, which is to say perform outside of the confinement of strict compositional notation, making discoveries in real time and in response to an immediate environmental context, anticipating some of the central concerns of her eventual Deep Listening strategies; and third, an innovative sense of how one might engage with technological interfaces, toward greater human/machine reciprocity, often building up these relationships into a dense, complex synthesis.

This last word is particularly important here, especially in consideration of Oliveros's proximity to the development of the modular synthesizer. She was unquestionably one of the first people to see the Buchla Box 100 Series Modular synthesizer, which was built by Don Buchla to support the needs of Subotnick and Sender. The Buchla arrived at the Tape Music Center in late 1964 or early 1965; but despite Oliveros's close involvement in the development of the Tape Music Center and its community of composers, and her own pioneering contributions to early tape music, she largely refrained from using the Buchla in the first few years of the center, often returning to more conventional scoring and instrumentation, relatively speaking . . .

119

Arguably, synthesis would emerge as one of the most significant aspects of Oliveros's work for the next half-century, regardless of the equipment involved. Often, in fact, there is no equipment beyond human voice. A significant example of this is *Sound Patterns* (1961), a four-minute acapella work for mixed chorus, built from phonetic sounds chosen for their timbre. While the sounds are entirely human-made, they specifically emulate electronic sounds, which Oliveros would have recently encountered, as Heidi Von Gunden notes in a thorough analysis of the composition:

> In electronic music white noise (the presence of all pitches sounding randomly) is frequently colored by selecting certain areas or band widths of noise to be heard. This creates a variety of possible noise-like timbres. The initial sound of Oliveros's piece is "sh," a vocal example of white noise that sonically permits a broad band of hissing sound. She colored this "sh" white noise by substituting various consonants, such as s, z, wh, p, t, h, ct, d, ch, th, k, and sw to change subtly the quality of the sound.

Von Gunden further describes how Oliveros's score imitates other electronic sounds, including ring modulation through rapidly changing the vowel content, percussive envelopes through a series of "lip pops," "tongue clicks," "snap fingers," and "flutter lips," and muting the mouth with one's hand, sounding the consonant "m" through tightly closed lips, or singing through clenched teeth, and so on.

Sound Patterns earned Oliveros the prestigious Gaudeamus International Composers Award in 1962, which brought her to Europe for a premiere and her first substantial engagement with the continent. She was the first woman to receive the award since its inception in 1957 and would be the only woman to do so for many years. The influential composer György Ligeti was on the jury, and within a year, his own choral compositions began to use non-conventional vocal sounds. Oliveros returned to San Francisco and the Tape Music Center milieu, working in the studio but on her own terms that were implicitly gendered. As she later described it:

I worked most often in the studio from midnight to dawn when the daily hubbub was over and there was quiet and a peaceful space. I had no training in electronics, mathematics, or physics. I had to teach myself about the hardware in the analog studio. Though well meaning, the "boys" were not necessarily helpful. The tech-oriented attitude put me off more often than not—mostly because of lack of vocabulary and knowledge on my part. Men have a way of bonding around technology. There seemed to be an invisible barrier tied to a way of treating women as helpless or hapless beings. I wanted to learn and be in on the latest gadgets, but it was difficult to make my learning needs known. I also had my pride. I learned by drawing pictures of every piece of equipment, noting every term, then searching in references for their meanings. After this research, I asked questions and gradually learned how to operate the equipment that had accumulated in the studio. This was hands-on, trial-and-error learning. My procedure was to work from sound sources that were mostly found objects or unorthodox ways of playing instruments...

120

In 1965, Don Buchla gave a public demonstration of his 100 Series modular synthesizer at the Tape Music Center's concert hall. Immediately after the demonstration, Oliveros went upstairs to the studio and made *Bye Bye Butterfly*, which is now regarded as one of the most important early examples of electronic music. Notably, *Bye Bye Butterfly* did *not* make use of the Buchla, but did make use of Oliveros's own synthetic discoveries in the electronic studio: First, her tape delay techniques, resulting from her realization that the physical distance between the recording head and the playback head on the tape recorder could be used to create temporal delays, particularly when threaded through multiple recorders (what Riley defined as a Time Lag Accumulator); and second, her innovative use of two Hewlett-Packard oscillators to produce difference tones, also known as heterodyning. Together, these techniques represented a breakthrough that further opened up the field of sound to her. The latter discovery echoed an early excitement over the idea of combination tones, which her accordion teacher taught her to listen for at the age of sixteen. Oliveros invented the idea of amplifying difference tones, created by playing two otherwise inaudible tones against each other, as a tool of musical composition. Heterodyning is a more commonly used technique for detecting bats, which can hear frequencies beyond the range of human hearing. One electronic studio director accused Oliveros of "black art" in her use of frequencies beyond the spectrum of human hearing. "I felt like a witch capturing sounds from a nether realm . . . " she noted, embracing the accusations of sonic heresy. "For recreation, [I] would ride my bicycle to the town power plant where I would listen for hours to the source of my newfound powers."

Bye Bye Butterfly also incorporates a recording of Puccini's opera *Madama Butterfly* (1904), which is, in the composer's account, the record Oliveros randomly picked up in the studio and fed into this remarkable synthesis. Her *Bye Bye Butterfly* pulls open—butterflies?—Puccini's opera, destabilizes it, distends it in time, makes it her own.

I was really happy with the super heterodyne technique that I had developed. I set those oscillators to superaudio and then amplified the difference tones. And beat them against the bias of the tape recorders. And I was running a tape delay. So, I had all these artifacts and instability that created those wonderful sounds. I had an ambivalent feeling about this new development, the Buchla. It was taking away my old toys. It didn't feel like an addition at the time because I couldn't get the sounds that I could get with the oscillators.

While Oliveros credits serendipity for the use of the record, there is much one could read into the gender politics of remaking Puccini's opera. Certainly, in retrospect, it is possible to see *Bye Bye Butterfly* as a critique of the Buchla, and the gendered entitlements of those who brought it to the Tape Music Center, as well as a demonstration of Oliveros's own inventions. One could also be tempted to take the title metaphorically: the following year Oliveros departed San Francisco for an extended stay at the University of Toronto . . .

121

MY STRATEGY WAS INSTABILITY

In residence at the University of Toronto in 1966, and far removed from the milieu of the Tape Music Center, Oliveros explored the possibilities of her heterodyning discovery combined with tape delay and other techniques afforded by an electronic music studio. Presumably, she felt at home quickly because her output from this period is profuse, with at least two dozen of her finished works as evidence. The titles of some of the works plainly render the speculative nature of her exploration and encounter with this equipment, and even embrace the potential "mistakes" she was using to her advantage and apparent delight, most notably in the work called *The Day I Disconnected the Erase Head and Forgot to Reconnect It*. Other titles—*Bottoms Up*, *No Mo*, *Something Else*, *Big Mother is Watching You*, and *Another Big Mother*—revealed an abundant, sometimes giddy sense of humor that would hardly be expected in early electronic music, though this humor would not surprise anyone familiar with the composer's more frankly outrageous multimedia theater works, such as *Pieces of Eight* (1964), which was loosely based on Robert Louis Stevenson's *Treasure Island*, or *George Washington Slept Here* and its sequel *George Washington Slept Here Too* (both 1965).

Word play—especially her use of puns—becomes an important aspect of Oliveros's titling, breaking away from the stodgy and burdensome legacy of classical music, while also articulating her own profoundly unique voice as a lesbian feminist composer. A prolific author, Oliveros wrote texts in a wide variety of modes, from scholarly essays to poetry, with a significant number of her scores using purely textual notation. The pleasure of her language play seems to acknowledge the precedent of poet

Gertrude Stein, a significant lesbian forerunner, perhaps first evidenced in Oliveros's non-semantic phonetic construction in *Sound Patterns* (1961) but becoming more emphatic while in the electronic music studio at the University of Toronto. If the idea of *Sound Patterns* was to emulate exotic new electronic sounds by use of the human voice, Oliveros's later *Sonic Meditations* (1971–1973) were a series of text scores predicated on the concept of finding one's voice and directly connected to the composer's increasingly urgent and unreserved feminist politics. The first *Sonic Meditation*, *Teach Yourself to Fly*, was dedicated to Amelia Earhart, and clearly demonstrates these emerging values:

Any number of persons sit in a circle facing the center. Illuminate the space with dim blue light. Begin by simply observing your own breathing. Always be an observer. Gradually allow your breathing to become audible. Then gradually introduce your voice. Allow your vocal cords to vibrate in any mode slowly. Continue as long as possible, naturally, and until all others are quiet, always observing your own breath cycle . . .

122

Oliveros's tape music titles are often funny, or at least accessible, and explicitly materialist, seemingly to demystify the conditions or processes that determined the otherwise "abstract" work. For a listener, these works can be demanding, often fifteen minutes to a half hour in length with maximum duration limited only by the final output tape. Oliveros was averse to editing or splicing tape, preferring to treat each magnetic reel as a document of an event occurring in real time, even as she is destabilizing the listeners' understanding of time, and presumably her own, in the listening process. These compositions are in fact improvisations, as are the vast majority of Oliveros's electronic works, yet another way of breaking away from the staid edifices of classical music.

There is a history of improvisation within the classical tradition, but it is typically subservient to a score. John Cage's indeterminate music is one useful example, and unquestionably, his precedent loomed large for Oliveros and her cohort. But, as Heidi Von Gunden argues, "Oliveros certainly has been influenced by Cage, and although they share an interest in the material aspects of sound, Oliveros's ideas about composition are quite different."

> Her manner of writing is personal and controlled, where Cage's is impersonal and determined by chance operations. Frequently, Oliveros's presence is an important aspect of her work, especially when it includes audience participation. Her body language of sitting cross-legged on a stage or in the center of a circle with house lights dimmed communicates her attitudes about sound and performing.

Oliveros is rarely cited as a significant figure in the development of improvised music, but she should be. Her physical presence is central to the performance of many of her compositions, from the reverberatory bathtub explorations of *Time Perspectives* (1961) to the guided *Sonic Mediations* of the early 1970s and beyond. Chronologically situated in-between, her real-time electronic works serve as an example of the threads of composition and performance becoming one tightly knit totality. Improvisation—especially "free improvisation"—is of course much more closely associated with jazz, and the expanding field of improvisation would indeed be the defining aspect of jazz in the 1960s. Ornette Coleman's album *Free Jazz*, often considered the clarion call for this movement, was released in 1961. Oliveros was exploring her own understanding of improvisation by 1958, most notably in a trio with classmates at San Francisco State College, Terry Riley and Loren Rush. The initial prompt was a film by Claire Falkenstein, titled *Polyester Moon* (1957), for which Riley was invited to devise a soundtrack. With a limited amount of time to write a score, Riley turned to his colleagues, and they turned to improvisation, recording in the KPFA studios, with Riley on piano, Rush on bass and koto, and Oliveros on French horn, an instrument she played early in her musical development. "The first session piqued our interest in improvisation," as Oliveros recalled:

> We were amazed that we could make music together this way. We decided to meet regularly for more sessions. We learned an all-important lesson in these early sessions: if we talked first and tried to impose guidelines or structure for the improvisation, the attempt would likely fall flat. If we played first without talking about it, then listened to the recording critically, our improvising would improve naturally. We liberated ourselves from unnecessary controls and developed trust in process

through spontaneity. As far as we know, we were the first in avant-garde art music to engage in "free improvisation." Our process was new: play and record, listen to the recording, enjoy, talk, judge, criticize, analyze, and play again.

This process—playing, listening, enjoying, talking, judging, analyzing, playing again—is a feedback loop of sorts, and is the root of the theory and practice of Deep Listening that Oliveros would develop and more fully articulate several decades later. It was also behind her exploration in the electronic music studios in Toronto, and later at Mills College and the University of California San Diego (UCSD), one that fully entangles studio hardware and human software in real time . . .

123

While there is no traditional notation for these electronic works, the rigorously structured schematic diagrams for each acts as a kind of *de facto* score—one that sets a process in motion, establishing parameters and a directional flow while also enabling and inducing new possibilities during a real-time improvisation made with and committed to magnetic tape. As evidenced by Oliveros's journal article "Tape Delay Techniques for Electronic Music Composers" (1969), each studio set-up is carefully planned and diagrammed with the sequence of "playing, listening, enjoying . . . as a circuitous relay system." Some diagrams were also accompanied by a set of written instructions. *The Bath* (1966), composed as a score for Anna Halprin, used the sound of the dancers as an inaugurating material that was then fed back into the mix during live performance. Oliveros described the diagramming of the work to Tara Rodgers:

> I was recording a dance piece, recording the sound of the dancers, and eventually opening up the delay to change the shape of the room, the feeling of the room. I would play back what I recorded, and play back much later what had been recorded into the whole piece, so that eventually it was a very complex texture but it was all made of sounds that they had already made and were making.

The diagrams for these compositions grew increasingly complex, toward extraordinary synthetic density. Even while looking at the diagrams, it would be difficult if not impossible for most listeners to interpolate the schematic process—or parts from the whole—while confronting the incredible thicket of electronic sound in any of these recordings. Oliveros later described her approach to improvisation in the electronic studio in an interview with Andrew Deutsch, remarking, "I had this interaction of delays, echoes, and combination tones. But I was making a system that was unstable, so my strategy was INSTABILITY. I would have to react instantaneously to reconcile anything that came out. And that was my strategy." Prompted by Deutsch's suggestion that her approach was "Dionysian," Oliveros replied, "Well, I think it was both because I had an Apollonian system, and the system was like the container for the Dionysian approach. The sensuality of the sound was what I was after."

Given that Oliveros performed each of these works in the studio, each schematic diagram inevitably represents a kind of mnemonic device for her, and a point of departure for the next, more complex assembly. One could also read each diagram as an expansive map without a particular destination. In contradistinction to the classical tradition, circularity replaces linearity, though given the continual accumulation of sounds and Oliveros's real-time adjustments, repeatability is out of the question here, and for Oliveros, was never the question in the first place . . .

124

ANTICIPATING THE FUTURE

By the end of 1966, Oliveros had returned to the Bay Area with a one-year contract from Mills College to direct the Tape Music Center, which she did alongside Tony Martin, a friend and early collaborator who had provided inventive visual components for Oliveros and many of her peers. The Rockefeller Foundation provided substantial funding for the Tape Music Center, but with need of a fiscal agent and increased administrative oversight, the center was transferred to Mills College. Meanwhile, Morton Subotnick had departed for New York University, and Ramon Sender, deeply involved in the psychedelic scene, left the center to start the Trips Festival with Stewart Brand.

Working in the newly established Mills College Tape Music Center, and presumably with a growing sense of agency if not urgency, Oliveros continued to develop and expand the complex electronic synthesis she developed in Toronto. And following a two-year delay, whether by choice or circumstance or both, Oliveros finally began to explore the Buchla 100 synthesizer, working it into the already dense mesh of her studio set-up. The works resulting from this new arrangement include at least six works with the word “bog” in the title, and another she called *Beautiful Soop* (1966)—with “bog” and “soop” serving as useful descriptions of the sounds she was producing with Buchla’s synthesizer subsumed into her own idiosyncratic studio synthesis.

By now a master of the tape delay techniques she helped innovate, the Buchla presented a new set of challenges to encounter. If the modular synthesizer promised endless possibilities for sonic experimentation, it also presented the possibility of systemic chaos and confusion with the opening and closing of its envelopes in real time. The relentlessness of the machine's signal flow paralleled the constancy of the looping magnetic tape, Oliveros deftly navigating their intertwined trajectories. If "mistakes" were made, it would be difficult to locate them in the "alien" sounds of the resulting compositions, which have little precedent. Oliveros observed other limitations with the Buchla: "I felt the loss of the sound of the old tube oscillators, and it took some time for me to adapt to the coolness of transistor-generated sound," she later described:

> The oscillators also did not have the high-frequency range above hearing like the tube oscillators. By 1967, I had made some pieces with the Buchla Box, still using my tape delay system, which included *Beautiful Soop* and *Alien Bog*. I designed a four-channel mixer to be used for performance. Nothing was available for performance except the input splitters from Radio Shack. We still had no mixer in the studio. Carl Countryman, a young engineer, undertook the construction of this mixer, which had eight inputs, four outputs, and DC voltage-control outputs. I used the mixer in a few performances before I left my one-year position at Mills . . .

125

In retrospect, it is easy to see Oliveros at an impasse, or at least at a moment of transition, with evidence of seven resulting works with the word "bog" in the title: *Alien Bog*, *Big Slow Bog*, *Boone Bog*, *Bog Bog*, *Mind Bog*, *Bog Road*, and *Mills Bog* (all 1966–1967). Despite a common title, and a similar duration, with each *Bog* lasting just over a half hour, the works are extremely varied, each wresting wildly different results from a more-or-less constant but complex set-up. The bog in the title of these works refers directly to the pond outside the Mills College Tape Music Center. In the liner notes for a belated release of *Alien Bog/ Beautiful Soop* (1997), Oliveros recalls, "I was deeply impressed by the sounds from the frog pond outside the studio window at Mills. I loved the accompaniment as I worked on my pieces. Though I never recorded the frogs I was of course influenced by their music. Since that time many other composers have also been influenced by sounds from the pond." Elsewhere, she connects the Mills bog to the Houston-area landscape that shaped her relationship to sound at an early age:

> As far back as I can remember I was always listening to what was happening around me. I lived in a rich environment of sound. In the Texas wetlands, there were lots of insects—it was really like a thick canopy that changed through the season: tree frogs, cicadas, crickets, all these wonderful sounding critters.

Taking the titles and Oliveros's description of the pond at face value, it is obvious that the landscape is the subject of these works. While they are not field recordings, these *Bog* pieces anticipate later work shaped by the specificity of her environmental context, including numerous collaborations with Deep Listening Band. Oliveros's first notable use of the phrase Deep Listening appeared over twenty years later in 1989 as the punning title of an album recorded in the massive underground Fort Worden cistern in Port Townsend, Washington. The group continued in various configurations, always including Oliveros and Stuart Dempster, as Deep Listening Band. Oliveros subsequently initiated occasional week-long Deep Listening retreats and in 2005, founded the Deep Listening Institute . . .

In 1967, Oliveros worked inside the Tape Music Center at Mills with the window open, listening to the rich sound environment outside, while improvising with her expansive studio set-up, the Buchla synthesizer included. The approach suggests another kind of feedback loop, a call and response reminiscent of the critical improvising process Oliveros, Riley, and Rush developed some nine years earlier. This analytical process also anticipates the intense reciprocal relationship between awareness and attention she would begin to articulate in the early 1970s with a mandala diagram serving as her primary compositional structure for many years following. The most basic version of the diagram is a circle, representing awareness, with a dot in the center, representing attention. Awareness is passive listening, attention is focused listening. Later, she revised the terms to "global attention" and "focal attention." In the case of the *Bogs*, one can picture her focal attention inside the Tape Music Center with her global attention open to the vast external environment outside her window—the pond, of course, but whatever else was happening on the Mills campus, or even beyond, as well. These two states—awareness and attention—are not fixed, but constantly in flux, representing a listening continuum.

One can learn to train their attention and much of Oliveros's work that followed attended to that practice and its implications with compositions that depended on the active engagement of performers responding to one another and/or the larger sound environment. Her later theory of Deep Listening emerges out of this same relationship:

Deep Listening for me is learning to expand the perception of sounds to include the whole space/time continuum of sound–encountering the vastness and complexities as much as possible. Simultaneously one ought to be able to target a sound or sequence of sounds as a focus within the space/time continuum and to perceive the detail or trajectory of the sound or sequence of sounds.

While there are obvious precedents for this approach—Cage's *4'33"* (1952), with its shifting of emphasis from performer to audience and the total sound environment, is the most well-known example—the mandala represents another way of Oliveros extricating herself from the burdensome past of the European classical tradition (and perhaps from the compositional strategies of Cage, too). Her approach develops out of the improvisations she began in 1958 and continued in her bathtub with *Time Perspectives* in 1961, and then into electronic music studios in San Francisco, Toronto, and at Mills. All require active listening in real time (or reel time) and encourage the performer or performers to focus attention in a highly rigorous way.

127

By 1967, "bog" served as a ripe metaphor—surely an extension of Oliveros's word play. After all, she could have called these "pond" pieces but didn't. The word "bog" does not typically connote something playful or good. For example, in British slang, a bog is a toilet. But my sense is that this particular bog for Oliveros was a bog of both fecundity and ambivalence. The ambivalence was perhaps twofold, resulting from her uncertain future with only the guarantee of a one-year contract at Mills and her uncertain relationship to the electronic studio. "Tape delay was cumbersome," she admitted many years later. "For some reason, I'm not interested in going into a studio anymore, I'm not sure why. I guess I prefer the contact of nice warm bodies to the cold isolation of the studio."

By 1967, Oliveros was bogged down. She had pushed the envelope for what was possible in the studio, perhaps toward a kind of mastery over her individual powers, and she sought another kind of synthesis—one that was bodily, shared, communal. Such a shift certainly represents the ethos of the historical moment, but also returns Oliveros to the joy of working with others, for which she demonstrated fondness and aptitude in her early years in San Francisco. This is precisely the work she would do again, with new forms and renewed attention upon her arrival at UCSD, where she was offered a long-term teaching contract. There she would find the contact of nice warm bodies with nice warm voices, both trained and untrained, and would develop the *Sonic Meditations* that would define the next important phase of her development.

She would not abandon the promise of technology, but largely limited her engagement with it to the classroom. Heidi Von Gunden was a student of Oliveros's at UCSD and describes Oliveros's approach to teaching electronic music at length in her monographic study of the composer:

Oliveros demanded an orderliness about our work. Tapes were to be correctly labeled with leaders, and we were to come prepared with our own empty reels, high-quality tape, splicing block, stopwatch, pitch pipe, and good razor. She remarked that it was wise to have your own equipment that way you could depend on it. She also stressed that when you meet the machine (the synthesizer), you meet yourself. In her terms, "You had better walk into the studio with good vibes. If you are disturbed, you will most likely make mistakes."

In the late 1980s, Oliveros would elaborate her synthetic approach with the development of her Expanded Instrument System (EIS), a reciprocal human-machine interface that further imbricated composition and performance. Oliveros's description of the Expanded Instrument System, with its potential to rupture linear time, explicitly recalls the complex synthesis she achieved in the Tape Music Center:

I think about using all of these delays as a time machine. Because when I play something in the present, then it's delayed and comes back in the future. But when it comes back in the future, I'm dealing with the past, and also playing again in the present, anticipating the future. So that's expanding time. That's the idea there. It's not about just one delay, it's about a whole lot of them. I've got it up to the point now where I can actually use about twenty delays. If you're in a space, you're hearing delays all the time, different time-scales. What I got interested in, long ago, was the coloration of sound that happens in a space. This happens because of delays, so I wanted to work with that.

This description returns Oliveros—and us—to the bog, particularly if we think of a bog as a large composting bin for organic matter. While a bog is a dense record of decay and delay, it is also fecund and supportive of new growth. It is self-sustaining, both one with the larger environment and apart from it. It compresses and expands time, much in the way Oliveros connected the pond outside her studio at Mills to the wetlands of her Texas childhood, time traveling in her head and in her studio, collapsing past, present, and future. In short, the bog is a great synthesizer, and for Oliveros, it was inevitably more of a beginning than an ending.

129

I woke up this morning to "Hear the Weird Sounds of a Black Hole Singing," as advertised by a headline in the *New York Times*, in their (wonderful) Out There section. The description of these "sonified ripples" actually reminded of a conceptual score:

Sound waves of the Perseus galaxy cluster were resynthesized after boosting their frequency quadrillions of times, scaling them 57 to 58 octaves—or about seven piano-lengths—above their true pitch.

The result was not unlike the sound of an electric ceiling fan that threatens to detach from its mooring. I consider (once again) the relationship of sound to music, and which category a "Black Hole Singing" belongs too. Or

What constitutes music to the universe?

A few hours later, I found myself in F200, a classroom in CalArts where I had taught Pauline Oliveros for Artists and was reminded of the intense oscillations of the fan in the ceiling projector, which often became the unwitting focus of my attention during our listening meditations and otherwise.

130

Summer Reading (provisional, aspirational, and in no particular order):

Deborah Miranda
"Teaching on Stolen Ground"
Jennifer Sinor and Rona Kaufman (editors)
Placing the Academy: Essays on Landscape, Work, and Identity
Utah State University Press, 2007

Robin Wall Kimmerer
Braiding Sweetgrass
Milkweed Editions, 2013

Stuart Dempster
The Modern Trombone: A Definition of Its Idioms
University of California Press, 1979

Daphne A. Brooks
Liner Notes for the Revolution: The Intellectual Life of Black Feminist Sound
Belknap/Harvard University Press, 2021

Sarah Ahmed
Queer Phenomenology: Orientations, Objects, Others
Duke University Press, 2006

Nicole Rudick
What Is Now Known Was Once Only Imagined: An (Auto)biography of Niki de Saint Phalle
Baker and Taylor, 2022

Charles Mingus
Beneath the Underdog (re-read)
Alfred A. Knopf, 1971

131

Thoughts gradually turn to summer, but perhaps prematurely, as I remain stuck in a thick bog of the present trying to wrap up an overwhelming school year, with numerous events for my exhibition piled on top. I wake up and send my condolences to a colleague whose mother died. Between the war in Ukraine and the end of *Roe v. Wade*, the news is almost unbearable.

This morning, I'm listening to Oliveros's album *Tara's Room* which was originally released on cassette in 1987, and released on vinyl (and digitally) by Important Records in 2019. It is dedicated to "all who have lost loved ones whose lives were taken by war." Subtitled *Two Meditations on Transition and Change*, the album consists of two long sides: *The Beauty of Sorrow* and *Tara's Room*. Both compositions are (seemingly) works for solo accordion, though the latter incorporates voice (chanting) and some kind of percussion (yes, the accordion can be a percussion instrument, but there is also a bell and a drumstick striking a wooden block), and here often sounds like a flute (it does it all, really). Oliveros is clearly using her Expanded Instrument System (EIS) to delay and layer herself. *The Beauty of Sorrow* often sounds like an accordion duet; according to the album notes, the piece is "intended to assist the listener in connecting and relaxing with deep feelings." One is aware that it likely functioned in a similar way for its composer. The dense, repetitive *Tara's Room* is described as "an invocation for wisdom especially during an unfamiliar journey." (What is she chanting? I can't make it out. Is it in English?) In many ways it recalls her early tape music: The EIS essentially turns her just-tuned accordion (and her voice, too) into a synthesizer. I am surely repeating myself when I say that all of Oliveros's work is about synthesis.

132

Thinking about Pauline Oliveros's understanding of improvisation in proximity to jazz while answering morning email—a playlist:

Pauline Oliveros + Connie Crothers
Live at The Stone
Important Records, 2016

Connie Crothers
Perception
SteepleChase, 1975

133

This evening I will be standing on stage for graduation at CalArts—the first in-person version of the ceremony since 2019. I will be reading the names of the graduating students from the School of Art as they cross the stage. At CalArts, graduation is far from formal and usually very festive—sometimes it is quite wild. Usually there is a gamelan concert before the ceremony, greeting people as they enter the school, and the African drum ensemble leads the procession of administrators and faculty as they (we) enter. This year our honorary degree recipients are Wayne Shorter, Charles Lloyd, and Esperanza Spalding. What a cool bunch. Unfortunately, they won't be there in person.

It's difficult to predict what this year's "post-COVID" version will look like. But at least one tradition remains: Each graduating student gets to select nine seconds of music to accompany them as they cross the stage and get their (placebo) diploma. I love hearing each student's choice of music because it defines them in such a succinct, if obviously limited way.

What constitutes your musical universe?

I often contemplate what my nine seconds would be—thankfully I've never had to make this difficult decision! It's hard enough to decide what I'm going to listen to on the way to graduation. (It will probably be Wayne Shorter.)

134

The morning after graduation—a playlist:

Charles Lloyd Quartet
Forest Flower: Charles Lloyd at Monterey
Atlantic, 1966

Wayne Shorter
Etcetera
Blue Note Records, 1980 (recorded in 1965)

Esperanza Spalding
Songwrights Apothecary Lab
Concord Records, 2021

Wayne Shorter
Super Nova
Blue Note Records, 1969

Charles Lloyd & The Marvels
Tone Poem
Blue Note, 2021

135

Last night, Charles Curtis and Peter Ko performed Tashi Wada's *Duets* (2014) at Arlington Garden in Pasadena. The late spring heat was oppressive, even in the early evening. I was impressed with the performers' focus as they moved through the four scores, each one technically and (apparently) physically demanding. As Charles observed in our Q&A after the performance, the compositions operate around a central paradox, in which an idea of unison between the two stringed instruments (celli) is at odds with the constant and gradual movement demanded by each score. I'm not articulating this as well as Charles did, but he is a professor of music. (In his notes that reside on the back cover of the album, he asks, "How far can we enter into a single moment, such that for that brief speck of time, for an instant, unison is registered? This would suggest a different sense of unison, as a state of complete integration hidden behind the disparity and change caused by the passing of time.") During the performance, my attention was pulled back and forth between the two cellists, who were seated facing each other, just a few feet apart. I fixed on their bows, and (with the second) on their hands as they plucked the strings, and I occasionally observed their eyes following each other's movements. Did their constant attempt at unison emphasize vision or listening? The answer is surely both. I should have asked during the talk.

The event was also intended as a tribute to Marcia Hafif, a mutual friend whose painting from 1965 appears as the cover of the *Duets* album. Marcia introduced me to Tashi and Charles when she played the album for me in her immaculate studio on St. Ann's Drive in Laguna Beach. She showed it to me, then played it as we sat in rapt silence, surrounded by her *Shade Paintings* (2013), which I had the pleasure of including in an exhibition at the

Hammer Museum's *Made in L.A. 2014*. The *Duets* album was released that year, but I don't remember if the studio visit was before or after the exhibition. My daily log indicates I visited Marcia in Laguna in September and December after the show ended. I do clearly remember the intensity of the act of listening to the album, unspeaking, while sitting across from Marcia, and then the inevitable pause when the first side of the album ended and she flipped it over. Marcia did everything with tremendous deliberateness, and for her, listening to music was no different.

Marcia was deeply fond of music and felt connected to Tashi's album, in no small part because her painting served as its cover. But as Tashi said last night, not every artist connects to an album just because they made the cover art. It was a soundtrack Marcia used when making the *Shade Paintings*. In the conversation, Tashi, Charles, and I triangulated the words "basic," "weird," and "logical," which are somehow helpful in describing *Duets* and the *Shade Paintings*. The *Shade Paintings* are monochrome canvases in which a tiny amount of black was added to familiar colors, rendering them weird or complex. In Marcia's work, a process is initiated and then followed to a logical conclusion. Tashi's scores work the same way. They seem to demand something simple, but the realization or performance of them is anything but perfunctory. These connections are not an exact parallel but are a kind of dialogue, between one distinct medium and another.

136

The Monday after the weekend that wasn't really a weekend—a playlist of works (all found online) by Raven Chacon, who just won the Pulitzer Prize in Music, and is the first Indigenous composer to do so:

Raven Chacon
The Journey of the Horizontal People, 2016
Performed by Kronos Quartet as part of *50 for the Future: The Kronos Learning Repertoire*

Raven Chacon
Voiceless Mass, 2021
Performed by Present Music at the Cathedral of St. John the Evangelist, Milwaukee

The Creative Destruction (Raven Chacon and Timothy Archambault)
Mirror (Live), 2022

137

Last year I bought a lithograph by Raven Chacon, published by Crow's Shadow Institute of the Arts, located on the Confederated Tribes of the Umatilla Indian Reservation in the foothills of Oregon's Blue Mountains. Each print in the series titled *For Zitkála-Šá* (2020–2021) is a one-page score dedicated to a different Indigenous woman composer. The one I acquired is dedicated to Heidi Senungetuk. It was difficult to choose one—not all were available. (By now, none of them are available.)

The score *For Heidi Senungetuk* (2020) consists of five figures or diagrams that recall bars or measures (I resort to this conventional musical term for lack of a better one), each with five horizontal lines, recalling the staff paper familiar to Western notation but also tweaking those lines to point in new (or perhaps old) directions. The top measure is five horizontal lines, parallel, but apparently hand-drawn. The second measure rises to form a point before descending to another point, then rising again. The third suggests waves, with three crests. The fourth is a diagonal descent. The fifth and last features a pinch in its center and to my eye resembles a whale's tale or a fancy bracket balanced on its pointy back. There are no notes, nor is there any text indicating how these lines are to be interpreted. To this amateur interpreter, each represents a journey following a specific narrative movement or shape in which details are left indeterminate.

This interpretation is given some credence when I happened upon Chacon's score for *The Journey of the Horizontal People* (2016), commissioned by Kronos Quartet. By comparison, *The Journey of the Horizontal People* suggests a more conventional, classical (European) idea of notation, including my assumed reading from left to right, but his notes offer important clues for a reading of *For Heidi Senungetuk*:

The Journey of the Horizontal People is a future creation story telling of a group of people traveling from west to east, across the written page, contrary to the movement of the sun, but involuntarily and unconsciously allegiant to the trappings of time. With their bows, these wanderers sought out others like them, knowing that they could survive by finding these other clans who resided in the east, others who shared their linear cosmologies. It is told that throughout the journey, in their own passage of time, this group became the very people they were seeking.

As Anthony Huberman observes, in his essay "On Raven Chacon":

When writing a score, a musician is making music but is also *giving* music. [Emphasis mine.] As a set of prompts, guidelines, or instructions, a score comes alive when it is read and interpreted, and, as such, it's a language that begets [other] languages–it doesn't tell people what to think as much as it asks to be transformed into something else. It's a way to provide direction in the form of a question.

It is useful to think of this score, which I have yet to get framed, as a set of five questions. I am also connecting the dots of Huberman's essay and thinking about a question as a gift.

138

Two avant-garde bands, badly remembered:

Today, for reasons that mostly escape me, thoughts turned to two bands I remember from my college years in Madison, though my memory of both is cloudy at best. Somehow both confirmed my nascent interest in the avant-garde. One, I heard only once; the other I never even heard—I only heard of it.

The latter was a duo that included my friend Todd, whom I worked with at Helen C. White College Library at UW-Madison. (Sadly, I can't recall his last name at the moment.) Todd was consistently disheveled despite the fact that he always wore a suit and tie, which invariably seemed to come from a thrift store. (At the time, most of my clothes came from thrift stores, too, though I wouldn't wear a suit, even ironically.) He played the trombone, and his bandmate played the drums. The band was called Birdbrain Shitstain (or, perhaps, Bird Brain Shit Stain—alliterative and rhyming either way). I don't really know what they sounded like; I can only imagine, truly. And I have no idea if they ever played for an audience. If so, I'm sorry I missed them. (And I wish I had their band T-shirt.) Todd was always down for the most avant-garde music, and he and I got front-row tickets to see John Zorn's Masada play at the Barrymore Theatre in 1993. (The internet reveals it was November 21, 1993 to be precise—sandwiched, so to speak, between Dick Dale and Wisconsin's favorite sons, the Violent Femmes.) Somewhere I have a bootleg of that show on cassette. It was an early Masada show, before they had released any albums. I also remember happily shelling out twenty bucks each for most of the early Masada CDs, titled with the letters of the Hebrew alphabet, and released on the Japanese import label diskUnion.

The second band was called Platypus, and they played a show in the basement of a big old house on Franklin, one block away from the big old house I lived in on Hancock. I don't remember much about the band, but there were at least five or six members, and a woman in the band was playing . . . What, exactly? An accordion, or perhaps bandoneon? It could have been a xylophone or a saw, but for some reason I'm remembering bellows and the undulating push-pull of the music. I do remember thinking the instrumentation was unusual, at least for an "alternative" band. It might have been entirely appropriate for a Wisconsin wedding band—I don't remember much about Platypus, but they didn't strike me as a likely wedding band. But I don't actually remember what they were playing or much about their music. The way I'm remembering it, it might be described as post-rock, but I didn't know that term until a few years later. So, maybe I can call them pre-post-rock. (There's another band called Platypus that existed in the late 90s, but the Platypus I'm describing seems like a wholly different animal.) One thing I do remember is what happened after the show, though I can't really explain it. When the band stopped playing, everyone went upstairs and one of the people who lived in the house started jumping on furniture, trashing the couch. Eventually others, including me, were encouraged to join in, laying waste to the entire living room set. It too was likely sourced from a thrift store, but still. I can't explain why this happened. Surely everyone was drunk or high or both. In retrospect, it was entirely stupid. But at the time it felt somehow fitting and welcome, and my reading of Aristotle's *Poetics* would have allowed me to think about this in terms of *catharsis*. (And therefore as *Art*.) I remember thinking the guy who lived in the house was cool, and I felt like *I* was cool to get invited to his party and then obliterate his furniture. (Twenty-seven years later, I don't remember his name at all.) Was *every* party there like this? I never returned, and I only have the vaguest memory of him now.

139

This morning Dave Muller texts me with two links: one to Michael Brewster's *Falls From the Sky* (1994) from the Treasury of Claremont Music SoundCloud, which is a series of descending sounds; the other to James Tenney's *For Ann (rising)* (1969), which is based on the "Shepard-tone" (named for the experimental psychologist R. N. Shepard, a pioneer of multi-dimensional scaling who Tenney met and worked with at Bell Labs), and is perceived as a continual ascent. "Down & up!" as Dave succinctly put it. I listen to them in that order, then play them simultaneously, with Tenney starting before and ending after the Brewster.

140

Yesterday, I returned to see and hear Simone Forti's show before it closed. Once again, I didn't allow myself enough time. I got chatty, which is a hazard of the profession and knowing most everyone I encountered in the gallery. One item was resolved on my second visit: the gong, which I find listed on the checklist as *The Very Big Sound* (2022). I asked Mara McCarthy about it, and apparently the gong is struck once a day. The mallet, which is included on the checklist, resides in the front desk of the gallery. Once a day the gong is played. As luck would have it, I happened to be there at the appointed time, which was 3 p.m. Emma, the friendly gallery assistant who had greeted me, walked up to the gong, and began to play it with a series of quick taps or blows, not very hard. It was still quite loud, and the sound permeated the space. Emma returned to the desk, and I left the gallery to get back to my car, just as my meter ran out.

141

One answer to the question, "What constitutes your musical universe?," courtesy of Charlie Morrow:

The music in the outer world is a great soup, in which there is ambiance, a sense of location and specific sounds in different places. The other universe is the inner world, the music that is inside, that comes to life when it hears music from outside or in the creation of music for that outside. The two work together toward fulfillment–inside, outside, or together. The inner music is, in fact, I think a kind of steady heartbeat that runs through your whole life, a beat that has its own dimension.

142

In recent days I've been exploring the Bandcamp page for New Wilderness Audiographics, a cassette label started by Charlie Morrow in the late 1970s, while also returning to the double CD set *From The Kitchen Archives—New Music New York 1979*, which was released in 2004. (I've been listening to the former on my laptop at home and the latter in my car while driving around.) There are a lot of overlaps between the two, with a number of composers represented by the 1979 concert series at The Kitchen who were also contributors to New Wilderness Audiographics—Charlie Morrow, Tom Johnson, and Barbara Benary among them. Pauline Oliveros makes an appearance on the second side of Jackson Mac Low's Audiographics cassette, *Homage to Leona Bleiweiss* (1977), which is what led me to the Bandcamp site in the first place. The recording quality is poor, but it's of archival interest (obviously). I'm familiar with Mac Low's poetry and was aware that his circle overlapped with Oliveros's, but this performance marks a specific confluence, as does the Audiographics series in general. It draws a Venn diagram (of more than two circles) connecting Fluxus-adjacent poetry and New American Music (a phrase worthy of further scrutiny), as well as some "world music" and related field recordings. Oliveros's contribution to The Kitchen CD is a version of her *Tuning Meditation* (1979). It was an important, early point of connection with her work for me, one I often played on repeat. I eventually included this recording of the work in my *Routine Pleasures* (2016) exhibition, with the speakers hiding in the bushes of the garden at the Schindler House. I wanted the undulating swell of voices, veering between consonance and dissonance, to fill the enclosed yard. I always wanted it to be louder than it was. What's done is done, and this week, I am enjoying my rediscovery of composers and compositions I might have overlooked. Barbara Benary's

Exchanges (1971) for three violins gets my renewed attention. I should know more about her. (I am more familiar with her collaborative project Gamelan Son of Lion than with her solo compositions.) She, Meredith Monk, and Oliveros are the only three women composers on the set. Gordon Mumma's *Schoolwork* (1970), for the wholly unlikely trio of melodica, bowed saw, and bowed psaltery, seems particularly fresh as I listen with new ears, and Tom Johnson's *Secret Songs* (1976) stick in my head and on my lips, even after I try to sing/recite/chant along with them.

143

Walking in Kenneth Hahn this morning, I listened to the newly expanded release of Sun Ra's *Disco 3000*, a quartet recorded at the Teatro Ciak, Milan on January 23, 1978. The group included John Gilmore, Michael Ray, and Luqman Ali, but often sounds much bigger than a truncated Arkestra thanks to the Crumar Mainman synthesizer prototype Sun Ra plays here. The title is both topical but tongue-in-cheek. We'll need to wait another nine hundred seventy-eight years to discover if Ra's prophecy for the fate of disco holds true. Meanwhile, in the present of 1978, he's exploring the outer limits of what is sometimes called experimental jazz. I'm thinking about this in the context of the "New American Music" that I've been listening to in recent days, on The Kitchen anthology from 1979, and the recordings from New Wilderness Audiographics. This music, too, was often called experimental. "Experimental" is a term that is often used in describing the historical mission at CalArts, along with its close cousin "radical." I am often prone to interrogating this terminology: What exactly *is* the experiment? (Or, if we follow the more rigorous scientific understanding of the term, then what is the control for the experiment?)

Alongside these terms, I'm thinking about how white most New American Music is. (I'm also thinking of Robert Ashley's *Music with Roots in the Aether* and the Walter Zimmerman book *Desert Plants: Conversations with Twenty-Three American Musicians,* first published in 1976—of which I believe all twenty-three are white and only two are women.) The New Wilderness Audiographics trove is incredible, but it is also overwhelmingly white and reveals an ethnographic impulse toward world music (another bad term) that many would likely label as cultural appropriation or extractive or colonialist in the discourse of the present. I think it's hard to argue with an expansive curiosity about the world and its cultures, but it's also glaringly true that most of the composers whose curiosity is centralized in this regard are white. I believe George Lewis is the only artist of color on The Kitchen anthology from 1979, and in the 1980s he became the musical director there.

So, George made the cut, and thankfully so, but I also am thinking about his friends and collaborators Anthony Braxton and Wadada Leo Smith among those who emerged from Chicago as part of the Association for the Advancement of Creative Musicians (AACM) and are routinely excluded from round-ups or collections of New American Music. (Julius Eastman is getting belated and posthumous attention as part of this scene, deservedly so.) Lewis was nineteen when he joined the AACM, and much later (in 2008) wrote and wrangled its collective and plural story in his extraordinary oral history *A Power Stronger Than Itself: The AACM and American Experimental Music*. (There's that word again.) Importantly, the composers and musicians who were part of the AACM assiduously avoided the word "jazz" and its baggage—they refused to play standards at clubs, focusing instead on their own compositions. The Art Ensemble of Chicago adopted the slogan "Great Black Music, Ancient to the Future." Much of the development of Great Black Music from the 1960s onward was explicitly focused on notions of liberation in all senses, including liberation from music as a form of entertainment. (Of course, Braxton would later return to standards and jazz idioms, which are among my favorite recordings of his, but there is also a scholarly aspect to these retrospective considerations, albeit a fiery and occasionally mischievous version of scholarship.) I understand why these divisions exist if we see these scenes as geographic, as a result of certain academic training, and contextualized by certain markets and venues and support structures. The "experimental" white composers were trying to undo the conservatory; "experimental" Black composers were mostly not welcomed into it in the first place. Many of the musicians I'm talking about were born during segregation. There is a reason Sun Ra claimed to come from another planet. In many contexts and venues, he was from another planet.

My taste runs in both directions at once, and everywhere in between. My snobbery tends toward the avant-garde in any color—it's the music of the proletariat that I'm largely indifferent toward. I'm also aware of how the artists associated with the AACM crossed over the "invisible" racial boundary line and worked (and still work) with many of their white contemporaries: Braxton with Derek Bailey; Lewis with John Zorn; Smith with Carol Emanuel and Henry Kaiser; and so on. Free improvisation is a space in which these various tendencies could enter into conversation. ECM, a label formed in Munich in 1969 that became home to Art Ensemble of Chicago and Steve Reich, is another example of where these circles (or color lines) overlapped in a fascinating way. See also: Circle's *Paris Concert* (ECM, 1971) with Chick Corea on piano, Braxton on reeds, Dave Holland on bass, and Barry Altschul on drums; or Holland's own *Conference for the Birds* (ECM, 1972), also featuring Braxton and Altschul, with Sam Rivers on reeds.

I am oversimplifying by talking specifically about Black and white composers, as one could and should bring other ethnicities into the conversation as well: Indian "classical" music looms large here, circa "experimental" American music circa the late 1970s, as does the microtonal music of Bali and Indonesia, as does music from the entire African continent, music from South America, and beyond. Still, the history of music in America (popular or otherwise) is largely a complex tale of Black and white. The integration of these extraordinary composers and musicians of diverse training, lineages, instrumentation, and improvisational methodologies has produced some of my favorite music, much of which becomes hard to classify despite the prevalence of certain labels ("experimental," "minimalism," "new," "avant-garde," etc.). It's part of what makes Don Cherry's development, or his development of "organic music," so engaging for me—continually shifting and embracing and synthesizing without a sense of hierarchy.

144

Last night I saw the world premiere performance of Wadada Leo Smith's *String Quartet No. 11* (2019) and *String Quartet No. 13* (2020) at LAXART. The latter was a five-minute excerpt with the RedKoral Quartet accompanied by soprano vocalist Karen Parks. The former quartet consisted of nine movements and totaled an hour and half in duration. It was constantly engaging, despite the length of the performance, the comfortable folding chairs, and the stuffy room, with everyone in the room except the singer wearing masks. Smith's music is always engaging, though I find it consistently allergic to hooks or anything remotely catchy. That might be a compliment. But for the same reason, it evades my memory's capture and mostly exists in the present moment as I'm listening to it.

The performance was preceded by a conversation between Smith and LAXART Director Hamza Walker. In the talk, Smith revealed that he began composing (creating?) when he was twelve, and he wrote his first string quartet in 1963, after hearing Ornette Coleman's "Dedication to Poets and Writers" on *Town Hall, 1962*. "His work illustrated that one could use creativity and freedom as a major source in addition to inspiration in constructing a work of art." One senses the musicians finding their way through these scores in real time, following one another musically and visually—Smith defines this as creation rather than composition. He uses some combination of classical Western notation and his own highly idiosyncratic notation he calls *ankhrasmation*, which are by all appearances abstract drawings made with a full deck of colors. The latter especially leaves a lot of room for interpretation—*creation*. Today, I read the program notes on the LAXART website. It offers support to my idea about the musicians finding their way(s) through the score.

A majority of my string quartets have some elements of the create and ankhrasmation language, and the ensemble forms. The scores are essentially non-metric, and a full page represents a complete "bar" length, with no maintaining of the concept of downbeat and upbeat idea. The ensemble's leadership articulation continuously fluctuates from person to person as the decision for continuity keeps changing from page to page.

Walker included Smith's work in the 2016 edition of *Made in L.A.* I've also seen his scores exhibited in *The Freedom Principle: Experiments in Art and Music, 1965 to Now* (2015) at MCA Chicago, a fantastic show that expanded outward from the parallel AACM and AfriCOBRA scenes. (There's that word again—"experiments.") During the talk, there was an enjoyable anecdote about Smith's first recording session, on Anthony Braxton's *3 Compositions of New Jazz* (1968) and Braxton's decision to include Smith's composition *The Bell* (1967) on the record. I love the detail that Braxton addressed his colleagues by their last name—"Hey, Smith . . . " Seems to match the formality of the pipe and cable knit sweaters.

I briefly talked to "Smith" after the concert. Technically speaking we were colleagues at CalArts, but our paths never really crossed. I was aware of his presence (I mean generally, though I did see him in the halls) and classes (I will forever regret not crashing his seminar on Miles Davis's 1970s period—his take on this material with Henry Kaiser on *Yo Miles!* [1998] is nearly as good and sometimes perhaps even better than the originals, dare I say), but he retired before I could work up the gumption to seek him out. I tell him some version of this, more or less. He is disarmingly warm and sweet, and now I feel even sillier for not going out of my way to find him when we worked in the same building.

145

Braxton and Smith, the early years—a playlist:

Anthony Braxton with Muhal Richard Abrams, Leroy Jenkins, Wadada Leo Smith
3 Compositions of New Jazz
Delmark, 1968

Anthony Braxton with Leroy Jenkins, Steve McCall, Wadada Leo Smith
B-X0 NO-47A
BYG Records, 1969

Anthony Braxton with Leroy Jenkins, Steve McCall, Wadada Leo Smith
This Time . . .
BYG Records, 1970

Anthony Braxton with Wadada Leo Smith and Richard Teitelbaum
HM 421 (RTS) 47
Trio and Duet
Sackville Recordings, 1974

Anthony Braxton, Leroy Jenkins, Leo Smith
Silence
Freedom, 1974

146

Braxton and Smith, the later years—a playlist:

Wadada Leo Smith & Anthony Braxton
Organic Resonance
Pi Recordings, 2003

Wadada Leo Smith & Anthony Braxton
Saturn, Conjunct the Grand Canyon in a Sweet Embrace
Pi Recordings, 2004

147

Yesterday, an excursion to Amoeba yielded a bigger-than-expected bounty. New and used, mostly vinyl, but some CDs, too. I guess when I go there less frequently, I find more things I want. (I almost wrote "things I need," but that's not exactly accurate.) At least I remembered to bring a tote bag. My haul included a new CD by ensemble 0, which is directed by Stéphane Garin and Sylvain Chauveau, and is dedicated to the work of contemporary composers. Their newest release, titled *Musica Nuvolosa* (*Cloudy Music*) (2022), includes performances of Pauline Oliveros's *Horse Sings from Cloud* (1975) and György Ligeti's *Musica Ricercata* (1951–1953). It is the former that catches my attention. (It's also filed under "Oliveros" in the 20th Century Classical section of the store, which is how I found it.) I listen to it on the way home, its glacial pacing over nineteen minutes taking about half of the drive home. The ensemble consists of flute, violin, viola, cello, marimba, vibraphone, piano, and clarinet. No accordion, no vocals. It sounds quite distinct from any of the versions featuring Oliveros, including those under different titles: *Rose Mountain Slow Runner* or *The Pathways of the Grandmothers*, though those all performed by Oliveros seem immediately connected. The difference from the ensemble 0 interpretation is inevitable, given the subjective prompt of the score:

Sustain one or more tones or sounds until any desire to change the tone(s) or sound(s) subsides. When there is no desire to change the tone(s) or sound(s), then change.

What would be strange, really, is if the performance of the aggregated desire and change by ensemble 0 sounded like any of Oliveros's performances of her desire and change. One wonders how much the changes of the individual performances weighed on one another. Are they all measuring their own desire, and resisting desire for change, independently? To what extent are they communicating (desire), to each other, as an ensemble?

There is more to be said about the composer as the primary interpreter of their own work. I am also thinking of someone like Charlemagne Palestine (my Amoeba haul included two new records of his early performances), where it is nearly impossible to imagine someone else performing his music—the performance and the performer are inextricably bound, or at least that's my sense of it. Someone like Anthony Braxton also comes to mind. I don't recall hearing too many musicians taking on his graphic scores unless they're playing with him or have played extensively with him. (Marilyn Crispell, Mark Dresser, and Gerri Hemmingway's *Play Braxton* [2012] is one of few examples that come to mind.)

Oliveros is a more complex case, perhaps, because her text scores (not to mention other scores) were meant to exist beyond her. They are utterly accessible, which was clearly one of their goals. In the version of her *Tuning Meditation* that appears on The Kitchen anthology from 1979, she provides a spoken introduction to set the performance in motion for "those who want to do it," and then, "while you're at it, I'm going to see if I can disappear." It's hard to know if she does disappear or is part of the undulating chorus of *Tuning Meditation*. But her absence from this new performance of *Horse Sings from Cloud* is notable, if only because her own interpretations of the score are decisively imprinted in my head.

A second listen. This one is indeed more *nuvolosa* than the original(s), and therefore lacks some of their tension or drama, and certainly some of the "personality" of Oliveros's husky voice and reedy, but warm accordion swell. Nevertheless, it's pleasurable to hear another take on it and to hear it expand beyond its point of origin.

148

Snap, crackle, pop: listening to new (or new to me) records—
a playlist:

Charlemagne Palestine & Simone Forti
Illuminations
Alga Marghen, 2010

David Daniell
I-IV-V-I
Table of the Elements, 2008

Eleh / Tara Jane O'Neil
Circle Four: 100 Gongs for Arieto / Medusa Smack
Important Records, 2015

Sébastien Roux
Inevitable Music #1: Variations on Sol LeWitt's Wall Drawing #260
Future Audio Graphics, 2014

Mikrokosmos
Another time, this time, one time
Western Front Records, 2020

Dick Slessig Combo
Rock Your Baby
75 Records, 2013

Charlemagne Palestine & Simone Forti
Meditative Sound Environments
Alga Marghen, 2021

149

Listening anew, listening again—a playlist:

Michael Snow
Musics for Piano, Whistling, Microphone and Tape Recorder
Song Cycle Records, 2016 (originally issued by Chatham Square in 1975)

Yoshi Wada
Off the Wall
Saltern, 2016 (originally issued by FMP Records in 1985)

Tashi Wada
Gradient
De Stijl, 2012

Simone Forti
Hippie Gospel Songs
Box Editions, 2018

150—Pauline Oliveros's ninetieth birthday

Listening to one record inevitably makes me want to listen to at least two other records—a playlist:

Terry Riley / Calder Quartet
Two Early Works
75 Records, 2010

Alvin Lucier
Dark Matter
God Records, 2015

Eleh / Pauline Oliveros
The Beauty of the Steel Skeleton / Drifting Depths
Important Records, 2008

Judith Hamann
Peaks
Black Truffle Records, 2020

151

Four sides (be)for(e) the road—a playlist:

Werner Durand with Amelia Cuni and Victor Meertens
Processions
Besom Presse, 2019

152

Today, I was listening to the ocean arriving at the constantly evolving threshold of Gaviota State Beach, just before low tide.

153

Last night, in a surprisingly quiet hotel room, I was listening to the oscillations of the mini-fridge before falling asleep.

Today, after returning home and opening the kitchen window to get some fresh air, I was listening to a neighbor's weed wacker.

154

I returned home to find a package from Milwaukee, Wisconsin had arrived. I ordered a letterpress print by Pauline Oliveros from Woodland Pattern Book Center, from a signed edition of 200 printed by Black Mesa Press. It's the text score for *Horse Sings from Cloud*—more precisely, a text score for the composition, which (as I've noted) changed its name over time, and in fact also changed in its content, too. The poem is printed in all-caps on this thin, tall (6 x 19.75 inches), and pale blue sheet, and "was written in January 1984 to reflect Oliveros's growing understanding of *Horse*." This I learn not from the print itself but from Oliveros's *Anthology of Text Scores*, which includes the original score from 1975 ("Sustain one or more tones until any desire to change the tone(s) or sound(s) subsides. When there is no desire to change the tone(s) or sound(s), then change.") followed by the revised version. Oliveros's poem begins with the phrase

LISTEN
DANCING BREATH
LISTEN

Here it's worth noting (for the sake of hyperspecificity if nothing else) that the type setting on the print (in Gill Sans) is actually quite different from the way it is set in the book version. Here, I'm following the version on the print, which is lying next to me on my desk. The anthology was published in 2013, nearly three decades after the poem was written. The print also features a dedication, "To Dancing Breath," who I imagine is the dancer Deborah Hay, who was in a relationship with Oliveros in the early 1980s. *Horse* was previously called *Rose Mountain Slow Runner*, in reference to Oliveros's romantic merger with Linda Montano. The changes to the score represent not only a growing understanding of it, but also the way the work is imbricated in daily life—and love.

LONG SOUND
SOUND LONG
BREATHE LONG
LISTEN
SOUND STRONGER
BREATH LONGER
SOUND LONGER
BREATHE STRONGER
BREATH SOUND
SOUND BREATH

The core of the original (or more succinct) score, with its entanglement of desire and change, arrives in the following "stanza."

LISTEN
DANCING BREATH
LISTEN
NO CHANGE
WHEN DESIRE
TO CHANGE
CHANGE WHEN
NO DESIRE
WHEN DESIRE CHANGE
CHANGE DESIRE
WHEN NO DESIRE
NO CHANGE
LISTEN
BREATHE SOUND
WHEN NO SOUND
BREATH CHANGE
WHEN NO CHANGE
BREATHE DESIRE

As I try to replicate this typography, more or less exactly, I am noting its shifting contours as it descends on the page. To type it is to read it, which is also to perform it.

LISTEN
          DANCING BREATH
                    LISTEN

indicates a transition between one section (or stanza) and the next, often serving as a beginning and ending. A threshold. A sequence of thresholds, changes.

CHANGE
BREATHE
SOUND
DESIRE

DESIRE
CHANGE
BREATHE
SOUND

SOUND
CHANGE
DESIRE
BREATH

BREATHE
SOUND
CHANGE
DESIRE

In this recombinatory reordering, the presumed linear order of the earlier score gives way to something less precise, more intuitive. I am also noting the subtle shift between "breath" and "breathe"—

the former a noun, a gaseous thing; the latter a verb, an action, an instruction.

"Change," "sound," and "desire": I am reminded that these are all nouns that are also verbs, actions, instructions.

LISTEN
DANCING BREATH
LISTEN
WHEN NO BREATH
NO CHANGE
NO DESIRE
NO SOUND

DEATH

Thankfully, it doesn't end with "death," but offers another threshold of transition.

LISTEN
DANCING BREATH
LISTEN

And then it ends with the title, which is also its beginning, more or less.

HORSE SINGS FROM CLOUD

As I write this, I listen to the previous version of *Horse Sings from Cloud*, circa 1982, on vinyl, loud enough to blot out any other sound beyond my fingers tapping on the keyboard.

155

I am reminded of a Xeroxed flyer, found at the Olin Library at Mills College, for a performance by Oliveros at Woodland Pattern in Milwaukee on February 3, 1984. Simply advertised as "PAULINE OLIVEROS ACCORDION & VOICE," the event undoubtedly coincided with the release of the print I just received in the mail and followed the release of the record of the same name on Lovely Music. The ticket price for the show was four dollars. The flyer uses a familiar, square, black-and-white photo of a barefoot Oliveros playing her accordion in an outdoor setting. It was taken by Becky Cohen, a frequent accomplice. The two collaborated on a photo/text book titled *Initiation Dream* in 1981. It is also square and black-and-white, and the picture on this flyer appears there, too.

It also appears on numerous other flyers found in the archive. One is for a performance at the Madison Art Center on February 13, 1984—ten days after the Milwaukee show. What else was Oliveros doing in Wisconsin? On this flyer, Cohen's photo is set in a more dynamic geometric design. The ticket price was five dollars. The venue in which Oliveros played has changed considerably over the years, and in 2006 reopened as the Madison Museum of Contemporary Art with a sleek facelift. The adjoining theater became the Overture Center for the Arts. In my time living in Madison (1991–1995), I enjoyed many concerts in the Civic Center, as it was called then, and its more intimate Oscar Meyer Theater, including Philip Glass (twice) and Kronos Quartet. Another memorable show happened on October 11, 1991, with Pearl Jam and Smashing Pumpkins opening for the Red Hot Chili Peppers. Pearl Jam was still largely unknown, and there was only a small crowd in attendance when their show started. No venue better represents the transition in my own music interests at that time.

Sustain one or more tones until any desire to change the tone(s) or sound(s) subsides. When there is no desire to change the tone(s) or sound(s), then change.

156

Abrasions—a playlist:

Joshua Abrams
Excavations 1
Feeding Tube Records, 2012

Radio/Guitar (Peggy Ahwesh + Barbara Ess)
Thrum
Table of the Elements, 2003

Ju Suk Reet Meate
Solo 1975–1980
Alga Marghen, 2017

Ellen Fullman
Through Glass Panes
Important Records, 2011

Carefully strew atop a lace mandala situated on the floor: framed photographs, divination cards, paper currency (real and play), battery-powered candles with a candy-colored remote control, a JBL speaker, a plastic water bottle, and a pleasing array of musical instruments—bamboo chimes, rattles, singing bowls, a metal tongue drum, a shruti box. And nearby, a small library of books set in snaking pathways like stepping stones one would never step on. These were among the objects activated by Gabrielle Civil and Kenyatta A.C. Hinkle, for a performance they titled *invocations* (2022), which in turn inhabited and activated my exhibition *how we are in time and space: Nancy Buchanan, Marcia Hafif, Barbara T. Smith* (2022) over the course of two hours. I had asked them to consider the collaborative works of Nancy Buchanan and Barbara T. Smith, given their own previous collaborations in Civil's *Experiments in Joy*. Here, the two began by sounding the chimes, and gradually circled the space. Hinkle, who has trained in sound healing practices, had brought most of the instruments in a suitcase, arriving from Oakland shortly before the performance. Civil contributed most of the books, which were primarily (or possibly all) titles by Black femme authors: Audrey Lorde, Thulani Davis, Ntozake Shange, Mari Evans, Erica Hunt's *Arcade* with woodcuts by Alison Saar, Civil's own *(ghost gestures)* among them. Civil invited viewers (some of whom came to the show unaware that a performance would be happening) to choose a book, and then read from it in a private act of bibliomancy. At times they both engaged specific artworks in the exhibition: Civil setting stones on the floor below a constellation of shells on the wall by Smith, then splaying open two books in front of Buchanan's giant wedge of metal shavings (the sculpture summoning a pubic mound); Hinkle writing a journal entry next to Smith's *Hot Peppers* (1982–1983), a "spine"

(Hinkle's characterization) of objects and notes written on pink index cards, dangling from the ceiling. Hinkle, wearing a striking white wig and a tiara of crystals, played a variety of instruments, occasionally sounding the singing bowl. Improvising, the pair would go their separate ways and then converge, again and again, like two satellites orbiting in contrary motion. Always highly deliberate and unhurried, they would also pause to converse from time to time, with each other and with viewers. On one occasion, I assumed the performance had ended, but it had only ebbed into friendly socializing before once again flowing into purposeful movement. In this way, the event was refreshingly casual, despite its ritualistic moments. At some point the JBL speaker burst into the immediately familiar but unexpected voice of Nina Simone, in response to one gallery visitor's spontaneous written recollection of seeing the singer in concert. Civil and Hinkle danced to the music, cracking open the exhibition in ways I could not have imagined when I installed it.

158

The Long String Instrument &—a playlist:

Ellen Fullman and David Gamper with Stuart Dempster
Pink Sea Thrift
fo'c'sle, 2020 (recorded 2009)

Ellen Fullman & Okkyung Lee
The Air Around Her
1703 Skivbolaget, 2018

Ellen Fullman / Monique Buzzarté
Fluctuations
Deep Listening, 2008

Ellen Fullman / Konrad Sprenger
Ort
Choose Records, 2004

Ellen Fullman & Theresa Wong
Harbors
Room40, 2020

Deep Listening Band and the Long String Instrument
Suspended Music
Periplum, 1997

159

Yesterday and today I have been listening to a variety of albums by Ellen Fullman, mostly duets or larger collaborations, some very familiar to me and others completely new. Her website is fairly comprehensive with links to many of the albums on Bandcamp or elsewhere. I encountered Fullman and her Long String Instrument during the pandemic in my many hours of exploratory listening, and on November 1, 2021, I attended a lecture she gave in the music school at CalArts for a seminar called Graduate Composer's Forum, held on Zoom. One of the other gifts of the pandemic—beyond the long bouts of exploratory listening—was the ability to drop into lectures I might not have otherwise attended (or been able to attend). Fullman was in her studio in the Bay Area, and was able to demonstrate her Long String Instrument, which she invented.

In the transition to Zoom teaching (and, in this case, learning) I adopted the habit of taking notes with a pencil on loose-leaf bond paper held in place by a clipboard. I have piles of these notes now, loosely categorized and held in place with binder clips. My notes taken during Fullman's lecture are quite cryptic. She spent quite a bit of time talking about the Long String Instrument (LSI) and its tuning system, which follows the logic of just intonation—the long strings perfectly, diagrammatically demonstrate waveforms and harmonics—and sometimes employs the 43-tone system developed by Harry Partch. The LSI at times recalls an organ with its extraordinary, immersive scale and sustained drones; at other times, it suggests a sprawling horizontal harp or the world's longest guitar, especially when played with an idiosyncratic device Fullman calls "the shoveler," which is basically a big wooden plectrum (also her invention). One note I made that resonates now (pun certainly intended) is the phrase "walking—architecture," which, as I recall, refers to a discussion of the instrument connecting the building (wherever it is installed) to an ambulatory body, and how the instrument necessitates both. This seems obvious but also radical in some way, thinking about the taut strings and the resulting waveforms connecting an immobile site to a mobile performer or vice versa. Videos of Fullman and others performing the LSI immediately conjure a slow, contemplative choreography.

I believe I first encountered her because she had collaborated with Deep Listening Band on *Suspended Music* (1997), though her more recent duet album with cellist Theresa Wong, *Harbors* (2020), was a mainstay of my pandemic listening. One of my discoveries yesterday was *Pink Sea Thrift* (2018), a recording of a performance by Fullman with David Gamper of Deep Listening Band playing ("natural") flutes, bells, conch, melodica, and electronics (presumably the Expanded Instrument System or EIS), with Stuart Dempster joining in on two tracks playing trombone and didjeridu. The performance took place in 2009 at the Headlands Center for the Arts in Marin County, just north of the Golden Gate Bridge. I spent a cool, foggy August in residence there the following year. The arts center is situated in a former military base, and Fullman installed the Long String Instrument in the old gym, which as I remember has incredible acoustics. The titles ("Tidepool," "Hawk Hill," "Monterey Cypress," and so on) all refer to that magical coastal environment. The music, in collaboration with my distinct memories of hiking in the foggy, fecund hills of Headlands, transports me there.

160

A note on time and space:

It's important to have an outlet for music where time isn't an issue.

—Bitchin Bajas

161

Suspended Music (1997) brings together Ellen Fullman and the Long String Instrument (she is abetted here by performers Elise Gould and Nigel Jacobs) with Pauline Oliveros, Stuart Dempster, and David Gamper of Deep Listening Band. The album documents the performance of two long compositions, one each by Oliveros and Fullman, at the Candy Factory in Austin, Texas on November 12, 1994. Oliveros's *Epigraphs in the Time of AIDS* (1994) is dedicated to the memory of her half-brother Peter. (An excerpt of this is also found on DLB's compilation album *Tosca Salad*.) Oliveros describes the composition in the liner notes:

> There are fifteen epigraphs in the piece. Each time whoever is performing in the quartet is commemorating their own person, so that the epigraph takes on the energy of those who are being remembered; and that informs how the epigraph sounds.

I am unclear if this "quartet" refers to the Deep Listening Band (a trio) plus the Long String Instrument (which is being performed by Fullman, Gould, and Jacobs), or if there are different configurations of four players with each epigraph. Elsewhere (on *Tosca Salad* [1995], for example), Deep Listening Band engages that kind of "round robin" strategy, with all combinations of duets from the trio. At times it's clear who's playing: Oliveros's accordion and singing voice are distinct, as are Dempster's trombone and didjeridu. But many of the instruments played by Gamper, and especially the effects generated by Expanded Instrument System, are harder to identify, particularly when coupled with the shimmering Long String Instrument—described here as "175 strings suspended at waist height" and theatrically spotlit from above to make the rest of the space disappear while "allowing the suspended wires to *float*." Even two members of this group can produce a very full, complex sound.

Nearing forty minutes, Fullman's *TexasTravelTexture* (1994) is perhaps the composer's longest composition, which she describes as "kind of like a road trip landscape in which moods and environments seamlessly transform, gradually."

Unconventional modulations possible in Just Intonation are important to this piece and occur step by step, one part changing at a time. In effect, I composed a harmonic framework with the Long String Instrument, upon which Deep Listening Band improvises. Improvisational elements exist within the string parts as well.

It is instructive to consider the Long String Instrument as "harmonic framework," as Fullman describes, for Deep Listening Band as well as its "site," which conditions their group improvisation. If, as Dempster has argued, "the [Fort Worden] cistern is an instrument that you learn to play," then Fullman's Long String Instrument defines an unconventional site *within which* one plays. A description of DLB in these liner notes is as succinct as any I've read: ". . . the purpose of the Deep Listening Band is to explore alternative listening strategies, unusual acoustic environments, expanded instrument technologies and new relationships with audiences."

On a related note, there is also more that needs to be said about the EIS (pronounced "ice" by those in the know). In many ways it is as prominent here as Fullman's Long String Instrument, and one could even see this album as a duet between the EIS and the LSI, each performed by a trio.

162

5 a.m. question: Is there a point at which deep listening can go . . . too deep? At times I become preoccupied with certain frequencies, particularly as layers of other sound begin to peel away. It's a depth where awareness has become attention and can't ease back to awareness. This is particularly true with the oscillation of certain electric equipment, like my refrigerator or the fan of the digital projector in the classroom where I taught my seminar Pauline Oliveros for Artists. It was certainly true of the HVAC (heating/ventilation/air conditioning) system at the Biltmore Hotel, where I stayed on this particular night, along with a suite of exquisite art works by Kang Seung Lee. The art was utterly silent, the room perfectly chilly. But the hum—emanating from an HVAC system massive enough to heat or cool the hotel's 683 guest rooms as well as its palatial banquet halls and lobby—grabbed my undivided attention and wouldn't let go. "Hum" is too pleasant of a word for what I was hearing. Far from the kind of elegant drone I tend to enjoy listening to, this sound was thick with partials and overtones. A real wobbler, it was hard to measure its pattern or how often it was repeating. I pictured a sawtooth wave that became increasingly snarled the longer I listened. Would most people ignore this? I suspect yes, which also makes me question whether I am listening too closely to the world sometimes. The discourse around Deep Listening (meaning the practice and pedagogy as defined by Pauline Oliveros) seems to assign positive value to the phrase, but I wonder if we should instead imagine it as value neutral. Meaning: Deep, yes, but at what cost? Is the tradeoff for good listening a short night of sleep? Would earplugs be cheating?

163

Round trip to Pasadena and back, for the closing of my exhibition *how we are in time and space: Nancy Buchanan, Marcia Hafif, Barbara T. Smith* (2022), with a quick stop in Chinatown for the closing of Josh Cloud's show *The Only Way Out Is Through* (2022)—a playlist:

Charlemagne Palestine
The Apocalypse Will Blossom
Yesmissolga, 2007

V/A
Trojan Dub Box Set (Disc One)
Trojan Records, 1998

164

Lake / Waves / Air / Vesper—a playlist:

James Rushford
Lake from the Louvers
Shelter Press, 2021

R.I.P. Hayman
Waves: Real and Imagined
Recital, 2021

Annea Lockwood
Becoming Air / Into the Vanishing Point
Black Truffle, 2021

Kim Myhr & Australian Art Orchestra
Vesper
Hubro, 2020

165

One of the composers/musicians I've grown to know and love during the long listening exercise of the pandemic is Judith Hamann, who I intially encountered playing cello alongside/against Charles Curtis on Tashi Wada's *Duets* (2014), first heard in Marcia Hafif's Laguna studio. I pre-ordered her two albums from Blank Forms, both issued in 2020, and seemingly waited an eternity for their COVID-delayed revival: *Shaking Studies* (which I got on vinyl) and *Music for Cello and Humming* (which was only available on CD). Both are demanding records, meaning they encourage attention and repeated listening. I also got her album *Peaks* on vinyl, also released in 2020, on Black Truffle. It begins with the cello, but then transitions into a collage of field recordings, which are a kind of concrète (in the sense of mixture, as well as musical lineage) that represents a wandering, migrating sense of place:

Southern California nightscapes heard through windows, San Francisco bathroom fans, snatches of recordings of friends, hand organs, and engines. *signal/centinela* draws primarily on recordings from Hamann's time living in San Diego, and carries with it a certain sense of nostalgia in the sense of homesickness, longing, and displacement of distance and time. Side B is composed from recordings gathered on a different continent, Europe, weaving piano with recordings of sleep, breath, church organ, and the act of climbing. *under/over* emerges as it recedes, overlapping moments of arrival to create another kind of "spire" in the sense of spir (breath).

There is also another recent recording, *Hinterhof* (2021), which is a single thirty-two-minute work that combines cello and humming with "field" recordings. In this case, the field is the small guest apartment in Berlin that Hamann was living in during the pandemic. I want to listen to all four of them again as I write this, but to be honest I'm too tired for the kind of listening they demand, which is hardly a complaint, at least in my case. Perhaps this is tomorrow's project.

How often, in writing this daily meditation, am I actually projecting into the future or ruminating on the past, rather than being in the present? In text, and in my head, all temporalities tend to intermingle. Memory is about the past but happens in the present. Likewise, planning in anticipation . . .

166

Humming along (to Judith Hamann)—a playlist:

Judith Hamann
Music for Cello and Humming
Blank Forms, 2020

Judith Hamann
Shaking Studies
Blank Forms, 2020

Judith Hamann
Peaks
Black Truffle Records, 2020

Judith Hamann
Hinterhof
Longform Editions, 2021

167

Hum

humming

hummed

to utter a sound like that of the speech sound

Hmm

humming along with the music

Hum / along with me / hum along to the TV (Jane's Addiction, "Stop!" [1990])

to make the natural noise of an insect in motion or a similar sound : DRONE

mmmmmmmmmmmmmmmmmmmmmmmmmmmmmmmmmmmmmmmmmmm
mmmmm

From the Middle English hummen*; akin to Middle High German* hummen*, meaning to hum, or Middle Dutch* hommel*, meaning bumblebee.*

ho-hum

listening to the bees hum in the garden

Or a hummingbird furiously fluttering its wings.

humdrum

to give forth a low continuous blend of sound

hmmmmmmmmmmmmmmmmmmmmmmmmmmmmmmmmm mmmmm

At times the hum becomes indistinguishable from the cello.

It seems to me that Judith Hamann's *Music for Cello and Humming* is concerned with activity–not the activity of the instrument in itself or the activity of the hummed voice in itself, not these together (because it is a question, whether they are together)–but the activity of the void between the serration on the strings and the mouth's suppression of its own sound. When these works set cello and hum to harmonics, to scalar drifts, to sustained loops, to electronic decays, one senses the rigor of Hamann's investigations; one senses that the music is an investigation into a kind of nothing that acts or forces action that a music is able to track.

–Nora Fulton, "Notes on the Production of Opacity" (2020)

vibration, vibrato—vibrant

the sound of children's voices with which the house was always humming

I haven't been able to do much of what I perhaps *should* have been doing this last two weeks, instead I might find myself going for long windy walks, or spending the afternoon humming and modulating feedback with a washing basket (spoiler alert), or finding just practicing scales on cello incredibly comforting, or reading an unauthorized biography of Black Sabbath I found in the laundry room etc.

–Judith Hamann, liner notes for *days collapse days collapse night* (2020)

mmmmmmm mmmmmmmmmm mmm mmmm mmmmmmmmmmmmm

So, I started humming along with the heating and the contours of voices leaking from upstairs, playing cello along with the low-mid range resonances of the hinterhof, weaving in recordings of people's voices who are far away and who I miss so much, fabricating a kind of imagined shared space. The pitched material is drawn out from the frequencies I hear in the hof recordings, via the mediation of listening to/with the apartment. From extending them outwards, through that process I uncover harmony, relational connections, gestures, interplay. In a way, I am mapping and then feeding back into the space the same territories, just through different filters: through voice, electronics, through the mediating bodies of the cello and my own body.

—Judith Hamann, liner notes for *Hinterhof* (2021)

to run smoothly

to be busily active

the museum hummed with visitors

Though something like humming may often be normatively described as "less determined" and "more emotive" than the verbal terrain of language, there is clearly a regulatory power in the hum which is under scrutiny here. The moments in which the hum benevolently shepherds Hamann's beautiful, dissonant playing in "Étude for Multiphonics and Humming: One Cello, One Voice and One Shadow Voice" must be set alongside the moments in which it unfolds into that same type of dissonance in the two "Fragments," and appears, if you'll forgive my psychologism here, a bit hypocritical. We picture a musician humming to find the right note—the body containing a "wise character"—but there is something lost if one cannot be seen as enveloped by the other, with one prodding the other on.

—Nora Fulton, "Notes on the Production of Opacity"

the business started to hum

hum a tune

Abbey Lincoln humming and expanding upon the melody of Langston Hughes's "Six-Bits Blues" (1942) for Max Roach's quartet performing ("Scene B") on Toshiro Mayuzumi's soundtrack for the movie *Black Sun* (1964), directed by Koreyoshi Kurahara.

(

Gimme six-bits' worth o' ticket
On a train that runs somewhere.
I say six-bits' worth o' ticket
On a train that runs somewhere.
I don't care where it's goin'
Just so it goes away from here.

Baby, gimme a little lovin',
But don't make it too long.
A little lovin', babe, but
Don't make it too long.
Make it short and sweet, your lovin',
So I can roll along.

)

humdinger

to sing with the lips closed and without uttering speech sounds distinctly

hummer—slang, meaning blowjob

to express by making a vocal sound with the lips pressed together : to affect by humming

I am trying to remember grief is weird and that all of this is ok. (Hamann)

hummed his displeasure

humble pie

hmmmmmmmmmmmmmmmmmmmmmmmmmmmmmmmmm
mmm

168

Pauline Oliveros, *Lullaby for Daisy Pauline*:

For Daisy Pauline Oliveros, born September 19, 1979

Sing MMM the sound of pleasure.
Sing MMM to your favorite infant or to yourself.
Sing MMM in the style of a lullaby for deep relaxation.
Sing MMM and play with MMM by singing vowel sounds between each M.
MAMAM MOMOM MUMUM MIMIM MAMOM MUMEM etc.
Sing independently, remaining aware of others.
Sing until the lull is complete.

Commentary
Lullaby for Daisy Pauline was composed for a large group to sing with a tape accompaniment of natural sounds such as frogs and cicadas. The piece can also be sung as a solo.

April 1980
St. Paul, Minnesota

169

As far as I can find, there is just one recorded performance of *Lullaby for Daisy Pauline*, which appears on a record called *Sleepers*, released in 1985 on Finnadar Records, an imprint of Atlantic. This compilation of "lull music" was organized by composer Doris Hays, who contributed the first track, and also includes Daniel Goode, Tom Johnson, Alison Knowles, Annea Lockwood, Ilhan Mimaroglu, Ann Silsbee, and of course, Oliveros. I bought the record at least five years ago at a hip boutique in Chinatown, New York for eighteen dollars. Next to the price sticker is another sticker that says "dead stock." What could be more appealing? I can't imagine this album was a big hit in its time. I could have gotten it for cheaper on Discogs, but the point is I didn't even know I was looking for it until I happened upon it. I bought it for Oliveros's *Lullaby*, but I also liked the mix of composers (Knowles, Lockwood . . .) and the concept of music intended to put one to sleep. In 2015 I taught a seminar called Resistance to Work, which was often referred to (by students and me) as the laziness class. It's one of the seminars I've taught only once, before it became something else. Here's the course description:

What constitutes work? When is an artist not working? This course will consider both the imperative and resistance to work—as well as related concepts of idleness, sleep, procrastination, waste, and pleasure—with particular emphasis on the labor (and refusal) of artistic production, historically and in the present. If art making has shifted from producing objects to providing services, as many have argued, what are the implications for artists? We will discuss critical texts by authors including Julia Bryan-Wilson, Jonathan Crary, Bruce Hainley, Caroline Jones, Maurizio Lazzarato, and Sarah Lehrer-Graiwer, alongside the work of artists such as Charlie Chaplin, Marcel Duchamp, David Hammons, Lee Lozano,

Yvonne Rainer, Frances Stark, Sturtevant, and Andy Warhol. Students will be expected to participate in class discussion and maintain a written account of their time and relation to course materials throughout the semester.

We spent a lot of time—say, three or four weeks—talking about sleep, and I screened Warhol's film *Sleep* (1964) in its five-hour, twenty-minute entirety. (Most of the class gradually disappeared, but a few of us lasted until the end. One person fell asleep, snoring loudly through the silence.) Shortly after teaching the seminar, I had a chance to travel to Cali, Colombia to teach a related workshop for *escuela incierta* (the uncertain school), which I proposed to teach as a very long lecture with live Spanish translation (by Tupac Cruz). The lecture was titled "I AM GOING TO SLEEP FORGET IT," after a line from a telegram sent by On Kawara to Michel Claura. I had hoped to teach for sixteen hours, based on the "ideal" of working eight hours a day and sleeping eight hours a day. It didn't really go as planned, which in context was totally fine. It lasted about fourteen hours, including a number of breaks and a long walk around the neighborhood. A few students seemed to fall asleep. No judgment!

Needless to say, I am invested in sleep as a topic of historical and theoretical interest (not to mention "embodied experience"). So, when I found the *Sleepers* record at the hip Chinatown shop, I didn't hesitate to take it home. *Lullaby for Daisy Pauline* was performed by the Queens College Choral Society. It only lasts two minutes and twenty-seven seconds: Daisy Pauline must have been a mellow baby. Listening to the record yesterday, none of the lullabies put me to sleep.

170

Some possible uses for music:

spiritual / religious / worship
entertainment
dancing
romance (love songs)
accompaniment to drinking, partying
accompaniment to driving, road trips
accompaniment to exercise
accompaniment to performance, a play, opera, figure skating, the circus, etc.
movie soundtrack
selling stuff (jingles)
music videos (at some point the video was no longer the illustration of the song, but the whole reason for the song in the first place)
ceremonial: memorial / honoring the dead
ceremonial: honoring the living (e.g. royalty, the birthday song, etc.)
ceremonial: national (or regional) anthem
parade / marching band
support for military or athletics
work inducement (e.g. the Seven Dwarfs whistling while they work, etc.)
communication (storytelling, mnemonics)
education
protest (fight songs / songs of resistance / songs of liberation)
lullaby
meditation / relaxation
healing
growing plants
drowning out other sounds
environmental ("elevator music," *Music for Airports*)

tripping out
measuring time
killing time
hold music
warfare (psyops)
"waking the dead"
historical (organology / musicology)
perpetuation / conversation of tradition ("classical music")
art / "experimentation"
etc.

171

These categories are in no way intended to be exhaustive, and I'm sure I'm missing something obvious. They are, hopefully, transhistorical and transcultural. Some of the categories are extremely broad ("entertainment") and are likely to overlap with other categories. Jazz scatters around this list of categories in a complicated way. What once functioned as dance music (swing) or marching band (or Dixieland) music eventually evolved into music of liberation and experimentation (art), among other things. Amiri Baraka's *Blues People* is the best analysis of this development. "Jazz" is a complicated word. Maybe more complicated than "art." I don't know.

I think there is also an important distinction to the reason someone performs music to the reason one listens to it. For example, if I listen to Alice Coltrane or gospel, it is not because I am seeking "spiritual" meaning from this music, even if that was the intention of the people performing it. I am aware that the overwhelming majority (~80%?) of my musical universe is best described by the last category on the list ("art / 'experimental'"), but that other ~20% begs the question of how much nonconsensual music one is subjected to in what is euphemistically and optimistically called late capitalism. For example, Blackstreet's "No Diggity" was in my head recently (and repeatedly) for reasons unknown until I realized it was being used as a jingle on a television commercial for Instacart. (Yes, I still watch "live television," as one student recently called it.) That's a case where a song goes from one category ("romance"? "storytelling"?) to another ("selling stuff"). I was only peripherally aware of the song when it was a pop hit in 1996. I am often only aware of pop hits peripherally, and might not know whose song it is until it gets stuck in my head, at which point I have to Google it in hopes that locating the source will also somehow help exorcize the affliction. I could also add "songs playing in one's head" to yesterday's list of places where music appears. Isn't that one of use of music: to be catchy, infectious?

I often go days without listening to what might conventionally be called "songs." This sounds really pretentious, even to me, but these days I'm usually not that interested in songs as a form, especially the kind with lyrics (which can be distracting). I am tending to favor music that instead comes in "compositions" or "pieces" or "tracks." That said, yesterday I listened to a lot of songs, really great songs—by Nick Cave and the Bad Seeds, Low, Nina Simone, Cat Power, Arleta—while reading Warren Ellis's terrific book *Nina Simone's Gum* and while making dinner after. I also listen to music when I exercise (go for walks), though a lot of that also falls under the category of "art."

Is it more or less pretentious to mention that I'm not that crazy about most classical music, which is probably obvious in the boring way I've described it: "perpetuation / conversation of tradition"? I am also aware that what I find entertaining, many (most) would not, especially when it comes to music. I suspect that a larger (global) survey sample would conclude that less than 1% of music listened to in the category of "art."

Most people listen to songs, and I don't begrudge them, really. The people I really wonder about are the people who don't have any use for music at all.

172

Sometimes I ponder if my neighbors with whom I share a driveway sometimes wonder about the sounds emanating from my house, or even recognize it as "music." I don't mean this in a snooty way, but in a self-conscious way because the only music I've ever heard come from their side of the driveway is a lively Guatemalan house music mix, which my neighbor Luis plays, most often on Saturdays while working on one or more of his several cars. It's always the same mix, and he plays it loud when he plays it. I can relate because I also like to listen to my music very loud, except in my case it might not register as "music," especially when I'm listening to something that contains no recognizable musical instruments. Case in point: Aki Onda's *Nam June's Spirit Was Speaking to Me* (2020), which I recently purchased on vinyl and which I'm playing for a second time in several days. The sound is wild, seemingly out of control, and the effect is hypnotic, engrossing. I am acutely aware that others might find it wildly irritating. It is an homage to the Fluxus-associated artist Nam June Paik (1932–2006), but also (apparently) a communication with his ghost. According to Onda's notes, "*Nam June's Spirit Was Speaking to Me* occurred purely by chance."

In 2010, I was spending four days at Nam June Paik Art Center in South Korea for a series of performances and had plenty of free time to wander. The building was packed with Paik's artwork and related material. I have always felt a close kinship with him as an artist, and so it was a great opportunity to immerse myself in his works and ephemera.

It was that night I made the first contact, via a hand-held radio in a hotel room in Seoul. It was literally out of the blue. Scanning through the stations, I stumbled upon what sounded like a submerged voice and I began to record it in fascination. I concluded this was Paik's spirit reaching out to me.

The project continued to grow organically as I kept channeling Paik's spirit over long distance and receiving cryptic broadcasts/messages. The series of séances, conducted in different cities across the globe, began in Seoul in 2010, and continued in Köln, Germany in 2012, Wrocław, Poland in 2013, and Lewisburg, USA in 2014. The original recordings were captured by the same radio which has a tape recorder, with almost no editing, save for some minimal slicing and mastering.

"Channeling the dead" might be another category on my list of "Some possible uses for music," or at least be paired with "waking the dead." Similar concept. Onda refers to Paik's shamanism, "a practice that constantly surfaces in his works all through his career"—a side hustle I was totally unaware of, despite regularly teaching Paik in some of my classes at CalArts where he legendarily taught in the School of Film and Video, and seeing a rather big exhibition of his work a few years ago.

In an interview, he stated, "In Korea, diverse forms of shamanism are strongly remained. Even though I have created my work unconsciously, the most inspiring thing in my work came from Korean female shaman Mudang." Paik himself was a master shaman and vividly used shaman rituals and symbols for staging his performances and installations.

These recordings also became a way for me to explore the mythic form of radio—a medium which is full of mysteries. The transmissions captured may be "secret broadcasts" on anonymous radio stations. There are in fact hundreds of those stations around the world, although the numbers dwindle as clandestine messages can now be sent via encrypted digital channels. Some of these stations were likely for military use or espionage or relics of the Cold War. But many others continue without apparent explanation. These are just some of the questions that remain unanswered.

Onda's attempt to summon the ghost of Nam June Paik through the radio reminds me of my own Philips brand AM/FM clock radio, which my parents bought for me at an electronics store in Madison, Wisconsin in the early 1980s. It was my first AM/FM clock radio, which I listened to often during my childhood and woke up to for many, many years. I had it during my four years living in Madison as an undergrad, and then I brought it with me when I moved to Los Angeles in 1995. At some point the big knob that allowed one to shuttle between stations no longer operated as intended, and my radio was stuck in one place. When I moved to Los Angeles, it was stuck between a station that played country music, and another that played pop or R&B. Neither would have been my first (or second choice), but I continued to use the "radio" alarm function anyway. Usually, I would wake up to the sound of "the radio," meaning some static limbo between stations, and then the signal would eventually move in one direction or the other, like a slow sonic tug-of-war between competing frequencies. By that time, I was usually awake and getting out of bed. But sometimes I would lie there and listen to it as it struggled to land on one station or the other, enjoying the resulting sound as I emerged from my hypnagogic state.

I eventually replaced this with a CD/radio alarm clock, and for many years woke up to the song "Sixtyten" by Boards of Canada from the CD *Music Has the Right to Children* (1998), though I rarely heard more than a few notes of the song because the sound of the CD starting to spin would wake me up. In fact, I would often shut off the alarm before a single note would play, usually with my eyes closed. (The CD stayed in the device for many years, and for all those years I never listened to it beyond the tiniest snippet of that one song. It's a good album, but I could no longer listen to it in any other context.) Presently, I have my alarm on my iPhone set to Brian Eno's song "The Ship" (from his 2016 album of the same name), which begins with a series of long, droning synth tones. It's pleasant enough to wake up to, hardly *alarming*, but in reality I'm usually awake and reading the *New York Times* long before the alarm goes off. My *de facto* wake up is usually the stirring harp alarm on Leslie's iPhone.

I should add "music to wake the living" to my provisional list.

173

Some music never goes out of style (because it was never fashionable in the first place), or getting to know Timeless Pulse—a playlist:

Timeless Pulse
(Pauline Oliveros, accordion; David Wessel, electronics; George Marsh, Jennifer Wilsey, percussion)
Live at CNMAT 2002
Deep Listening, 2002

Timeless Pulse
(Pauline Oliveros, accordion; David Wessel, [live] electronics; George Marsh, Jennifer Wilsey, percussion; Thomas Buckner, voice)
Quintet
Mutable Music, 2007

Timeless Pulse
(Pauline Oliveros, accordion; George Marsh, drumset and percussion; Jennifer Wilsey Marsh, percussion; with guests IONE, spoken word; and Joyce Kouffman, violin, on "Real as Any Dream")
Trio
Taiga Records, 2010

174

Timeless Pulse, Triple Point, The Space Between, Deep Listening Band, New Circle Five, Cicada Dream Band, Carrier Band . . . Pauline Oliveros was a total jammer. I know I am repeating myself, but this innovative, influential composer was a wildly prolific and promiscuous improviser, bringing her V accordion into frisky dialogue with a broad plurality of instruments and the like-minded musicians who play them. This describes the bulk of her output from the last two decades of her productive career. There is also a profusion of recordings from this period put into circulation, as if to make up for the paltry number of albums from her first two decades of professional work. I'm gradually trying to seek them out and listen to them.

"Leaning into the moments of sounding I rest in the music of my friends and enjoy being," she remarks on Timeless Pulse's *Quintet* (2007). This impulse—ethos?—defines all of her improvisatory group efforts, but it also describes most of her compositions for multiple performers as well, whether text-based or notated (often, mandala-based) scores, both of which leave ample space for interpretation, exploration, negotiation. It might be helpful to remember this dedication to group improvisation began in 1958, in cahoots with her San Francisco State colleagues Loren Rush and Terry Riley. (In this trio, Oliveros played French horn, with Rush on bass and koto, and Riley on piano.) "We were amazed that we could make music together this way," Oliveros recalls in *The San Francisco Tape Music Center: 1960s Counterculture and the Avant-Garde*.

We learned an all-important lesson in these early sessions: if we talked first and tried to impose guidelines or structure for the improvisation, the attempt would likely fall flat. If we played first without talking about it, then listened to the recording critically, our improvising would improve naturally. We liberated ourselves from unnecessary controls and developed trust in process through spontaneity. As far as we know, we were the first in avant-garde art music to engage in "free improvisation." Our process was new: play and record, listen to the recording, enjoy, talk, judge, criticize, analyze, and play again.

This process continued for nearly sixty years. I don't love each of these efforts equally; some I don't love at all. (It would be weird if I *did* like them all.) Some I have yet to track down, let alone listen to carefully. But each of the many examples I have spent time listening to teases out the widest variety of Oliveros's approaches to the accordion and the broadest spectrum of colors from it (with the accordion often abetted by the Expanded Instrument System). In all of them, Oliveros is an instantly recognizable presence the moment she sounds the accordion, listening and leaning in.

175

Dear Janice,

I hope this finds you well.

As per my previous emails, I had hoped to get up to Mills this past spring, but an exhibition project and my teaching and administrative duties at CalArts kept me close to home. I would love to spend a few days with the Pauline Oliveros archives this summer, if possible. (I got a faculty development grant to cover my travel and stay.) The week of July 25 would be ideal for me (there is an Alison Knowles exhibition opening at BAMPFA I'd also like to see). Please let me know if this is possible, and if you'll be around. I see there's a finding guide now, which is very helpful.

Many thanks,

Michael

Hi Michael,

We are planning to be around this summer (as long as nothing happens due to the merger, COVID, fires, murder hornets, invasion from outer space, etc.). I will be on vacation from July 19–26 but my colleague Rebecca Leung will be here. We should be open Monday-Friday, 1-5pm.

best regards,

Janice

176

What constitutes your musical universe?

In my months-long attempt to answer this question, I have largely avoided discussion of most everything else in my universe, including "the news." The news has often been bad, and in fact one of the first things I do upon waking, nearly every day, is to read (and/or doomscroll) the *New York Times* on my phone. Despite what is usually a surplus of terrible news, I always get out of bed. Yesterday's bad news—a majority theocratic Supreme Court overturning *Roe v. Wade* and intimating further erosion of individual liberty and privacy—arrived after I was already out of bed, caffeinating, responding to email, probably listening to music, though I have no recollection of what I was listening to at the time. I got an email alert about it, and immediately turned on NPR. The decision was foretold weeks ago, thanks to a leak from within the hallowed halls of Justice, but sadly I saw it coming on the night of November 8, 2016—which didn't make the official announcement any less painful or angering. That I was born less than three months after the *Roe* decision, almost fifty years ago, means that I have only lived in a society in which women had more rights than the unborn. That changed yesterday, at least in many parts of the country. Among many other thoughts and feelings, music has felt inconsequential, at least for the moment. (Everything else in the universe colors the music I listen to, just as music colors everything else in my universe.) And at this moment I'm listening to Nina Simone's "I Put a Spell on You" (1965), hoping for the situation to improve, at least the music situation.

Though some may reach for the stars
Others will end behind bars
What the future has in store no one ever knows before

Yet, we would all like the right to find the key to success
That elusive ray of light that will lead to happiness

Tomorrow is my turn
No more doubts, no more fears
Tomorrow is my turn
When my luck is returning
All these years, I've been learning to save fingers from burning

177

Yesterday, I made the rounds to visit galleries and see some art. What was notable was the proliferation of sound—or visual signs standing in for sound—at so many of the shows. This concluded with a pleasantly overwhelming exhibition of posters and other subcultural ephemera, titled *Torn Apart, 1976–1986: Punk, New Wave + The Graphic Aftermath* (2022), curated by my CalArts colleague Michael Worthington at the Pacific Design Center gallery. A DJ was set up outside, but in the gallery the actual music was thankfully left to the imagination. The buzz of the crowd was the only sound needed.

At the beginning of the day's journey at LAXART, a video by Nikita Gale titled *Takers* (2022) depicted a ridiculous, Hollywood-style fight between two white men, oblivious to the soundtrack of Big Mama Thornton's version of "Hound Dog." The gallery was once the home of Radio Recorders, the studio where Thornton recorded "Hound Dog" in 1952. The video was shot in the gallery, which was now pocked by holes apparently caused by the fight, which explains why there were holes in the wall when I saw Wadada Leo Smith's performance here a month earlier.

A few blocks east, Kevin Beasley's exhibition at Regen Projects included a utility pole that stretched from the gallery's floor to its ceiling. Titled *THE SOURCE* (2022), the pole was outfitted with a white Coleman cooler (I was tempted to open it, but didn't), a pair of dangling black-and-white Nike Cortez sneakers, and cables extending to speakers arrayed throughout the gallery. A field recording was playing from these, though its density suggested several overlapping tracks taken from different locations. The sounds (and some of the surrounding imagery) conjured a place that was rural, but industrial. I heard traffic, I heard the drone of an HVAC unit or other electrical equipment (perhaps a similar utility pole?). I found it compelling and listened for some time. I was told by a gallery employee that the sound was different every day, which struck me as ambitious, but some people who worked in the gallery had taken to wearing ear plugs.

Further east at Michael Benevento, an exhibition of paintings by Benjamin Echeverria unexpectedly included a sound work titled *Breather* (2022), which (I was informed) consisted of a found field recording of hundreds of monks praying or in meditation. It was a static drone, nearly subliminal, with the two speakers positioned out of immediate view, though I quickly perceived the sound in the gallery and sought out its source(s). One painting was situated in an (intentionally) awkward spot in the hallway, near one of the speakers, and to pass through meant being in close proximity to both.

Most engrossing, for me, was a show by Alison O'Daniel at Commonwealth and Council, provocatively titled *The Ownership of Onomatopoeia* (2022). Most of O'Daniel's work considers sound. She is hard of hearing (HoH) and relies on the use of hearing aids and lip reading, which makes her chosen subject matter all the more urgent. The exhibition, which included a surprising range of objects, is related to her ongoing production of a film called *The Tuba Thieves*, which the artist has described (in a 2018 interview in *Bomb* magazine) as "derived from an ongoing collaboration with composers, deaf athletes, musicians, and performers—began in the wake of tuba robberies from Los Angeles schools in 2012, and tells the story of marching band students reconciling with missing sound, a deaf drummer, the 1952 premiere of John Cage's *4'33"*, and the last punk show at the Deaf Club in San Francisco in 1979." That description is really just the tip of the proverbial iceberg of this enjoyably convoluted (at least for this viewer) and gently absurdist project. (I've seen numerous fragments in various contexts over the years.) One constant is O'Daniel's interest in accessibility (or dis/ability) and complicating every viewer's or listener's access to the work, often by pitting those two positions (looking vs. listening) in a playful game of substitutions.

One thread that winds through the densely packed exhibition is the sonic boom—an instance of sound becoming visible (and felt). This takes the form of wallpaper, filled with images of this event along with stills from *The Tuba Thieves* in which its characters discuss their experience of a sonic boom. Several sculptures, in which transducers adorn cast glass ears like acupuncture needs, protrude from the gallery walls and emit a low drone. One can feel the sound as it vibrates the wall, apparently at the same frequency experienced at houses on the flight paths near LAX. (A side note: I considered buying a house in Lennox, but the constant sound pollution seemed unnerving.) My favorite works in the show were a series of *Sound Segregations*, textual "captions" cut from long white steel angles situated at the intersection of floor and wall circling around the gallery. According to O'Daniel, the title of these works "describes inequities in access to sound or safety from sound, wherein precarity can be manifest in ways ranging from airport-adjacent communities being denied access to soundproofing (and thus air conditioning) to the Deaf and Hard of Hearing fighting for access to language."

178

[LEAF BLOWERS THROW THEIR LOW FREQUENCIES.] [THE TONES TRAVEL 800 FEET, PENETRATE WINDOWS AND WALLS.] [IT'S 95 dB AT THE EAR OF THE OPERATOR, BUT THE HOMEOWNERS COMPLAIN.]

—Alison O'Daniel, *Sound Segregations—Leaf Blowers* (2022)

Alison O'Daniel's show reminded me of my privilege as a hearer, but also the occasional burden of having to hear. Yesterday morning, I was subjected to a barrage of sound through the bedroom window. I was already awake, but I was happy enough to enjoy the tranquility of the morning while lying in bed. It started with the shrill bark of the neighbor's little dog, which was followed soon after by the neighbor's lawnmower rumbling to life. It was 7:30, a half hour before one is supposed to create unnecessary noise in Los Angeles. This seemed especially egregious on an otherwise tranquil Sunday morning. He tended to his yard for three hours, which also seems preposterous. (It's a modestly scaled urban yard. And I've mowed many yards, and even did so professionally one summer, so this is an expert opinion.) I ventured to the farmer's market and came back, and he was still at it. I have observed that my neighbor is probably HoH because there have been a number of occasions when I've tried to get his attention to no avail. (He's friendly whenever I talk to him.) So perhaps he is unaware of how annoying three hours of lawn mowing and edging can be, even through double-pane glass windows. This doesn't explain why it took him so long. Later in the day, long after the yard work had ended, I went to the backyard to check on the tomatoes Leslie is growing. I interrupted a very lively conference of birds, who were chattering loudly. Some quickly fluttered into nearby trees or the electrical wire overhead when I suddenly popped out the back door, as they do. I hated to break up the party. Some noises are better than others.

[BIRDS AND CONSTRUCTION ACCOMPANY ONE ANOTHER.] [THEY CAN'T HELP IT.]

—Alison O'Daniel, *Sound Segregations—Birds and Construction* (2022)

179

Twice as nice with EIS—a playlist:

Pauline Oliveros / David Gamper
At the Ijsbreker Jan 24, 1999
JdK Productions, 1999

Deep Listening Band
(Pauline Oliveros, David Gamper, Stuart Dempster, and guests)
Non Stop Flight
Music & Arts, 1998

180

I'm finally getting around to talking about the Expanded Instrument System or EIS (pronounced "ice" and subject to many frozen liquid-related puns by Oliveros, Gamper, Dempster, and company). According to legend (i.e. documents found in the Oliveros Papers at Mills), the earliest version EIS was first used in 1983, and I take that to be a rather basic use of effects pedals (delays, etc.) to process the sound of Oliveros's accordion. The idea was further developed by Panaiotis, who was part of the Deep Listening Band in its early years. David Gamper considerably expanded the reach of EIS in his time working with and playing with Oliveros and Deep Listening Band. Panaiotis and Gamper briefly overlapped, though Gamper was initially part of the group's technical support team before becoming a bona fide member. In a paper titled "The Expanded Instrument System (EIS)," Oliveros and Panaiotis outline the early history of the technology:

The Expanded Instrument System (EIS™) for live performance has been under continual development since 1983. The EIS in its current form is a performance environment consisting of a network of time delays, mixing routes, microphones and a multichannel speaker configuration. Acoustic instruments are the preferred signal sources. Performers are able to "expand" the sound of their instrument through interaction with the various parameters of the delay and effects processors, which can modulate the sounds and change the perceived quality of the space in which the performer is playing. The delay processors are controlled through a non-MIDI based control network using foot pedals and computers. The current delay processors will be replaced by a Reson8 processor that will provide digital mixing, resonance processing, and will potentially handle DSP via a MAC II computer.

Unfortunately I didn't manage to scan the whole paper or note its date, though the Apple Mac II was on the market from 1987 to 1990. This period also coincides with the first few Deep Listening Band albums; however, there is no mention of the EIS™ on the albums in which Panaiotis appears. Fwiw, DLB first mentions the EIS in the liner notes for *Tosca Salad* (1995). Gamper and Panaiotis overlap on the third DLB album, *The Ready Made Boomerang* (1991), which saw the band return to the Fort Worden cistern, though Gamper is listed as "technical assistance." (David's wife Gisella Gamper took the photographs used on the *Boomerang* CD.) While these albums did not make specific use of the EIS, recording in the cistern or the Tarpaper Cave (for *Troglodyte's Delight* [1990]) was full of technical challenges, given the naturally occurring reverb of these sites, and was inevitably informed by collaborative development of the EIS by Panaiotis and Oliveros, and eventually Gamper. The EIS would later be used to replicate some of the reverberative and other acoustic properties of these sites.

In all of the language around DLB's use of the EIS, it is emphasized that all of the sounds produced were initiated acoustically by human beings playing acoustic instruments (accordion, trombone, piano, etc.) or using their voices, before becoming transformed through the EIS. It might be said that to "expand" an instrument also means to defamiliarize it. A technical diagram for a DLB performance, "Hall Configuration" circa 1990–1991 (probably drawn on a Mac II), situates Panaiotis and Gamper at a mixing console, away from the stage, and in the middle of the audience. Eight speakers line the edges of the hall, with four on either side of the audience. Dempster and Oliveros are positioned on stage, with exact microphone positions indicated—two for Dempster, three for Oliveros (perhaps accounting for accordion and voice). Next to Panaiotis and Gamper are four Lexicon PCM 42 and four Lexicon PCM 70 digital delay processors. This also closely resembles a diagram from the same time period for a solo performance by Oliveros, in which the delays are on stage with her, with the mixing console (presumably operated by an unnamed accomplice) situated in the middle of the audience, with four speakers in the corners of the room.

A few observations on the EIS and DLB:

The DLB diagram marks the band shifting from performance in unusual acoustic sites to constructing unusual acoustic sites digitally, or what could be called "virtual sites" or perhaps "virtual space."

Along with this shift, DLB began to reimagine David Gamper's role as a full member of the group. Soon, and following the departure of Panaiotis from the band, Gamper's role grew to include the playing of acoustic instruments such as piano, flute, and percussion, along with his development of the EIS. (Gamper's bio on DLB's *Non Stop Flight* [1998] lists him as the "director of development" for the EIS, a funny use of that phrase.)

It is useful to consider the EIS as a meta-instrument in the same way the cistern or the cave serve as mega-instruments. (Dempster: "The cistern is an instrument that you learn to play.") In this sense, the human performers are situated in a dynamic ("three-way"?) relationship with nature and technology.

181

In Oliveros's solo performances, the EIS is an obvious extension of the accordion, which (as I've already argued) is an inherently synthetic instrument. Oliveros has, since her introduction to the instrument in her teenage years, sought to reveal the extraordinary range of its sonic possibilities and to invent some new ones in the process. At times she renders the accordion illegible as such. Historically, the primary place of the accordion has been as a significant instrument of folk or popular music, with a fairly global reach (if we include the concertina, bandoneon, and other family members), but not as an instrument of classical or academic music. Oliveros has almost single-handedly accorded the accordion a place in "new" music, leveling hierarchies and presumed orders. (Guy Klucevsek is part of the story, too, but Oliveros has further reach beyond the accordion, too, and multiple audiences.)

Oliveros returned to the primacy of the accordion after exploring the possibilities of music attained through the most basic of means—the human voice, alone and with others, along with a variety of ready-at-hand objects—in her *Sonic Meditations* of the early 1970s. The *Sonic Meditations* followed her pioneering exploration of the electronic music studio. A return to her deep exploration of the accordion (with *Horse Sings from Cloud* and so on, circa 1975) was followed, relatively soon after (circa 1983), by the development of the Expanded Instrument System.

I think about using all of these delays as a time machine. Because when I play something in the present, then it's delayed and comes back in the future. But when it comes back in the future, I'm dealing with the past, and also playing again in the present, anticipating the future. So that's expanding time.

The EIS represents Oliveros's return to the possibilities of the electronic music studio, by other means: As ever, Oliveros is always synthesizing. Importantly, all sounds are initiated by the performer (Oliveros and her accordion and/or voice) and processed through the EIS, in many ways replicating the way she used her tape delay system, sometimes augmented by the Buchla synthesizer, in the 1960s. In both cases (EIS and electronic music studio, EMS), a system is created to create certain possibilities and to set certain limits. In the case of Oliveros, this generally becomes a space for improvisation—an opportunity to push against perceived limits while exploring the sonic possibilities. It is therefore no surprise (if unremarked upon) that the EIS diagrams for live performance closely resemble Oliveros's tape delay diagrams from the electronic music studio. See, for example, the "Sound Speaker Schematic" for *Crone Music* (1989–1990) next to the diagram for *Beautiful Soop* (1967) in her article "Tape Delay Techniques." In both cases, Oliveros the composer is essentially designing a maze in which Oliveros the performer can get lost—or, to take her metaphor, travel through time.

182

More sound observed in galleries: Yesterday, I ventured to see—and hear—*Sonic Terrains in Latinx Art* (2022), a group exhibition at the Vincent Price Art Museum at East Los Angeles College, followed by Nour Mobarak's solo show *Dafne Phono* (2022) at JOAN.

Sonic Terrains filled most of the museum's three floors. Given that most of the work was time-based (sound/video), it was a lot to take in. At times, particularly as sound from various works overlapped in space, it became overwhelming. But there was plenty to enjoy, including some contributions by friends and former students that were already familiar. Some of these artists (ASCO, Nervous Gender, Pauline Oliveros) also appeared in the exhibition *Axis Mundo: Queer Networks in Chicano L.A.,* curated by C. Ondine Chavoya and David Evans Frantz in 2017. It's curious that Oliveros appeared in both exhibitions, despite the fact that she never defined or described herself as Chicana or Latinx. As far as I know, her surname is Spanish. But who am I to argue against her inclusion? Her radical approach to music, sound, art, and pedagogy makes her an important point of reference in both of these networked exhibitions. (L.A. punk icon Alice Bag, née Armendariz, would have been a nice inclusion.) In any event, I was happy to see the postcards from Oliveros's *Postcard Theatre* (1974), a humorous collaboration with Alison Knowles, as well as some color photos of her performance *Cheap Commissions* (1981), which would have benefitted from some contextualizing information. It's a funny performance—I showed her punning, punky flyer for it in my *Routine Pleasures* exhibition in 2016.

Oliveros's sense of humor, often poking fun at serious music ("BRAHMS WAS A TWO-PENNY HARLOT," etc., etc.) informed many of the works in the show. A video by

Los Jaichackers (Eamon Ore-Giron and Julio Cesar Morales), *Subterranean Homesick Cumbia* (2014), subjected an accordion to a variety of indignities, from dragging it on the ground to drowning it in the sea, in a retelling of one of the origin myths of Cumbia, "in which a German shipwreck scattered accordions across the Caribbean shore of Colombia. Black enslaved people and locals found the instrument and created a folk style that would later emerge in mainstream big band orchestras across the Americas." A nearby piano, or what remained of it, was evidence of other indignities performed by Raphael Montañez Ortiz. Like a wreck on the freeway, it was impossible not to look and appreciate its demolished form. The relic had been given to the museum, and I enjoyed imagining the care taken to pack and unpack the obliterated object.

Massagem Sonora (*Sonic Massage*), a 2014 performance by Carmina Escobar, was shown on a monitor in a corridor. In the performance, which took place in San Pedro, next to the Friendship Bell (a gift from South Korea), Escobar placed her mouth against the backs or chests of various passerby with their consent and sometimes bemusement, as she applied therapy with her considerable pipes. Another highlight included the performance video *Aztlan, Babylon, Rhythm & Blues* (1990) by Rubén Guevara, a Chicano Renaissance man who appeared in Cheech and Chong movies and fronted a real band, Ruben and the Jets, that started as a fictional band created by Frank Zappa. This work, as well as the recent Ulysses Jenkins retrospective at the Hammer, reminded me that there is a lot I don't know about the performance art scene in Southern California in the late 1980s and early 1990s, much of it existing at the boundaries of punk, experimental music, theater, film, pop culture, and so on. I am reminded of Jay Sander's excellent 2014 exhibition *Rituals of Rented Island: Object Theater, Loft Performance, and the New Psychodrama—Manhattan, 1970–1980* , which pulled together Jack Smith, Laurie Anderson, Yvonne Rainer, Richard Foreman, John Zorn, and many more who worked independently but in proximity on the island of Manhattan, but the L.A. version I'm imagining is a decade or so later, more colorful (less white) and more queer—an area for future research.

183

A found sound or loaned moan: a quote by Renee Gladman, from her Bagley Wright Lecture "Lines Into Grasses," repurposed for the curatorial text by Fía Benitez and Simone Zapata for their exhibition *Tense Renderings: The Will and Won't of Spatial Logics* (2022) at the REEF, Los Angeles:

Space is not a static field. It does not wait for our offerings or our movements. It is not blank and has never been blank. Spaces moan. They are of another order.

184

"IMPORTANT
NOTICE"

𝄞 CHEAP COMMISSIONS 𝄢
written while u wait
$1.00 PER MEASURE
25¢ extra per ledger line
MEET YOU AT THE BAR
CONCEPTUAL MUSIC–SONIC MEDITATIONS
DO IT YOURSELF your price or mine
USED MUSIC
SECOND HAND COMPOSITIONS
(a dime a dozen)
GOOD SOUNDS BOUGHT-SOLD-TRADED
new music opera negotiated separately
futures (see my staff 𝄞)
NEW MUSIC FORTUNES
(told for a song)
EIGHTH NOTES 5¢ A PAIR ♫
ALL RHYTHMS AT BARGAIN RATES
(your sound or mine)
THEMES FOR SALE
buy one now!
PAY NOW PLAY LATER
THIS IS A PITCH ♩

© Pauline Oliveros APRIL, 1986

185

Cheap Commissions was a live performance or perhaps "happening" in which Oliveros wrote bespoke scores on the spot for a nominal fee. Here's an example of one I found on crinkled stationery in her papers in the Olin Library at Mills College:

AUG 10 - 1980

CHEAP STAKES

COMMISSIONED BY

WARREN BURT

FOR RON NAGORKA

FIND A WAY TO GET YOUR NOTE

TO THE FINISH LINE FIRST

ALL CAN PLAY

ALL CAN PLACE BETS

AND THERE THEY GO . . . !

WINNER PLAYS ALL

P.O.

Apparently, *Cheap Commissions* took place at least a few times over the years, at various locations. The documentation I've seen (the color pictures I saw at Vincent Price Art Museum last week, as well as the black-and-white pictures I encountered at Mills) apparently date from March 7, 1981 and took place at the flea market in Leucadia, California. (I took a picture of the back of one of the b&w pictures, dated and credited to Pat Szydelko in Oliveros's handwriting.) In the Leucadia version, Oliveros is situated at a stand that recalls Lucy Van Pelt's ad-hoc therapy stand from Peanuts, which was of course, based on a classic American lemonade stand. Oliveros's stand is fitted with a big handwritten sign, reading with two columns of balloons adorning either side. (The composer is in.) It's a funny work, meaning in the ha-ha sense, but also funny in how it fits in her body of work. Certainly it recalls her earlier theater pieces, which often incorporated props and poked fun at the pretensions of classical music. (The scores written for *Cheap Commissions* are full of musical puns, often aiming high and low at the same time.) The suburban enclave of Leucadia was home to Oliveros at the time, and the San Diego context also aligns with Oliveros's close proximity to Allan Kaprow, Eleanor Antin, Linda Montano, and other artists working in performance—all of whom participated in a semi-regular series of happenings called *What's Cooking?* organized by the Center for Music Experiment at UCSD in the late 70s and early 80s. 1981 is the year that marks Oliveros's departure from UCSD, so perhaps the performance was a going away party? (Thrown for herself, much like the 1967 Tape-athon that concluded her time in San Francisco?) The balloons are certainly festive, and her sailor's cap—shades of Captain Stubing from *The Love Boat*—connotes voyage.

Oddly, *Cheap Commissions* is one of the specific works that led me to Oliveros, but more strangely, I no longer recall how I knew about this particular (and relatively obscure) work of hers. I met Oliveros on September 30, 2015 at EMPAC, the Curtis R. Priem Experimental Media and Performing Arts Center at Rensselaer Polytechnic Institute, where she taught and frequently performed. I was there with Jennifer West to present a project (reading) on film memory the following night. When I told the curator Vic Brooks I had been trying to contact Oliveros, she quickly arranged a meeting. I was amazed and grateful she was able to bring us together. Like magic. We met in the cafeteria outside the big theater at EMPAC. It was late afternoon; Oliveros had just finished teaching. I was surely nervous and tried to cloak my excitement. Her presence was reassuring if not relaxing. I have always loved her speaking voice, its husky and calm sonority, and was happy to hear it in such close proximity.

I told her about the premise of my forthcoming exhibition *Routine Pleasures*, which would open at the MAK Center for Art and Architecture at the Schindler House in May 2016. (I knew she knew the venue, having performed there at the invitation of SASSAS years earlier.) I explained how the artist and longtime UCSD professor Manny Farber was central to the exhibition (and to Jean-Pierre Gorin's 1986 essay film, *Routine Pleasures*, from which its title was stolen), and how I also saw her own work as an artist and educator (also at UCSD) as a parallel version of Farber's "termite art." I was also thinking about the ♀ Ensemble that performed many of the *Sonic Meditations* as a counterpoint to the (♂) model train enthusiasts who also feature in Gorin's film. The premise of the show (not unlike Gorin's film) was admittedly convoluted, but Oliveros demonstrated great patience as I tried to describe it and somehow rope her into my scheme. We discussed *Cheap Commissions* and *Sonic Meditations*, and she encouraged me to visit her papers at Mills College, giving me the name and contact information for Janice Braun, the librarian there. Going big, I also took the opportunity to invite Oliveros to perform during the exhibition (which wasn't possible given her schedule) and to contribute some writing to the catalog for the show (which she did).

Soon after, we corresponded by email, and she followed up with some scores, mostly unpublished, for me to choose from. I chose four, which seemed to make sense in context: *Sound Listening*, *For Claire*, *Occupy Air*, and *Sounding Secret Spaces*. At Mills, I would find the flyer for a 1986 edition of *Cheap Commissions*, which I borrowed for the show, and a photo of the ♀ Ensemble, a scan of which I included in the catalog. With Oliveros's permission, I also included a recording of *The Tuning Meditation* (1979) in the Schindler garden, with speakers tucked in the bushes. I sent her a copy of catalog when it was done, shortly after the show closed. I don't know if she got it or if she looked at it. A few months later, she died.

I met with Oliveros for an hour. Time stopped, then flew by. As a teacher, I am keenly aware of the generosity of meeting with me (a complete stranger, potentially a stalker) after a long day of teaching. She was still teaching fulltime at age eighty-three when I met her. She was tired, ready to hit the road back to Kingston, an hour away. I totally understood, and thanked her for her time. She told me to give our mutual friend Simone Forti a hug when I next saw her. When recounting this meeting to those who cared to hear about it, I was left with few salient details to share. She hadn't really said that much, beyond providing some helpful information about the works in question and directing me to her papers. I left with a realization, hardly surprising: She's a good listener.

186

Resonance Studies (Music for Very Big Spaces)—a playlist:

Paul Horn
Inside
Epic, 1968
(Later reissued as *Inside the Taj Mahal*, Kuckuck, 1983)

Stuart Dempster
In the Great Abbey of Clement VI
1750 Arch Records, 1979
(Later reissued with an additional track by New Albion, 1987)

Bill Fontana
Landscape Sculpture with Fog Horns
KQED-FM, 1982
(Later reissued with an additional track, featuring a performance by Stuart Dempster, by Other Minds, 2020)

James Newton
Echo Canyon
Celestial Harmonies, 1984

187

I finished reading Dempster's *The Modern Trombone: A Definition of Its Idioms*. To confess: I could not have predicted reading a book on the trombone, modern or otherwise, let alone enjoying it. But Dempster has a friendly, accessible voice, and there's plenty there for the non-specialist, provided they have some fundamental interest in the trombone or in Dempster as a historical figure, which is more precisely my point of entry. The book provided crucial insight into Dempster's role in shaping the trombone as a worthy avant-garde instrument, demonstrating its potential for composers and performers alike. It also proved particularly helpful in understanding Dempster's role in shaping Deep Listening Band. (He also has a really precise grasp of punctuation.) A few sound observations:

1. "The trombone, of course, is an extension of the body, and in that capacity acts as a resonator, just as we have seen the body itself act as a resonator." In the reverberant spaces favored by Deep Listening Band, it is sometimes difficult to discern instrument from voice. So, it is useful to think of Dempster's chosen instruments—which include other resonators like the didjeridu and the garden hose—as an extension of the body, which is actually somewhat different than the way Oliveros's accordion parallels or imitates her voice. He also notes that through the trombone, "various vocal sounds, particularly the scream, can effectively mimic the sounds of electronic music," such as a ring modulator. This recalls the "lessons" of Oliveros's early compositions, including *Sound Patterns* (1961), in which human voices are used to mimic electronic sounds, and *Time Perspectives*, an early (1961) tape piece in which she sounded a cardboard tube in the bathtub to unusual effect—both anticipate the sonic "palette" of her

work in the electronic music studio utilizing humble means. Both Dempster and Oliveros seem interested in this kind of mimicry and the way the voice performs in specific resonant conditions.

2. Dempster was among the very first American musicians to use a didjeridu, and he spent time in Australia learning it. He tends to use a handmade PVC version of the instrument, rather than fetishize an exotic Aboriginal object outside its indigenous culture and cultural significance. (I'm paraphrasing.) "The trombone may seem old when compared to western orchestral instruments, but it is only a five-hundred-year-old baby when compared to the possible two- to four-thousand-year-old tradition of the didjeridu," he notes in a short, but sweet appendix on the instrument.

3. The garden hose is an unlikely musical instrument, though Dempster uses it frequently on DLB recordings. I love thinking about the familiarity and accessibility of this suburban object, which, like PVC pipes, one can buy at a hardware store. "The garden hose is a nonadjustable-length trombone," he argues, "just as the trombone is an adjustable-length garden hose." Beyond this sort of logic, the garden hose allows for many surprising applications, the most ambitious (and frankly wacky) of which is certainly Dempster's own composition *Ten Grand Hosery*, "for Musician, Dancer, Sculptorchestra, Dancers, and Audience," which he premiered at the University of Illinois-Urbana in 1972:

   Place ten grand pianos on the stage with the lids raised and sustaining pedals blocked so that the strings will be free to resonate ... Ten garden hoses with as many trombone mouthpieces should be stretched, one from each piano, to the center of the stage, the ends of the hoses being hooked in the sounding board holes so that they will not slip out.

4. "*All* music is theatrical; that is, the performance of any piece is of interest visually as well as acoustically." Dempster, influenced by examples like Spike Jones and certain jazz performers, understood the theatrical potential for the trombone as well as anyone, and was among the most pioneering of its practitioners in the avant-garde context. John Cage's *Solo for Sliding Trombone* (1957–1958), Luciano Berio's *Sequenza V* (1966), Oliveros's *Theater Piece* (1966), and Robert Erickson's *General Speech* (1969) each receive considerable attention in the book. He gave the premiere performance of the latter three and cites many other works that make rather outrageous demands. "In all these works I never appeared as a 'trombonist' but rather as an outer-space being, a larva, a speech giver, and a mechanized robot," he notes, deadpan. Needless to say, Dempster (like Oliveros) has an abundant sense of humor.

5. Dempster's interest in what he calls performance space has an obvious relation to the collective, resonant interests of Deep Listening Band, and help articulate this understanding a decade in advance of their first recording in the cistern, with its 45-second echo:

   Performance space is part of the trombone, and, like trombones and players, every space is different. These spaces are extensions of the trombone, just as the trombone is an extension of the body within which the vocal or lip buzzed sound functions. The performer must "play" the space just as much as one would the trombone or body cavity. The trombone has perhaps more control over its acoustical environment than any other instrument because of its dynamic range and directional quality. It is, like a trumpet, an instrument that can be literally "aimed," and this allows for tremendous control of acoustics. Performance space resonance can allow for imaginative thinking in terms of the creative process; it can also cause tremendous problems if this resonance is not clearly understood.

The awareness of resonance is best begun in a room with a long reverberation time. A cathedral will serve this purpose, or a cement stairwell.

This reflection follows quite directly from his own (indispensable!) solo album *In the Great Abbey of Clement VI*, recorded in 1976 while working with David Behrman and David Tudor at the Popes' Palace in Avignon.

With the kind assistance of John Fullemann, sound technician, I not only performed from this "Great Abbey" but I also made several tape recordings in this chapel dealing with its fourteen-second echo. The trombone sounded beautiful in this space, perhaps due to the irregular surface of the sandstone, and much compositional material was obtained. I have titled these works and sketches *Standing Waves* to reflect the actual acoustic process taking place.

In a footnote, he also calls the reader's attention to Paul Horn's albums of solo flute music performed inside the Taj Mahal and the Great Pyramid, which are undoubtedly precursors to Deep Listening Band's performances in the Fort Worden cistern or the Tarpaper Cave.

6. Famous last words: "Who is to say at this point that the peaks and valleys have all been reached?"

188—Stuart Dempster's eighty-sixth birthday

There's a promo photograph of Deep Listening Band taken by Gisela Gamper, found in in the Olin Library, that points to the group's frisky sense of humor. Dated 1991, it marks the brief period when David Gamper and Panaiotis were both in the mix. Gamper is at the far left, processor in his left hand with his right hand playing the keys of Oliveros's Titano accordion; Oliveros grins despite the fact that a garden hose suggestively rings her neck; Panaiotis blows into a mouthpiece connected to one end of the hose, held to his lips by Dempster; and Dempster bookends the scene on the right, with the garden hose snaking around his turtleneck shirt. Gamper, Oliveros, and Dempster are smiling widely. Panaiotis might be suppressing a laugh, while maintaining his embouchure. Corny, to be sure, the image nevertheless makes a case for *entanglement* as a primary feature of the band, despite also suggesting each individual member brings a distinct personality. (Isn't that *every* band picture—a tug-of-war between individual personalities and collective identity?) The promo shot also emphasizes extension (likewise symbolized by Dempster's hose, but also manifested in the resonant spaces favored by the band and/or the use of the EIS), interchangeability (who's playing what?), and what Dempster calls "theatrical consciousness" ("*all* music is theatrical; that is, the performance of any piece is of interest visually as well as acoustically"). The blank photo studio background also reminds me how far we're removed from the exotic spaces favored by the band on its earliest recordings (e.g. cistern, cave), here with the DLB situated in virtual space, setting the scene for future explorations.

189

Two records purchased from Dave Muller's Record Pavilion in his exhibition *Sunset, Sunrise (repeat) b/w The Record Pavilion* (2022) at Blum & Poe, Los Angeles—a playlist:

Arthur Doyle
No More Crazy Women
Qbico, 2005
Note: Single-sided yellow vinyl with octagonal cover and yellow borders

Alan Nakagawa
Organ of Corti
Not on label (manufactured by Bill Smith Custom Records), 2013

Suggestions [from Nakagawa's album notes]: Listen at 35 [*sic*] or 45 rpm. You can listen normally or alternate by wearing earplugs and holding an inflated balloon near the speaker (feeling vibrations through your fingertips) or put speakers under a coffee table and lay on the coffee table.

190

With *Sunset, Sunrise (repeat) b/w The Record Pavilion*, Muller looks back on his life of growing up in record stores. In a tribute to the slow and physical act of touching, browsing, and looking at records, this exhibition presents the artist's treasured pastime, one that is becoming extinct as music consumption is increasingly intangible.

Among the works in the show are a series of (six, I believe) paintings, each titled *Youth Misspent (in Record Stores)*, depicting larger than life collages of price stickers and "hype stickers" from the artist's "personal collection of roughly 1,500 unique decals from albums purchased," all lavishly reproduced in acrylic paint. Each of these is subtitled with the amount of money paid for the records in the currency indicated on the sticker. The painting I'm most drawn to, for example, is subtitled *$157.96 + 41.49 £ + 1,365 ¥ + Bs.S40 + R4.99* (2022). In addition to the price stickers, there's a round yellow sticker that says "SUN CITY GIRLS." This sits atop an upside-down sticker, a little white rectangle that says "THIRTY THREE" (the name of a Japanese record store, I suspect), though reading its old-fashioned font upside down and in proximity to the Sun City Girls, I initially misread it as "DIRTY THREE." I guess I have a dirty mind that way. The sticker that really gets my attention is for a record that cost "$16.00" and is hand-annotated with the provocative phrase "LOCAL WEIRDOS." Because I am at the opening and the artist is present, I ask him about it. "That's a great question," Dave enthuses. "I'm glad you asked about it." It turns out the local weirdos are a postpunk (or "artpunk") band called Bpeople, which is a great name, though Local Weirdos would also be a fantastic band name. (If you're reading this, you can have it.) It turns out Bpeople included Fredrik Nilsen on bass and Tom Recchion on drums, both local weirdos I happen to know, though embarrassingly, until yesterday, I didn't know about Bpeople which had its brief heyday in the earliest 80s. Nilsen and Recchion are both in Extended Organ and part of the Los Angeles Free Music Society (LAFMS). (Nilsen is the proud owner of the LAFMS California license plate and was overjoyed when he saw me at the Mar Vista Farmers Market wearing my LAFMS cap a few years ago.) Nilsen is also one of the best art/exhibition photographers in the business, which is how I met him in the first place. Some of his color images grace either side of the Bpeople's self-titled LP (Faulty Records, 1981) with a sleeve designed by Recchion. There is also a posthumous collection with the excellent title *Petrified Conditions 1979–1981*, released on Restless Records in 1986. I'm listening to all of these on YouTube this morning, continuing my education in a never-ending seminar called Local Weirdos.

191

Leslie and I have been watching the new series about the Sex Pistols, with the awful title *Pistol*, based on the account of the guitarist Steve Jones. It's entertaining, and I suppose educational. I don't know that much about British punk beyond the basic outline, and I've never felt much connection to the music or its aesthetic. (For what it's worth, many years ago I read Noel Monk and Jimmy Guterman's *12 Days on the Road*, an account of the Sex Pistols short and ill-fated US tour, and I've seen Alex Cox's movie *Sid and Nancy* [1986]. Every account of the band is a salacious one.) Which isn't to say I don't *appreciate* the music or aesthetic, but is there a more milquetoast compliment one could pay to a music style that practically demands to be loved or loathed? For me, it's neither. Meanwhile, I'm finally getting around to reading Derek Bailey's *Improvisation: Its Nature and Practice in Music*, first written in 1975/1976, which exactly coincides with the formative years of the Sex Pistols. In 1976, Bailey also formed Company, a constantly evolving group of improvisers that mixed British and European free improvisers with Americans like Anthony Braxton, Wadada Leo Smith, and Steve Lacy. It's funny to imagine these things happening at the same time in Great Britain, and it's hard to imagine a less-punk name than Company. But whatever Bailey was doing in the 1970s (and after) seems far more musically radical or ambitious than the Sex Pistols—though the media spectacle of the Sex Pistols was surely more culturally radical, and presumably dangerous or at least annoying to the conservative cultural establishment. Because what Bailey was doing was small and presumably never aiming for a big audience (probably the exact opposite really), whereas the Sex Pistols were fashioned (quite literally, by "impresario" Malcolm McLaren and designer Vivienne Westwood) for maximum attention. Bailey also dressed like a square and wore glasses, but circa 1977 his idiosyncratic, "non-idiomatic" brand of freely improvised guitar playing was probably more likely to annoy an unsuspecting listener than "God Save the Queen." And, perhaps more importantly, it would *still* annoy an unsuspecting listener, whereas the filth and the fury of punk has largely been assimilated by the mainstream and crass commercial culture. Admittedly, I'm whistling past important class considerations in this hypothetical duel. And I'm writing from the perspective of someone who was an infant when the Sex Pistols changed the world, though it's always worth considering why certain historical figures or moments recirculate in pop culture and what it says about the present. (We're in a very conservative moment, in which institutions seem especially feeble and vulnerable and corporations seem to continually gain a greater hold on our collective imagination.) In other words, I'm not holding my breath for FX on Hulu to make a television series about Derek Bailey.

192

"the basic characteristic of music-making is improvisation," or listening to Derek Bailey while reading Derek Bailey—a playlist:

Evan Parker, Derek Bailey, Han Bennink
Topography of the Lungs
Incus, 1970

The Music Improvisation Company
(Christine Jeffrey, Derek Bailey, Evan Parker, Hugh Davies, Jamie Muir)
The Music Improvisation Company
ECM, 1970

Anthony Braxton & Derek Bailey
First Duo Concert (London 1974)
Emanem, 1996

Derek Bailey
Improvisation
Cramps Records, 1975

Maarten van Regteren Altena, Tristan Honsinger, Evan Parker, Derek Bailey
Company 1
Incus, 1977

Evan Parker, Anthony Braxton, Derek Bailey
Company 2
Incus, 1977

193

This morning, I accidentally started a Spotify "radio" program by playing the song "Ya Habibti" (2021) by Mdou Moctar. It's the song that plays over the opening animated credit sequence of the HBO limited series *Irma Vep* (2022), which is a reimagining of the 1996 film by Olivier Assayas. It was one of my favorite films of the 90s, an indie "cult classic." The new show (also directed by Assayas) is really meta and mostly a light diversion, but a rather infectious one. Moctar's music is also infectious, which makes the use of "Ya Habibti" an auspicious opener. (Thurston Moore contributes some incidental jingle jangle to the soundtrack.) While preparing my morning coffee, I played the song on my living room speaker from my phone via Bluetooth. When the song ended, the "radio" station started, choosing songs algorithmically based on their proximity to Moctar or based on my own listening habits, or possibly both. It chose artists I listen to often, like Alice Coltrane, Bitchin Bajas, and Jeff Parker; it also chose many artists I've never heard or even heard of: Jupiter & Okwess, Ben LaMar Gay, Alabaster DePlume, L'Rain, and more. It was a fun mix, and well-suited for reading and answering email, which was this morning's task. I don't usually like letting the bots make decisions for me, especially when it comes to choosing what I'm listening to. But one could argue that I "chose" this myself, setting it in motion with my algorithmic unconscious. I'm skeptical of this or at least reluctant to even participate in it, though they surely know many of my weaknesses. It's also fun and educational to learn about new things, expand my reach, shake things up. Maybe especially after a day of listening to Derek Bailey. I imagine there are some (many?) who are perfectly content to let the machine make decisions for them, the way one used to let the radio DJ make all their listening decisions. It's convenient, though convenience is rarely one of my highest values or top priorities, for better or worse.

194

Most musicians learn to improvise by accident; or by a series of observed accidents; by trial and error. And there is of course an appropriateness about this method, a natural correspondence between improvisation and empiricism. Learning improvisation is a practical matter: there is no exclusively theoretical side to improvisation. Appreciating and understanding how improvisation works is achieved through the failures and successes involved in attempting to do it.

I'm working my way through Derek Bailey's *Improvisation: Its Nature and Practice in Music*, which has long been a "definitive" treatise on the subject at hand, even as he takes pains to avoid making any overarching theoretical point about it. He's more interested in presenting a comparative study of improvised music, with considerations of raga, flamenco, organ music in churches, and the Grateful Dead, among other eclectic practices. Of primary interest (to me, but Bailey too) is free improvisation, which is the area the author is most closely associated with as a practitioner. Perhaps his most important claim, which we could call theoretical whether he likes it or not, is that free improvisation is, in fact, the very origin of music—not only that music is inherently non-idiomatic, which is a term he likes to use, but *pre-idiomatic*. "Historically," he argues, "it predates any other music—mankind's first musical performance couldn't have been anything other than a free improvisation—and I think that it is reasonable speculation that at most times since then there will have been some music-making most aptly described as free improvisation." Which he also intends as a way to preempt any claims that one person or another was the first to discover or invent free improvisation. The proverbial caveman got there first. In a footnote, he dates his own entry into the field of improvisation, which at first rendered him "totally confused and alienated" to 1957. (He also notes that free improvisation is accessible to trained musicians and non-musicians alike. "The skill and intellect required is whatever is available.") Oliveros is not mentioned in the book, but it's of interest (to me, at least) to think about her relation to free improvisation alongside Bailey's. Oliveros first explored this area in 1958 with Terry Riley and Loren Rush. One of the most engaging areas for Bailey, who has no shortage of his own solo improvisations committed to tape, is the way in which group improvisation works. I think this is also true for Oliveros and her revolving cast of fellow explorers, and the way other players can coax new tricks out of an old dog. One trick used by Bailey, in the annual Company gatherings he organized, was to stir the pot (apologies for mixed metaphors) by including a highly trained musician or two who were not regular improvisers. Bailey was largely hostile to composition itself, whereas Oliveros seemed to use composition as a way of opening a liberatory ("free") space for performance. I could expand upon this point. For now, I'll end with an anecdote by Evan Parker about fellow saxophonist Steve Lacy (who worked with a wide range of improvising musicians including Bailey, Don Cherry, and Frederic Rzewski, among many others), committed to the page by Bailey:

In 1968 I ran into Steve Lacy on the street in Rome. I took out my pocket tape recorder and asked him to describe in fifteen seconds the difference between composition and improvisation. He answered: "In fifteen seconds the difference between composition and improvisation is that in composition you have all the time you want to decide what to say in fifteen seconds, while in improvisation you have fifteen seconds."

195

One of the most compelling considerations in Derek Bailey's *Improvisation* book is the question of documentation. If the fundamental goal of improvised music is to be ever-always in the moment and never do the same thing twice, why would someone make it endlessly repeatable by recording it? Good question. There is also a related question of audience: Who is this music for? I would argue that improvised music, first and foremost, is for the person or people performing it, which makes group improvisation all the more vital. (It's for a bigger audience, even if it's inevitably a small one.) But there are those of us who enjoy listening to it, even though we weren't involved in the making of it, because we are listening to a performer or performer operating in a risky, uncharted space, sometimes teetering on the edge of the unknown. Bailey described this precipice in a 2002 interview in *Jazziz* magazine:

There has to be some degree, not just of unfamiliarity, but incompatibility [with a partner]. Otherwise, what are you improvising for? What are you improvising with or around? You've got to find somewhere where you can work. If there are no difficulties, it seems to me that there's pretty much no point in playing. I find that the things that excite me are trying to make something work. And when it does work, it's the most fantastic thing. Maybe the most obvious analogy would be the grit that produces the pearl in an oyster, or some shit like that.

I've come back to this quote a few times over the years—not just to make sense of my own interest in listening to improvised music, but in order to make sense of my own interest in finding somewhere where *I* can work, as a writer, curator, teacher. Curating and teaching are essentially group activities, and regardless of the power dynamics, there is usually plenty of open space for give and take that shapes the outcome. Working in this collaborative/collective/codependent space has its obvious challenges and rewards, much as Bailey describes: "The essence of improvisation, its intuitive, telepathic foundation, is best explored in a group situation." When I'm writing, I'm doing it alone, but also usually working with some constraints—writing on some *thing* (e.g. a painting, a piece of music, etc.) or somebody (i.e. an artist or musician), and therefore I'm always already working in a space of friction. The essay is my preferred form, rather than fiction or poetry. I can't write fiction, or perhaps I can but I don't (not for many years at least) because I'm more interested in writing that engages with a set of given conditions. The present text is an obvious example, prompted by Pauline Oliveros's *Sonic Meditation XXI* with a duration imposed by myself at the outset: writing for a year, day by day. 195 days in, writing *this* has often been a pain in the ass, given the limits of time determined by everything else on my daily agenda (work, sleep, or otherwise), and given the structural imperative to keep moving according to the calendar, I'm certain some of this is pretentious, obsessive, arcane, indigestible, a shaggy dog story, and perhaps total crap. But given the predetermined structure and the continual growth of the thing, I have to just keep going, rather than reworking or even rereading. (Though I occasionally go back and reread passages or search for keywords to re-engage certain things.) Also, given the performative nature of the thing, what I might ambitiously call a kind of improvisation, I can't go back and restructure it or do it over. I'm way beyond the point of worrying whether it's good or not, and I know I'm the worst person to attempt such a judgment anyway. As a critic, I am usually resistant to the very idea of calling something "good" because it essentially kills conversation. "Good" or "bad" is rarely the point of art, so why should it be the point of criticism? Perhaps a year of rubbing up against the grit will produce a pearl or two. But will anyone even read it? (Neil Doshi sweetly said he would when I told him about it. So that's one. Ha.) Very few people are even aware I'm doing this "performance," which indeed is an intensely private one. (Writing is usually intensely private, at least it's always been that way for me.) Perhaps only Leslie is aware of its daily demands and how often it structures the rhythm of my day. Is it even for an audience? Maybe I'm just rehearsing, but for what exactly? Sometimes (usually?) the rehearsal is more energetic or meaningful than the official thing which one is rehearsing for—Bailey talks to several improvisers who confess they do their best work when no one else is listening. I can relate. I'm also reminded of one of my favorite quotes by Roland Barthes, from his eponymous 1975 book:

I delight continuously, endlessly, in writing as in perpetual production, in an unconditional dispersion, in an energy of seduction which no legal defense of the subject I fling upon the page can any longer halt. But in our mercantile society, one must end up with a work, an "*oeuvre*": one must construct, i.e., *complete*, a piece of merchandise. While I write, the writing is thereby at every moment flattened out, banalized, made guilty by the work to which it must eventually contribute.

Barthes wrote a lot of books—a lot of *important* books, to me and certainly to many—and I don't really think of them as *merch*. Likewise, Derek Bailey's recordings. I prefer to think of them as documents of "perpetual production." Documents provide an opportunity for deferred evaluation. For that, right now, I am grateful.

196

A residual reaction to reading Derek Bailey's *Improvisation* is a reconsideration of John Zorn's game piece *Cobra* (1984), which he discusses in an interview with Zorn for the book. (The two tangoed, or tangled, on numerous occasions.) *Cobra* uses an elaborate set of available rules and cues, based on war games, in order to structure a wide variety of group improvisations. A complete visual guide to these cues, along with a thorough description of the composition, can be found on the first CD version of it released by Hat Hut in 1991. (There are several versions of the Hat Hut/hatART recordings, which include a live performance from 1985 and a studio session from 1986. I don't know if all of them feature the same notes and other inserts. Mine includes a postcard with a drawing by Kiriko Kubo, who also drew the *kawaii*—cute!—artwork on the front and back cover.) Some of the *Cobra* recordings are hit-and-miss, which is probably to be expected given the highwire act of improvisation, and presumably risk compounds with the addition of each musician to the mix.

In my car, I've been listening to the 2002 version of *Cobra* released on Zorn's own Tzadik label, in part because Bailey appears on two tracks. It's quite masterful, given the number of quality musicians involved—most or all of whom are part of Zorn's circle and are highly skilled in the widest gamut of avant-garde performance styles, including improvisation. By 2002, many of these characters were already quite familiar with *Cobra* or the game pieces in general. Zorn is also the "prompter" here, akin to a conductor, which surely helps give the whole thing a kind of coherence. By 2002, he clearly knows how the composition works, who to pair or oppose, how to build tension, how to cut, and how to switch it up for maximum effect. Zorn's music has long been known for its hard cuts, in which the music can change on a dime. His Naked

City project is perhaps the best example, and it grew quite directly out of *Cobra*, *Locus Solus* (1983), and his other game pieces.

Cobra is probably more fun to watch than listen to, or to watch it helps elucidate how it's working, who's playing when, which cues are being delivered when, and so on. A *Cobra* rehearsal session is featured on the first episode of the 1992 television series *On the Edge: Improvisation in Music* based directly on Bailey's book and produced by Channel 4, a British free-to-air public service television network. I was fortunate to see a version performed at the Barrymore Theatre in Madison, Wisconsin on March 6, 1994. I still have a small ad for it, clipped out of a local newspaper (*The Isthmus* or possibly *The Onion* which was a local paper), now yellowed and stored in my Hat Hut *Cobra* CD jewel case. The group of musicians assembled, and arranged in a semi-circle on stage, was extraordinary: Chris Cochrane, Anthony Coleman, Erik Friedlander, Eyvind Kang, Zeena Parkins, Jim Pugliese, Marc Ribot, David Shea, David Slusser, David Weinstein, and William Winant, with Zorn prompting.

What I remember most is how much fun Zorn was having the whole time as prompter. Sometimes the musicians were clearly having fun too, though they all seemed quite serious and exceptionally focused on following the cues and responding with bespoke virtuosity, served up à la *minute*. It seemed exhausting, at least from where I was sitting. On stage, one was always either playing or anxiously awaiting the next cue. (I also remember the ticket price was quite reasonable, so I also wondered how much, or rather, little all those musicians earned to play this little gig, most nearly a thousand miles from home. For me, it was a lot cheaper than a trip to the Knitting Factory.)

But maybe all improvised music is as visual as it is aural, and especially group improvisation because communication between musicians is so crucial. At one point, Zorn began pointing at each musician inducing the briefest burst of creativity from this collection of individuals, and after a few trips around the horn, pointed to the audience to get us tangled in the performance, too, closing the circle.

197

Yesterday I went into one of Los Angeles's high temples of conspicuous consumption, also known as The Grove, and bought a pair of AirPods Pro from the Apple Store. It was a seamless $277 transaction. I always seem to have a minor existential crisis at shopping malls, and this has been the case since I was an undergrad or even earlier. I remember my mom took me to a mall in Madison, and I muttered, "Karl Marx would be rolling over in his grave right now," a week or two after first reading *The Communist Manifesto*. I can still be a drama queen about capitalism. But, I've been overdue for better personal listening technology for some time. The issue came to a head when my old-fashioned earbuds, still connected to my iPhone with a wire, kept abruptly coming unplugged with the slightest jostle, stopping the music. Very annoying, especially in the midst of listening to an epic jam while climbing a hill at Kenneth Hahn. I really should have invested in noise-canceling earbuds, or (ahem) AirPods, during the long stretch of quarantine where I was teaching on Zoom while my neighbor was (almost invariably) playing basketball. With the new AirPods Pro, I can easily switch between noise cancellation and transparency mode, which the Apple salesperson kindly explained. I immediately thought of Oliveros's mandala, and the shift from awareness (transparency) to attention (noise cancellation). I also considered (for the first time?) the term "shallow listening," as the obvious inverse of Deep Listening. I also considered (not for the first time) that I've so far spent surprisingly little time, in a text ostensibly about Oliveros, writing about the concept of Deep Listening—a branded term, not unlike like AirPods Pro—and its larger implications and influence. In fact, I tend to avoid the term when writing or talking about Oliveros, which is almost willfully perverse. (I've written about Deep Listening Band a lot, but not so much the concept or practice of Deep Listening.) It's a term I see used a lot, and not always in conjunction with Oliveros. So: I hereby promise to discuss Deep Listening, and its many uses and abuses, in coming days.

198

Today I've been listening to Lou Reed's *Metal Machine Music*, a double album released in 1975. It's a notorious album, controversial in its time, a commercial flop, pulled off the shelves by the record company three weeks after it first appeared; it was also widely panned by critics, even reviled. Strangely, it's the first time I'm listening to it, even though I've listened to the Velvet Underground since college, and I have owned a variety of Lou Reed's solo material. (*Transformer* has long been a favorite of mine.) I'm listening to *Metal Machine Music* on Spotify, which is somehow appropriate. ("Corporate Machine Music"?) It's obviously no longer 1975, and the album has had a bit of a critical reexamination if not total redemption, but it's never going to win over a large audience. I'm trying to keep some historical perspective, imagining a dedicated Lou Reed fan putting this on the record player in 1975 and expecting his usual brand of lightly transgressive rock and roll. Lou Reed is a poet, but there are no lyrics here. No verses, no choruses, no hooks, no licks, no melodies. Just "noise." Its primary materials seem to be feedback and tape manipulation, but it's actually quite active and varied. Relatively speaking, of course. There are also occasional squeals that sound like puppies or babies being tortured, though it could be the actual baby next door (screaming because it can hear me playing *Metal Machine Music*), or it could be magnetic tape being rewound very quickly. Whatever the case, it covers the sound of traffic outside the open window. It's one of those works where observers tend to say nothing is happening, when in fact *a lot* is happening if one is actually paying attention. (When I finally saw Warhol's *Sleep*, in all of its five-hour, twenty-minute glory, I was shocked by how active the camera and cutting were compared to the descriptions.) But despite "nothing happening," it is likely to send the many listeners running from the room, or (circa 1975) yanking the needle off the record. Some of the reviews of the album from the time are pretty funny. It's the kind of work that's off-putting and just pretentious enough to give critics a big, fat target. (The Wikipedia entry on the album is far more entertaining than the album.) It might now get some grudging respect. It's certainly a classic among those who appreciate or indulge in noise music, which is perhaps the ultimate crossover genre where one might find the converging cognoscenti of obscure and/or loathed examples from rock, jazz, classical, and "experimental." Of course, I am often digging happily in the Venn intersection of those circles. So it's weird I've never listened to this. I have Tony Conrad's box set and all of John Cale's early solo albums and whatever La Monte Young stuff I could get my hands on—all obvious and immediate precedents for this. But Lou Reed was a rock star, and therefore this experimental noise record was primarily taken as a kind of "fuck you" gesture, rather than as a work of art (even a failed one). Rock stars (or even art stars) are only allowed to wander so far beyond the familiar boundaries of their well-cultivated *terra firma*, lest they are deemed lost in the wilderness. Better, I suppose, to be an avant-garde kook at the outset and not have to suffer the indignity of expectations. Or, even better, to be an avant-garde kook and shock the onlookers by making a "pretty" or "catchy" album, rather than the other way around.

199

Dear Razan,

This note is terribly overdue. I've had a draft email started to you right after we met, and then I kind of became a puddle after graduation and after my show closed. I hope this finds you doing well in the "afterlife." Are you still in Los Angeles? Still working on your film?

As promised, so long ago, I wanted to share some music with you. Whatever I intended to share with you a few months ago has probably changed somewhat, though rest assured I am still in deep with Pauline Oliveros, with my research and listening. (Next week I'm going to Mills College to spend time with her papers.) You might have found some things on your own, but if not I always like to recommend her *Accordion & Voice* as a good starting place, which pares things down to the basics, featuring her favorite instrument and yours! The first *Deep Listening* album is also exquisite—it was recorded in an enormous underground cistern (hence the pun "deep listening") in Washington State, with collaborators Panaiotis (vocals and percussion) and Oliveros's college buddy Stuart Dempster on trombone and didjeridu, and . . . garden hose! The cistern has a natural echo of forty-five seconds, which structures their slowly evolving jams. In addition to the accordion, Oliveros also plays a conch shell and sings. The album led to the formation of Deep Listening Band and Oliveros's extensive use of that term. Because you are also interested in electronic music (I remember we discussed *Sisters with Transistors*, right?), I'd also like to point you toward Oliveros's early tape and electronic music. She was a pioneering figure (and token sister) in the San Francisco Tape Music Center in the 1960s. The *Reverberations* box set is an extraordinary document of this period (1961–1970). It's all decidedly "experimental" and pretty demanding. I especially like the "Bog" pieces from 1966–1967, which incorporate the Buchla synthesizer; she made these at Mills College shortly before taking a teaching post at UCSD. And then, if you're curious about how she eventually integrated electronics (with her so-called Expanded Instrument System) and the accordion, *The Roots of the Moment* or *Ghostdance* are both recommended.

On a different note, I know I also mentioned Don Cherry, whose music I've enjoyed for many years. Thankfully, more of it keeps getting unearthed. I've been really into *Organic Music Theatre: Festival de jazz de Chateauvallon* (1972), which was recently released by Blank Forms. *Organic Music Society* (1973), *Brown Rice* (1973), and *The Codona Trilogy* (1979/1981/1983) are all terrific, too—he was such an eager collaborator and kept expanding his circle, geographically and stylistically. This is really some of the first great "world music." In recent weeks I've been really into *Music/Sangam*, his collaboration with Latif Khan from 1979/1980.

Also in heavy rotation: Bitchin Bajas's *Switched on Ra*, a Sun Ra tribute album that is quite faithful to the original material, but at times recalls Kraftwerk, Cluster, Susan Ciani, Wendy Carlos (the album title is an obvious homage to the last of these) . . . All of Bitchin Bajas's stuff is great, despite their stupid name. I was thrilled they did a Sun Ra tribute album, and even more thrilled it's so good. I've also been digging *Vivification Exercises* by Ka Baird, anything by Sarah Davachi (she's prolific, but *Cantus, Descant* has been a favorite since quarantine), everything by Judith Hamann (who also writes great album notes!), and the new Kali Malone is really, really good.

I also wanted to plug my friend Lorenzo's Occasional Radio, which is always fun to listen to and a nice relief from the Spotify algorithms. I met Lorenzo in a little club in Torino where he was

DJing, and we had a lot of common musical interests. (He actually designed an album for Oliveros.) I've contributed five episodes to his site, but not recently, so they're buried pretty deep if you're curious. Probably better to just enjoy what's in reach!

I'd love to know what you're listening to, and what you've been working on, but—needless to say—at your leisure!

Warmest regards,

Michael

200

How do you demonstrate deep listening?

What is the difference between active and deep listening?

Is Deep Listening a type of listening?

What is the deepest level of listening?

Oh, the things people ask Google. When I do a search for "deep listening," the first thing that comes up isn't related to the person who (I think) coined or at least trademarked the term. The first item that pops up is from the Earl E. Bakken Center for Spirituality & Healing at the University of Minnesota. It defines Deep Listening as "a process of listening to learn. It requires the temporary suspension of judgment, and a willingness to receive new information—whether pleasant, unpleasant, or neutral." It goes on to define the principles of Deep Listening, as well as its benefits, and provides references for further reading, none of which includes Pauline Oliveros who wrote prolifically on the topic. The second entry is for a post by David Rome and Hope Martin, from 2010 on the website mindful.org. According to the bio at the end of the post, "Hope Martin has taught Deep Listening for ten years with David Rome. She has taught the Alexander Technique since 1987 and has a studio in New York City. She's a teacher in the Shambhala Buddhist tradition." Again, no mention of Oliveros.

The third entry is, thankfully, for the Deep Listening Institute (DLI), which was founded by Pauline Oliveros and is now overseen by her partner IONE. The splash page, crowned by the question "HOW MANY SOUNDS CAN YOU HEAR ALL AT ONCE?" and the familiar Deep Listening spiral logo, is a lovable hodgepodge, a virtual information kiosk with a memorial tribute to its founding mother and a link to the DLI store (where you can score all the hot CDs I've been listening to in my Scion) among other connections. There is no real description or definition of Deep Listening—one has to veer off to the Center for Deep Listening at Rensselaer for that, for which one will also be rewarded with a nicely designed website with some great pictures of its founder.

One measure of the influence of Deep Listening or at least the term is its relative pervasiveness, its ability to be scattered like seeds. It's an easily graspable concept with a catchy name (even more than *Sonic Meditations* before it), even if the practice in question is decidedly more difficult to achieve or sustain. Undoubtedly and admittedly, Oliveros borrowed many of its key concepts from Buddhism and other Eastern spiritual practices. Her book *Deep Listening: A Composer's Sound Practice* (2005) is the clearest delineation of those sympathies and appropriations. (It follows closely from her earlier lecture "MMM: Meditation/Mandala/Music," which is included in *Software for People*.) Needless to say, Eastern spiritual practices have become a huge industry, and the appearance of "deep listening" in this context only adds to my sense of aversion. But I can relate with Oliveros's investment in a secular practice of listening, or at least not letting the trappings of spirituality get in the way of the personal and political possibilities of it. (This is likewise true for the *Sonic Meditations*.) For Oliveros, Deep Listening is a pedagogy (with its own certificate program), but more importantly it's also a practice, one that manages to dissolve the presumed boundary between life and art. "For me," Oliveros observed, "Deep Listening is a lifelong practice." The very notion of such a sustained practice, which by all accounts she genuinely realized, seems strangely at odds with a disposable culture that has prioritized the instant over all other measurements of time. This is the appeal of Deep Listening, as Oliveros defined it, but also, when in the wrong hands, its potential as a shallow marketing term.

201

Only the performer knows that she is performing.

Throughout the semester, these pieces are done in connection with meditations. The performances are a series of examples.

All encounters are to be considered as performances. Principles prevail. What are those principles? What are the examples?

1. Always be moving toward a goal. Always be actually doing something. Never be aimless.
2. Always speak your native language (determine what that is).
3. Always observe your state of mind behind what you do or say.

Pauline Oliveros
"A Series of Mini Pieces"
(May 15, 1992, San Diego)

"Doing Life, consciously, was a compelling notion for me. When you do life consciously, however, life becomes pretty strange," Allan Kaprow notes in his 1979 essay "Performing Life," which also happens to be the name of one of the recurring seminars I teach at CalArts. Kaprow's essay and his notion of "performing life" follows a gradual transition from his early influential Happenings, which were scripted and relatively elaborate, to his pared-down Actions, which were often written for two people, to an understanding of performance that was completely privatized and eschewed the idea of an audience. "The Happenings were not as lifelike as I had supposed they might be. But I learned something about life and 'life.'"

I mention Kaprow because I cannot think of Deep Listening, or at least Oliveros's version of it, without thinking of Kaprow's notion of Performing Life. Both, for me, bring with them a question of intentionality and specifically doing something that's necessary or involuntary with intentionality. One is performing life when they are aware they are doing so; one is deep listening when one is conscious of the act of listening. (Oliveros: "Only the performer knows that she is performing.") Kaprow and Oliveros both taught at UCSD. Oliveros arrived from Mills in 1967; Kaprow arrived from CalArts in 1974. Prior to Kaprow's arrival at UCSD, the two appeared in a 1972 video "about artists, their work, and thoughts; in an epicurean setting" (per Alice Dusapin), titled *A.T.E.*, produced by Wolfgang Stoerchle and Daniel Lentz who also appear in the video along with Emmett Williams, Clare Loeb, and Helene Winer. In 1977 under the auspices of UCSD's Center for Music Experiment, Oliveros initiated a series of performance programs called *What's Cooking?* that brought together faculty from the university's music and art departments, and beyond. Oliveros and Kaprow were participants, as well as Dick Higgins, Eleanor Antin, Charlie Morrow, Carolee Schneemann, Paul McCarthy, Nancy Buchanan, and Linda Montano, among many others from the (often overlapping) fields of art, music, and poetry.

In her 1981 book *Art in Everyday Life*, Linda Montano defines the term "living art," a contractual performance practice for an individual, pair, or group:

> Living art is any work play which artists/nonartists are willing to perform together or alone. The rules can be determined by the needs of the participants. For example they may explore silence, fasting, psychic discoveries, eating, basketball, etc. in the search for new styles of relating. LIVING ART becomes LIVING ART when the time in activities which the artist perform are intended to be art. The announcement may be public or private.

It is important to consider the concept of Deep Listening in relation to Living Art and Performing Life. Montano and Oliveros converged in 1975, during Montano's performance *Three*

Day Blindfold at the Woman's Building in Los Angeles. Oliveros, a complete stranger to Montano, became her guide for those three days. They soon became lovers and collaborators—partners in art and life. How fitting that they would meet in a performance that prioritizes listening over seeing. (Kaprow: "A new art/life genre therefore came about, reflecting equally the artificial aspects of everyday life and the lifelike qualities of created art . . . I also became aware that artworks of any kind could be autobiographical and prophetic.")

Shortly after their merger at the Woman's Building, Oliveros and Montano traveled to the Mojave together in Oliveros's VW van and enacted what Montano would title *Living Art: A Complex Theory Which States That Life Can Be Art (Living with Pauline Oliveros in the Desert for Ten Days).*

ART Pauline Oliveros and I lived in the desert for ten days and agreed that everything we did would be considered art. We documented the event.

LIFE Living art was incredibly exhilarating . . . I thought that the life/art transference was finally made because I began interacting more truthfully and spontaneously. I called each day art and not life.

I was happy and making art at the same time.

As I've noted previously, the influence of Oliveros and Montano on one another is enormous. I believe it is necessary to consider Deep Listening at a form of Living Art, one that in Oliveros's case was all-pervasive, shaping not only her work but her *understanding* of her work as a continuous practice. My understanding of Deep Listening is a synthetic concept, arrived at (circa 1990) gradually and building upon everything that came before it. So, it is worth noting that Oliveros would eventually define Deep Listening in this sense, going so far as to backdate the concept to include the *Sonic Mediations* composed in the early 1970s.

202

Leslie sometimes wonders aloud how I can listen to what I listen to when I'm driving. *Traffic in Los Angeles is crazy enough, do you really need to listen to [pick a berserk free jazz saxophonist] on top of it?* (I'm paraphrasing.) But for me, it's often better to steer into the skid. It can actually make the traffic seem less crazy when the music is even more nuts. I have to admit I don't always realize I'm listening to something crazy, in the car or otherwise, given my highly developed tolerance for noise. It helps to have someone point it out and, if I'm feeling diplomatic, I recalibrate for the situation. Today I was driving to Pasadena while listening to a CD compilation of Los Angeles Free Music Society (LAFMS), *Unboxed* (1999), a kind of "greatest hits" collection culled from their box set *The Lowest Form of Music* released by the Cortical Foundation in 1996. I was driving alone, but at some point while traversing the thicket it occurred to me this might not be the best music to play when passengers are in the car. (Duly noted for future reference.) The LAFMS, founded by Joe and Rick Potts and Chip Chapman in 1973, is both a band and an umbrella for a loose and convoluted confederation of offshoots and side hustles of and by its various members and co-conspirators: Le Forte Four, Doo-Dooettes, C.V. Massage, Smegma, Extended Organ, and Seldom Melodic Ensemble among them. Local weirdos all. Most of what's on the compilation is early LAFMS, often structured around tape collage and a refusal of any and all expectation of "musicality," let alone tasteful or "good" musicality, is at once "ahead of its time" and often deliriously (and self-consciously) dumb and abject. Literally loopy. The same could be said of the many offshoots and side hustles in the years since. It's music that has never been in fashion and will likely never be palatable to a large audience. As far as driving music goes, it's nearly equal to the perpetually bonkers nature of the Los Angeles freeways and therefore a perfectly fitting soundtrack for today's solo expedition.

203

What constitutes your musical universe?

I'm easily distracted. I'm sure I'm not alone. I don't think I have (or have ever had) ADHD—I once took an Adderall out of curiosity and decided it was the wrong drug for me, even if it made for an exceptionally productive afternoon. (If you don't have ADHD Adderall works like speed.) But can we agree there are different kinds or levels of distraction? The present text is evidence of my ability to focus on a long-term or protracted project (despite many other demands and sometimes against all odds), but also evidence of my capacity for distraction, digression, drift. I often have a loose plan for what I'll be writing about on a given day that can easily change if I don't write first thing in the morning. There are many topics I have intended to write about but don't get to because I get involved in something else. Sometimes I return to them; often I don't. There is also so much music I listen to that I never mention here. As with my daily log, no matter how many data sets I tracked, there is always plenty more I didn't—stuff that slips through the cracks, whether inadvertently or by design. I couldn't begin to tell you all of the things I listened to today, in the car, in the park, at home. Or could I? Spotify could surely tell you some of it. At times I let my agency give way to the creative decision making of their bots. And, less invested in the process, I am often listening without paying attention. (I'm also doing a dozen other things like making passata di pomodoro with the abundance of Genovese tomatoes from the garden, washing dishes, doing laundry, packing for my trip to Mills, pecking away at a letter of recommendation, checking and avoiding email, closing tabs on my browser, writing this, and so on.) So, call it Shallow Listening. Or Ambivalent Listening. Or Distracted Listening. At the moment I am Haphazardly Listening to a "radio" program based around Nala Sinephro's (lovely but subtle) album *Space 1.8* (2021) and recognize roughly half of the music that passes through my ears. A few heretofore unknown things snare my less divided attention: a song from Branko Mataja's *Over Fields and Mountains* (released 2022), a song from Amaro Freitas's album *Sankofa* (2021). I "heart" these and add them to my bottomless Spotify library, optimistically, while the bots take notes on my behalf.

204

Listening to a pair of late Oliveros albums that I haven't listened to recently, both featuring IONE, while preparing for my visit to Mills College and while trying to ignore my neighbor's house music—a playlist:

Pauline Oliveros and Musique Nouvelles
Four Meditations / Sound Geometries
(A: *Four Meditations for Orchestra* [1991–1997]. B: *Sound Geometries for Chamber Orchestra, Expanded Instrument System and 5.1 Surround Sound System* [2003]: *I. Contemplative: Into the Dreaming; II. Travelling By Any Means: Walking, Running, Floating, Swimming, Flying; III. Arriving Anywhere, Nowhere, Somewhere*)
Sub Rosa, 2016

Pauline Oliveros and IONE
Water Above Sky Below Now
Morphine Records, 2015

205

Michael Henderson died at seventy-one. He lent his funky brand of electric bass to Miles Davis in the early 1970s, which is why I know about him, but he also played with Stevie Wonder, Aretha Franklin, Marvin Gaye, and the Temptations among many others. And then in the late 70s, he went on to have a successful pop/funk/soul career as a singer with sex appeal. (See, for example, his electric-blue thong on the cover for his winkingly titled 1981 album *Slingshot*.) His single "Take Me I'm Yours" reached #3 on the *Billboard* R&B chart in 1978. I first encountered his insistent pulse on Miles Davis's *Agharta* (1975), that divisive masterpiece which was such an important gateway drug for me. He first played on Davis's *A Tribute to Jack Johnson* in 1970. He's a driving force in that period of Miles Davis, holding together something often nebulous and evolving. The story of how he joined Davis's band at the delicate age of nineteen or so is infamous. As Henderson recalled, "I was playing a gig in New York with Stevie Wonder. Miles was in the audience. After the show Miles walked backstage and told Stevie in a raspy voice, 'I'm taking your fucking bass player.'" And he did. This morning, I am listening to *Get Up with It*, Davis's double album from 1974, with Henderson dropping the anchor and holding the whole thing in place.

206

Yesterday I flew to Oakland and immediately headed to BAMPFA (Berkeley Art Museum and Pacific Film Archive) to see a beautiful and reliably strange show by my friend Candice Lin and *by Alison Knowles: A Retrospective (1960–2022)* (2022–2023). Candice's exhibition, titled *Seeping, Rotting, Resting, Weeping* (2022), was first shown at the Walker and came together during the pandemic. I was privy to seeing much of the installation-in-progress in her studio and her backyard. I took off my shoes to enter the cat shrine, and I was invited to fondle two carved stone table sculptures, as well as a sumptuous artist book full of Candice's madcap drawings, indigo dye tests, COVID journaling, and an abundance of feline fantasy. *by Alison Knowles* held similar tactile pleasures—and frustrations. Most of the show was "look but don't touch," though one could run their hand ("gently") through a big vat of dry garbanzo beans. One young person, who misheard the security guard, stepped into the beans barefooted. The guard gently encouraged the stepper to step out. I'm not a "viewer" who is often tempted to touch things in galleries or museums—I take a few more liberties during studio visits—but I would have enjoyed playing with Knowles's Bean Turners, big noisemakers made of hardened flax paper shells with a number of beans inside. Now they are sculptures, meant for looking, not listening. But the tactile prohibitions (perfectly understandable for irreplaceable objects) were supplanted by the racket of the show, from video performances, some with headphones, and punctuated by the rather loud and semi-regular plotting of the algorithmic poem *A House of Dust* on a vintage Oki Microline 280 dot matrix printer in the corner of the first gallery. *A House of Dust* was a collaboration with James Tenney, realized at CalArts in its first years, resulting in the computer-generated poem and an organic, cave-like structure situated at the edge of the campus that served as a site for numerous Fluxus-oriented events. Among many other delights, I was also happy to see *Rice and Beans* (c. 1995), a tapestry of sorts with string, red lentils, and flax on muslin. It is, I believe, the score she made for Charles Curtis, for a solo cello performance that I once heard (and saw) him play at Marcia Hafif's memorial in New York in 2018. After seeing the score, I can only say his interpretation is quite brilliant. It's a score that definitely demands interpretation!

207

The Mills campus was mostly deserted when I arrived by Uber. It can be startling to be reminded that small colleges, including the one I teach at, become ghost towns in the summer. Mills was recently taken over by Northeastern University, which saved it from total collapse, though not without new anxieties about what its new conjoined future would hold. So, the absence of humans felt particularly eerie. The landscaper operating the weed wacker was an affirming sign of life, even as his power tool shredded into the tranquility. I arrived almost two hours before the Olin Library opened, so I wandered the campus taking in the architecture, with its charming variety of historical styles, and the landscape with its towering groves of redwood (or sequoia, I never know) and eucalyptus. Very Californian. The scent of eucalyptus was pervasive and perfectly paired with the shower gel from my hotel. Everything felt tidy but shaggy at the same time. I couldn't help but focus my listening. Beyond and between the weed wacking this was a hushed environment, secreted from the urban context beyond. A few cars drove around; there was a golf cart driven by campus security. Surprisingly, there were little children playing, apparently in a summer school program of some kind. But there were more birds than humans, and I followed the development of their networked communication system as I circled the campus, stopping for a long stretch on a well shaded park bench. My first stop was the Music Building, and next to it I found the adjacent bog that inspired Oliveros's numerous compositions using the original Buchla synthesizer. For whatever reason, I didn't really notice this the first time I visited the campus. I looked up to the window to the room I imagined her in, based on her own description, expanding her attention to the bog below, even as she negotiated the intricate tape delay system she had devised in the electronic music studio.

I was deeply impressed by the sounds from the frog pond outside the studio window at Mills. I loved the accompaniment as I worked on my pieces. Though I never recorded the frogs I was of course influenced by their music. Since that time many other composers have also been influenced by sounds from the pond.

Currently the bog is drained, dry, silent. Perhaps it, too, is on summer break. (I found two vending machines that were likewise emptied and dormant). At first (or, really, second) glance, it's hard to imagine this as a mecca for the development of electronic music, but I appreciate that perceptual discrepancy. At 1 p.m. I entered the Olin Library and went immediately to Special Collections in the Elinor Raas Heller Rare Book Room. Rebecca Leung was ready for me. She got me updated in their system and brought Box 9 of the Pauline Oliveros Papers to the table I had claimed as my own, not that there was any competition to be had. I chose a different table than the one I had used nearly seven years ago. For some reason I picked the one next to the portable air purifier—surely a COVID-era addition. I embraced the relentless hum of the thing as my soundtrack. I could also hear the weed wacker in the distance through the windows, cutting into the calm, but eventually that faded and the air purifier did too, as I gave my attention over fully to looking.

If my first encounter with the Oliveros Papers in October 2015 was a quick contour drawing, then this visit is all about intricate shading. The iPhone also allows me to ingest relatively quickly for future delectation, but I'm also giving myself time to luxuriate in details. The five folders devoted to *Sonic Meditations* hold many gems, including hand-written (and drawn) drafts of the text scores. It also offers some clues to the proliferation of the *Meditations*, which took place in firsthand encounters at colleges and universities, the Metropolitan Community Church of San Diego, and Merce Cunningham's dance studio, among other venues, and in the dissemination of the scores in journals and by other means.

These five folders provide overwhelming evidence of the palpable excitement around this body of work in and between the fields of contemporary music and art. As early as July 9, 1971, Stanley Lunetta, editor of the journal *Source: Music of the Avant-Garde* (for which Oliveros had written "Some Sonic Observations" in 1967), sent Oliveros a brief but emphatic inquiry, requesting the *Sonic Meditations* for an issue of the magazine guest edited by Alvin Lucier:

Dear Pauline,

Just got a letter from Alvin Lucier and he really wants to use SONIC MEDITATIONS. Send the stuff as soon as possible. (Well as soon as it is ready/within a month?) He seems to feel it is a very important part of the issue.

On March 27, 1974, composer and pianist Yūji Takahashi writes to Oliveros: "Dear Pauline, I would like to have your *Sonic Meditation* [*sic*] for my magazine *tranSonic* #3—special issue on learning (out in the end of June). Mieko Shiomi will translate the version in *Something Else Yearbook*." Having seen it in *Source*, he was also urgent: "Could you send some as soon as possible?" In a 1975 letter to Ms. Oliveros, Hildegard Westerkamp of the World Soundstage Project at Simon Fraser University, wrote, "I am interested in your *Sonic Meditations*. Is it possible to get a copy from you? During my stay in San Francisco I heard a lot about you and your work, and I am now curious to hear and learn more. Much of it seems to touch on areas I am concerned with."

On January 28, 1974, the Los Angeles-based Womanspace Exhibition Committee—Carol Kerlan with Suzanne Lacy, Susan Mogul, Laurel Click, and Meg Harlam—reached out to Oliveros, presumably with interest in *Sonic Meditations*. After articulating the mission of the organization, they make their request. It's worthy citing at length:

Womanspace was formed to provide women artists with a space of their own. In this space women have found a place to exhibit their art, meet and communicate with each other, and develop self-confidence in themselves as artists and women. Shows are chosen by a rotating exhibition committee which is selected from the membership. A new show is mounted each month, and an evening program of discussions, lectures, performances, and films is planned by the committee around the theme of the exhibition.

We have proposed a show which will exhibit documentation of women's performance art. We are also planning a month of performances, activities, and events which will be documented as they are presented. The committee sees this exhibit as a landmark in historical terms as this is the first extensive show of women's work of this nature. The exhibit will serve to educate the public on this often obscured area and provide an enriched context for performing artists. The rationale for documentation is to begin to build an archive of work in this genre. This will permit us to begin to formulate definitions of performance, an underestimated art form, to explore interrelationships between the work, and to make women's contributions in this field manifest.

We would like written statements of work, scripts, photographs, preferably 8x10's or llx14's, slides, video tapes, films, and actual objects used in performance if feasible. Non-returnable entries (photo, slides, statements, and scripts) would be kept on file at Womanspace a beginning to a permanent documentation collection.

We would also like proposals for possible performances, performance sketches, films, video, happening, and art history lectures in this field if you would like to participate in the month's activities. You may also wish to come and discuss your work.

The message of the typed letter is prescient in its understanding of the way in which many contemporary women artists were currently working, in performance and other ephemeral forms, and the value in preserving this "stuff" when there was little to no commercial or museological interest in it, which is still generally the case. That Ms. Oliveros received the invite also points to the immediate significance of the *Sonic Meditations* work in the context of the field of ("visual") art. It marks an important moment in the development of her "crossover" appeal. It's also worth noting Oliveros became extremely dedicated to the task of reproducing and distributing the *Sonic Meditations*, as well as her other scores. The *Sonic Meditations* folders reveal many copies of the scores, often painstakingly rewritten by hand. Subtle alterations happened but it's more likely it was a way of committing them to memory. The papers also reveal constant reiteration and preparation—signs of a serious composer, performer, and educator (a triumvirate self-description on one later letterhead).

I found one letter in the *Sonic Meditations* files particularly touching, in part because of its peculiar, spidery, and spacious handwriting that crosses diagonally across three horizontal sheets of paper. It is from poet and artist Linda Smukler (now dba Samuel Ace), though Oliveros notes the name as "LINDA SMULLER / 45 E. BROADWAY / NYC 10002" in her own rounded, all-caps handwriting at the top of the first page. There is no greeting, or salutation, but what the letter lacks in formality, it more than makes up for in raw affirmation:

> I was a part of Tuning Meditations in New York on Teus night . The work moved me deeply. It was so clearly to the point · of imagginning being and around the end of the things , I have not been able to work since . My own work seems so pale in the light of such clarity . If ever we should meet , which I hope might happen some day , my name is Linda Smukler. I have in the last months begun some work down at Princeton through the generosity of Jim Randall. I am in the midst of realizing some works with the aid of the computer there . I was just moved to write to thank you for showing me some light .
>
> Lin

209

Funny that it took me three days to notice the bellows in the painting hanging in the Elinor Raas Heller Rare Book Room. In the dark (chiaroscuro, I guess) oil on canvas, a girl wearing a ruff hovers over a set of bellows, perhaps belonging to a concertina. The details get lost in the shadows. When I ask the Rebecca the librarian about it, she sends me an informative email indicating the painting is by Joseph Raphael—a fateful name for a painter—a Bay Area artist who spanned nineteenth and twentieth centuries and, as I observed in my quick Google search, seems to have made a lot of paintings of innocent girls. Strange this historic women's college would have so much art by dudes on display, including all of the outdoor sculptures I've identified. But when the "accordion painting" finally nabs my attention during a brief intermission from having my head buried in the Oliveros Papers, I take it as an auspicious sign. I think I might have laughed out loud.

On Monday, after wrapping up at the library, I went to Old Weang Ping, a delightful and delicious mom-and-pop Thai restaurant near Mills. There, amid the abundant, eccentric, colorful decor, were two accordions. One was on a stand next to a bottle of hand sanitizer and toggled on the "bassoon" setting. The other was prominently perched under the front counter, next to a mixer and equalizer. There was a microphone, too, and I immediately thought about the Expanded Instrument System diagrams I had just been perusing an hour or so earlier. I likewise took the accordions as an auspicious sign. I overheard a customer asking the woman running the restaurant about it, and apparently her father plays. For better or worse, he's also the cook, so he's usually too busy to entertain.

210

Even more auspicious signs were quietly on display when I finally found my way into the Music Building. On my previous attempt, all the doors were locked, but yesterday one of the doors at the ornate front entrance was open, so I wandered in. In the distance I could hear a rhythmic chime, perhaps a marimba? I never found the source, but it might explain why the door was open. As I've already noted, the Mills campus is a ghost town, but I don't really believe in ghosts. At least not the literal kind. But, I'm certainly no stranger to metaphorical hauntings. Speaking of which, I found the Center for Contemporary Music, which is essentially a wing of the building, and went down a hall, past tiny faculty and staff offices and practice rooms. I've been taking note of the (mostly, but not quite empty) bulletin boards around the campus, a habit I picked up from Fiona Connor, who has remade many "community notice boards" with loving exactitude. (I've sent her a few pictures of my finds, including the bamboo-framed board in the entrance of Old Weang Ping.) The bulletin boards in the Music Building seem to exist out of time, somehow, with fliers or yellowed newspaper clippings for things that happened months or even years ago. A few notices revealed the pervasive anxiety at Mills, with its institutional future uncertain. "We Want Answers Now!" read one small pink flier for a Students, Faculty & Staff Solidarity Rally from May. I also observed little embellishments of various door placards: one (Room 109) noting, "BEETHOVEN WAS QUEER," an apparent reference to the *Postcard Theatre* by Oliveros and Alison Knowles; another (Room 233) featured a little black-and-white picture of Robert Ashley with the phrase "LONG LIVE THE AVANT-GARDE!" layered atop. Indeed. At the end of the hall on the second floor, I arrived at the *sanctum sanctorum*, The Pauline Oliveros Room:

Named in honor of a distinguished
composer, feminist, humanitarian, and
beloved member of the Mills Community

Doctor of Music, honoris causa
2004

Darius Milhaud Professor of Composition
from 1996 to 2001

Distinguished Visiting Composer
in 1985 and from 2002

Director of the Mills Tape Music Center
from 1966 to 1967

This engraved brass plaque was situated next to Room 234, the Center for Contemporary Music Recording Studio, and near Room 238, the Hybrid Studio. I suspect she created many of her tape and synth works in one or both of these studios when she directed the Tape Music Center. The hallway outside the studios was cluttered with an old leather sofa, a well-used wooden table with boxes piled below, an empty coat rack, a Shark vacuum cleaner. Bless this mess. Between the rooms, there was another bulletin board, prominently featuring a color production still of Oliveros gussied up in lady drag in Ashley's *Music with Roots in the Aether* (1975–1976), taken by Patricia Kelley. In (and out of) character, wearing a blonde wig and a leopard-skin blouse, with an extravagant bouquet as a backdrop, she is beaming her biggest smile. Below the picture is a full 8.5 x 11-inch printout of Question 40, the very last of Oliveros's "Listening Questions," in *Deep Listening: A Composer's Sound Practice*:

What sound would you like whispered in your ear?

Well?

211

Staying on it, or: Catching up with my Spotify library, the day after returning from Mills, and listening to anyone besides Pauline Oliveros (just kidding, but really)—a playlist:

Mary Lou Williams
Nice Jazz 1978
Black and Blue, 2016

Mary Lou Williams & Cecil Taylor
Embraced
Pablo Live, 1978

Julius Eastman / Sō Percussion, MEDIAQUEER, Adam Tendler, Alex Sopp, Beth Meyers, Shelley Washington, Greg Mcmurray
Stay On It
Sō Percussion Editions, 2021

Julius Eastman / Wild Up
Julius Eastman Vol. 2: Joy Boy
New Amsterdam Records, 2022

Cheri Knight
American Rituals
Freedom to Spend, 2022

212

The full promise of my AirPods Pro was realized in the Oakland airport, while waiting for my flight back to Los Angeles. I was listening to a recording of *Teach Yourself to Fly*, with Oliveros and Stuart Dempster from April 11, 1971. I couldn't hear a thing beyond the walla walla surrounding me. Other versions of *Teach Yourself to Fly* take time to get started, even longer to get cooking. They begin with breathing and an observation of the breathing before sound is introduced:

Any number of persons sit in a circle facing the center. Illuminate the space with dim blue light. Begin by simply observing your own breathing. Always be an observer. Gradually allow your breathing to become audible. Then gradually introduce your voice. Allow your vocal cords to vibrate in any mode which occurs naturally. Allow the intensity to increase very slowly. Continue as long as possible naturally, and until all others are quiet, always observing your own breath cycle.

Variation: Translate voice to an instrument.

After six or seven minutes, I turned up the volume, but with no discernable change. Then I switched my AirPods setting from transparency to noise cancellation, and the surrounding din almost completely vanished. I could finally hear Dempster (on didjeridu) and Oliveros (voice) vibrating sympathetically. I switched back and forth a few times, almost in disbelief of the sheer chatter and ambient noise in the surrounding environment. And then I would return to the concerted effort of Dempster and Oliveros, flying. The experience was a tidy demonstration of Oliveros's mandala, and the relationship between awareness and attention.

On the plane I took a window seat just above one of the engines. Again, I switched between transparency (awareness) and noise cancellation (attention). When the theatrical flight attendant came over the plane's speakers, I yielded to his groan-worthy paronomasia, sufficiently amused. He earned some chuckles from his captive audience; only his co-workers know how many times he's done this act. I also observed a kind of Robert Ashley sing-song quality to his patter, specifically reminding me of his vocal performance on Éliane Radigue's *Mila's Journey Inspired by a Dream* (1987). Discreetly, I made a 20-second recording on my phone. And then he was done, the lights went out, I switched back to noise cancellation and resumed Flying while staring out the window.

213

My final day with the Oliveros Papers was a bit of a whirlwind: too much to look at and listen to, too little time. But in some twenty hours, over five days, I uncovered a lot of useful stuff, even if it will take me daysweeksmonthsyears to sort through all of it. On the last day, two folders of correspondence proved particularly revelatory. Tonight, I'll address a folder labeled "Nonesuch Records" from 1971. I was curious about it in part because I wasn't aware of Oliveros recording for Nonesuch in the 1970s, or ever. First, the vintage Nonesuch letterhead is really special, from the eccentric folksy/futurist typography with a magenta logo with the big lowercase "n" and "nonesuch" blind debossed near the top. The folder revealed four letters from Teresa Sterne (director of Nonesuch from 1965 to 1979), written between January 21 and May 17. (There are no "carbon copies" or drafts of Oliveros's replies; one wishes there were.) In four short months, the one-sided conversation centers around a potential record of Oliveros's *Teach Yourself to Fly*, perhaps with *Theater Piece* on the other side. Stuart Dempster had brought Oliveros's music to Sterne's attention, and Sterne's initial tone is friendly and enthusiastic, with a faint whiff of caution. There is a clear sense that they are on track to make a record, provisionally planned for early 1972. But the plan is derailed when Sterne receives a demo recording from Dempster—a twenty-minute version of the first *Sonic Meditation* he performed with Oliveros. One can only guess what Sterne was expecting, but clearly this slow developing duet wasn't it. By 1970, Nonesuch has begun slowly transitioning from a fairly conventional classical label (with releases by Bach, Beethoven, Brahms, Hayden, Handel, and so on) to a growing interest in world music and new music, with releases by Stockhausen, Cage, Crumb, Foss, and so on. Closest to home, Nonesuch released Tape Music Center colleague Morton Subotnick's *Silver Apples of the Moon* (1967), with what would prove to be a highly influential electronic music release. But *Teach Yourself to Fly* and Oliveros's *Sonic Meditations* in general, were like none of the above.

There are multiple recordings of *Teach Yourself to Fly* from the early 1970s, several including Dempster, and at least one by the ♀ Ensemble. Oliveros performs on all of them, usually with vocals. Ironically, the twenty-minute version, with voice and didjeridu, feels rushed, as if there is a specific point of making it fit one side of an LP. There are other versions twice as long, and they truly come into being at their own pace, almost as if time ceases to exist. In the final analysis, Sterne writes,

> At this point, I must unhappily report that after a good deal of consideration we feel that *Teach Yourself* will not be well served by the record medium, partly because its effectiveness calls for a listening environment that simply cannot be presumed among the general record audience. For this principal reason, we believe that it is not to its advantage to issue the work on the album we had in mind. As we are aware that *TYTF* is strongly representative of your creative directions at this time, I honestly do not feel it wise or fair to suggest another piece as substitute for it in this context. The goal of our commission series is indeed to present a composer's work (in the large sense) at a stage where it can *best* be transmitted via the record medium. In the present instance, I submit that the shape and substance of *Teach Yourself to Fly* will *not* be well reflected in record form.

Well, ouch. I've often wondered why there is so little recorded output from Oliveros in the 1970s—really, there's almost nothing. I naïvely assumed this was her choice, that she was focused on the intimate, interpersonal aspects—both pedagogical and performative—of the *Sonic Meditations*, and was interested in how they circulated in parallel to the composer's travel itinerary, or they were easily distributed as text scores. In my earlier research focused on the remarkable run of electronic recordings in 1966 and 1967, Oliveros was burned out on the recording studio: "For some reason, I'm not interested in going into a studio anymore, I'm not sure why. I guess I prefer the contact of nice warm bodies to the cold isolation of the studio."

But the correspondence with Nonesuch makes me think Oliveros was *actively* invested in putting records in the world—and who, teaching in the Music Department of a tenure-track university system, wouldn't be? So, she was likely discouraged by the Nonesuch experience, and wouldn't release a solo record until *Accordion & Voice* on Lovely Music in 1982. [I am coming back to this after reviewing Oliveros's early discography and re-remembering that her "*Outline for Flute, Percussion, and String Bass* (An Improvisation Chart)" was included on a 1970 Nonesuch anthology titled *The Contemporary Contrabass*, alongside Cage and Ben Johnston, with all performances featuring Bertram Turetzky on double bass. This does little to diminish the disappointment of not getting a bigger, solo opportunity with Nonesuch. She never appeared on the label again.] I also get a sense (here and elsewhere) of hard lessons learned, with Oliveros increasingly taking business matters into her own hands: starting her own record label, her own academy, and so on. Deep Listening is, among many other things, the culmination of these entrepreneurial endeavors.

I am not entirely certain of what Sterne actually means when she writes, "its effectiveness calls for a listening environment that simply cannot be presumed among the general record audience." That the Nonesuch audience won't have the right audio equipment? That it is better heard in a live setting? I presume the latter but can only speculate. What fascinates me, with the remarkable benefit of hindsight, is how this dismissal also sets the stage for Deep Listening Band—Oliveros and Dempster's most significant and lasting collaboration—with its foregrounded investment in the listening environment. By my count, Deep Listening Band has (so far) released fourteen albums since 1989, on labels including New Albion, Deep Listening, Mode, Important Records, and Taiga—and none on Nonesuch.

214

6. Do you listen for sound in your dreams? What do you hear? How does it affect you?

I rarely remember my dreams, or if I do, I don't remember much about them. But for the past few nights I have been trying to pay attention to sound in my dreams. Last night I had a dream where I was talking to Stuart Dempster. Other people were there, but I don't remember who. And I don't remember what we talked about. Probably Deep Listening Band. (In waking life, I have plenty of questions for Stu, and even more so after visiting Oliveros's papers. I should finally reach out.) In my dream, I had a strong sense we were in Seattle, which makes sense, though there were no identifiable landmarks. And I hazily remember we were in or around a car or van, in a parking lot what seemed to be a garden supply store. Presumably we were there to take a look at (listen to) their garden hose selection. Dempster looked younger than he does now—I've recently been looking at many pictures of him over the years, including a baby picture. He's one of those people that looked like an old guy when he was young, and then looked more and more boyish as he got older. I found some nice shots of him in the April 2006 issue of *International Trombone Association Journal*. He's on the cover, sitting cross-legged on a Persian rug, with (of course) his trombone, and there's a lengthy article ("on the eve of his seventieth birthday") with great pull quotes inside, titled "Sedimental Journey." There's a great black-and-white shot of him, looking like a beat poet in black framed glasses as he played Berio's *Sequenza V* in 1968. The article discusses Focal Task Specific Dystonia: "In Stuart's case, as is typical of trombone players, this manifested as a quivering embouchure among other symptoms." I also learned a little more about his therapeutic *Sound Massage Parlor*, circa 1986, including a few of the titles:

"Acuhosery," "Aura Fluff," "Didjeriatsu." (Do recordings of these exist?) Trombone magazines are strange, though this is the only one I've looked at. Inevitably, I found an accordion magazine or two, too, digging through the Oliveros Papers.

215

I've been listening to Roger Reynolds in the past few days—primarily the compilation *All Known, All White* (2002), which incorporates both tracks ("Traces" and "Ping") from his 1971 LP *Electronic/Instrumental Music* along with the composition *. . . the serpent-snapping eye*, which appeared on a 1984 anthology of works by three composers. I've never paid much attention to Reynolds; I knew his name, but not his music. He is a Pulitzer Prize-winning composer. His music has been released by Mode, Wergo, Neuma, New World, Lovely Music, and (yes) Nonesuch, among many other labels. According to one critic in the *Village Voice* (cited on Wikipedia), "his reputation rests, in part, upon his 'wizardry in sending music flying through space: whether vocal, instrumental, or computerized.'" Reynolds taught in the Music Department of UCSD and eventually became its chair, but his faculty appointment was not without some controversy. Witness this undated letter (c. 1969?) to then-chair Will Ogdon from junior faculty member (lecturer) Pauline Oliveros—but was it sent? It's worth quoting in its entirety:

Although I strongly support your stand against the arbitrary position of the CEP [Committee on Educational Policy] on hiring composers as assistant professors, I definitely cannot support the appointment of Roger Reynolds.

It seems obvious from your stand that you wish to hire Mr. Reynolds at a higher rank and salary than my own. Since I consider Mr. Reynolds a peer, in my present position this would be an insulting slap in the face. If Mr. Reynolds possessed a Ph.D. and twenty years teaching experience, I could easily except the difference in salary and status. My first-hand knowledge of Mr. Reynolds is limited to his appearance here as Regents Lecturer, to the performance of his "Ping" and to an article, *It(')s Time*, which appeared in a recent issue of "Electronic Music Review." I have seen no recommendations for him, but two of our faculty members who know him well have expressed strong opposition to his appointment. My impressions are not good. I am told Mr. Reynolds has no teaching experience. What is his interest in education? "Ping" is a slick but naïve use of the material of mixed means. The quality of electronic sound was poor (limited frequency response and IM distortion) and indicated the use of inferior circuitry. I have heard the same techniques as developed and presented some years ago by David Tudor and Gordon Mumma in a vastly superior way. There is no reason why anyone should not appropriate techniques for his own use, however the techniques should become his own through imaginative assimilation. Mr. Reynolds claims the credit for the film involved in "Ping." Any filmmaker would credit the Japanese cameraman and the actor for their collaborative effort. These two names were not offered in the program nor acknowledged by Mr. Reynolds in conversation. In my opinion this indicates selfish accumulation of credits and is inexcusable. In his article *It(')s Time*, Mr. Reynolds gives the impression that no one but he and the psychologist have given any thought to time. Time, however, is generally ignored (or is it avoided?) and the result has been some unfortunately misplaced allegiances. This generalization is never illustrated by specific examples nor is the work of numerous contemporary composers whose chief concern is the passage of time, ever mentioned, i.e. Karlheinz Stockhausen's *How Time Passes*, Die Reihe, Volume Three, Musical Craftsmanship, 1957, which begins, "Music consists of order-relationships in time; this presupposes that one has a conception of such time." The comparison of these two articles would uncover many more difficulties with Mr. Reynolds' article.

If Mr. Reynolds is hired your faculty will not be in unanimous agreement on the appointment.

Pauline Oliveros

I don't want to offer a rebuttal on behalf of Roger Reynolds or his music. He got the job, and far beyond the molehills of academia, he's clearly defined his own legacy as a contemporary composer. University hierarchies are brutal; faculty hires are usually as political as they are pragmatic, and often messy. But the letter—one of several I found addressed to Will Ogdon that express Oliveros's outrage or exasperation, often addressing a lack of bureaucratic transparency—nevertheless provides some insight into her precarious position as a junior member of the faculty, and the sole woman in the Music Department, following her arrival in 1967. It also sheds light on the period just before the development of the *Sonic Mediations* in the early 1970s. The very premise of the first *Sonic Meditation*, *Teach Yourself to Fly*, is finding one's voice:

... gradually introduce your voice. Allow your vocal cords to vibrate in any mode which occurs naturally. Allow the intensity to increase very slowly.

With her letters to Ogdon, Oliveros was finding her voice in a new institutional context. There is also a complaint about being left out of the selection of graduate students and teaching assistants, as well as a complaint about the squalid conditions of the Music facilities. I don't think of Oliveros as a complainer—quite the opposite, in fact—but that is surely because much of her career was developed on her own terms. But this is why it's important to remember that Deep Listening, as an all-encompassing practice and brand, didn't just come out of nowhere. It was a practice and brand that emerged gradually, its intensity increasing slowly. She had to *teach herself* how to do it.

Despite her distinguished career of teaching in the academy (at UCSD, Mills, Rensselaer, and elsewhere) and her reverence for her own music teachers (from Robert Erickson to her own mother), Oliveros was always something of an autodidact. Her understanding of education, I'd argue, is giving others the tools to teach themselves. Of her litany of complaints regarding Reynolds (and one could call this an emerging rivalry, given the overlapping interests and parallel accomplishments of these "peers"), the one that feels most direct and personal is the one about teaching: *What is his interest in education?* To ask that question, one must have a fairly developed sense of their own interest in pedagogy. The *Sonic Meditations* would emerge as further evidence of a pedagogical investment even beyond the classroom, one inextricably, emphatically woven into the very form and structure of her compositions. The twenty-five *Sonic Mediations* are, among many other things, proof of that commitment to teaching.

As with the Nonesuch letdown, the letter provides further evidence of Oliveros's exit from institutional academia in 1981, shortly after Reynolds became chair. But like the first *Sonic Meditation*, it happened gradually, slowly, naturally. In her fourteen years at UCSD, she taught herself to fly—and many others along with her. Then she flew away.

216

An undated (unsent?) letter on University of California San Diego Department of Music letterhead:

COMMUNICATION GAP

Everyone here and every where else is a value to me personally.

We are joined by a common environment.

Everything you do affects me personally.

Everything I do affects you personally.

There is an alienation and communication crisis everywhere now and especially here in our department.

If <u>You</u> write a memo to someone, it is ignored, forgotten, disregarded, undelivered, distorted, or generally abused.

If <u>You</u> give someone information verbally, the same things occur.

The results of this are usually insulting or just plain dumb.

Do you wish to address yourself to this problem?

Do you think that emergency solutions to everyone's wishes or desires, without treating the basic problem which is lack of direct communication and concern for the environment which acts upon us and shapes our lives as a breakdown in an ineffective system?

How can we illuminate buck-passing, evasiveness, and disregard of human rights?

The alternatives are: Accept the system, change the system, or drop out of the system; otherwise we will continue to hurt each other and generally make an irreversible mass.

You are effective.

Pauline Oliveros

217

Two excerpts from the article "Oliveros—Composer Moving East" by Daniel Cariaga, Calendar section, *Los Angeles Times*, Sunday, June 14, 1981:

"I am not leaving the university for another institution," Oliveros explained, several days after the birthday in which she turned forty-nine.

"For a long time, I had been thinking about leaving the university—taking an early retirement at, say, fifty-five. But, then, when I was in the Catskills last summer, I thought, why not now?

"Leaving music? Oh, no—actually, I'll be more into it. There was a conflict between my university life and my outside work—my traveling, performing, and making music away from the school. It made me have a conflict of interest because, if you teach, you have to be here, and if you do other things, you have to be there . . ."

What will Oliveros miss most about La Jolla?

"Probably the sun, the ocean. The temperate climate. The people, of course.

"But I am just answering a call. I feel that I've been called there. Whenever I go to the Catskills, it always feels like I'm going home."

Would she advise young composers to follow the path she has followed?

"Well, it depends on their constitution. A long time ago, I vowed to do what I wanted to do until someone paid me to do it. You really need a strong constitution for that."

I am still trying to get to the bottom of the Deep Listening Band. I just culled an album from my photos from Mills, dedicated to DLB and related material: EIS (Expanded Instrument System), collaborations with Peter Ward/Panaiotis, collaborations with Stuart Dempster, etc. I encountered a lot of in this territory: correspondence (fax and, later, email) related to various performances, including a short European tour and a concert at the Panasonic Hall (P/N) in Tokyo; flyers and programs for various concerts; notes (in Oliveros's handwriting, perhaps from a band meeting or just a solo ideation session, including a business plan for DLB); tech and stage diagrams; photographs; press; etc.

Among other things, I am trying to assemble a chronology of live performances by DLB, its various expansions and offshoots. There is, I think, something a little perverse or at least conventional about the idea of a live Deep Listening Band concert, given the band's sequestered origins in an unusual acoustic setting (the Fort Worden cistern, followed by the Tarpaper Cave), but the transposition of the band's interest in sounding spaces in more conventional settings also gives way to an increased exploration of virtual space. The framework of DLB is highly adaptable and evolves considerably in the years from its signal moment in the cistern on October 8, 1988 to its final manifestation (?) almost exactly twenty-five years later on October 5, 2013, at the Dunrobin Sonic Gym in Ottawa. Twenty-five years is a long existence for a band: That *is* deep. And long.

My understanding of Deep Listening Band is that it was the most consistent collaborative project for Oliveros and also the most complex in its intersection of concerns regarding improvisation, with an expanding cast of contributors; the integration of eclectic acoustic instruments with electronics (the EIS); and the exploration of usual or compelling acoustic spaces and/or virtual space. And while it is fundamentally a collective endeavor (Dempster is always involved, along with David Gamper or Panaiotis—and for a short but crucial period, both), DLB is also a part of a larger network of Oliveros's concerns and pursuits, all under the umbrella of Deep Listening. The Papers reveal how all of these concerns parallel one another and feed into the larger concept. I always want to call it a brand, which sounds icky and corporate, but cuts to the quick—Oliveros was always looking holistically at ways of sustaining the operation, and DLB was a small but important part of that. There's much more to say about all of the above, but meanwhile, I'm enjoying flipping through the badly (or weirdly—I rather like them) exposed color 35mm pictures of the band in and around the Tarpaper Cave that I carefully rephotographed in the Olin Library.

219

In my effort to construct a more complete chronology of DLB, I am indebted to the WBM (the Internet Archive's Wayback Machine) where I locate an official DLB chronology, prepared by Stuart Dempster (et al.). It's fourteen pages printed out or made into a PDF. I already know it's not complete because it doesn't include the (final?) performance on October 5, 2013 at the Dunrobin Sonic Gym or the resulting album (CD) *Dunrobin Sonic Gems* (2017). The last concert it lists is October 29, 2011 at Lawrence University in Appleton, Wisconsin, where Loren Dempster is on the music faculty. The show took place just over a month after David Gamper died. Between then and the Dunrobin show was a concert at EMPAC celebrating Oliveros's eightieth birthday. Oliveros and Dempster perform *From Now On* (1995), a composition by DLB—a version appears on *Tosca Salad* (1995)—and are joined by guest Brian Pertl (who also joined for the Lawrence concert). I don't know if there were any other DLB outings after Dunrobin. A complete chronology of DLB may not be possible. In any event, Stuart Dempster and the WBM saved me a lot of time, but I still have plenty of homework to do.

220

Today I'm taking a brief respite from Deep Listening (Band) and listening to K-pop while packing for my trip home to Wisconsin. It's good to mix it up to keep the senses sharp. I also tend to like vocal music when I can't understand a word. I received an email from my former student Christine Yerie Lee who just returned from Memphis:

> It's funny that I yet again ended up back home for this residency. My friend Ezra let me take over his radio show and I put a very poppy mix together for it titled "An Ode to toughgurl5" (my old AIM screenname), plugged some muff too. You can listen to it here [Dead Wax on 91.7 WYXR], it's the 7/26 episode. I apologized to him in advance because he usually only plays rare Memphis soul records, and I blasted 90s k-pop and middle school jams (lol).

For the record, "plugg[ing] muff" refers to the handle of artist and musician Steven Chen, also a former student of mine, who wrote and performed the catchy soundtrack for Christine's likewise catchy video *BUL* 불 (2022), based on the mythological Korean monster Bulgasari. It's the first time I've heard the song detached from the video. It's still catchy. There's a fun part of the episode where she talks about cleaning out her old CD collection from her parents' house. Christine is a generation or two younger than me, so it's gratifying (or perhaps bewildering?) to learn we were both listening to Aphex Twin in the late 90s. Her middle school jams were my post-college jams. Yesterday I had to make some hard choices in deciding which CDs I would bring with me to listen to in my mom's car. In deference to my mother, Aphex Twin was not one of them.

221

Deep Listening (/ Band) at ~35,000 feet, with my Apple AirPods set to noise cancellation mode, on American Airlines flight 669 between LAX and O'Hare—a playlist:

La Monte Young and Marian Zazeela
The Tamburas of Pandit Pran Nath
Just Dreams, 1999/2021

Pauline Oliveros, Stuart Dempster, Panaiotis
Deep Listening
New Albion, 1989

Deep Listening Band
The Ready Made Boomerang
New Albion, 1991

222

I am reading Donald Brackett's enjoyable enough biography *Yoko Ono: An Artful Life*. But, I can't help but wonder: Who is the audience for this book? John Lennon fans? Fluxus fans? The special club where these overlap on the Venn diagram? The author clearly tries to strike a balance between these constituencies. He makes a convincing case for Ono as an important artist, long before she meets John Lennon (her third husband), and especially in her role as a conduit (and figurehead) between the avant-garde scenes in New York and Tokyo. I already know a lot of the story of her contribution to what would become Fluxus, shortly after she met George Maciunas, and teach her early work regularly. I also know plenty about her relationship to the Beatles in the final years of the band. What I know less about are her own musical efforts, with and without Lennon. Brackett argues for her influence in music, which is indisputable, but he goes to considerable effort to make a case for her being years ahead of her time. This is only really true in the sense that pop and rock music were, in so many ways, always behind the avant-garde. That is, by definition, what an avant-garde is. There was an interest in noise in the avant-garde (noise is the inevitable flipside of Cage's silence) before it became idiomatic in rock music. There are things that Pauline Oliveros (or Morton Subotnick or Pierre Schaeffer or Bernard Parmegiani, et al.) was doing in the electronic music studio long before the advent of IDM (intelligent dance music) in the 1990s. The latter was surely innovative in many ways, but mostly in the context of dance or pop music. In the Oliveros Papers I found a really great argument on this topic by OIiveros. (It's in the folders for the composition *Tashi Gomang* from 1981.) "I don't think of composers being 'ahead of their times'—I think of them as being 'at present' with their times, and that perhaps there are others who are looking too far back, or too far forward," she opines.

"But perhaps those who are exactly in the present might be a new kind of avant-garde which is exactly in the center. It's just simple geometry—it's just a circle with a dot in the center!" Context of time and place seem crucial to the equation. Ono seems to have gradually left the avant-garde in favor of a larger crossover audience. There is no judgment implied in this. Once she married John Lennon she became "famous for being famous," in Brackett's words. Inevitably so. But the avant-garde artist will always be time traveling when they transpose their ideas to a pop context.

223

Concerto for cicadas and other unidentified critters, air conditioners, and pick-up basketball lit by lightning bugs and the Sturgeon Supermoon, overheard near Bond Park, Janesville, Wisconsin.

224

This morning I am listening to the *Cicada Dream Band* (2014), a one-off album by a band comprising Pauline Oliveros, David Rothenberg (clarinet and critter sounds), and Timothy Hill (voice). The album was recorded at Dreamland Studios, West Hurley, New York in August 2013, coinciding with the arrival of millions (a so-called brood) of periodical cicadas to the area. Cicadas are famous for showing up in big numbers every seventeen years, but there are plenty of cicadas that follow their own rhythm and appear out of sync with the larger broods. I am reading about the relative regularity of cicadas on the University of Wisconsin's Horticulture site, hastened by my experience of listening to their late-night jam session around my mom's house last night. Mostly I am taken with their impressive collective vibration, a joyful noise I am tempted to describe as ecstatic, though for the cicadas it's probably just business as usual. According to the Wisconsin Horticulture Division of Extension, "Most people wouldn't notice the well-camouflaged cicadas at all if it wasn't for the noise they make." (Surely this is especially true at night.) "Their persistent hum is the soundtrack of summer afternoons in the Midwest as the males 'sing' to attract mates."

The buzzing sound is created by rapidly flexing thin drum-like membranes (tymbals) on the underside of the abdomen at a high speed and amplifying the sound in enlarged chambers derived from the tracheae. The noise can be deafening when lots of males are calling all at once. Some cicadas produce sounds over 100 decibels! The repertoire of mating songs and other acoustic signals is unique to each species. That of the dog-day cicada is often described as a loud, high-pitched whine similar to a power saw cutting wood lasting for several seconds before fading away. Females lack the tymbals so do not make the buzzing noise but both can also make a different sound by flicking their wings.

225

Today I'm listening to Yoko Ono's album *Approximately Infinite Universe* from 1973, the year of my birth. It's taking me a few passes to get through, in part because it's a double album and in part because my mom's Wi-Fi is so difficult to deal with, and I'm listening to it on Spotify. But the album is terrific, starting with the sublime title. I'm also in the home stretch with the Ono biography, which for many pages has felt more like a John Lennon biography, though hardly an uncritical one. Ono sometimes disappears in the narrative, and maybe there's no way to write a thorough biography about such an enigmatic figure. (*An Artful Life* is pretty conventional as far as biographies go. I probably should have read Nicole Rudick's *(Auto)biography of Niki de Saint Phalle instead.*)

I also had a flashback to my first trip to New York City in 1987, at age fourteen. I was on a bus trip with my mother and grandmother. It was an exceptionally exciting and memorable trip. I often say I learned how to walk in New York (i.e. consciously). I also remember our hotel room, in a Howard Johnson near Times Square. Times Square was still squalid. There was a porn theater on the block. The television in the room was chained to the wall. Of course I loved every minute of it, but it's remarkable my mom let me wander around the neighborhood by myself. I have a vague but certain recollection of a cable access television show or segment called *The Man Who Smelled a Little Too Much Like Urine* that I watched on the TV chained to the wall. My efforts at Googling it have revealed nothing, but I'm not quite ready to give my admittedly active fourteen-year-old imagination credit for it. I keep thinking it will turn up somewhere in my encounters with New York culture, circa 1987.

Among the things I remember about that trip, which only included about two days in Manhattan with a heavy emphasis on the usual tourist fare—the Statue of Liberty, the World Trade Center, South Street Seaport, etc., I recall the tour guide alerting us to the Dakota, the storied apartment building on the corner of W. 72nd St. and Central Park West, which is where John Lennon and Yoko Ono lived and where Lennon was shot and killed by the enraged and mentally ill Beatles fan Mark David Chapman on December 8, 1980—still recent history when I encountered it. At that time, I don't know how much I knew about the Beatles or how much of their music I had heard growing up—not much, really. My mom loved the Beatles in their early years but never followed their later, ever shaggier moves, and she mostly listened to country after getting together with my father. But "everyone," including me, knew who John Lennon was. I don't remember if anything else about the hotel or its many famous inhabitants was mentioned during the tour; I only remember the most salacious detail. Many years later, when trips to New York became more regular, I saw Yoko Ono coming out of a jewelry store on Madison Avenue, not far from where the Whitney was. I took it as an auspicious celebrity sighting. It's funny I'm remembering all of this while in sleepy Janesville, Wisconsin.

226

One of the things I often have to re-remember is that my own experience of music is contextualized by whoever else might be listening, too. I've been listening to DLB's *Sanctuary* (1995) while driving my mom's Cadillac. Like me, my mom still has a CD player in her car. I was playing it quietly, so as to not arouse her attention or suspicion, and to allow for unfettered conversation. It was just loud enough that I could hear it and follow it, but I was hoping she might not even notice. No avail. "What is that?" she inquired skeptically. "Just some old people jamming, mom." I should have also mentioned it was recorded in a church.

In teenage years after my dad died, my mom put up with all sorts of more serious noise pollution, from my own electric guitar "studies" or whatever I was listening to—most often metal, in progressing states of heaviness (Iron Maiden, Black Sabbath, Metallica . . .), but also rap (Beastie Boys, Run-DMC, Public Enemy . . .), lots of Jimi Hendrix, grunge, etc. She was almost always a good sport and was certainly "ahead of her time" in hearing Nirvana before they went mainstream. I had purchased the cassette of *Bleach* from Commander Salamander in Georgetown on my eighteenth birthday (April 11, 1991—almost exactly five months before the world premiere of their "Smells Like Teen Spirit" video), which I then listened to endlessly upon my return, often driving around in her car. We had, and still have, a rule that whoever is driving gets to choose the music. It was a good incentive to drive. She thought the song "About a Girl" was reminiscent of the Beatles, and she was right. In a few short months Nirvana would transcend whatever grunge is (or was) to become a legitimate pop phenomenon, for better or worse. The only thing I remember my mom flatly objecting to was PainKiller's *Buried Secrets* (1992), which was released—quite appropriately—on the Earache label. I was listening to it in the basement, at the highest volume possible for my CD boombox, and she came to the top of the stairs. "What the hell is that?" she inquired, shouting over the din, but pacing her words. "PainKiller, mom." That name surely seemed ironic, but that music was a painkiller, for me, in a way. I turned it down. At least I hope I did. It was my last summer living at home.

227

Some sound observations

I am able to hear my mother's voice through walls and even in busy places where there is a lot of competing sound activity. If she's talking to someone else and I am several rooms away, I can't always make out what she's saying, but I usually can detect her tone and timbre. This makes perfect sense, given that her voice is surely the first one I heard, and heard with frequency even before entering the world. I don't hear it as often now—once or twice a week on the phone, and a few weeks each year unmediated and in close proximity—but even at a normal speaking volume it cuts through the din at home and elsewhere. She is a retired elementary school teacher, so she also has a "classroom voice" as she describes it and in part explains why she can cut through the din.

That said, it's remarkably quiet here at her house, which is also the house I grew up in. I always forget how quiet it is here, or more accurately, I remember that it's quiet, but it's hard to imagine the quietude without actually being in it—say, from the noisy vantage of Los Angeles. A few recurring sounds here, beyond my mother's familiar voice: local talk radio on WCLO from a small boombox in the basement; the hum of the central air conditioning; the neighbor's noisy vehicles (some things never change) and sporadic "traffic"; dogs barking; the train about a half mile away, which I mostly hear in the middle of the night when the rest of the world recedes. The swell of the critters outside is ferocious (wonderful, really, especially at night), but the house is buttoned up tight, so they only exist when I go outside.

It also smells really good here, which I already knew, but (likewise) it's hard to imagine how good it smells without actually smelling it. And at night you can also see a handful of planets and countless stars.

228

Fractured folk songs

Driving between Chicago and Janesville, I listened to Deep Listening Band's *Looking Back* in my mother's big red Cadillac. Recorded on June 14 and 15, 1999, at Deep Listening Studios in Kingston, New York, the sessions were apparently lost or forgotten, but recovered and released in 2013 in memory of David Gamper. On the recording, the triangle of Gamper, Oliveros, and Stuart Dempster is augmented by Joe McPhee (a semi-regular guest of DLB) who plays pocket trumpet, percussion, and wooden flute, and Randy Raine-Reusch who contributes an impressive list of instruments to the mix (biwa, didjeridu, keene/khaen, ney, sho, suling—he sings too). As with other DLB albums, it's not always easy to suss out who is playing what, or what is even being played. In addition to their primary instruments—accordion, trombone, didjeridu—Oliveros and Dempster play conch shells and lend their voices, too; Dempster plays the garden hose, a piece of garden equipment he transformed into a legitimate instrument; Gamper operates a Max/MSP Realtime Interactive Computer (a.k.a. the EIS); most of the group plays "toys," which are unnamed but recall the "little instruments" played by the Art Ensemble of Chicago. The interplay is intricate, often dense, evolving.

Increasing the volume reveals detail—I believe I've read this phrase in the notes on at least one DLB album, and it's true. Morton Feldman and Steve Roden explicitly favor *pianissimo*, but with DLB, higher volume is rewarded. I want to believe I'm in the middle of the swell, overwhelmed by it. In the swell, I consider the relation of folk and the avant-garde, which I had probably thought of as representing opposite ends of a spectrum, but when thinking about (listening to) DLB, I envision those endpoints curling up and forming a circle in which these categories are fully imbricated or at least gently touching. Of course, when one uses these terms, one must be mindful of audience and other contextual details. The very notion of an avant-garde is intentionally limited and self-selecting, whereas folk is, by definition, broad and inclusive. But something about playing a garden hose makes me think about True Value hardware more than, well, Feldman or Bartók or another emblematic figure of the musical avant-garde. And the accordion and trombone have their own populist histories, not to mention conch shells. (I am always reminded of the conch representing the seat of power in *Lord of the Flies*.) All of Raine-Reusch's instruments are "exotic" in a Western context but traditional and utterly familiar in their countries of origin. Something about the very idea of a "band" and its implication of regularity or ongoingness is very folksy, though I'd hardly confuse DLB with, say, the Five Bear Rugs from Country Bear Jamboree, even if Raine-Reusch played a washboard rather than a biwa, or if Oliveros set down her conch and took up the whiskey jug instead. *Looking Back*, especially with its corny, punning album cover and odd assortment of instruments, even the T-shirts worn by the band and (especially) Raine-Reusch's impressive mullet), all take me to a very folksy place. (Grateful Dead, with their idiosyncratic mix of popular genres and spacey improvisation, also comes to mind—maybe splits the difference between the Five Bear Rugs and DLB.) I'm tired, so my logic is likely loopy, or leaky. I guess what I'm trying to get at, or what I imagine Deep Listening Band is trying to get at, is something fundamental and foundational about music itself, maybe even something ontological, where the impulse for banding sounds together is coterminous with the act of listening—something as familiar to us, as it was the troglodytes, or at least I'd like to imagine that's true.

229

Looking Back (2013): a chart of its instrumentation (with thanks to Discogs)

Song:	Dempster	Gamper	McPhee	Oliveros	Raine-Reusch
"Roi Et"	didjeridu	-	percussion	accordion, toys	khaen
"Luolong"	trombone, garden hose, voice, toys	EIS, toys	pocket trumpet, flute, toys	accordion, voice	biwa, voice
"Orcis"	trombone, didjeridu, toys	EIS, keys, toys	pocket trumpet, toys	accordion, toys	ney
"Tremper"	conch	EIS	pocket trumpet	conch	suling
"Kuranda"	trombone	EIS	-	-	didjeridu
"Kamakura"	trombone, didjeridu	-	-	accordion	sho

230

The Sing★a★ma★jigs!™ are a line of terrycloth-covered, battery-powered singing toys introduced by Mattel in 2010. *Time* magazine rated them the #1 toy of 2010. "Mattel's plush Sing-a-ma-jigs have become this year's must-haves for the little ones," Allie Townsend notes in the magazine.

The eerie-toned talking and singing dolls each belt out a different note when their stomachs are pressed. Play them alone or grouped together for synchronized harmony. Navigate between chatter and crooning by pressing the left hand and then press the stomach to activate a motorized mouth that moves as you control its sound.

Each toy in the series is a different color—vaguely recalling the Teletubbies but with rabbity or bearish ears rather than single antennae—each color has corresponding vocal range and signature song, from "A-Tisket, A-Tasket" (alto, hot pink) to "John Jacob Jingleheimer Schmidt" (tenor, lime)—twenty-two American public domain classics, all told. On January 15, 2011, the Sing★a★ma★jigs!™ appeared in concert with Deep Listening Band at Town Hall in Seattle on the animalistic jam "Great Horned Howl." The concert was preserved on the CD *Great Howl at Town Haul*, released by Important Records the following year, and you can see two of the 'jigs dangling expectantly from Stuart Dempster's microphone stand on the CD cover. If I'm not mistaken, *Great Howl* was the very first work by DLB I heard, and it remains one of my favorites. Of all of their recordings, it has certainly spent the most time in my Scion and has made the most commutes to CalArts and back. The relatively concise trio of Oliveros, Dempster, and Gamper fully exploit the harmonic possibilities of the Sing★a★ma★jigs!™ as well as their playful, chattery nonsense, bringing the toys into dynamic interplay with accordion, piano, trombone, conch shell, duck call, flute, (human) voice, and the ever-present Expanded Instrument System. In some ways, The Sing★a★ma★jigs!™ are like a cuter, portable, more squeezable version of the EIS. Inhuman, they nevertheless made a joyful noise.

231

While thinking about the Sing★a★ma★jigs!™ and their use in (ahem) "serious music," I am also recalling the bewildering array drums and of little instruments used by the Art Ensemble of Chicago (AEC), which I never encountered in concert but was more than thrilled to see, even inert, at the MCA Chicago in 2015, in the exhibition *The Freedom Principle: Experiments in Art and Music, 1965 to Now*. AEC's percussion rig is one of the best things in an extraordinary, and one of my favorite things I've ever seen in a museum. There's something very provocative about imagining all of those potential sounds. I also imagined the effort in lugging this expansive "kit" around. It arrived at the museum courtesy of Roscoe Mitchell. And I imagined the considerable task of the museum's registrar, sorting through all of the drums, bike horns, toys, and noisemakers. I also imagined the empty space in Mitchell's house (?) while the arsenal of instruments was on loan. A banner with the AEC slogan—"GREAT BLACK MUSIC ANCIENT TO FUTURE"—hung above and behind the rig and efficiently annotated it.

On Tuesday, I was at the museum again, seeing Nick Cave's exuberant exhibition, curated by Naomi Beckwith, who had co-curated *The Freedom Principle* with Dieter Roelstraete—that show was the first place I had seen Cave's work in person. (For the record, I'm referring to Nick Cave, the gay Black artist, not Nick Cave the Australian musician who played with The Birthday Party and The Bad Seeds.) There, in 2015, one of Cave's elaborate sculptures appeared alongside scores by Anthony Braxton and Wadada Leo Smith, and work by Cauleen Smith, Pope.L, Charles Gaines, Stan Douglas, Nari Ward, and lots of AfriCOBRA stuff I knew nothing about. It's also where I first saw the dazzling banners by Lisa Alvarado, which often serve as backdrops for performances by Natural Information Society. I also saw a lively concert by Douglas R. Ewart Clarinet Choir, titled "Homage to Malachi Maghostut Favors" coinciding with the opening of the exhibition and celebrating fifty years of the AACM (Association for the Advancement of Creative Musicians) with dance, poetry, and a wide variety of reeds. I even dragged my mom along for the show before we flew to Florida the following day.

232

Gee, ain't it funny how time slips away?

I spent a good parcel of the morning *and* afternoon reading "Willie Nelson's Lengthy Encore," a lengthy feature by Jody Rosen in the *New York Times Magazine*. It is entirely appropriate that I'm reading about Nelson while staying with my mom. She's a longtime fan of his music and the man, and I've bought her many of his CDs and a book or two over the years. (Perversely, I've been reading it while listening to Joe McPhee's *Soprano* [2007] album—twice. More on that later.) At eighty-nine, Nelson is a gravity-defying marvel, and his long, gradually evolving career, with success at most stages of the journey, would be enviable to most any musician. There are few equals, though I do consider Oliveros as something of an unexpected parallel in those respects, albeit on a smaller (avant-garde) stage. Both artists also share a time and place, with their formative years in Texas: Oliveros was born in Houston in 1932; Nelson was born the following year in tiny Abbott, some two hundred miles northwest. Both had early success and became influential figures in their field; both have collaborated with a wide range of their peers in many contexts; both grew increasingly prolific with age. Both are also "outlaws" in their respective musical contexts: Oliveros, a successful and brash feminist, lesbian presence in the deeply patriarchal classical, electronic, and "new" music communities; Nelson, of course, literally defined his style as "outlaw country" in the early 1970s.

When I met Oliveros she was at the tender age of eighty-three, she had been teaching all day, then met with me for an hour before hitting the road to Kingston, another hour away. She was preparing for a show at The Kitchen and in Belgium; she showed no signs of slowing down until the moment she bowed out entirely the following year on November 24. It's hard, but fun, to imagine these two legends playing together—a duet for trusted just-intonation V-accordion and trusted, ruinous nylon string guitar ("Trigger"), or perhaps two singularly lovely voices ("Husky" and "Raspy"?) harmonizing—that only exists in my waking dream. Of course, they never did play together, though curiously enough, both played with Nels Cline. How cool is Nels Cline?

233

Two degrees of Nels Cline—a playlist:

Carla Bozulich
The Red Headed Stranger
Dicristina Stair Builders, 2003

Thollem [McDonas] / Oliveros / Cline
Molecular Affinity
Roaratorio, 2016

234

As the days of my vacation evaporate, I'm finally getting down to business digging through the "archive" preserved in my mother's closet, spanning early childhood to the first years of college, give or take. There is an absurd number of drawings and stapled handmade books, some of which I remember distinctly, most of which I don't. There are also boxes of comic books, which fueled my imagination, and assorted toys. I also found papers written in high school and college, along with some course readers and syllabi, and a trove of research documents on the National Endowment for the Arts. The NEA was my research topic for AP US Government, a class taught by one John Eyster that included a weeklong trip to Washington, D.C. in order to conduct field research. I still remember elbowing my way into Jesse Helms's Senate Office, where I interrogated his legislative assistant John Mashburn about his boss's NEA policy and was treated to some very graphic descriptions of Robert Mapplethorpe photographs, while I attempted to maintain a straight face.

I turned eighteen while in D.C., and that April 11 was a day full of music. First, (as I recently described) my friend Salomon and I went to Commander Salamander in Georgetown where I bought the cassette of Nirvana's *Bleach* (1989). I had heard *about* Nirvana, probably due to their connection to Sonic Youth and their signing to Geffen, but I had yet to actually *hear* them. As I recall, I had looked for *Bleach* on weekend trips to Madison and B-Side Records, and came up empty-handed. Sometimes you just have to go to Georgetown. Commander Salamander was sold out of the CD, which was my medium of choice then, but I was happy to walk away with the cassette, which I played much later that night when I finally got back to the hotel, and then in heavy rotation for many months after.

In the evening, our class went to the Kennedy Center to hear the National Symphony Orchestra. Digging through the closet yielded the program for the concert, conducted by Lorin Maazel and comprising Wagner's *Siegfried Idyll* (1870), Druckman's *Windows* (1972), and Mendelssohn's *Symphony No. 5 in D Major, Op. 107 ("Reformation")* (1830). We had already been to the Kennedy Center earlier in the week—twice!—to see the Dance Theatre of Harlem and Wendy Wasserstein's *The Heidi Chronicles* (1988). My fieldwork on the NEA coincided with a heavy dose of high culture, but Nirvana balanced things out—as did a strictly prohibited trip to a lively Irish pub along with some of my colleagues and a few congressional assistants from Wisconsin's 1st District. (I can't determine which Irish pub we went to—the capital has quite a few.) The drinking age was twenty-one, but nobody carded us (the congressional assistants were of age and, I suspect, regulars), and we imbibed in pitchers of beer while listening to an anonymous singer with an acoustic guitar performing folk/protest/drinking anthems. After a few beers, we are all singing along.

Did he ever return? / No, he never returned / And his fate is still unknown / Bullshit!

235

Cleaning out the closet—a playlist:

Talk Talk
Laughing Stock
Polydor, 1991

Michael Jackson
Thriller
Epic, 1982

Le Tigre
Le Tigre
Mr. Lady, 1999

236

Among the treasures and traumas uncovered in the closet of what was once my bedroom, I found my copy of Michael Jackson's *Thriller* (1982) on vinyl, with its famous gatefold image of MJ lounging with a tiger cub. Surprisingly pristine (NM+?) considering how often it had been played, once upon a time. My other favorite records from that time period have vanished, probably sold in a rummage sale many years ago. No pop star loomed larger in my childhood than MJ. I still remember where I first saw the videos for "Billie Jean" (in my friend David Swaim's living room) and "Thriller" (the world premiere on MTV, watched with cousins in my grandmother's family room); I remember impatiently rushing my mom home from an evening event in the basement of St. William Catholic Church in order see network debut of *The Wiz* (1978); I remember seeing his first moonwalk on the American Music Awards; I remember buying a single white spangled glove (a cheap imitation, almost needless to say) from a bin of them at Shopko at the height of Michaelmania: At age nine, when *Thriller* was released and became an instant phenomenon, I was at the height of pop fashion. At age nine, I could never have imagined I would eventually meet the complicated and possibly monstrous manchild he would become. In my twenty-seven years of living in Los Angeles, I've met many celebrities, big and small, real and imagined—movie stars, rap stars, art stars, "starchitects." None had the surreal (I use the word sparingly, but it seems perfectly appropriate here) presence of Michael Jackson, who I encountered three times while working at Hennessey + Ingalls bookstore on the Third Street Promenade in Santa Monica in the late 90s. I worked there from 1997 to 2000. Maybe the less I say about these encounters, the better, to preserve some of their mysterious energy. I will report he was a regular there, and often appeared in the store immediately after sensational stories or lurid allegations would appear in the headlines. Art books were a balm for him, and probably another addiction. In this sense, I felt genuinely connected to him, albeit in a different way than when I bought a single white glove in a naive act of identification. Despite his many trials and tribulations, which were shocking and heartbreaking, I always felt empathy for the King of Pop—a being who was, by design and circumstance, an alien in our earthly kingdom. (In 1983, he was nearly as close to E.T. as Eliot.) I remember where I was—my desk at USC Roski School of Fine Art, preparing for my exit to CalArts, June 2009—when I learned he had died. This morning, I put my copy of *Thriller* in my thick suitcase, with as much care as possible, in order to get it to Los Angeles, where it was recorded. It will join my other records as another kind of an alien presence.

237

Some sound observations

After lunch and some big box adventures, my mom drove me to the little bus terminal to initiate the beginning of my journey to Chicago, then back to Los Angeles. Nothing played on the stereo, but the air conditioner of the big red Cadillac made a sound—roughly halfway between a wheeze and a whine—that had become familiar in the two weeks spent in the car. We had commented on it before, but on this occasion she noted that it reminded her of the music I had been playing—meaning, Deep Listening Band. I laughed. She had made a few comments over the course of my stay as I played various examples from the DLB discography, maxing out my puny MacBook Air speakers. "Oh, I thought the air conditioner was falling apart," etc. In earlier years I might have been annoyed, but in my earlier years I was listening to Michael Jackson or Nirvana or whatever, not Deep Listening Band. I love that a band of old codgers could provoke such ontological questions about music. Not that my mom thinks about music ontologically, but everyone has their line for what makes sound *music* . . . or, well, something else. My line tends to be much (much) more permissive or, I suppose, "generous." But my mom hasn't read Cage (nor listened to him). It's nearly impossible to hear music as others hear it.

What constitutes your musical universe?

238

Two walks

If there was any question I was no longer in Wisconsin, look no further than Kenneth Hahn State Recreation Area, where I headed the morning after my return to Los Angeles. On the Bowl Loop trail there was a thick congregation of nearly a dozen dogs on leashes, led by (or really, leading) three dog walkers, two of whom looked like professionals. And then down below, near the big pond, was a mass of people gathered that included at least three Mighty Morphin Power Rangers, including two wearing the red uniform. I couldn't tell if it was a legit Hollywood reboot, or a cosplay session, or possibly a wedding. I watched for a few minutes from the other side of the water; the ducks had a better view than me, and I continued back to my car. For that walk, I listened to Willie Nelson's *Red Headed Stranger*, which I've only heard once or twice before. I've heard parts of it many times—"Blue Eyes Crying in the Rain" is a staple from my childhood diet of country and western—but a hit single loses its context as part of one of the first concept albums in country music. Released in 1975, *Red Headed Stranger* is often considered the birth of outlaw country, a subgenre devoted to the mythologies of the West. Much of the same could be said for Terry Allen's *Juarez*, which was released the same year. Both are really great country concept albums. Nelson's is famous; Allen's is perhaps infamous, or at least decidedly more obscure, or cultish—it's the only record released on its label, Landfall Press Inc. Terry Allen is a visual artist as well as a musician, and his country concept album is further contextualized by his proximity to conceptual art. I bought *Juarez* on vinyl a number of years ago, before its recent reissue, and played it for a listening party at Fiona Connor's one-year apartment gallery Laurel Doody. It was almost excruciating to listen to the record with a room full of people who mostly felt obliged to shut up and listen to the music. I kept thinking, "They probably hate this." And also, "Do they wonder why I'm making them listen to this?" I don't really remember why (of all the things I might have chosen) I chose *Juarez* for the listening party, but I liked (and still like) the record very much, and the idea of a record as an artwork, or vice versa. *Juarez* also included a series of intricate and surreal drawings (prints) by Allen, practically forcing the correlation. Today, if I got invited to pick a record for a listening party, would I choose Nelson's *Red Headed Stranger* instead? Perhaps I would choose Carla Bozulich's more obscure cover version of the record—a cover version of a whole record is its own kind of concept, so her version is extremely conceptual. It's also really lovely.

Today I returned to the park and listened to Pelt's *Effigy* (2012), which is perhaps my favorite album by a band I love but have yet to mention. I would probably not choose it for a listening party because, well, it's a really fucking intense album. Somehow I'm just noticing this, or perhaps remembering this, undoubtedly colored by a few weeks of trying to not rattle my mom with my music selections. But even listening to *Effigy* in the privacy of my own head, courtesy of my AirPods, I was newly awakened to its visceral charge. I was listening on Spotify, though I have the double vinyl version with its psychedelic gatefold design by Jake Blanchard. The album was recorded in Wisconsin at Bodhi Yoga Studio in Mt. Horeb and the Gates of Heaven Synagogue in Madison—quite a pair! Its title refers to the Indigenous effigy mounds which are abundant in the southern half of my home state, and are the subject of Blanchard's intricate and surreal drawings; it also refers to Jack Rose, a founding member of the band who had died shockingly young of a heart attack in 2009, several years after leaving the band to pursue a solo act. The album is dedicated to him, and while not strictly a concept album (there are no lyrics, which usually spin the yarn), there is something of a spiritual arc that seem to trace a trip through the bardo, a trip both elegiac and ecstatic. Song titles are certainly allusive: "Of Jack's Darbari" (the opening track), "Ashes of a Photograph," "Last Toast Before Capsizing," and so on. Rose's virtuoso guitar work, clearly descending from John Fahey's signature brand of American Primitive fingerpicking, used to be the driving force of the band and how I found them in the first place. Following Rose's departure, co-founders Mike Gangloff and Patrick Best brought Nathan Bowles and Mikel Dimmick (both are also members, with Gangloff, of Spiral Joy Band) on board for the ride. Here, their instrumentation, which is unspecified on the sleeve, favors singing bowls, violin, jaw harp (or is it a mbira?), harmonium, bells, cymbals (bowed?), and gongs. Despite Rose's (physical) absence, the album really rips. Pelt, rather knowingly, dwells at an unlikely sweet spot where the massive drones of Theater of Eternal Music intersect with exuberant Appalachian jamboree. It might come down to whether one calls a violin a "violin" or calls a violin a "fiddle": a distinction with a difference.

239

A Pair of Paik Pairings

This morning, I am listening to Nam June Paik's *Works 1958–1979* (2007), while my neighbor runs his leaf blower. With the windows closed and the music turned up relatively loud, I can still hear the whir. Paik has met his match. The intermittent blowing adds a degree of Cagean indeterminacy and a touch of Fluxian humor to the music, while Paik's compositions, mostly for prepared piano or found sounds (records? radio?), bring an element of playful sophistication to Saturday's chores. (I'm procrastinating from doing my 2021 taxes, for which my extended deadline is running out.)

Two days ago, when I unpacked my suitcase, I put my copy of Michael Jackson's *Thriller* (1982) in the walk-in closet (a.k.a. book nook) of my home office. Out of one closet and into another. I have several stacks of unfiled records that sit on the ground, facing out, and I put MJ on the end face of one stack. The face of the other stack is Paik, on the cover of Aki Onda's *Nam June's Spirit Was Speaking to Me* (2020). The image is a still from Michael Snow's absurdist structuralist film *Rameau's Nephew by Diderot (Thanx to Dennis Young) by Wilma Schoen* (1974), which I saw once in its epic two-hundred-sixty-seven-minute entirety at UCLA. In the film still, Paik is either yawning or perhaps making a sound by slapping his cheek with his mouth forming a perfect O, with a microphone pointing toward his face from out of frame (and held by critic Annette Michelson, if I'm remembering correctly). MJ and NJ make for an odd couple, both in suits but intimating casualness or even lassitude. The pairing speaks to two (or even three) eras of my personal history and the gradual expansion of my musical universe.

240

A few days ago, Leslie observed that I had become a music historian, or something to that effect. I don't think of myself as a historian because I tend to think of a historian as someone with a degree in history. But of course I also believe in such a thing as an "armchair historian" and I am surely that. If my interest in art history is somewhat limited, my interest in music is highly specific. (e.g. I know a lot about jazz but not much about classical; my pop knowledge is extremely Western, etc.) I've taught art history off and on for many years at CalArts and was hired as a "contemporary art historian," but there's sometimes an audible gasp when I reveal to the class that I've never actually studied art history. For the record, I do have a master's degree in art theory and criticism, and I've read a lot of art history in grad school, but mostly on my own. I've never studied music history in a formal setting. I did take a film history class in college, as part of my communication arts degree. But, the overwhelming amount of history I've consumed was self-motivated. (History is, by definition, a narrative ordering of factual information; but that story need not be told in a linear way. My scholarship likewise tends toward nonlinearity, which is also a nice way of saying haphazard or erratic.) I consume history all the time and produce some too. The present text is one example, though I tend to think of it as a "performance in writing" that incorporates history, criticism, (auto)theory, memory writing, (play)lists, and whatever else happens on a given day. I'd argue that most of my work as a writer, curator, and teacher is built on a foundation of history. I'm also a fan of counter-histories or (especially) "minor histories," to use a phrase favored by Mike Kelley who was one of my teachers, following from Deleuze and Guattari's notion of a "minor literature." I recently observed to a former student that CalArts is an expensive school for autodidacts—which sounds perverse for several reasons, but the reality is that most artists or scholars need to forge their own path into research, often out of sheer necessity or libidinal curiosity. School becomes a context where all of the autodidacts can bring their findings into the stew of conversation. In a few weeks, I'm going to be teaching my Routine Pleasures seminar, which I intend as a place to foster that exact kind of stewy conversation.

Implicit in Leslie's observation is that I am currently obsessed with music and music history, and less obsessed with art and art history. That is surely true. With a limited number of hours in a day, something has to give. I've been seeing fewer and fewer shows and have slowed down my usual gallery grind, reading and writing less about "art" (or the art world) while spending more time reading and writing about music. I've been listening to a lot of music, but that's always the case.

Two points toward—what, exactly, a thesis? A credo? A conclusion?

First, I consider Pauline Oliveros an artist as much as a composer, and in a similar sense, I think of Deep Listening as a practice (and pedagogy) in which life and art are deeply, inextricably imbricated, a notion which derives from the work and writing of artists including Allan Kaprow ("performing life") and Linda Montano ("living art") who, not coincidentally, were emphatically part of Oliveros's world. Or, to say it another way, her work is as dependent on (contemporary) art history as it is music history—or, yet another way, she uses her findings from the former to interrogate the latter. This is one of the reasons I titled my seminar Pauline Oliveros for Artists. I'm often most interested in the intersection or overlap of fields and their attendant discourses—art/music, art/film, film/architecture, etc.

Second, and above all else, I'm in favor of works of art that, regardless of media or categorical boundaries, continue to give and reveal with repeated viewing or listening. My favorite work of art is the inexhaustible kind, one that is in fact practically demanding of return visits, and with each visit rewards one (me) with rich new details or additional layers of complexity: a work of art that keeps on giving, in which no amount of historicizing or theorizing can diminish its impact. As a writer, my inability to have the last word about an artwork, no matter how astute or enlightening my analysis, is one of the reasons I keep writing.

Is *Sonic Meditation XXI* Oliveros's "best" or most important work? In a word, no, but it is one that reframes her whole (holistic) enterprise while perpetually and economically asking its vast, vexing question: *What constitutes your musical universe?* Even when I am far beyond exhausted, the question never is.

241

Summer dwindles, and there's much too much left to do on my to-do list. I'm a world-class procrastinator, and a deadline can turn the most mundane tasks into a kind of performance. Today, I managed to get my 2021 taxes under control, following an extension filed in April; and before that, I applied to the Centrum Artist Residency, which just happens to be located in Fort Worden Historical State Park, north of Seattle, where Deep Listening Band first banded together. The Dan Harpole Cistern is closed indefinitely, but I am still drawn to that landscape and the larger environment context. Besides, I will be on creative leave and away from CalArts in the spring, so it would be nice to take some pointed adventures. Maybe if I get an invite, excursions to the Tarpaper Cave and Kingston (home of the Deep Listening Institute and the birthplace of the *Tosca Salad* [1995]) will follow. Stay tuned.

242

This morning's playlist for my walk at Kenneth Hahn: *Artlessly Falling* (2020) by Mary Halvorson's Code Girl, one of my favorite albums to be released during the long slog of the pandemic. Halvorson's rangy, pitch-shifting guitar work—effortlessly veering from *burble* to *bloop* to *ZZZJJJUNNNNGGG!!* and back again—is typically the centerpiece of her records, but here it is well matched by the equally rangy vocals of Amirtha Kidambi and occasional guest turns by Robert Wyatt. Their contrasting voices are set in proximity, alternating, but rarely overlapping. In fact, it's not until the third song, "Walls and Roses," that the guitar playing reaches full Halvorson. It turns out she is a gifted lyricist, too, serving up choice material to two idiosyncratic vocalists.

It's ridiculous it's taken me 242 days of writing to even mention Robert Wyatt.

Sometimes when I go for a walk, I have something specific I want to listen to. And sometimes I decide once I get to the park. Today, I decided on *Artlessly Falling* because I was thinking about it yesterday, while encountering some other projects by Amirtha Kidambi. Now I am thinking about Robert Wyatt, and my mind continues to wander, as does my listening plan for the rest of the day.

243

Yesterday, man (wandering after Wyatt)—a playlist:

Mary Halvorson's Code Girl
Artlessly Falling
Firehouse 12 Records, 2020

Isotope 217
The Unstable Molecule
Thrill Jockey, 1997

Nick Mason
Nick Mason's Fictitious Sports
Harvest, 1981

Scarnella
scarnella
Smells Like Records, 1998

Geraldine Fibbers
Butch
Virgin, 1997

244

The end of summer is always bittersweet, as I ruminate on all of the projects I imagined getting to, but didn't start, or the books I bought, moved around, planned to read, but didn't even open. Whether owing to lingering apprehension around the pandemic or my daily immersion in *Sonic Meditation XXI*, or likely both, I've been less social than usual. And now, fittingly, I'm hunkered down, polishing the edges of my syllabus for Routine Pleasures, which I will begin teaching two weeks from today. The class will be quite different from the version exactly ten years ago, presumably due to gradual shifts in my own routine pleasures. But it will begin in the same place it did in 2012—with Jean-Pierre Gorin's essay film *Routine Pleasures* (1986) and with Manny Farber's notion of termite art—before swerving elsewhere, from Gee's Bend, Alabama to West Hollywood (EZTV) to Hong Kong (Simon Leung) to Watts (Don Cherry, Noah Purifoy, Horace Tapscott, et al.) to Tågarp (Don and Moki Cherry and Organic Music Theatre) to the Tarpaper Cave in upstate New York (Deep Listening Band).

Writing on Farber's paintings, Gorin and Patrick Amos observed, "Everything is assigned a materiality of its own: an image is never freed from a material context, but remains a flower illustration on a seed packet or a picture in a book, creased by its binding. It is the specific weight Farber gives to his objects, their definition and claim to space, their near-equal standing which pushes to the fore the questions of what links and separates them—of the in-between." This is exactly how I'm thinking (have been thinking) about the syllabus and bringing these different examples together, or rather, of luxuriating in the spaces between them. (Thanks again, JP.) For all of its digressions and in-between, the class has always been predicated on the axial relationship between solitude and the collective, and the axial relationship of work and pleasure. In art making, those relations are particularly vexed as they intersect. Yesterday I turned this into a kooky diagram, using Google Drawings, my new favorite tool. Simultaneously, I'm also considering the "performance-in-writing" of the present text as another example of my own termite tendency, almost entirely solitary, an activity that is both work and pleasure, though somedays much more of one than the other.

245

September, man—a playlist:

Robert Wyatt
"Maryan"
Shleep
Hannibal Records, 1997

Mary Halvorson Septet
"Nairam"
Illusionary Sea
Firehouse 12 Records, 2013

Philip Catherine
"Nairam"
September Man
Warner Music, 1974

North Sea Radio Orchestra
"Maryan"
Folly Bololey (Songs from Robert Wyatt's Rock Bottom)
Dark Companion, 2019

246

It's been brutally hot. Yesterday was devoted as much as possible to reading as I laid low, blotted out the sun, and put the finishing touches (yes?) on my syllabus for Routine Pleasures, taking in lengthy essays about the Gee's Bend quilters and Godzilla, the Asian American artist network that started in New York in the 1990s. I also finally got around to reading Deborah Miranda's "Teaching on Stolen Ground," which was on my summer reading list. It's a beautiful essay, provocative and moving. It should be required reading for anyone teaching in the United States. There is much in it that I will continue to dwell with into the future, as a teacher and as a white man on stolen land, but there was one passage in particular that seemed particularly fitting to this daily consideration of my musical universe.

Miranda is talking about the way knowledge is summoned. "I want to argue that intangibles (or as [Linda] Hogan calls them, *intelligences*) are in fact inherent in all of us, perhaps just deeply hidden or needing the right language to bring out . . . What if these knowledges, *always here*, can be *evoked* from one being to another—in a moment of resonance?" She then gives the example of tuning a drum, which she describes as a whole-body effort.

When tuning a drum, you lean down with your face right over the drumhead and hum the note you want the drum to hold, while adjusting the sinews on the back or bottom or sides of the drum (depending on construction) that tighten or loosen the drumhead accordingly. I learned this not as a young Indian girl in traditional training, but as a junior high student who bucked her counselor's advice to take typing or accounting and followed, instead, a powerful yearning toward tympani and snare (where tradition is lacking, perhaps the body remembers). I have since discovered that it's the same for any drum, though, whether symphonic or native, machine- or handmade. Tuning a drum is a whole-body effort—foot, leg, diaphragm, lungs, breath, lips, hands—because you must stand with your feet firmly planted, knees bent a little to keep the body's energy open, humming and simultaneously tapping the drumhead with a stick or finger. And as you hum out into the drum, tap the drumhead, and pull or release the drumhead ever so slightly, the drum searches for the note. And when everything coalesces—the pressure of the drumhead, the humming in your mouth, the angle and punctuation of a strike—the drum sings the note back to you. Then your whole body, starting with your head (and teeth!), continuing down to the very soles of your feet, is enveloped in the totality of *rightness*; the note sings its way back up your spine and out through your molars and connects with the drum's note. Then, it's complete. Then, you *know*.

I immediately thought of my friend Elisa Harkins, who has made her own drums; Judith Hamann, who dwells in the hum; and Milford Graves, who understood the true complexities of the heart's rhythm.

This dazzling account is followed by a line that will also continue to resonate in a personal way: "Writing, the art of literature, is like tuning a drum: a whole-body experience." I had really only considered that idea this year, since initiating my ongoing performance of *Sonic Meditation XXI*, in which writing is so intimately connected to the ceaseless practice of listening—though for years I have said I tend to do my best writing when I'm walking or driving or taking a shower.

247

Today's soundtrack for heat beating includes Joshua Abrams & Natural Information Society's *Mandatory Reality* (2019), or at least the first half of it, as I drive to the farmer's market and various other pitstops, as the morning temperature rises toward triple digits. Since its release, it's often been in heavy rotation in my car. (I have the double CD; it's not on Spotify.) Repetitive, hypnotic, insistent, it's also a reliably mellow match for a molten Sunday morning, as the coffee gradually takes hold. At home, cowering in front of the portable air conditioner, I take my first plunge into Bitchin Bajas's new release, *Bajascillators* (2022). No strangers to bad puns (see their 2017 album *Bajas Fresh*, presumably named after the burrito chain founded in Southern California), not to mention their silly name, the band is serious and seriously good, often great, and sometimes capable of scratching the surface of sublime. As it turns out, they also paired nicely with Natural Information Society on the collaborative LP *Automaginary* (2015). *Bajascillators*, as the title suggests, continues the group's exploration of the synthesizer, following closely on the heels of last year's Sun Ra covers record, *Switched On Ra* (2021), which I listened to as much as any album that came out last year. *Switched On Ra* manages to be remarkably faithful to its ostensible subject while also conjuring Wendy Carlos (who is insinuated in the title), Suzanne Ciani, Cluster, and especially Kraftwerk—Krautrock has long been part of their foundation. If *Ra* had me thinking about *Autobahn* (1974), mostly with its vehicular intimations and proto-autotune vocals, *Bajascillators* calls to mind Kraftwerk's two earlier, eponymous albums (*1* and *2*, from 1970 and 1972) as well as the third, *Ralf & Florian* (1973). But with its euphonic marimbas, the first of the four tracks, "Amorpha," at first suggests Steve Reich, and then, when the synths fully announce their arrival, Stereolab. I'm feeling some late 90s flashbacks of Stereolab and Tortoise—

both of which clearly knew their Steve Reich, too. (Does it really sound like these things, or are just my nearest points of reference? Leslie mentioned Reich at the same time I was thinking about him, as we listened to "Amorpha.") Armchair historians, but hardly stuffy about it, the Bajas don't hide their references but explore, exploit, and explode them. As with the *Ra* tribute, *Bajascillators* makes me want to follow this chain of references, which I likely will before I return for a second hearing.

248

Trio for Ralf & Florian & Honeywell portable air conditioner.

249

Today, I returned to CalArts for the first time since mid-May, and to a poorly air-conditioned building under 110-degree-Fahrenheit assault, for the beginning of an ominous prelude to the new school year. My soundtrack for the morning commute? Pauline Oliveros's *The Roots of the Moment* (1988). I lent the CD to my graduate assistant in 2019 and never got it back. (This happens.) So, I recently bought a shiny new copy, mostly to have Joe McPhee's liner notes. It's been a long time since I've listened to in full, and with relatively complete attention. Traffic was a beast, though the tuff gnarl of the city eventually gave way to the majesty of the sunbaked mountains and . . . SPACE. Ostensibly a solo accordion performance, the album is also (among) the first to employ an "interactive electronic environment," which is to say a series of delays and other effects, a precursor of the Expanded Instrument System (EIS) as it would come to be known, developed by Oliveros's former student Peter Ward or Panaiotis as he would come to be known. The album anticipates many of the concerns that would soon preoccupy Deep Listening Band, which initially included Panaiotis, yet it sounds quite distinct from those collective efforts. *Roots* shares DNA with *Accordion & Voice* from some six years earlier, with its two album side jams, *Horse Sings from Cloud* and *Rattlesnake Mountain*. Oliveros's voice is absent from *Roots*; beyond that, or because of that, *Accordion & Voice* is distinctly warmer in tone. (The cover of *A & V* shows Oliveros resplendent in overalls, shaggy dog at her side, in the expansive rural setting of upstate New York.) Comparably, the tone of *Roots* is a little more shiny and metallic, even a little frosty, suggesting a less earthy or even a slightly alien environment. (In his notes, McPhee even refers to *Star Trek*—for which he and Pauline apparently shared an affinity.) On *Roots*, Oliveros and her accordion are further meditated by the presence of the studio-machine (EIS), while *Accordion & Voice* (and especially *Horse Sings from Cloud*) is built around the composer-performer's breathing. While similarly unhurried, the rhythmic logic of *Roots* is harder to fathom or humanize—it blends, smears, and slurs time. This is Oliveros embracing her cyborg potential, leaving the earthen bumpkin persona of *Accordion & Voice* behind, or at least updating it with the next generation of software for people.

250

I had no doubt multi-instrumentalist Joe McPhee was multi-talented, but I only recently learned he was a vice president at Hat Hut Records for some time, which helps explain how he came to write the liner notes to Pauline Oliveros's *The Roots of the Moment*, first released by hat ART in 1988. My version of the CD, with McPhee's commentary, dates from 2006. His notes are, well, expansive, considering Oliveros in the context of (outer) space and their mutual admiration for *Star Trek*: "In fact," he speculates, "Pauline would be as able a captain of any Starship in the fleet of the United Federation of Planets. A bit of difference here though, for Pauline Oliveros space is not necessarily the final frontier and the barrier at the end of the universe is just another interesting challenge. For Pauline, like Sun Ra, Space is the place." McPhee takes the metaphor further, though he means literal space, too, in his analysis. In it, he takes up Oliveros's notions of "quantum improvisation" and Deep Listening, and brings them into dialogue with his own way of organizing improvisation, calling it "PO music" while noting the two letters also happen to be the initials of his ostensible subject:

> The PO music to which I refer comes from the work of the philosopher Dr. Edward de Bono's *Lateral Thinking* and is a language indicator to show that provocation is being used to move from one set of fixed ideas in order to discover new ones (PO?). Drawing from a concept of Positive, Possible, Poetic Hypothesis, PO Music too relies more on listening than reading and writing conventional notation to make music … IMPROVISATION. Is this the Twilight Zone or what?

251

In order / to hear / what I say / you have to listen / deeply.

—Joe McPhee, "In Order to Hear" (2007)

252

It's like a heat wave
Burning in my heart (It's like a heat wave)
I can't keep from crying (It's like a heat wave)
It's tearing me apart

In a much-needed moment of levity at the beginning of the inaugural faculty senate Zoom meeting at the end of a very long, very hot first week of school in which the CalArts HVAC system broke down, the new dean of the art school Steve Lam took an open request for some music while we waited for everyone to arrive. Steve leaped to the occasion and played "(Love is Like a) Heat Wave," the 1963 Motown classic by Martha and the Vandellas. An appropriate choice given the continuing string of 90°F-plus days. Two of my colleagues noted their own Detroit origins and felt the love.

My own go-to heatwave theme song is Lee "Scratch" Perry's "City Too Hot," which is included on the *Trojan Upsetter Box Set* that tends to stay in my car's semi-regular heavy rotation. I haven't listened to it yet during the current heatwave because I've been sitting on Zoom for three days and not in my car.

Why, why, why, why . . .
This city too hot
I'm a got to cool out, upon the hilltop
This city too hot
I'm a got to cool out, upon the hilltop

But, no need to choose a favorite. There are plenty of too-hot days to go around.

253

Between the intense heat and the intense beginning to the school year, with three days of (unanticipated) Zoom meetings, I suddenly haven't had much time for music. And I've been distracted from my plan to write about Joe McPhee's *Soprano* (2007) album, which recently arrived in the mail. I hope to return to it soon. I finally got out of the house today and went to see some exhibitions. My soundtrack was Alice Coltrane's *Translinear Light*, her final studio album from 2004. I haven't listened to it as obsessively as some of her earlier albums, but in many ways it's a return to the muscular piano playing of her earlier years, with and after John Coltrane—her takes on her husband's *Leo* (1967) and *Crescent* (1964) are idiosyncratic and reveal new thoughts about those classics. There are some jammy Wurlitzer workouts too. There's no harp on the album. The blues, in its most expansive (cosmic) sense, pervades her work, and this album affirms that, including a rendition of the traditional "This Train," a gospel song first recorded in 1922, which is also something of a sly self-portrait, perhaps?: Train/Trane. Today my new graduate assistant Bethlehem told me about a concert in celebration of Alice Coltrane that took place in Downtown Los Angeles on August 27, which would have been her eighty-fifth birthday. I'm sad I missed it.

254

On Thursday night, Leslie kindly treated me to a concert by Peter Hook & The Light, fronted by the Joy Division and New Order bass player, who was playing both albums (*Unknown Pleasures* [1979] and *Closer* [1980]) by the former band, preceded by a set of hits by the latter. The show was at the opulent and deeply eccentric Theatre at the Ace Hotel, where we had previously seen Spiritualized play their classic album *Ladies and gentlemen we are floating in space* (1997). This is of course a lucrative opportunity for yesteryear's favorite band—provided they stay alive long enough to do so—to play full albums for new and old fans, and who's to blame them? A block away, Pavement was playing on the same night. For most people, including me for many of my formative years, this is what music is: bands playing songs and albums on repeat, taking the perfection of the studio product and adding the visceral energy and residual star power in presenting the material live, no matter how old and weathered the vessel. If you know the words, you can and probably will sing along. How many times had Peter Hook heel-tapped through these songs?

Joy Division is Leslie's band, not mine, meaning their music was crucial to her at a formative moment, which happened to be when I was six years old. I missed it the first time around and for many years later, and never exactly caught up. At some point, very belatedly, I got into British postpunk—some but not all. Wire and Gang of Four especially, but also Mission of Burma. My high school sweetheart was obsessed with the Cure and the Smiths, so I already knew both of those bands by osmosis, but didn't go out of my way to listen to them on my own. I absolutely love the Raincoats, which I discovered through Kurt Cobain—does that count? But for whatever reason, I never dug into Joy Division or New Order, perhaps sensing a hard and fast cult to which I was already too late to join, symbolized by the iconic *Unknown Pleasures* T-shirt which has launched an unknown number of funny parodies. (I've threatened to make a tie-dyed version; this would have been the perfect occasion.) Leslie adores Joy Division but is fairly repulsed by New Order. Obviously the loss of brooding singer Ian Curtis is the overwhelming difference, but the distinction isn't so perfectly distinct to me.

I enjoyed the show, but as a fairly neutral observer—neither loving nor hating the music. Damning by faint praise, I suppose, to say I enjoyed it. My own Proustian version of this would be something like a concert by Metallica's second bass player Jason Newsted, leading a backing band called The Heavy through renditions of . . . *And Justice for All* (1988) and *Garage Days Re-Revisited* (1987), with some early Flotsam & Jetsam songs thrown in for good measure. Above all else, the show clarified something about where my musical values are at this moment: I prefer bearing witness to the unknown pleasures of telepathic improvisation over the heel-tapping familiarity of tried-and-true numbers. But then again sometimes it's nice to have something to hum along to.

255

I listened to Joe McPhee's *Soprano* (2007) this afternoon. And then I immediately listened to it again. The LP, with a tipped-on silkscreen on rice paper by Judith Lindbloom, is very special, and what's on the record is even more so. It was recorded at St. George's Church in Guelph on September 10, 1998, as part of the Guelph Jazz Festival, a year or so after Pauline Oliveros performed there. Oliveros supplied the album notes, and there's clearly a two-way jolt of Deep Admiration between her and McPhee. "A Night on Rose Mountain" seemingly refers to a Deep Listening Retreat, which had often taken place at Rose Mountain, Las Vegas, New Mexico. Not mentioned, strangely enough, is that the first two tracks, titled "Response Ability I" and "Response Ability II" are actually performances of an Oliveros text score from 1978:

RESPONSE ABILITY

Listen for a call. When the call comes, answer with your own call.

Call until you receive an answering call. Echo that call.

Reading this text, I think one might easily assume a duo performance. And McPhee is certainly no stranger to the duet as form, but here he interprets Oliveros's score as a solo for soprano saxophone. Or, one might call it a duet between McPhee and St. George's Church. The call, from McPhee, is answered by the echo of St. George's generously reverberant space. Beautifully recorded to reveal that acoustic expanse, it's a solo and duet at the same time, reminding me of the jazz title "Alone Together."

One of my favorite exhibitions last fall was a duet between McPhee and photographer/filmmaker Ari Marcopoulos at LAXART in Hollywood, titled (no coincidence) *Alone Together* (2021).

The show consisted of a video by Marcopoulos of McPhee improvising in the exact same empty gallery in which one watched the video. As a former recording studio where Charlie Parker—among many other notables—once appeared, McPhee decided on the alto saxophone. And he played a plastic alto in honor of Ornette Coleman, extending the lineage another generation or two.

In his insightful curatorial notes for the exhibition, LAXART director Hamza Walker comments that

Alone Together is named for a poem written by McPhee and recited in the video's opening minutes. While the title's immediate reference is to a collective isolation engendered by the pandemic, the poem itself is an invective whose sentiments are fueled by COVID's death toll. It is a scathing indictment of the Trump administration to the degree that the virus and the presidency are referenced interchangeably throughout the poem.

The poem begins, "On a day the world stood still/it arrived in the dead of winter/ushered in on a cold wind from hell." It is not until a few lines later, when McPhee references "Morning In America," the slogan for Ronald Reagan's 1984 presidential campaign, that it becomes clear that winter as a season not only marked the arrival of the virus but also Trump's inauguration. With or without COVID, Reagan's Morning in America, under the auspices of Trump, has become mourning in America.

The poem's directness renders it a précis announcing a performance taking up the task of mourning. Courtesy of its integral connection to breathing, the saxophone already lends itself to a rhetoric of the soul. Abiding by these notions, McPhee grounds the performance in breath. But here, the essence of life is at the service of singing of and for the dead. McPhee's brusque and strained vocalizing cannot help but come across as a form of channeling, his horn an instrument for all the souls who, unable to be in the presence of loved ones at the time of death, "began their journey to forever/alone together."

Heavy, that. The audience for that channeling was Marcopoulos's crew and a few people from LAXART. By presenting the resulting video in the same space, the rest of us are invited to bear witness, too, if belatedly. Breathing is also integral to McPhee's "Response Ability": There is in fact a dynamic relationship between call and response that manifests more like

listening / sounding / echoing / breathing / listening / sounding / echoing / breathing . . .

There was presumably an audience for this performance at St. George's because it was part of the Guelph Jazz Festival, but much like McPhee's plastic alto solo at LAXART, the "dialogue" is between performer and interior architecture. The audience is (it seems) a mere, if fortunate, bystander. The emphasis here, as with Deep Listening Band, is on SOUNDING SPACE. Everything else, including my/our eventual delectation, committed to vinyl, is so much icing on the proverbial cake.

256

Joe McPhee's interpretation of Oliveros's *Response Ability* (1978) subtly (or perhaps not so subtly) conjoins it with the blues and its long history of call and response. Perhaps it also makes perfect sense he did this in a church, as "the call" of call and response is one often made to someone or something beyond the earthly realm.

This score, like so many of Oliveros's text scores, is so open to interpretation—presenting a framework or structures or perhaps a guidepost for how to approach playing (through listening, breathing, etc.), without ever telling you what note(s) to play—that one could almost take it as a "traditional," like "This Train." Oliveros was not one for playing cover versions, but perhaps many or most of the works in her own catalog operate like meta-traditionals. They remind us of our most basic and universal impulses toward making music, alone or together, sounding spaces, and the deep history of those impulses.

257

When You Hear Music / After It's Over / It's Gone in the Air / You Can Never Capture It Again—a playlist:

Joe McPhee
As Serious as Your Life
hatOLOGY, 1998

Sun Ra
Outer Spaceways Incorporated
Black Lion Records, 1993

Joe McPhee
Po Music / Oleo
hatOLOGY, 2004

Psychic Temple
Plays Music for Airports
Joyful Noise Recordings, 2016

258

Deep looking, deep listening

This morning, I am reading an article in the *New York Times* about the James Webb Space Telescope. The headline: "The Search for Intelligent Life is About to Get a Lot More Interesting." Among the findings (for me), is the term "technosignatures," coined in 2007 by astronomer Jill Tarter. The author of the article asks, "Does a telescopic reading suggest a life-sustaining atmosphere? Or is it possibly a sign of technology, too? Scientists looking for biosignatures, in other words, may encounter marks of technology as well." Would aliens create as much space junk as we have? That's my own armchair astronomer question. Humans seem exceedingly good at creating garbage, and leaving traces of our colonial missions wherever we go. It's nice to imagine aliens would be tidier.

I am also thinking about *Response Ability* (1978) in light of Joe McPhee and Pauline Oliveros's mutual affection for *Star Trek*—and now in light of the idea of technosignatures.

Listen for a call. When the call comes, answer with your own call.

Call until you receive an answering call. Echo that call.

259

Friday into Saturday—a playlist:

Sarah Davachi
Two Sisters: Chamber Music for Consorts in Yellow, Green, and Bronze
Late Music, 2022

Kim Gordon & Loren Connors
at Issue
Alara, 2021

Steve Roden
Dark Over Light Earth
New Plastic Music, 2007

260

It's remarkable, in retrospect, how luxurious my summer was. By luxurious I mostly refer to time, much of which was devoted to listening. It's not as if I have stopped listening now that the school year has resumed, but it is true that my attention has been diverted toward other pressing matters: my two classes and various administrative duties. Yesterday I listened to new finds on Spotify while "pencil pushing" (approving independent contracts with my lazy digital signature, though I was taking notes with an actual pencil on paper) and doing two loads of laundry. The reality is that most of my listening accompanies another activity, but it's ideal when that activity actually helps focus my listening. Walking in the park is one example. Driving is another, though sometimes I get caught up in the snarl of traffic and focus on my safety—or my mind wanders elsewhere in a fugue state. It's hard to stay in the music, but I am now acutely aware that it's much easier for me to do so in the summer. Likewise, the present text, which is suddenly much more difficult to accomplish, given my need to get on the road promptly in the morning and my diminished energy by the time I get home. It's a loss, really, to let go of that luxury, though I am excited to train my attention on my students, on preparing lectures, on spending time in the classroom and meeting colleagues in the hallways of CalArts. Thursday evening, at a welcome party for new faculty, I talked to MPA and Alan Poma about my "performance" of *Sonic Meditation XXI*. Alan, who is an experimental musician from Lima, had met Pauline Oliveros when she came to Peru; MPA has performed in an interpretation of Oliveros's *Telepathic Improvisation* by Boudry / Lorenz and had narrowly missed meeting the composer. No matter how brief or seemingly straightforward the prompt—*What constitutes your musical universe?*—my explanation of my response tends to initiate a longer conversation. This text, which I most often write at home, regardless of where my listening takes place, is extremely private and tends to feel like a secret when I reveal it to people. Now, some eight and a half months into it, I can already imagine this text coming to an end, and am wondering how that ending will transform my listening and sense of time. Will the future anterior reveal another loss, or a kind of gain? Only time will tell.

261

Tomorrow Will Be Nothing Like Today Will Be Nothing Like Tomorrow seems like a useful mantra for my year of intentional listening, if not for any given year. It is also the title of a neon sculpture by Madeline Hollander that I saw yesterday in the vault room at Jeffrey Deitch's new gallery outpost at 7000 Santa Monica Blvd. The space was most recently LAXART, which is vacating to a new location, and many years ago it was Radio Recorders recording studio. Several projects at LAXART called attention to this history, including Joe McPhee's performance-for-video recorded in the space last year. For the inaugural show under new ownership, the main space was devoted to Hollander's light and sound installation *Sunrise/Sunset* (2022), in which 96 BMW headlights are installed *en masse* as a 4 x 24 grid on a curved wall. The lights occasionally flash on and off, but in a rhythm that is difficult to apprehend, if it is a rhythm at all. Further investigation (reading the press release) reveals, "The headlights form a global time zone map that performs with the earth's rotation. As the sun rises and sets across the globe, the headlights react, turning on when moving into the night and off when entering daylight, blinking and shifting in real-time according to their location in the world." I'm also informed that, "The result is an image of global connectedness emerging from the interaction between individual actions, technological automation, and cosmic forces." I'm not sure that's immediately clear, but the installation is strange to behold and provocative in its insinuation of an inhuman scale of time. I mean nobody is going to experience the full twenty-four-hour cycle of the work, but the work seems willfully indifferent (?) to a human perceiver. The blinks rather maddeningly query: *What does the machine want?* That BMW-funded the work complicates whatever utopian aspiration ("cosmic forces"?) the work hopes to propose—for me at least. But what held my interest was the musical accompaniment, by Madeline's sister Celia Hollander, who I met and worked with a little when she was a student in the music school at CalArts. The sisters have collaborated frequently; Madeline trained and first emerged as a choreographer, and Celia often composed scores for her dances. The present score reminds me that the installation of headlights is a kind of choreography, too, albeit for machines and not people. Celia's music was similarly machine-like in its affect and its relentlessness without actually feeling repetitive. It's varied and suggests a kind of regularity. It might take an hour—or twenty-four—to figure out or, really, several cycles. This reminds me to return to Celia's album from last year, titled *Timekeeper* (2021). I listened to it when it first came out but haven't given it a recent listen. I should. Maybe tomorrow (which will be nothing like today, which will be nothing like . . .)?

262

Today (Time / No Time) x 2—a playlist:

Celia Hollander
Timekeeper
Leaving Records, 2021

Celia Hollander
Recent Futures
Leaving Records, 2020

263

Tbh I don't think about genre very much when it comes to music and what I'm listening to—particularly with contemporary music. Which isn't to say I'm not interested in genre as a concept, only that I tend toward music that 1) at least bends or expands our understanding of a given genre, or 2) mashes two or more genres together, or 3) demands its own genre, or 4) evades or actively resists genre altogether. Immediately after delineating these possibilities, I realize that my own tastes have gradually evolved from 1 toward 4. What *Bitches Brew* (1970) did to jazz is a useful example of #1. John Zorn's *Naked City* (1990) is a textbook example of #2. Steve Roden, and the naming of the lowercase genre (not by him), exemplifies #3. Pauline Oliveros's *The Roots of the Moment* (1988) might be a perfect example of #4. A lot of what gets called "new music" falls under the fourth category. When does "new" music become old music?

Yesterday, while looking up some of Steve's records on Discogs, I noticed that his EP *ecstasy showered its petals with the full peal of the bells* (2009), which is actually a little 3-inch CD, is classified as "Electronic, Non-Music." Listening to it now, I can assure you it's music, even if it doesn't sound like what my mom thinks music is. For the record, the spare notes on the tiny CD indicate the sound is made using a small hand bell, "generated and organized" by Steve. This classification is further articulated, by Discogs, through style: "Drone, Music Concrète, Sound Art." No reference to "lowercase," a genre that Steve was tagged with because he always writes in lowercase, and his music is (seemingly) so modest and unassuming. On Discogs, his other releases are given a wide assortment of other descriptors: electronic, minimal, experimental. But "Non-Music" actually strikes me as a kind of perverse achievement for this dedicated follower of Cage, who entered the music world through a teenage punk band and then art school, rather than the conservatory. For its part, Discogs notes:

The Non-Music genre is for releases without music, such as speeches, comedy, audiobooks, poetry, PSAs, special effects, interviews, and other forms of non-music.

The Non-Music style is to only be used on releases that do not contain music. Do not apply this style to releases that don't follow the rules of music; despite the mindsets of the artists, styles such as noise, experimental, etc. are still music.

So, I think it's fair to say that *ecstasy showered its petals with the full peal of the bells* has been miscategorized. (The style categories provided—"Drone, Music Concrète, Sound Art"—immediately reveal this contradiction.) I won't even touch the phrase "rules of music." For now. Maybe that will be next year's meditation.

And then, looking up Celia Hollander, I note that her album *Recent Futures* (2020) is tagged as "Leftfield." What the heck is that? (Presumably not music about baseball, which in fact describes a few of Steve's compositions. He's a fan of the Dodgers.) According to Discogs:

. . . this term tends to be applied to anything with a "quirky" component, or anything that's atypical of its genre, or to which no other style really seems to apply.

Sometimes it is used as a less-alienating alternative for the term Experimental.

There is major potential for overuse of this tag, and as more styles are added, they can potentially be used to replace this tag where there was previously no better description.

Well, "Experimental" is easily abused (as I've already pondered weeks ago). "Quirky" is at best a back-handed compliment. But a quick glance at what has been tagged as "Leftfield" reveals a pretty wide swath of music, from Talking Heads's *True Stories* (1986) to Moby's *Play* (1999), MF Doom and Madlib's *Madvillainy* (2004) to Terry Riley's *Reed Streams* (1967). A lot of what it describes is very popular music, if not exactly Top 40 popular. (Terry Riley is an outlier here, though his *Church of Anthrax* [1971] record with John Cale has some serious hook. According to Discogs, that record is "Modern Classical, Abstract, Minimal, Avantgarde.") I suppose I prefer Leftfield to Centerfield—and certainly to Rightfield. Yikes.

Categories tend to fall apart. I'm not here to say they're inherently bad. They might help someone discover something they've never heard before, and in that sense they offer some useful navigation. Mostly, they are signposts (literally, in a record store or on Discogs or Bandcamp or Spotify). They are about marketing, social segmentation, algorithms, norms. But they are also lazy descriptors, ultimately more limiting than revealing, I think, and they don't do many favors for the actual music. Best to avoid them, whenever possible, but good for a chuckle when your friend makes a delightful little 3-inch CD in an edition of 500, with a very poetic title, that manages to qualify as *NON-MUSIC*. Congratulations are in order!

264

What constitutes your musical universe?

How is it that I just realized this sonic meditation is a more elegant (and perhaps even sublime) rephrasing of one of my least favorite questions in the world: *What kind of music do you like?* It's also one word shorter. Funny that I would devote so much time to answering a question that I hate so much.

265

15–30 Hz Greg Anderson (USA)

31–65 Hz Jana Winderen (NO)

66–90 Hz Minoru Sato (JP)

91–140 Hz Jimena Sarno (AR/USA)

141–180 Hz Bethan Kellough (UK/USA)

181–250 Hz Tom Recchion (USA)

251–350 Hz JG Thirlwell (AUS/USA)

351–500 Hz Alba Triana (CO/USA)

501–1000 Hz Jónsi (IS/USA)

1001–2000 Hz Lawrence English (AUS)

2001–5000 Hz Yan Jun (CN)

5001–12000 Hz Richard Chartier (USA)

266

What constitutes your musical universe?

Yesterday I elevated my listening game and drove to Mt. Wilson Observatory, perched in the Angeles Crest National Forest above Los Angeles. It was "on the way" to CalArts, though it's really quite a detour and would have better been its own day-long adventure. Other duties called in the afternoon, but first was a press preview for *freq_wave*:

> an immersive installation by pioneering new media and conceptual artist, Carl Michael von Hausswolff, who will transform the interior of the 100-inch Hooker Telescope at Mount Wilson Observatories with a visual and sound installation. The project brings together twelve individual sound works by twelve artists, each operating within a unique frequency range based on field recordings from the Pacific Ocean and amplified to act as a single, generative sonic zone.

The Hooker Telescope was the world's largest and most important telescope from 1917 to 1949. It's an extraordinary site, regardless of the art quotient. (Years ago, I visited the McDonald Observatory near Fort Davis, Texas with a group of art students from USC. It was a stunning experience.) Even the drive up the mountain, with the windows open and the gradual sensation of the air getting thinner and clearer, was transportive. I even saw a baby bobcat run across the road as I navigated the hairpin turns.

I usually hate press previews. And I don't even really consider myself "press," or what Connie Butler referred to as "the muffin eaters" when we co-curated *Made in L.A.* (2014). After that, I knew I wasn't and didn't want to be a muffin eater: I'm a person who looks at a lot of art (and affiliated culture) and writes about it, sometimes, and makes exhibitions even less frequently. Most often these days I'm just looking—or just listening. But the event sounded incredibly cool (it is) and was organized by Robert Crouch, a sweet curator and composer who I met years ago through our mutual friend Steve Roden. It was a low-key affair, with many of the esteemed composers and artists in attendance.

After some remarks by Robert and Carl Michael, the whole group entered the telescope, passing its collection of dusty relics, then climbing several flights of stairs to get to the top deck. Dark and awash in blue light, the effect was decidedly otherworldly. It took time for my eyes to adjust and to take in the massive telescope in the middle of it all. The collective composition by von Hausswolff et al. was dispersed around the space. Chairs were available for extended contemplation, but I found that walking in circles was the preferred way to apprehend the dense and undulating drone, and to begin peeling apart its ten layers. There's something perverse about resituating sounds generated by the ocean in a telescope 5715 feet above sea level. I mean that as a compliment. I'm still chewing on it.

Still, the music itself took second fiddle to the noble old telescope, which they rotated for the preview. The hatch above gradually opened up, and the room suddenly began to spin. It was difficult to comprehend what exactly was spinning. It looked like the telescope was spinning, but was it actually me or the deck I was standing on that was in motion? I mentioned the disorienting effect to Robert on my way out, and he said it gets weirder with repeat experiences. So I hope to experience it again, with or without music.

267

JOHN
LENNON
BROKE UP
FLUXUS

So says a T-shirt by David Horvitz that I purchased at the Hauser & Wirth bookstore yesterday.

268

Pharoah Sanders died, at eighty-one. I've written about him a few times in this text. His music has remained dear to me since I discovered some thirty years ago, coinciding with my first explorations of John Coltrane, Alice Coltrane, Don Cherry, Sonny Sharrock, and world music. The extremity of his approach to the tenor saxophone greatly appealed to me when I first started listening to jazz music. It made for an easy transition from my infatuation with Jimi Hendrix, who took electric guitar to its outer reaches, to Sanders and the outer reaches of jazz. Why blow when you can overblow? But over the years I've also grown to appreciate Sanders's gentler side: his capacity for smooth, majestic grandeur on the tenor is in fact equal to his capacity for ferocious, abrasive eruption. Both are, in my opinion, "beautiful," representing the extremities of lived experience.

As a coincidence, earlier this week I received a copy of *The Cricket: Black Music in Evolution, 1968–69*, which was just published by Blank Forms. The book anthologizes all four issues of *The Cricket*, a magazine founded by Amiri Baraka (née LeRoi Jones), Larry Neal, and A.B. Spellman—with Sun Ra and Milford Graves as advisors and contributors—which provided a ground level critical account of "the new thing" as it was happening. I've known about the magazine for years, and have seen fragments from it, but I was extremely excited to have it finally arrive in the mail. Among the first things I read in my first glance at the book was a review by Baraka of *Tauhid*, Pharoah Sanders's first album for Impulse, and one of my favorite albums ever, in part because Sharrock is so good on it. The review, in the very first issue of *The Cricket*, is something else. Here's an excerpt that makes a case for his expansive range—his power, his tenderness, his "completeness":

On *Upper and Lower Egypt* Pharoah just about gets off. The conception is so beautiful, and that funky earth noise ("tune") he has carrying him sweeps along all our feeling for completion. The scream in the midst of that long line, is the feeling for sublime direction in the midst of the constant business of looking waking breathing working, &c. Our old symbol the phoenix, it too from Egypt, is what that sound finally makes me think of, that black bord bursting out of flame. The ending of the *Japan* side (Venus-Capricorn Rising) is a replacing, a restating, of what is now the known contemporary black emotion. The bursting, the flight, the screaming.

But Pharoah has a mastery of tone, you can hear in person, he hasn't to my knowledge yet recorded [he had, but not like this]. A mastery of "harmonics," a breath control . . . to draw out the sound into infinitely sounded slivers of feeling. This is what we look for. The completion the rounding into "completness," [*sic*] with the whole battery blowing out. Pharoah has incredible power, and incredible tenderness soulfulness . . . like a love of playing, of sound, that will spread your consciousness dazzled among his notes.

269

Spirits Known and Unknown (Memories of Pharoah Sanders)—a playlist:

Sun Ra and His Arkestra
Sun Ra and His Arkestra Featuring Pharoah Sanders & Black Harold
El Saturn Records, 1976 (recorded in 1964)

John Coltrane
Meditations
Impulse!, 1966

Pharoah Sanders
Tauhid
Impulse!, 1966

Don Cherry
Where is Brooklyn?
Blue Note, 1969

Leon Thomas
Spirits Known and Unknown
Flying Dutchman, 1969

Alice Coltrane (Featuring Pharoah Sanders and Joe Henderson)
Ptah the El Daoud
Impulse!, 1970

Pharoah Sanders
Black Unity
Impulse!, 1972

270

Abstract Dark Energy—a playlist:

John Coltrane
Live at the Village Vanguard Again!
Impulse!, 1966

Bill Dixon
Son of Sisyphus
Soul Note, 1990

Bill Dixon with Exploding Star Orchestra
Bill Dixon with Exploding Star Orchestra
Thrill Jockey, 2008

Rob Mazurek / Exploding Star Orchestra
Dimensional Stardust
International Anthem Recording Company, 2020

271

There's just not enough time in the day—for listening, but especially for writing. I'm struggling to keep up with school, which is always especially intense in the opening weeks of the semester. I've given too much homework, which (alas, why do I always need to be reminded?) is reading that I need to do, too, though perhaps I need to read it twice as well. I do love putting together a lecture, which is also to say put together a slideshow. On occasions when someone mistakes me for an artist (lol) and asks what my medium is, I like to say PowerPoint. Though for several years PowerPoint has been replaced by Google Slides. Sometimes I find myself adapting old PowerPoint slides to Google's wider format. This is the case with Routine Pleasures, which I haven't taught in ten years. A class is never the same twice, anyway, and it always seems like I'm starting almost from scratch. Kind of like baking bread, where one has to add a lot of new flour and water to the old starter. This week's tangle of topics: the quilts and quilters of Gee's Bend, the Asian American artist network Godzilla, and the "queer microcinema" (per Julia Bryan-Wilson) of EZTV, which was a space and organization for videomaking in West Hollywood that began in the 1980s.

Meanwhile, a package arrived at the door: *After All Is Said and Done: Taping the Grateful Dead 1965–1995*, by my friend Mark A. Rodriguez. It's a beauty and a BEAST of a book, focusing on the termite-like activity of recording and sharing bootleg tapes of Dead concerts. It actually fits the Routine Pleasures paradigm perfectly, which I define in part with Roland Barthes's notion of "plural delectation," in his essay "The Rustle of Language." "For the rustle," asserts Barthes, "implies a community of bodies":

> in the sounds of the pleasure which is "working," no voice is raised, guides, or swerves, no voice is constituted; the rustle is the very

sound of plural delectation—plural but never massive (the mass, quite the contrary, has a single voice, and terribly loud).

I've long been fascinated by this aspect of the Dead, though I will note for the record I am not nor have ever been a "Deadhead," though I have been taken in by their music many times. (Leslie sometimes confuses me for a fan, but no Deadhead would ever take me for one. I express my interest with too much fine print and too many asterisks.) I am at the very least sympathetic to the cause and appreciate the band as a cultural phenomenon with a syncretic grasp of diverse American musical idioms. (If that sounds more like appreciation than fanaticism, it is exactly that.) But that conversation must wait, as must Mark's book. At the moment, I have other delectation to attend to.

272

On the road today, I coined a new term: megaminor. It was first used in a text message to Mark A. Rodriguez, in congratulatory reaction to his book and by extension his project of duping Dead bootlegs by the thousands and making those into artwork ("sculpture"). The term megaminor was coined to describe a termite-like project which accrues over time to become something BIG—and, this part is important, in deference to Manny Farber's earliest conception of termite art—without becoming a White Elephant. The termite tendency, as Farber concluded his 1962 essay, is a "buglike immersion in a small area without point or aim, and, overall, concentration on nailing down one moment without glamorizing it, but forgetting this accomplishment as soon as it has been passed; the feeling that all is expendable, that it can be chopped up and flung down in a different arrangement without ruin."

The Dead has a similar story: a band with a massive legacy, developed over many decades, but utterly termite-like in its devotion to the minor. Hence the band making space for bootleggers and multiple versions of the truth. In a Dead show, no song is too big to be subject to revision or at least some light tinkering, including the intricate group improvisations which seam these songs together, in ever-surprising variation. The idea of the minor follows from the can of worms opened by Deleuze and Guattari in their book on Kafka, whose writing they define as a "minor literature," which is to say a literature focused on the "small stuff" rather than the "obvious stuff" (quoting Jean-Pierre Gorin in *Routine Pleasures*), eschewing "gilt ambitions" (Farber) toward the Great Novel. Beyond Kafka, beyond Mark A. Rodriguez, beyond the Dead, I'm thinking about everything on this semester's syllabus as a version of the megaminor (including Deep Listening

Band). Farber seems to miss the notable fact that termites work collectively, but the true force of the termite is not located in size or even numbers, but in time and tenacity. The termite toils in the *longue durée*.

On the road today, I contemplated listening to the one Dead CD I have stowed in my car, but instead I listened to Sonic Youth's *SYR6: Koncertas Stan Brakhage prisiminimui* (a concert in memory of Stan Brakhage) stowed on my ancient iPod. The album was recorded live in 2003, with the band joined by Tim Barnes in an accompaniment of films by Stan Brakhage at Anthology Film Archives. (The Lithuanian title is courtesy of Brakhage peer Jonas Mekas. A film still portrait of Brakhage by Mekas graces the cover of the CD.) The three tracks are all titled "Heady Jam," and indeed, listening to these jams, driving over the mountains at 80 miles an hour following a slow slog through downtown, are my version of a Deadhead's ecstatic devotion. The secret sauce for heady improvisation is found in the perfect ratio of familiarity and surprise, even on repeat listening.

273

Heady Jams—a playlist:

Sonic Youth with Tim Barnes
SYR6: Koncertas Stan Brakhage prisiminimui
Sonic Youth Records, 2005

Xösen
In Chron
Radical Documents, 2021

John Oswald
Grayfolded: Transitive Axis
Artifact Music/Swell, 1994; Important Records, 2014

274

An abbreviated gallery itinerary trained my attention on three gallery exhibitions on Washington Blvd. in West Adams. The last of them, at Kristina Kite Gallery, was a group exhibition curated by Sabrina Tarasoff fashioned as a belated wake for Bob Flanagan. Flanagan was a poet, stand-up comedian, and artist, but is best known as a masochist. He died of cystic fibrosis in 1996, a few days after his 43rd birthday. His longtime partner in life and art, Sheree Rose, provided the countervailing sadism in their arrangement, and contributed a number of photographs to the show. (*The Pain Journal*, Flanagan's brutal diaristic account of his own demise, along with Kirby Dick's documentary, *Sick: The Life and Death of Bob Flanagan, Supermasochist* [1997], are recurring subjects of my occasional seminar Performing Life. Rose was once a guest in my class, and gamely participated in an Oliveros *Sonic Meditation* instigated by two of my students.) I had seen a lot of these works before, but it was nice to see them again, recontextualized. Altogether, the show had a heavy LA-in-the-90s vibe. Which is my kind of vibe. *100 Reasons* (1991), a video in the back room of the exhibition, focused on Flanagan's tender ass getting paddled, with Rose counting to one hundred while Mike Kelley annotates each blow with his distinct and nasally Michigan accent. The text Kelley recites is a list of nicknames or insults from his artist's book *Plato's Cave Rothko's Chapel Lincoln's Profile* (1986). Many of these are painfully appropriate: #34 FANNY TANNER, #47 MEAT BEATER, #75 REAR ADVANCE, #88 DADDY'S LITTLE HELPER, etc. (I first learned about Flanagan and Rose from the naughty insert card for Sonic Youth's *Dirty* [1992] CD, with its cover art by Kelley. Actually, it's where I first learned about Mike Kelley.) In the front of the gallery was Julie Becker's *Suburban Legend* (1999), which paired a projection of *The Wizard of Oz* (1939) with Pink Floyd's *Dark Side of the*

Moon (1973). This is, of course, a classic stoner pairing of two epic works that supposedly work together if one syncs them properly by starting the movie with the third roar of the MGM lion. I first learned about this "legend" in my college years which also happens to be when I was listening to a lot of Pink Floyd. I'm sure my roommates and I tried it at some point; if we did, I surely wasn't convinced by the results. Despite (or perhaps because of) its outsize popularity, I was never as taken with *Dark Side of the Moon* as I was with other Pink Floyd albums—*Meddle* (1971) and *Animals* (1977) were my favorites at the time. I was also a big fan of Adrian Maben's concert film *Live at Pompeii* (1972), in which the band performs in the ruinous grandeur of an ancient amphitheater for a tiny audience consisting only of the film crew. The concert is shot like a structural film, which was part of the appeal; it also includes scenes of the band at Abbey Road Studios recording *Dark Side of the Moon*. In the threshold of the gallery, one can listen to *Dark Side of the Moon* while watching Bob Flanagan get his moon darkened. It's an even less likely pairing, and it's not likely to become a new (sub)urban legend.

275

Last night at the Schindler House, architects Frank Escher and Ravi GuneWardena restaged *Pauline: An Opera*, based on the life of Pauline Gibling Schindler—socialist editor, wife of architect Rudolf Michael Schindler, homemaker, mother, and love interest of a twenty-two-year-old John Cage. The opera was initially performed at the house in 2013; I missed it the first time around. The libretto was largely drawn from the letters of the Schindler and Cage, and performed by Argenta Walther (as Pauline) and Charles Lane (alternating as "RMS" and Cage). They were accompanied by a trio of piano, cello, and flute, performing a pastiche of Cage, Henry Cowell, Sergei Prokofiev, and Edgard Varèse. At several points, the pianist (Todd Moellenberg) played the inside of the piano, in reference to Cage, of course, but also to Cowell and his influential and eccentric extended techniques, which included playing the piano strings like a harp. (Cage was a student of Cowell; Lou Harrison, Conlon Nancarrow, George Gershwin [!], and Burt Bacharach [!!] all were too.) This distinctly modernist vibe was extended by the vocalists, who delivered their lines using an aleatory approach. I do not know if the *I Ching* was involved. A proliferation of helicopters also provided "chance" accompaniment. I know the Schindler narrative well, but the opera left me especially curious about Cowell and his important role in the development of the West Coast avant-garde. (The 1999 anthology *New Music: Piano Compositions by Henry Cowell* was a pandemic discovery.) Some quick research reveals him as a controversial figure in art and life, from a riot in response to a concert of his in Leipzig in 1923, to four years of imprisonment for having sex with a minor. Sounds like a worthy subject for an opera.

276

Mr. John Cage's Prepared Piano—a playlist:

John Cage; John Tilbury, piano [prepared]
Mr. John Cage's Prepared Piano
Decca, 1976

John Cage; James Tenney, piano
Sonatas & Interludes
hat[now]ART, 2012

John Cage; Julie Steinberg, prepared piano
Sonatas & Interludes for Prepared Piano
Music & Arts, 1996

John Cage; Joshua Pierce, piano
Sonatas & Interludes for Prepared Piano
WERGO, 1989

John Cage; Maro Ajemian, piano
Sonatas & Interludes for Prepared Piano (1946-48)
Dial, 1951; reissued by Composers Recordings Inc. (CRI), 1965

277

A flyer, seen at CalArts today:

BANSHEE
QUEER TECHNO NIGHTCLUB PROJECT

/DJS
/PERFORMERS
/HOSTS

OPEN CALL

Is this a reference to Henry Cowell's *The Banshee* (1925)? Or do I just have Cowell on the brain? (Not) coincidentally, I checked out Michael Hicks's *Henry Cowell, Bohemian* from the library today. Will I actually find time to read it?

278

A week after considering the proposed category of "outlier" in my Routine Pleasures class, particularly in regard to the extraordinary Black women quilters of Gee's Bend, Alabama, I find myself now considering the term in relation to Henry Cowell—and any number of other composers and musicians. The term "outlier," as I'm using it, comes from Lynne Cooke, curator of the 2018–2019 exhibition *Outliers and American Vanguard Art*, which I saw at LACMA, and its immense catalog. "Outlier," as Cooke intends it, complicates the simple binary of inside and outside, and makes these categories spectral and relational. The very idea of a vanguard (as in avant-garde) already suggests an outlier—an artist or work that is literally ahead of the pack.

This morning, I read the first chapter of Michael Hicks's *Henry Cowell, Bohemian*, and my available attention has turned almost completely to Cowell and his West Coast context including Cage, Lou Harrison, and Harry Partch, among others. Some preliminary and inevitable Wikipedia-ing on Cowell leads me to "Category: Outsider musicians" a fascinating/puzzling/maddening grouping. Just under the letter "C," Cowell is joined by the Cherry Sisters, Corn Mo, and the band Cromagnon. It would have been an amazing, transhistorical show! The full alphabetical list includes Tiny Tim, who I once saw perform at a circus; Art Paul Schlosser, an "artist, cartoonist, comedian, journalist, musician, poet, singer, and songwriter" I regularly encountered on State Street in Madison during my undergraduate years (and honestly haven't thought about since); Red Krayola, which includes some of my grad school faculty at Art Center; and John Maus, who was briefly my classmate in the MA Program in Theory and Criticism at the same school (Maus had previously studied music as an undergrad at CalArts); fellow CalArtian Ariel Pink, who studied in the Art

Program before later becoming a Trumper, is also on the list. I keep thinking of weirdos who could also be on the "outsider" list, but aren't: Lo-fi musician and YouTube personality "Weird Paul" Petroskey made the list, but somehow "Weird Al" Yankovic didn't; Poetics, the group featuring Mike Kelley and Tony Oursler could easily be situated here, but aren't. Beach Boy and pop genius Brian Wilson does make the list, as does occasional Red Hot Chili Pepper guitarist John Frusciante; Yoshi Wada, who played epic drones on the bagpipes and made an elaborate pipe organ out of plumbing equipment, does not. I am reminded, once again, of my own mad obsession with categories despite—or perhaps precisely because of—their limitations and failure.

I generally tolerate (or straight up adore) kooks, but I don't necessarily go out of my way to find them. Or do I? Is Cowell really an "outsider"? Another Wikipedia page for "West Coast School" includes Cowell, Cage, Harrison, and Partch, united in their geographical connection to California, all with ears directed further west, across the Pacific, toward the "East" or "Orient," all—not insignificantly—queer. There's a lot I don't know about this group as a "school," and I am curious to learn more; as a school they must surely represent an important precedent for Pauline Oliveros and another West Coast school including Terry Riley, Stuart Dempster, et al., whose connection to Cage (at least) is most clear and well known to me. As always, there's more work to be done.

279

I am reminded that I had heard of John Cage before I heard his music. I believe I first encountered his name and picture—in his bearded, full denim jacket phase—in Michael Crichton's 1977 monograph on Jasper Johns. (Yes, *that* Michael Crichton, the guy that wrote *Jurassic Park*.) My high school art teacher Mrs. Belling encouraged me to look at Johns because of my interest in the American flag and my tendency toward thick impasto. So I found Crichton's book in the Janesville Public Library and checked it out. Johns's work was an important gateway to contemporary art for me—and art history, too. His work syncretized lots of things I was just discovering: Pop, Ab Ex, Dada. I suspect my first exposure to Marcel Duchamp was also in Crichton's wild essay from this book. Cage and Merce Cunningham too.

What is the first music of John Cage I heard? I believe the first music of his I bought on CD, circa that magical year of 1991, was *Music for Merce Cunningham* with performances of *Five Stone Wind* (1988) and *Cartridge Music* (1960) by Takehisa Kosugi, Michael Pugliese, and David Tudor. It was a weird opening gambit, I suppose. (Not unlike starting my Miles Davis collection with *Agharta* [1975].) I know I also found *The Perilous Night / Four Walls* (1991) soon after, with a work by Jasper Johns on the cover, and performances by Margaret Leng Tan (piano and prepared piano) and Joan La Barbara.

Among the first few Cage CDs I acquired was *Sonatas & Interludes for Prepared Piano* (1989), performed by Joshua Pierce. It's probably the one I've listened to the most. The work, composed in 1946–1948, precedes Cage's use of chance methodology, though the prepared piano was certainly a step in that direction. I was arriving to Cage's music after embracing Sonic Youth's noise and weird tunings, so for me *Sonatas* always struck me as an immensely pleasing piece of music, though it surely would have sounded discordant or even vulgar to much of its audience at the time, just as Cowell's piano performances did two decades earlier. I am also considering that I got into Thelonious Monk around the same time that I started listening to Cage, and it's possible to see both of them as inheritors of Henry Cowell's extremely physical and (to some) dismaying approach to the piano. It reminds one (me) that the piano, among other many possibilities, is a percussion instrument.

280

While preparing to read Adorno's "Free Time"—a playlist:

Morton Feldman; Darragh Morgan, violin; John Tilbury, piano
For John Cage
Diatribe Records, 2020

"A" Trio & AMM
AAMM
Al Maslakh, 2018

AMM
AMMUSIC
Elektra, 1967 / ReRMegacorp, 1990

281

Anton Fier died, at age sixty-six, by assisted suicide. As a drummer and longtime figure in the New York music scene, I've heard his work countless times, but I had never fully connected the dots of his resumé until reading the obituary in the *New York Times*. By their measure, he was a tormented soul. In his heyday, he played with an impressive list of luminaries from pop, the avant-garde, and everything in between. His evolving supergroup The Golden Palominos included everyone from John Zorn to Michael Stipe to Bernie Worrell to John Lydon to Richard Thompson . . . and that's just on the first two albums. (The family tree for King Crimson looks tidy by comparison.) Beyond his own project, Fier drummed for Herbie Hancock, Gil Scott-Heron, Yoko Ono, Mick Jagger, and Laurie Anderson. I first encountered him on Zorn's *The Big Gundown* (1986), a suitably raucous tribute to Ennio Morricone or possibly on the eponymous debut by The Lounge Lizards, both totally great albums. (Not coincidentally, Arto Lindsay is on both and was on a lot of records with him, including early Palominos and a lot of 1980s Zorn). Among his first recordings was the debut album by The Feelies, which is a band I've never (knowingly) listened to until today. Anton Fier, I hardly knew you.

282

For the past week or so I've had a JPEG of a painting by Morris Hirshfield on my desktop, extracted from a *New York Times* review by Roberta Smith of a Hirshfield retrospective at the American Folk Art Museum. Its redundant title: *Harp Girl II (Girl with Harp)* (1945). I've opened the JPEG a number of times and looked at the image in which the "girl" is framed—engulfed, really—by the elaborately decorated harp, which is further framed by an obsessive blue-and-yellow patterned background. She and the harp float in space; there is no ground. Most of Hirshfield's paintings situate their human and, often, animal subjects in wildly patterned environments which nearly swallow them alive. The paintings are flat in a perspectival sense, but vibrant, colorful; they are exuberant, full of bristling energy, but unfailingly stiff. The silence of the *Harp Girl* painting is nearly hyperbolic. Such contradictions are consistent across Hirshfield's paintings, which only began in his sixties when he retired and for seven brief years lived as an artist, celebrated by the American and European gatekeepers of the avant-garde flame. I first encountered his work in the exhibition *Outliers and American Vanguard Art* (2019), and now I wish I could see more of these strange, wonderful paintings in person. I might have to settle for the catalog, as I often do.

283

The following paragraph has already occurred in the program notes three times. Perhaps the idea of reading it a fourth time will not appeal to you. If so, you may want to read it very quickly this time. Or perhaps you will want to skip it entirely. But if the idea of reading it a fourth time does not seem too difficult or too restricting, you may want to read it again in much the same way you read it before. Perhaps, since you are now very familiar with it, you will find that it does not distract you from the music as much as it did before. Or perhaps you will find that it is more distracting than before. You may also find that it is more difficult to comprehend and relate to than it was when you read it before . . .

—Tom Johnson, liner notes for *An Hour for Piano* (1972)

284

An inventory of CDs in my car right now, alphabetical by artist*

Joshua Abrams & Natural Information Society
Mandatory Reality
Eremite Records, 2019

John Cale
Fear
Island Records, 1974

Don Cherry
Om Shanti Om
Black Sweat Records, 2020

Don Cherry
Organic Music Theatre: Festival de jazz de Chateauvallon
Blank Forms, 2021

The Circle Trio
Live at the Meridian
Sparkling Beatnik Records, 2000

Grateful Dead
Europe '72 Vol. 2
Warner Bros. Records/Rhino Records, 2011

Genius / GZA
Liquid Swords
Geffen Records, 1995

Catherine Christer Hennix / Chora(s)san Time-Court Mirage
Live at Issue Project Room
IMPREC, 2016

Bob Marley and the Wailers
Soul Revolution Part II
Upsetter, 1972

Thelonious Monk
Monk in Tokyo
Columbia Legacy, 2001

Pauline Oliveros, Roscoe Mitchell, John Tilbury, Wadada Leo Smith
Nessuno
I Dischi Di Angelica, 2016

Charlemagne Palestine + Rhys Chatham
Youuu + Mee = Weee
Sub Rosa, 2014

Pelt
Pearls From the River
VHF Records, 2003

Sebadoh
Bakesale
Sub Pop, 1994

Sun Ra and His Arkestra
At Inter-Media Arts, April 1991
Modern Harmonic, 2016

The Velvet Underground
Loaded (Fully Loaded Edition)
Rhino Records, 1997

V/A
Trojan Upsetter Box Set (Disc Three)
Trojan Records, 2002

285

*Many of which have been there for years. Their presence in my car also means they're not on my iPod. Most of these are CDs I've heard a countless number of times, know them "by heart," but nevertheless might want to listen to at a moment's notice—most often on the way home from school, late at night. Sometimes I have an overabundance of CDs in the backseat or in a tote bag. Like my library, the surplus is aspirational. But the number of CDs in my car at a given time is largely determined by the space allocated in the slot under the CD player, which holds four or five discs depending on their containers, and the console between the seats which holds about a dozen and also stows my iPod. Once a CD gets in the console, it tends to stay awhile. It's entered the "venerable" category. But I really should swap them out more often.

286

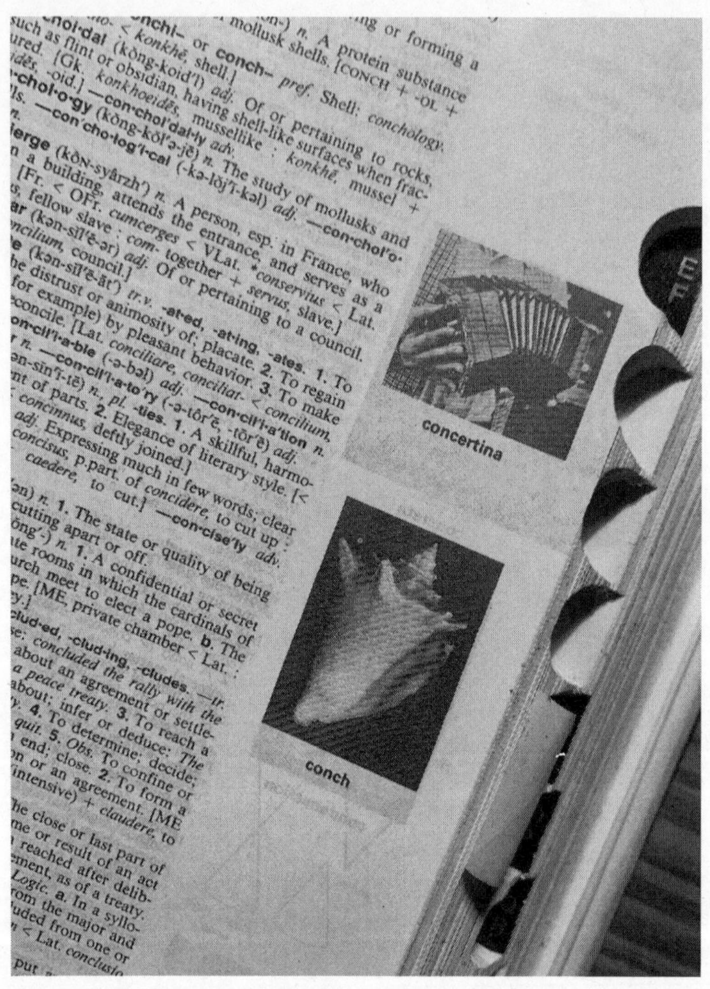

287

This week, a wonderfully provocative show of paintings and video animations by my student Vanessa Harding considered the gradual transformation of a song by the Norfolk Jazz and Jubilee Quartet, titled "Hide Me Over in the Rock of Ages" (1923) into Woody Guthrie's "This Land is Your Land" (1951) with the Carter Family's "When the World's on Fire" (1930) as a notable intermediary step. The Norfolk Jazz and Jubilee Quartet's "original" apparently derived from the eighteenth century "Hide Me Over in the Rock of Ages" by the poetically named Reformed Anglican minister Augustus Toplady. The category of "folk" has always implied cultural borrowing—hand-me-downing. But Vanessa makes the important point that such borrowing often carries with it an asymmetrical power in terms of legal and economic viability. (The intriguing, contemporary title of her show: *Transpose? I Suppose!*) In conversation, she notes that with the advent of the recording industry, the Carter Family was quick to claim legal ownership over hundreds of songs first performed by Black musicians who had less access to that industry, and presumably less of an immediate interest in questions of ownership. Vanessa's focus on Guthrie's well-known "This Land" provided a focal point for the larger and often unwieldy subject of cultural appropriation. Three large ("6 ft. and some") tondo paintings on unstretched canvas conflated historic record labels with landscapes—Guthrie's modernist and jagged; the Carter Family's a flaming hellscape; and the Norfolk Jazz and Jubilee Quartet record, a pastoral scene peppered with historical logos for Black Swan, OKeh race records, and Paramount, with two eagles soaring above its unspoiled mountains, one on the backside of a coin. (Paramount bought out the other two smaller catalogs and their labels.) Vanessa also wrote a substantial essay based on her research and kindly gave me a copy of it. The essay ends with a sweet letter by Vanessa to (long gone) Sister Rosetta Tharpe, who did her own version of "Rock of Ages" in 1951, coinciding with Guthrie's "This Land." (I was listening to her version of "This Train" a few months ago.) Vanessa writes:

Reflecting on history is so hard. The retrospective aspect leaves my thoughts in loops and contradictions, trying to rationalize why and how things were the way they were. I want to look into the future and see the world change, but I feel like I have to understand what happened in order to make the right choices about the future. EVERYTHING is always clear in retrospect. Maybe the fallacy of knowledge is what is confusing me.

288

This Land—a playlist:

Bill Frisell
This Land
Elektra Nonesuch, 1994

Don Byron
Bug Music
Nonesuch, 1996

Duke Ellington
Live at the Whitney
Impulse! / GRP, 1995

289

New York Contemporary Five
Togetherness
Don Cherry Quintet
Complete Communion Band
The Jazz Composer's Orchestra
International Quintet
Movement Incorporated
New Eternal Rhythm Orchestra
Liberation Music Orchestra
Organic Music Society
Don Cherry's New Researches
Organic Music Theatre
Mandingo Griot Society
Old and New Dreams
Codona
Bitter Funeral Beer Band
Don Cherry's Nu

290

Carrier Bag / Gathering-Work—two texts:

Ursula K. Le Guin
"The Carrier Bag Theory of Fiction"
Dancing at the Edge of the World: Thoughts on Words, Women, Places
Grove Press, 1989

Fumi Okiji
"Oriki for Don Cherry: To Be Part of a Gathering-Work"
Blank Forms 06: Organic Music Societies
Blank Forms Editions, 2021

291

To speak as part of the gathering-work is not only to place oneself in a crew. It is also to cultivate the manners of address appropriate to such a site of expressive energy. The gathering-work wants your body (which needs to be understood in its materiality-resonating chambers, ear drums, kinesics apparatuses), but it requires a body-space, a makeshift vector/host, a point of contact for the elusive, plastic gathering/dispersal. To speak as part of the work is . . . to become a "transducer," not for any original work but for the sociality constituted by constellations of response to a call we hear after the fact, if at all.

Don Cherry tells us: "It's actually not my music because it's a combination of different experiences, different cultures, and different composers that involves the music that we play together, or that I'm playing when I'm playing alone." Playing together or alone; playing alone, together.

> –Fumi Okiji, "Oriki for Don Cherry: To Be Part of a Gathering-Work" (2021)

292

School has been demanding, the art world too, and I've been rendered fuzzy with a good old-fashioned head cold. Writing has been a struggle, which isn't to say I've haven't continued devoting attention to what constitutes my musical universe when I can stave off various distractions (otherwise known as work and life) and the need for collapse. Among other considerations, this past week I've listened to new albums by Brian Eno and billy woods—both of which I want to hear again—and I visited the home studio of artist Lynn Marsh, which led to a music-heavy conversation about her experience of a recent Éliane Radigue concert that I missed, my own listening/writing performance, and her video work, which is structured around or against works by Strauss, Bruckner, and Verdi. Mostly though, I've returned to Don Cherry Studies, in preparation for my lecture on Don and Moki Cherry and Organic Music Society, and Watts Towers, for Routine Pleasures.

I've been chewing on Fumi Okiji's brilliant but dense essay "Oriki for Don Cherry: To Be Part of a Gathering-Work," which I assigned to the class. An oriki is a Yoruban praise-poem, though the essay in question is equally indebted to Okiji's ongoing interest in continental philosophy, from Hegel to Adorno. Like a good Hegelian, she is synthesizing these things while dialectically rubbing them against each other and their attendant cultural assumptions. Reading her essay leads me to further study of the donso ngoni, a stringed instrument of West African origin with a body constructed from a hollowed-out gourd covered with a taut goat skin. The instruments are beautiful and at once call to mind a harp, a guitar, and a mbira. I listen to various demonstrations of the instrument online and rewatch Urban Lasson's hour-long documentary *It Is Not My Music* (1978) on Cherry and extended family made for Swedish television. It's an amazing document(ary). One of my favorite scenes captures Don Cherry playing the donso ngoni and Naná Vasconcelos playing the berimbau as the pair walk down a New York City street, engaging an unwitting but enthused audience. Okiji's notion of a gathering-work is a compelling term for thinking through Cherry's syncretic and constantly evolving approach, in which music and living are one and the same. Rereading Okiji's oriki coincided with a rereading of Ursula K. Le Guin's "The Carrier Bag Theory of Fiction," which gloria galvez assigned to our Foundation class. Le Guin's notion of a carrier bag landed sympathetically in proximity to the gathering-work. The carrier bag is an emblem of constant gathering, an act of preserving and preparing for a future. The carrier bag carries meaning; it contains multitudes, a cosmos: "Still there are seeds to be gathered, and room in the bag of stars."

293

Way back there when Hell wasn't no bigger than Maitland, man found out something about the laws of sound. He found something before he even stood erect to think. He found that sounds could be assembled and manipulated and that such a collection of sound forms could become as definite and concrete as a war-axe or a food-tool.

—Zora Neale Hurston, *Folklore and Music* (1991), as quoted in Khaled Alqahtani, "On Modernity and Sound: An Interview with Dr. Fumi Okiji" (2021)

294

Every time I endeavor to return to a consideration of Deep Listening Band, I seem to swerve further off course. I will be teaching them soon enough, though not as soon as I'm teaching Don Cherry. (And I did listen to *Looking Back* [2013] a few days ago, though hardly deeply.) Among the many stops on my detour, I was reading about the Grateful Dead's Wall of Sound, courtesy of the Aquarium Drunkard blog:

> The Wall of Sound was the brainchild of the infamous LSD chemist-cum-audio engineer and early Dead benefactor, Owsley "Bear" Stanley, in collaboration with instrument manufacturer Alembic. The completed system (weighing 75 tons with 11 channels powered by 48 amplifiers, driving 586 speakers with 28,800 watts of continuous power) made its debut at Daly City's Cow Palace on March 23 (*Dick's Pick 24*). Now, even audience members in the upper reaches of the cavernous sports area could hear every strum of guitar, every plunk of piano and crash of cymbal. Phil Lesh reaped the biggest benefit of the new system with a quadraphonic encoder that sent signals from each of his four strings to a separate channel, and set of speakers, producing near subsonic notes that reportedly felt as if they were rising from the floorboards.

It's fun to think about the Wall of Sound in relation to DLB's Expanded Instrument System—especially Phil Lesh's elaborate sonic extension, which recalls DLB moving sound around space while stretching it in time. The phrase "Wall of Sound" is borrowed from Phil Spector, who in happier times was among the most influential producers of pop and rock music—his ideas around studio production were taken up by Brian Wilson and many others. But the Dead's version of the Wall of Sound is not designed for the studio but for the live context and an audience of thousands.

A link from the Aquarium Drunkard blog post leads me to Wikipedia and a schematic for the Wall of Sound. The rational, quantitative, silent black-and-white diagram is an unlikely stand-in for the psychedelic, qualitative, LOUD results.

It makes sense that Owsley Stanley's interests spanned from pharmaceutics to acoustics—two paths to altered consciousness that often work together. I'm also thinking of Pink Floyd's quadraphonic sound system and experiencing it with my already-altered consciousness at Camp Randall Stadium in Madison, summer of 1994, but that's a different detour.

295

Owsley Stanley's Wall of Sound summons a long history in the rock music context, from Phil Spector's Motown recordings to British shoegaze to Sunn O)))'s backdrop of namesake speaker cabinets. But my attention quickly turns to examples beyond the rock paradigm. Specifically, I am thinking of the Philips Pavilion, a collaboration between Le Corbusier, Iannis Xenakis, and Edgard Varèse, designed for the 1958 World's Fair in Brussels. The building, which was demolished less than a year after its construction, remains a significant early example of multimedia design, with architecture and music engaged sympathetically. The primary function of the building was to serve as a sound vessel for Varèse's eight-minute composition *Poème électronique*, which was accompanied by a film by Le Corbusier, ambient color washes, and spatialized around the interior through an array of speakers by sound projectionists using telephone dials—all about a decade before psychedelic rock and the first liquid light shows. The electronics company Philips sponsored the project and supplied the technology. While Le Corbusier is the architect of record, the extravagant form of the cast concrete building, structured around hyperbolic parabolas, is generally credited to Xenakis, who also contributed a brief composition—*Concret PH*—that served as exit music alternating with Varèse's "poem." The project also marked Xenakis's exit from Le Corbusier's office and architecture, and into a sustained focus on composition. (I believe I first encountered these two compositions by Varèse and Xenakis on *An Anthology of Noise and Electronic Music, Vol. 1* [2002], which also included Oliveros, Cage, Sonic Youth, and many others I keep in heavy rotation.) I probably haven't thought about the Philips Pavilion in a few years, though years ago I spent a lot of time researching the project. Thankfully, I have a copy of Marc Treib's definitive monograph on the subject, *Space Calculated in Seconds: The Philips*

Pavilion, Le Corbusier, Edgar Varèse, and I pull it off my shelf for a renewed consideration.

296

Music for Ephemeral Buildings—a playlist:

Edgard Varèse
Poème électronique, 1957–1958

Iannis Xenakis
Concret PH, 1958

Both on *An Anthology of Noise and Electronic Music, Vol. 1*
Sub Rosa, 2002

297

Infrequent Seams—a playlist:

James Ilgenfritz
Compositions (Braxton) 2011
Infrequent Seams, 2012

Pauline Oliveros & James Ilgenfritz
Altamirage
Infrequent Seams, 2022

298

Michael Ned Holte (Art)
Faculty Development Fund Application October 25, 2022

Project Description

I am requesting $1250.00 in order to travel to Ojo Caliente, New Mexico. I have been invited to stay at Labyrinth, a residency-program-in-formation founded by artists Mark A. Rodriguez and Sarah McMenamin. I have offered them some advice on running a residency program, and in turn they have invited me to visit.

The requested funding would support two weeks of travel, research, and writing. My continued research is aimed at a book-length study on Oliveros / Deep Listening Band, which I hope to complete during my creative leave in the spring 2023 semester. In August, with support of the faculty development fund, I visited Mills College in Oakland to study the Pauline Oliveros Papers at the F. W. Olin Library. Spending five days with this archive was incredibly productive, and provided me with an incredible trove of documents and information, which I will be sifting through for several months. I expect to arrive at the residency in a position to turn my notes into writing. I also intend to visit the Rose Mountain Retreat Center in Las Vegas, New Mexico. Rose Mountain was a frequent site for Oliveros's Deep Listening Retreats, which is part of my research. I would also like to visit the IAIA (Institute of American Indian Arts) campus while in Santa Fe.

My continued research and writing on Oliveros—as composer, performer, theorist, and educator—has been central to my teaching at CalArts. I have taught her work in many of my classes, including Art Foundation, Routine Pleasures, and Performing

Life. In fall 2019, I taught a seminar called Pauline Oliveros for Artists, which I hope to teach again in coming years. I appreciate your consideration.

299

Termite-like, I am still chewing on a line from Simon Leung's artist talk/reading, "Squatting Towards Hong Kong" at CalArts last night:

The work dilates and does its own thing.

It's a pithy, almost casual line in a text that is historically complex and temporally intricate. But it's a line that speaks to Simon's non-hierarchical understanding of his own work, in which a work may be "an image, a lecture, a screening, a conversation, a workshop," among other possibilities or really, all of those things, in sum. I can relate. The word "dilate" means to expand or become larger. One thinks (I think) immediately of the eyes and the cervix, not necessarily in that order. There is an old saw about the artist giving birth to their work. Simon's line describes something about his text, the work in question, as we read it or hear him read it. (I had read a PDF of the article, published in *October* 180, Spring 2022, as an audience of one, before he read it aloud to an audience of many last night.) I am no stranger to the idea of a work (or a project, one of my own preferred terms) expanding far beyond its initiating spark or impulse. The present text (meaning the one I am writing, and "you" are reading) is an example, developing and absorbing/demanding time in ways I couldn't really imagine. Simon's line—"the work dilates and does its own thing"—also suggests the afterlife of a work, once it has left the hands of its maker. I think about this in relation to *Sonic Meditation XXI*, and its pithy question, *What constitutes your musical universe?* Could Oliveros have imagined anyone spending a year answering it?

April 1, 2022

The time of a work of art, especially for its maker, does not begin or end with the moment it is made, but it is the convention that the time stamp of a work of art's making is when its relation to everything else is measured—when it gets released to the world, when it casts anchor in history. Where has the time gone?

300

In Routine Pleasures today, I screened Urban Lasson's *It Is Not My Music* (1978). No matter how many times I've seen something, watching it with a group (especially with my students) projected relatively large on a screen, changes the thing. It exacerbates the rewards or problems in a work, and the feel of the thing. Moki Cherry's role is rendered mostly silent and—at least by implication—subservient, being a wife and mother, tending to domestic chores, cooking and sewing, even when that sewing is the making of works of art—works of art that also double as stage backdrops, costumes, domestic decor. Thankfully, art historians and curators have already begun to right (rewrite) the story, one of complete communion between Don's musical universe and Moki's visual universe. On a related note, the documentary focuses so tightly on Don Cherry, it sometimes neglects to give full shape to his many collaborators, Moki first and foremost among many—a contradiction with the provocative refrain of, "It's not my music" at the beginning and end of the film, while deterministically pushing its central subject's authorship into the spotlight. A consummate sideman—to Sonny Rollins, Ornette Coleman, Albert Ayler—Cherry was also the lodestar in an endless variety of collaborative constellations. No documentary could account for all of these group efforts. A free improvisation by Cherry, Rashied Ali, and James "Blood" Ulmer in a Harlem club is compelling to behold. It's balanced and swinging, everyone is enmeshed. But it also feels strangely conventional—by 1978 so many of the idioms of "free jazz" are already familiar—whereas Cherry's spontaneous, ambulatory jam sessions with Naná Vasconcelos on a New York sidewalk or his lighthearted heuristic jam sessions with his son Eagle-Eye in their rural Swedish schoolhouse feel more urgent, true. Likewise Cherry playing music for/with himself, fully absorbed, while his family watches television. The overwhelming feeling of the documentary is one of propulsive movement, driven by the blues of Cherry playing the donso ngoni, summoning a train chugging along in a full-bodied engagement with the instrument. In this travelog, one gets the sense that Cherry only stops playing music long enough to answer the filmmaker's questions, which he does with an unhurried seriousness. In one explanation of his approach to playing the donso ngoni, Cherry describes a mandala that focuses our attention as he slaps the string percussively, throwing his shoulder into it, demonstrating his way back into propulsive motion, as if to say, "See?" even as we listen, too.

301

While reflecting on Simon Leung's talk on Tuesday and in preparation for this week's seminar, I looked through my personal documentation of the *Routine Pleasures* (2016) exhibition and its related events. One of the events was "A Friendly Party in the Garden of Schindler: Three Performances for *Routine Pleasures*." The three performances were by Steve Roden, Lucky Dragons, and Simon Leung with his frequent subject/collaborator Warren Niesłuchowski. I have quite a bit of documentation of all three sound checks and almost no documentation of the actual performances. There is presumably a video document because I see a camera on a tripod in a number of my photos, but I've never seen the documentation. I should inquire about it. In my own photo library, I found an eight-second video clip of Simon and Warren Niesłuchowski singing, which I shared with my class as a sound check for the borrowed speakers in the classroom. I was also struck, as I have been before, by a close-up of Steve Roden's partially closed laptop and a jumble of cables. Steve's performance was a solo improvisation for modular synthesizer, but in recent years whenever I look at this multicolored tangle and the fragmented screen of Steve's laptop, I see it as a kind of portrait of Steve.

Last night, after class, I returned home and received an email from Steve's studio that took whatever wind was left in my sails.

In 2017, Steve was diagnosed with Alzheimer's. Steve's family with the incredible dedication of his wife Sari are managing his progression into this horrific disease with great care. While Steve is in a safe and good place, he is no longer able to make art or music, is not able to communicate on his own or receive visitors. The family is grateful for your love and friendship with Steve as an artist, musician, and a wonderful human.

This did not arrive as new information. It was a confirmation of the inevitable. I was aware of Steve's worsening condition, with his wife Sari thoughtfully keeping me in the loop. Steve and I did a public talk at his gallery in 2019. It was incredibly hard, for him and me, albeit for different reasons. I knew it would be his last public talk. The jumbled pile of cables had become a heartbreaking metaphor. Likewise, a pair of incredible videos, *detritus* and *orrery*, which served as the backdrop for our talk carried a similar metaphoric charge. In them, we see Steve's hands rearranging bits and pieces from a pile of *Domus* magazines that belonged to his father, who had ended his own life when Steve was young. The videos suggested an attempt to make sense of a personal history marked by a tragedy, and to put the proverbial pieces in order, but its making also coincided with Steve's impairment—the pieces gradually falling apart. I was urgently aware of all of this when we spoke, but I withheld what I knew from the audience. Likewise, I had an urge to write about the videos, which are among my favorite things Steve has made, but a respect for his privacy overshadowed any desire to more fully elucidate the intricacies or import of the videos.

I can't overstate how important Steve has been for me as a writer, curator, fan, and eventually as a friend and collaborator—and how important he has been for this daily writing meditation, too: really, he's been on my mind almost every day. I was a fan of Steve's music and his art long before I met him. We always had a bottomless well of enthusiasms to share with one another. Our friendship felt almost effortless, as did our numerous collaborations and conversations, public and private. It's devastating to lose him, by which I mean my connection to him, but also to lose an artist putting so much wonder into the world. For the moment, I'm thankful for the vast amount of work I can always return to, including objects in my home I see every day, which lifts just a tiny corner of my sadness.

302

easy - to know
that diamonds - are precious

good - to learn
that rubies - have depth

but more - to know
that pebbles - are miraculous

303

Threads > Tapestries—a playlist:

Joe McPhee Quintet (with Stuart Dempster, Loren Dempster, Michael Bisio, Eyvind Kang)
Common Threads
Deep Listening, 1996

Bill Dixon
Tapestries for Small Orchestra
Firehouse 12 Records, 2009

Deep Listening Band
Dunrobin Sonic Gems
Deep Listening, 2014

304

I woke up in the middle of the night with several thoughts about the present text. They seemed remarkably crystalline at that moment, rendered in several precise phrases, but by the time I woke up they had all but evaporated, along with most of my dream activity. At the very least, I remember having dreams punctuated by crystalline thoughts. The closest I can get to them now, while simultaneously watching James Whale's horror classic *Frankenstein* (1931) on cable on Halloween, is this:

Repetition reveals information; duration fosters understanding.

Those aren't the exact phrases, but it occurred to me that while this daily text is a kind of representation of an ongoing activity, it hardly documents the totality of the project at hand—which is to say everything that accounts for my attempt to answer the question, *What constitutes your musical universe?* It's an approximation. So many loose threads never get woven into the tapestry. Some are too small or errant to articulate; others are too big and unwieldy. (I keep deferring on writing a substantial essay on Deep Listening Band. I should have done it in the summer when I had more headspace. But the deferral leads to repeat listening and renewed appreciation and renewed excitement.) Likewise, this text fails to capture the totality of my listening activity: minutes, hours, days spent listening to music on Spotify, Bandcamp, YouTube; listening to CDs in the car; reading liner notes; looking up albums and personnel on Discogs or Wikipedia. There are also the many albums I listen to over and over again, or semi-regularly—many have surely appeared on one of my notated playlists, which offer a sense of what I'm listening to but hardly account for the innumerable repetitions of my listening. (Lately it's been Bill Dixon, and on Saturday, on a trip to Amoeba, I bought a used copy of his *Tapestries for Small Orchestra* [2009] to listen to in the car.) Repetition is fundamental to my growing understanding of something, whether a gradual absorption of a piece of art or music or a movie or a text, or the flavor of a specific ingredient or dish. Repetition informs the way in which one navigates the world. There is much this text is likely to reveal to someone else, or to me, when I eventually read it. (Again, I have little expectation that anyone will read it, though a few kind souls have told me they would like to. Bless them.) Ten months into it, I've lost track of any sense of the whole and can't speak to its, ahem, *heuristic values*. I don't consider that a failure, but simply an inevitable part of the process. A year is an incredibly specific scale of time, and despite its correspondence to the earth's journey around the sun, it's ultimately a rather arbitrary measure. But as a unit of time, I prefer it to the instant, which seems to be the unit that largely shapes our collective imagination in the present. The instant is tied more immediately to the concerns of capitalism and (instant) gratification. Duration fosters understanding, but it is also a mode of resistance. Or at least that's my hope.

305

Because I was writing while "watching" *Frankenstein* (1931), I'm particularly attentive to its sound, including—rather unexpectedly—a scene with bandoneons, and another with (unseen) carillon bells.

306

The word *sounding* is deliciously manifold. To begin, nostalgically, with the definition found in my *American Heritage Dictionary*:

sound·ing[1] (soun′dĭng) *n.* 1. The act of one that sounds.
2. An environmental probe for scientific observation.
3. a. A measured depth of water. b. Often soundings. Water shallow enough for depth measurements to be taken by a hand line.

sound·ing[2] (soun′dĭng) *adj.* 1. Emitting a full sound; resonant.
2. Noisy but with little significance; high-sounding.

In its many folds, the word *sounding* is a useful tool in getting to the bottom of Deep Listening Band.

307

From: Michelle Hagewood
To: Michael Ned Holte
Subject: Invitation to a Centrum Residency

Dear Michael Ned Holte,

On behalf of Centrum, it is my great pleasure to invite you to be a 2023 Centrum Resident.

This year our review committee was comprised of Velda Thomas, Libby Pratt, and Robert Seifert Gage, who collectively represented expertise in writing, interdisciplinary art, and music/performance, as well as our local and national communities.

Our selection progress was our most rigorous yet, with well over triple the number of applications that we were able to accept. Your work stood out, your need for the residency was clearly articulated, and there is a timeliness to your work that we feel is very important. While our capacity for scholarships was limited, we worked hard to identify folks who demonstrated a strong need for the fee waiver. We were not able to accommodate all of the requests unfortunately. Each year, we increase our scholarship offerings as is possible through our funding. Fees charged to residents go directly towards operating costs and helps make it possible for others with financial barriers to come.

Given the tight schedule of our calendar this year, there is very little room for rescheduling, so we are very hopeful this offering works for you.

Dates: January 18–25, 2023
Housing: Private Cabin
Studio Access: (for wifi access), basement level room in 310
Total Fees: $500.00

If you are able to accept this, please let us know by Friday, November 11, 2022. After that time, we will need to extend offers to our next candidates. Following your acceptance, we will reach out with additional information, an invoice for a deposit (if applicable) to hold your spot, and a brief agreement form for you to complete.

308

Dear Meg and Sari,

I know this news was inevitable but is heavy and heartbreaking on arrival. I usually have words, but I've mostly been at a loss trying to get an email together.

Steve is incredibly important to me, as an artist, musician, and friend. I was a fan before I was a friend, and it's not always a given that an artist you like is going to be a terrific person, too! Steve always did things for the best reasons and the right reasons. I always trusted his compass and never had any doubts about any work made with him or time spent with him, some of which—like a certain Kaprow performance at LACE—pushed me out of my comfort zone (and his too) in ways that reshaped me and how I understood myself. A fellow enthusiast, we also never ever ran out of things to talk about, which is part of what makes his present reality so unfathomable. The (art)(music)world needs more Steve Rodens.

I've been reliving much of our shared history in my head since I got your email, and actually I've been writing about Steve a lot this year in a daily writing project that is heavily influenced by Steve's *365 x 433*, which remains one of my favorite works by him. It's been a mostly private project, initiated on January 1 and presumably ending on December 31, currently 360+ pages. It started as a prompt/score by Pauline Oliveros but Steve has been a big part of it throughout. I'd be happy to share a few excerpts if you'd be interested to read them.

Please don't hesitate to let me know if I can be helpful in any way, now or in the future.

Sending love,
Michael

309

Playing records in the dining room and (probably) annoying the neighbors—a playlist:

Mary Jane Leach
Pipe Dreams
Blume, 2017

Maggi Payne
Ahh-Ahh (Music for Ed Tannenbaum's Technological Feets 1984–1987)
Aguirre, 2020

310

Playing records, annoying the neighbors, Part 2—a playlist:

Terry Jennings, performed by Charles Curtis
Piece for Cello and Saxophone (1960)
Saltern, 2022

Eyvind Kang
Visible Breath
Ideologic Organ, 2012

311

The mission of the Deep Listening Band is to seek out, listen to, and interact with unusual spaces in order to make music. Space is an integral part of sound. One cannot exist without the other. We explore natural, constructed, imaginary, and virtual spaces to savor and enjoy their salient acoustical characteristics. This work is done with ears, voices, instruments, technology, shared experiences, and perceptions. Performance space is ordinarily held as a stationary paradigm in performance practice, but qualitative changes occur with our instruments and voices throughout the exploration process.

Listening to space changes space and changing space changes listening.

> —Pauline Oliveros, "Space for Listening and Listening to Space: A Musician's Way of 'Looking'" (2006)

312

The "accidental" origin story of Deep Listening Band has been repeated so often, it has reached the status of mythology—at least in new music circles. It is simultaneously the origin of the punning phrase "deep listening," which would become not just the name of the band, but also an all-encompassing term that, for Pauline Oliveros, at once describes compositional strategy, a pedagogy, and more generally, a life practice.

Stuart Dempster has written several versions of this history. "Deep Listening Band was formed by accident on 8 October 1988," begins one relatively recent account. "In fact, even after the recording session there was no hint that any such group would be formed."

Composer/performers Pauline Oliveros and Panaiotis were to be in San Francisco for a duo concert (Panaiotis and I had yet to meet). I convinced them to come by way of Seattle so they could view the Fort Worden cistern in Port Townsend. Word had it that Panaiotis was an electric designer–a veritable wizard–and I wanted him to hear the space and see if he could electronically recreate it. He later created a decent version of that space within the context of the EIS (Expanded Instrument System). My vision was that Pauline and I would play around in the cistern with our instruments and Panaiotis would listen; I didn't know he was also a vocalist and a composer. At the last moment, a week or two before they came, I arranged for the late Al Swanson of Location Recording to document whatever we did. This was somewhat of an afterthought–I had no inkling of what would transpire. Well, the rest, as they say, is history. The first Deep Listening compact disc came out in spring 1989 to critical acclaim.

–Stuart Dempster, "Bookends of Deep Listening's First 25 Years," liner notes for *Dunrobin Sonic Gems* (2014)

A detour to Seattle en route to San Francisco? Few would consider such a stop without a worthy lure—and Port Townsend is a hundred miles from Sea-Tac airport, a two-hour drive. But Oliveros was known for going out of her way for sound. "In New York, Terry Riley led me fifteen blocks out of our way to hear a building ventilator," she recounted in her 1968 essay, "Some Sound Observations." The object of acoustic intrigue in this case was a massive underground cistern on a decommissioned army base in northern Washington. The cistern is a marvel of quantifiable data: 14 feet deep, 186 feet in diameter, capable of holding two million gallons of water; most notably, for those traveling so far out of their way to visit it, the cistern produces a remarkable reverberation time of 45 seconds. It is also a source of abundant wordplay, for those who partake.

"The names Deep Listening and Deep Listening Band (DLB) came about through Pauline Oliveros writing her entry for the Deep Listening CD," Dempster recalls. "I saw it and said, 'That's it!' She replied, 'That's what?' I said that's the title for our CD and that's the name for our group. Pauline called it Deep Listening Ensemble. A day or so later she said it was Deep Listening Band, and the name was born." The recorded document of this initial visit to the cistern was in fact titled *Deep Listening* (1989), released on the New Albion label, though the name Deep Listening Band only appeared with the group's second release, *Troglodyte's Delight* (1990), recorded in the Tarpaper Cave in Rosendale, New York. It was the second of some of fourteen eventual albums by Deep Listening Band, assuming many different manifestations, between 1989 and 2014—all of these featured Oliveros and Dempster.

The "accidental" origin story of Deep Listening Band has been repeated so often, it has reached the status of mythology, but it is in fact only one point of origin. Dempster and Oliveros have a long-shared history, dating back to their first encounter in the music department at San Francisco State College (now San Francisco State University) in the mid-1950s, more than four decades before they would perform together in a cistern. Both were students of composer Robert Erickson, and their classmates notably included Terry Riley and Loren Rush. Among other things, Deep Listening Band is a friendship—between Dempster and Oliveros and many others—rendered audible.

313

Two concerts from 1964 consecrate the friendship and collaboration between Stuart Dempster and Pauline Oliveros. Both concerts took place at the San Francisco Tape Music Center, and both are significant in the development of "new music." The first, which took place in late March and early April, was a tribute to the composer David Tudor who was also the foremost interpreter of the compositions of John Cage. Six works by Cage were performed at *Tudorfest*, including *Music Walk* (1958); *Atlas Eclipticalis with Winter Music, Electronic Version* (1961); and *Concert for Piano and Orchestra* (1957–1958). Dempster and Oliveros performed in the ensemble for these three works, with Dempster on trombone and Oliveros on French horn. The event marked the West Coast premiere for most of these works. The festival was rounded out with two piano compositions by Toshi Ichiyanagi and Oliveros's own *Duo for Accordion and Bandoneon with Possible Mynah Bird Obbligato* (1963–1964), performed by Oliveros and Tudor, who were situated on a seesaw designed by Elizabeth Harris that swiveled full circle, with a caged mynah bird named Ahmed dangling above. The performance was largely improvised and is the first of many theater pieces staged by Oliveros over her long career.

The second significant concert at the Tape Music Center in 1964, the premiere of Terry Riley's *In C*, took place in November. The work is now regarded as a classic of American minimalism and a staple of the contemporary classical repertoire. The ensemble gathered for the premiere included Dempster, Oliveros, Jon Gibson, Steve Reich, Morton Subotnick, among other now legendary performer-composers. Dempster would go on to perform on the first recorded version of *In C* for Columbia Masterworks in 1968.

314

Few other instruments can approach the theatrical implications of the trombone: even when it is played normally, the slide moves at least three inches for only a half step. Musical site-sound relationship is probably nowhere more obvious than in the trombone glissando: everyone knows this visual cliché. When an instrument must extend the throat as well as the arm, the trombone is a much more logical body extender than other instruments. It is unique among instruments, and it is the only instrument of the body (resonator of body sounds) having a completely variable resonator length. This has implications both acoustically and visually . . .

Various references have been made throughout this book to garden hose instruments. As stated before, a garden hose fitted with a trombone mouthpiece is really a trombone of *nonadjustable* length, just as the trombone may be considered an *adjustable-length* garden hose. The first composition that ever considered this idea was a Pauline Oliveros is *Theater Piece for Trombone Player and Tape* (note the use of the word "player"). No trombone per se is used in this work but rather the acoustical and visual abstractions of it; however, this does not make it any *less* a trombone piece. If this piece were to be for a player of another brass instrument, it would be necessary to use different size hoses and mouthpieces, which would make it an entirely different venture. The hoses are simply resonators and, as such, are no different from any brass of similar length and bore.

These hoses in the Oliveros work were originally "woven" into two sculptures by the choreographer Elizabeth Harris. One, a "candle trumpet," has funnel bells on the end where candles are placed. An extremely tight interrelationship between sight and sound is achieved because the breath of the performer can control the amount and type of light that the candle gives. The other sculpture, a "sprinkler horn," allows for lawn sprinklers to rotate, spewing fourth baby powder, smoke, or whatever else might have been loaded in them. Many vocal sounds imitating animals are used.

My mixed media ballet entitled *Ten Grand Hosery* was inspired largely through my collaboration with Pauline Oliveros and Elizabeth Harris on the *Theater Piece*, and I will always be indebted to them. The sustaining pedals of ten pianos are blocked, the idea being to "send sound through space" from one piano to another. The same score calls for didjeridu, or an abstraction of it, to be used in the pianos (for the resonance). At one point, the performer is expected to dervish while playing the didjeridu. Also employed is "sculptorchestra"—that is, sculptured instruments or instrumental sculptures.

—Stuart Dempster, *The Modern Trombone: A Definition of Its Idioms* (1979)

315

110, 5, 2, 210, 134, 101, 405—a playlist:

Susan Alcorn
And I Await the Resurrection of the Pedal Steel Guitar
Olde English Spelling Bee, 2006

Eyvind Kang
Ajaeng Ajaeng
Ideologic Organ, 2020

Kronos Quartet
Pieces of Africa
Elektra Nonesuch, 1992

316

Reading "The Temporality of the Landscape" by Tim Ingold, with soundtrack by Susan Alcorn—a playlist:

Susan Alcorn
Touch This Moment
Uma Sounds, 2010

Susan Alcorn
Uma
Loveletter, 2000

Susan Alcorn
Curandera
Uma Sounds, 2003

Susan Alcorn
2.4.15
Liminal Sound Series, 2016

Janel Leppin, Susan Alcorn, Meghan Habibzai
Sister Mirror
Atlantic Rhythms, 2020

317

Another definition of "sounding" supplied by a friend, via text message, and not the *American Heritage Dictionary*: "Sounding is also a kink where people stick things in their urethra." Ouch.

318

A thorough if not necessarily exhaustive list of performers on fourteen Deep Listening Band recordings: Stuart Dempster, Pauline Oliveros, Panaiotis, David Gamper, Julie Lyon Balliett, Fritz Hauser, Thomasa Eckert, William O. Smith, Al Swanson, Joe McPhee, Joe Giardullo, Monica Wilson, Karen Jungens, Rachel Pollack, Ellen Fullman, Elise Gould, Nigel Jacobs, Urs Leimgruber, Ben Neill, Thomas Buckner, Maragit Shenker, Nego Gato, Carol Chappell, Jason Finkelman, Women Who Drum (Leaf Miller, Lorraine Demerest, Judith Muldoon), Randy Raine-Reusch, Chris Brown, John Bischoff, Phil Stone, Zero the Clown/Ramón Sender Barayón, Scot Gresham-Lancaster, Tim Perkis, William Winant, Joe Catalano, Karl S. Pribam, Maggi Payne, Toyoji Tomita, Bob Bialecki, Tom Dambly, Tom Heasly, David Abel, IONE, Jesse Stewart, Jonas Braasch, Johannes Welsch, "everyone"

319

A thorough if possibly redundant and not necessarily exhaustive list of instruments used on fourteen Deep Listening Band recordings: accordion/just-tuned accordion/Roland V accordion, alto clarinet, balloon, bamboo flute, bass clarinet, bawu, (other) bells, Brazilian percussion, Casio digital horn, cello, Cistern Simulation Technology, clarinet, conch shell/air and percussion conch, congas, contrabass trombone, didjeridu, djembe, drums, duck call, electronics, Expanded Instrument System (EIS), flutes, found percussion, French horn, garden hose, gongs, JDBBBDJ (John Diamond's Big Beautiful Brass Didjeridu), keyboards, khaen, Laos cowbell, little instruments, little sounds, Long String Instrument, Max/MSP realtime interactive computer, metal pieces, mutantrumpet, ney, ocarina, organ, overtone flutes, percussion, piano, pipes, pocket trumpet, reeds, Road Rage Racer, shekere, sho, Sing-a-Ma-Jigs, soprano sax, suling, tenor saxophone, THE HUB, Tibetan bell, toys, trombone, trombone mouthpiece whistle, trumpet, tuba, violin, voice, whistles

320

Beyond queering time, with the use of natural reverberation or the machine assist of the Expanded Instrument System, Deep Listening Band deploys other queer notions of banding together. Ever a fluid and evolving situation, the band favors interchangeability—one instrument for another, voice for instrument, instrument for body, space for instrument, body for machine, audience as performer, and so on—leveling familiar hierarchies, binaries, and categories that tend to define more stable concepts from classical, rock, and jazz paradigms. Space and time are leveraged toward disorientation, rather than the opposite. Abundant wordplay—e.g. "Tosca Salad," "Metalorgy," "Deep Hockets," and indeed "Deep Listening"—not to mention staged photographs of the band are forthrightly campy if not downright corny. Among many other things, Deep Listening Band is a model of "making kin," to borrow Donna J. Haraway's phrase from *Staying with the Trouble: Making Kin in the Chthulucene* (2016), an ever-expanding network of queer relationality that includes musicians and other performers, instruments, spaces, and machines.

321

The Complete Deep Listening Band at Town Hall—a playlist:

Deep Listening Band
Octagonal Polyphony
Important Records, 2012

Deep Listening Band
Needle Drop Jungle
Taiga, 2012

Deep Listening Band
Great Howl at Town Haul
Important Records, 2012

322

My conclusion that the landscape is the congealed form of the taskscape does enable us to explain why, intuitively, the landscape seems to be what we see around us, whereas the taskscape is what we *hear*. To be seen, an object need do nothing itself, for the optic array that specifies its form to a viewer consists of light reflected off its outer surfaces. To be heard, on the other hand, an object must actively emit sounds or, through its movement, cause sound to be emitted by other objects with which it comes into contact. Thus, outside my window I see a landscape of houses, trees, gardens, a street, and pavement. I do not hear any of these things, but I can hear people talking on the pavement, a car passing by, birds singing in the trees, a dog barking somewhere in the distance, and the sound of hammering as a neighbour repairs his garden shed. In short, what I hear is *activity*, even when its source cannot be seen. And since the forms of the taskscape, suspended as they are in movement, are present *only* as activity, the limits of the taskscape are also the limits of the auditory world. (Whilst I deal here only with visual and aural perception, we should not underestimate the significance of touch, which is important to all of us but above all to blind people, for whom it opens up the possibility of access to the landscape—if only through proximate bodily contact.)

This argument carries an important corollary. Whilst both the landscape and the taskscape presuppose the presence of an agent who watches and listens, the taskscape must be populated with beings who are themselves agents, and who reciprocally "act back" in the process of their own dwelling. In other words, the taskscape exists not just as activity but as *inter*activity. Indeed this conclusion was already foreshadowed when I introduced the concept of resonance as the rhythmic harmonization of mutual attention.

—Tim Ingold, "The Temporality of the Landscape" (1993)

323

Regularly at half past seven, in one part of the summer, after the evening train had gone by, the whippoorwills chanted their vespers for half an hour, sitting on a stump by my door, or upon the ridge pole of the house. They would begin to sing almost with as much precision as a clock, within five minutes of a particular time, referred to the setting of the sun, every evening. I had a rare opportunity to become acquainted with their habits. Sometimes I heard four or five at once in different parts of the wood, by accident one a bar behind another, and so near me that I distinguished not only the cluck after each note, but often that singular buzzing sound like a fly in a spider's web, only proportionally louder. Sometimes one would circle round and round me in the woods a few feet distant as if tethered by a string, when probably I was near its eggs. They sang at intervals throughout the night, and were again as musical as ever just before and about dawn.

—Henry David Thoreau, "Sounds," *Walden* (1854)

324

Some preliminary questions for Stuart Dempster:

How did the first New Albion album come about? (*Deep Listening* follows from your work with Paul Dresher on *Night Songs / Channels Passing* [1984].)

You had previously endeavored to get Pauline Oliveros a record contract with Nonesuch for *Teach Yourself to Fly* in the early 1970s. Can you talk about that process? It's notable to me that Pauline had very little recorded output in the 1970s, and you remained focused on getting her work recorded.

The first three Deep Listening Band albums, recorded in the Fort Worden Cistern and the Tarpaper Cave in Rosendale, New York, suggest a version of the band interacting with unusual spaces, albeit in fairly conventional ways in terms of the recording. And then, subsequent efforts seemed less focused on unusual acoustic environments and more on the development of the Expanded Instrument System—which is to say, using electronic means to move sound around space. Is that how you see it? And if so, what are the reasons for that transformation?

It's also notable that founding member Panaiotis left the band, and David Gamper emerged from a technical role as a full-fledged member of the group. Can you recount your understanding of those developments?

To what extent do you understand Deep Listening Band as an extension and demonstration of your pedagogy (including your book *The Modern Trombone: A Definition of Its Idioms*) and Pauline's pedagogy?

Can you discuss your sound massages? When and how did they emerge, and in what context did you do them?

In *The Modern Trombone* you elaborate some aspects of your friendship with Pauline, including her *Theater Piece for Trombone* (1966), choreographed by Elizabeth Harris. To what extent do you consider that work as a starting point for Deep Listening Band?

What was the relationship between composition and improvisation in DLB? For example, there were certain songs that got repeated in different contexts, live and recorded (e.g. "Deep Hockets," "Non Stop Flight"). Is there a score for these?

What is your recollection of the various Deep Listening Band concerts in Stockholm, Tokyo, and elsewhere? The paper trail suggests a kind of heroic collective effort to realize these tours, not to mention considerable expense. In Pauline's papers at Mills, I found a kind of business plan for Deep Listening Band. Was DLB a sustainable (pun acknowledged) project?

Beyond you and Pauline and David Gamper, who formed the core of Deep Listening Band, dozens of other musicians and performers contributed. How were decisions about inviting collaborators made? I am thinking about several examples that really stretch the "normative" DLB model, like the collaboration with Ellen Fullman and the Long String Instrument or with Joe McPhee's Quartet and Rachel Pollack on *Unquenchable Fire*?

The album *Non Stop Flight* (1998) documents a performance at Mills that seems the most elaborate and expansive manifestation of the Deep Listening Band project. It includes a performance of Cage's *4'33"* (1952), which I believe is the only example of DLB performing something composed by someone outside the immediate band. It also harkens back to you and Pauline performing several Cage scores at *Tudorfest* at the Tape Music Center in 1964. Can you explain how *Non Stop Flight* worked—and then, the way in which Cage served as a touchstone for the band?

325

More preliminary questions for Stuart Dempster:

Among all of your connections with Pauline over sixty years, perhaps puns and wordplay point most to the intimacy of your friendship, including the phrase "Deep Listening," and the importance of humor in your collaboration. How conscious were you both of this wordplay?

Are there other recordings from DLB out there? Any plans to release them?

Is there video documentation that has yet to be released—from Town Hall? From elsewhere?

326

What constitutes your musical universe?

I expect to be done with this text on December 31, exactly 365 days after I started it. Will I be any closer to answering the prompt, a sonic meditation written by Pauline Oliveros shortly before I was born, and performed by me, herein, on a daily basis since January 1? One trip of the earth around the sun is momentous, but given the cosmic nature of the question in question, it is also an arbitrary point of ending. There are times when I've considered wrapping it up early, rather than being at the service of the calendar. That might be the more radical gesture, but I'm not sure radical is really the point. And completion is perhaps only a state of mind. In fact, I have already come to realize that my musical universe is (and always already was) "every day," practically continuous, boundless, seemingly inexhaustible. Even my solemn (and occasionally irritated) daily dedication to the task of marking it, or remarking upon it, represents only a tiny portion of what music—or sound, an exponentially more expansive category—I'm listening to, observing. There is so much I have yet to get to, and will likely never get to, regarding Pauline Oliveros and regarding my musical universe. And there is surely more I could say beyond the boundedness of this "performance," but would I force myself to do it without those strictures in place? I think of Roland Barthes, who framed the dilemma so beautifully (of course—and of course I realize I'm repeating myself in citation). It's a dilemma I have made performative, hyperbolic:

I delight continuously, endlessly, in writing as in perpetual production, in an unconditional dispersion, in an energy of seduction which no legal defense of the subject I fling upon the page can any longer halt. But in our mercantile society, one must end up with a work, an "*oeuvre*": one must construct, i.e., complete, a piece of merchandise. While I write, the writing is thereby at every moment flattened out, banalized, made guilty by the work to which it must eventually contribute.

—Roland Barthes, *Roland Barthes* (1975)

Writing rarely pours out of me; still, text accumulates. But there is often a sense—not just here, in the present text—that I am merely scratching the surface of something. This is why I've hitched my wagon to the termite model, even as I've attempted to recontextualize that model and, at times, complicate it. The present *text* has been a *test*: whether of discipline, of commitment, of endurance, of stubbornness, of awareness and attention. But it's also a kind of *askesis*: a training or preparation for whatever comes next. Last Thursday, in reading my talk on Deep Listening Band ("Fourteen Ways of Looking at Deep Listening Band") to and for my Routine Pleasures class, I realized how important it is for me to share the work I'm doing, not only for the endorphic affirmation of an audience but also to allow ideas to circulate beyond the confines of my own head or this Google Doc. Following the talk, one of my students asked me if I was going to be writing a book on Deep Listening Band. I am aware that I have been writing that book for the past year, or at least thinking of what I'm doing as preparation for the next performance. I would be thankful for this daily routine to become an *oeuvre*, if anyone would actually be willing to read it. (*If You Won't Read, Then Why Should I Write?* is the title of a book by Jarett Kobek, and it's one I think about with knowingness and empathy.) Hit me up at the merch table!

327

Two tasks, one text

Peter Spirer invited me to contribute a paragraph for an upcoming book on his film *Rhyme & Reason* (1997). I've written about it a little bit here and there over the years, and there's probably more I could say, but today is the deadline, and this is what I shared:

> Working on *Rhyme & Reason* was my first job in Los Angeles, and as such a remarkable introduction to the city for a naive white kid from Wisconsin. I talked to Dr. Dre on the phone on my first day! And then got to meet a who's who of the hip hop community—in Compton and Lynwood, but also in Sacramento and the Hollywood Hills. What strikes me most about the film some twenty-five years later is the intimate, easy-going rapport Peter Spirer found in his surprisingly vulnerable subjects. We see Sean "Puffy" Combs (not yet Puff Daddy) getting a haircut at his executive desk, Craig Mack washing dishes, Biggie Smalls coolly unwrapping gold records like they were cough drops, and Nas opening his heart on a brownstone staircase. Then again, Tupac and Biggie were both murdered while the film was in post-production, and in retrospect one must confront the palpable end of a more innocent era: Rap had suddenly crossed a threshold from subculture to capital "C" Culture, and *Rhyme & Reason* marks that transition as well as any other document of its time.

328

Still and Moving (on Thanksgiving)—a playlist:

Alvin Lucier
"Clarinet"
Still and Moving Lines of Silence in Families of Hyperbolas
Lovely Music, 2002

John McCowen
Models of Duration
Astral Spirits/Dinzu Artefacts, 2022

329

Since jotting down some hypothetical questions for Stuart Dempster, I've spent some time considering—listening to—a number of the earliest releases from the New Albion record label, including Paul Dresher's *Night Songs / Channels Passing* (1984), seeming the second release from the label despite its catalog number NA003. The record arrived in the mail a few days ago, a promotional copy, "Not For Sale." I've been thinking about New Albion putting the first *Deep Listening* (*Band*) record (NA022) into the world in 1989, following a re-release of Stuart Dempster's *In the Great Abbey of Clement VI* (NA013) two years earlier. I didn't know about these albums until much later, though I purchased a few New Albion titles in the early 90s. The first was probably John Cage's *The Perilous Night / Four Walls*, performed by Margaret Leng Tan and Joan La Barbara (NA037, 1991), likely followed by Morton Feldman's *Rothko Chapel / Why Patterns?* (NA039, 1991), likely followed by Harold Budd with Zeitgeist's *She is a Phantom* (NA066, 1994), all on CD. I discovered Lou Harrison shortly after and bought many or most of his New Albion albums. The order of events for me are less important than thinking about DLB emerging in the context of these and other composer-musicians, also including Terry Riley, Alvin Curran, Anthony Braxton . . . Curiously, Steve Roden's brother Jeffrey even released one of the last albums on the label (*Seeds of Happiness*, NA133, 2007).

New Albion was founded by Foster Reed in San Francisco in 1983 or 1984, depending on the source, and much of its catalog reveals a West Coast focus or orientation. According to a brief paragraph on Discogs, the label "was named after what Sir Francis Drake named the San Francisco Bay after being the first European to see the area, which was near where the label was founded. During the mid-2000s, after over 20 years there, Reed relocated the label and his family to the upper Hudson valley of New York state. In 2010, the label ceased its retail operations. In 2012 the label closed completely and returned stock of unsold CDs to the artists." On the New Albion website, which still exists ten years later, Reed notes that, "We have moved through the eras of the LP, cassette, CD, and now the digital experience. For us the LP was the most intriguing medium, and it defined our idea of how a recording should sound."

A good recording is an experience that shares some values a good book, a visual work of art, and a moment in a daydream can offer–it has no literate meaning yet it is evocative. It creates and invokes feelings. It is what the mind sees when the eyes close. Some music is about a world that is far away, a distant universe; some of it is the cry of tragedy; some of it is the rapture of the ecstatic. It can make you laugh. It can make you cry.

On a related note, I am also curious about the role of Al Swanson, the engineer that Dempster brought along to the cistern for the fateful session that would become *Deep Listening*; he also recorded Dresher's *Night Songs / Channels Passing* and a number of other recordings for New Albion. Swanson died in 2012, around the time New Albion folded. (Bob Bielecki, who recorded DLB's *Troglodyte's Delight* [1990] and *Sanctuary* [1995], is still around. I should talk to him.)

330

Last night, in bed, I embarked upon reading a very long interview of Alvin Curran by David W. Bernstein, which put me to sleep almost immediately. No offense to Curran or his interlocutor—reading anything in bed usually knocks me out (especially if it's a heavy book, which this is). I don't get much reading done in bed unless it's in the morning, when I usually read the *New York Times* on my phone. (For better and worse.) So, this morning I read an article in the *NYT Magazine* titled "Could I Survive 'The Quietest Place on Earth'?" which in fact was a mostly silly report from a three-hour trip to an anechoic chamber in Minneapolis. Most people are—reportedly—terrified of silence, or what they perceive to be silence, which in the case of an anechoic chamber can sometimes include sound of one's heartbeat or blood pumping. (In reality, most people probably don't even think about silence; it's practically a philosophical concept, which means it's rarely a practical consideration for most.) While hardly an anechoic chamber, home was relatively silent when I woke up this morning. My usually noisy street was surprisingly still, an unspoken blessing of the sleepy holiday weekend. I got up, made coffee, and returned to the Curran interview, which is sidewinding but enjoyable. After Leslie got up, I began to play Curran's *Solo Works—The '70s* (2010) as accompaniment to the reading, but I've also been listening to my noisy refrigerator, to Arlington Avenue becoming more active, to my neighbor revving one of his many large vehicles, to another neighbor vacuuming, to Leslie on hold calling CVS Pharmacy. Somehow Curran's eclectic *Songs and Views from the Magnetic Garden* withstands all these aleatory sounds and perhaps embraces them, some fifty years later. Begrudgingly, I do as well.

331

"The art of free improvisation is so recent that I would say it has no tradition."

It's a virtuoso musical craft unlike any other. One of the fundamental [differences] is that the tradition of spontaneous music making does not have a tradition; it does not have a very long history, whereas most of the other musical arts do. The art of free improvisation is so recent that I would say it has no tradition. It's in constant development. My personal and momentary disappointment, stems from [the absence of] a constant critique that I've always applied to spontaneous music making, right from day one in the damp, dank, dark, dusty space in Rome where Musica Elettronica Viva began. Yes, it's total ecstasy from the word go. You throw yourself into this flow; you dive into a fast-moving stream, and you better be quick in order not to get hurt, and you really have to know what you are doing. This is all true. A lot of this has been said over and over again. From my personal perspective, the MEV group would have long discussions critiquing itself listening to recordings of our performances, sometimes with delight and sometimes with disgust, when long passages of nothing happened and saying, "Oh my god, listen to that, it's just disgusting. How could we spend so much of our lives doing nothing?" Of course today, the real, brilliant virtuosi, they don't waste any time. They don't waste any notes anymore. You listen to Frederic [Rzewski], to all these people, every single gesture, every single shape, every single sonic intention that's put out into the space is near perfect. You can hear that in players today, but those players are few. I can count them on a few fingers.

Free improvisation has not become a mass movement. Especially in the African American community, it has encountered severe opposition. Strangely enough, great masters—contentious experimentalists—like Roscoe, Braxton, and George Lewis, and Muhal Richard Abrams, and all these people who are very much like AMM people and MEV people, and Pauline Oliveros's people, are, it seems to me, really crying out into the wind. But while this has not become a mass movement, it has remarkably become a worldwide alternative music movement with strong cells and ongoing development in every urban center in the world including Asia. The African American case—the AACM and beyond—is a special one-full of the tensions and contradictions and inflammatory passions that surround any evolutionary or revolutionary step from a prized tradition such as jazz.

—Alvin Curran in conversation with David W. Bernstein, "An American in Rome," *Alvin Curran: Live in Roma* (2010)

332

BERNSTEIN: There are composers, like the improvisers of whom you are speaking, who also believe that improvisation isn't composition. They're both wrong.

CURRAN: In fact, I call myself more and more a composer because I'm openly, for a number of years, disappointed by the developments in collective improvisation. I am disappointed that there may be limits to this art, and that these limits may have been reached. It's hard for me to see where the future [may lead]. Of course, no one can be a prophet in this business, especially in an art form, which is always stepping into very vague and not easily definable categories. [These concerns notwithstanding, there's something] I feel I have to be very clear about: I consider any act of music making, whether it be composing or improvising, an act of composing. One is in real time; one is in deferred time, that's all there is to it.

333

Alvin Curran introduces the term "music outside the concert hall" in discussing his work *Maritime Rites* (*Riti Marittimi*), which was first performed in 1979 by a chorus of Curran's students positioned in small rowboats that were scattered on the *laghetto* at Villa Borghese, Rome. In 1984 the work was reconceived for National Public Radio, making use of the most massive and venerable foghorns along the Eastern Seaboard of the United States, along with an impressive list of invited soloists. (In some sense each is a duet with a field recording by Curran, including each foghorn, the voice of the horn's operator, and other elements of each landscape.) Pauline Oliveros was one of the soloists and performed *Rattlesnake Mountain* in this context. Its only other appearance that I'm aware of is on her *Accordion & Voice* record. This took place one year before Oliveros took part in *Vor der Flut* in the Cologne cistern, but Curran's "music outside the concert hall" is a useful term for thinking about that project and a prehistory of Deep Listening Band.

Very often, they were delighted that I wanted to go record their fog horns and their conversations and their codes and their machinery and the sounds of all of their electronic gear. I could have been a spy from Russia and just walked into these places. They were very welcoming and delightful people to work with I must say. The ten parts were posited on the concept that I would invite one soloist for each, one friend of mine basically.

. . . I wanted people like Leo Smith and George Lewis and John Cage to be heard in natural locations with the natural mixes from those locations, which I made. I didn't just play the location; I actually played with the location, creating composed soundscapes with site recordings at each one.

334

Yet another question for Stuart Dempster—or really, a line of questioning. I'm not quite sure how to ask it, and perhaps it's more of an observation with a question baked into it, but here goes:

Many of the DLB recordings take great pains to differentiate between a human-acoustic sound source, and any electronic processing that happens after, via the EIS, etc. What is the importance (implied value judgment) of making this distinction? I think of DLB as context in which an instrument as an extension of the human body and the EIS as a further extension of that instrument (as the name implies)—and a context in which the location (the cistern, a cave, etc.) is both another instrument and a kind of non-human collaborator. In fact, I think about DLB as a "band" that manages to decenter humans to an unusual degree—placing greater emphasis on location, electronic manipulation, and so on. Perhaps all of this boils down to a question of: where precisely is the human located in Deep Listening Band? (I suspect the answer is already in front of me, in the word "listening.")

And alongside this: What is the difference between Deep Listening Band performing for an audience, versus DLB performing only for itself? How does the medium of recording transform ("mediate") these experiences? Are the recordings an adequate representation of those experiences?

335

It needs to be said: There are some days, not many, when I don't have the time or inclination to listen to music. Which isn't to say I didn't listen to any music, but that I didn't have any real motivation or capacity for it. I am also aware: There are people, not many, who rarely listen to music at all. In my case, thankfully, it's a temporary condition, not even a setback, but something like a palate cleanser, a pause—a 𝄐.

336

Enough about 2022, let's talk about *you*
Welcome to your Wrapped, Michael Ned Holte
This year you ventured in the genre-verse

(Oh dear.)

You explored 45 different genres

Your top genres:
1 Free Jazz
2 Fourth World
3 Avant-Garde
4 Alternative Rock
5 Jazz

From sunrise to sunset, you kept it interesting

Your morning started with
Creative Fun Joy

You seized the day with
Love Chill Relaxing

You embraced the night with
Victorian Innovative Mayhem

(Uh . . .)

All that listening added up

In 2022, your total play time was 50,454 minutes. That's more than 92% of other listeners in the United States.

With one song, it was love at first listen

Your top song was "I caught a glimpse of the sea through the leafy boughs of the pines" by Kim Myhr & Australian Art Orchestra

You played it 10 times, with the most listens on Jan 11, 2022.

You played 5,856 songs, but these played again and again

And again.

Your top songs

1
"I caught a glimpse of the sea through the leafy boughs of the pines"
Kim Myhr & Australian Art Orchestra

2
"Elixir Reprise / Witchi Tai To"
Don Cherry's New Researches

3
"Sangam"
Don Cherry & Latif Khan

4
"We seemed to grow more and more pensive, but in fact we were less and less"
Kim Myhr & Australian Art Orchestra

5
"No walls, no ceiling, no wind"
Kim Myhr & Australian Art Orchestra

Your year can't be contained in a playlist
But we tried anyway.

You listened to 1,349 artists this year, but one ruled your world

Your top artist was Pauline Oliveros

(LOL)

You spent 1,648 minutes together. You were in the top 0.05% of Pauline Oliveros listeners this year.

You couldn't stop listening to "Non Stop Flight."

(By definition.)

Your top artists
1 Pauline Oliveros
2 Don Cherry
3 John Cage
4 Cat Power
5 Charles Lloyd

This year you had layers, like an onion
But you listened to music, unlike an onion.

Time to meet your listening personality . . .

(Drumroll please.)

The Adventurer

You're a seeker of sound. You venture out into the unknown, searching for fresher artists, deeper cuts, newer tracks—especially gems yet to be found.

✦ ENVU ✦

Exploration · Newness

Variety · Uniqueness

(Well, thanks Spotify. You just performed *Sonic Mediation XXI* for me, and didn't even break a sweat.)

337

Coincidence, confluence—a playlist:

Marja Ahti & Judith Hamann
A coincidence is perfect, intimate attunement
Second Editions, 2022

Annea Lockwood
Bayou-Borne / Jitterbug
Moving Furniture Records, 2022

Bayou-born, for Pauline (2016) is dedicated to Pauline Oliveros and was composed with her passions in mind. She was born in Houston, Texas, so I created a graphic score from a map of the six bayous which flow through the city to Galveston Bay, thinking that she would have known one or all of those rivers intimately as a child—swimming, wading, river mud between her toes. She was a superb improviser, so it is scored for six improvising musicians with each player reading one of the rivers as a guide. Their lines move independently at first, coming closer together at the confluences to form duets and trios, before converging at the red star, the whole sound darkening as they approach Houston in memory of the devastation and deaths caused by Hurricane Harvey in 2017.

This is one of eighty-five scores contributed to a memorial celebration of Pauline's life: *Still Listening: New Works in Honour of Pauline Oliveros* (1932–2016), held at McGill University, Canada, in 2017. I wish to thank Doris Yokelson for the design of the map.

> —Annea Lockwood, album notes for *Bayou-Borne / Jitterbug* (2021)

338

Dear Stuart,

I hope this finds you well.

I am a writer and curator based in Los Angeles, and I teach in the School of Art at CalArts. We have a mutual friend in Eyvind Kang.

I am currently engaged in research on Deep Listening Band, which will lead me to Fort Worden and the Centrum Self-Directed Residency next month. I have already spent considerable time with your discography including all the available DLB recordings, your thorough DLB chronology, and your wonderful book *The Modern Trombone*—CalArts has three copies!

I was fortunate to meet Pauline in 2015, when I was doing a project at EMPAC. I included some of her work in an exhibition called *Routine Pleasures* that I curated at The MAK Center in Los Angeles in summer 2016, and she provided some text scores for an accompanying publication. At her urging, I ventured to Mills to sift through her papers, and I taught a seminar on her called Pauline Oliveros for Artists at CalArts a few years ago. More recently, I've written a pamphlet on Pauline's early electronic music that will be published sometime in the next few months.

In the past year, my research has moved most decisively in the direction of Deep Listening Band. While I am not trained in music, I am compelled by: DLB's relation to site-based or site-responsive practice, its exploration and development of collective improvisation, its engagement with unconventional instrumentation and new technologies, its puns and other wordplay, and above all else your long-term friendship and collaboration with Pauline as a foundation of the band. (What

I think I am most interested in writing is actually a kind of prehistory of Deep Listening Band, extending back to 1964 or so.)

So, to finally get to the point: I would love to interview you as part of my research if you'd be game for it. I will be at Centrum from January 18–25, and could arrive a day or two earlier if that would be more convenient. I will likely fly into Sea-Tac and rent a car, so will have some mobility. I'm happy to come to Seattle or wherever you are. I've watched or read or listened to every interview with you I could find, but I still have some questions I'd like to ask, mostly related to Deep Listening Band and its prehistory.

Please let me know if you're able to meet with me. I really appreciate your time.

Kindest regards,

Michael Ned Holte

339

Mondays on Arlington Avenue—a playlist:

Jeff Parker
Mondays at The Enfield Tennis Academy
Eremite Records, 2022

340

3. If you teach a non-required but recurring course, how long have you taught this course? Has the course evolved over time? If so, how and what role does it play in the curriculum?

Pauline Oliveros for Artists (taught once, Fall 2019)
Routine Pleasures (second iteration, taught Spring 2022)
The Contemporary Exhibition (four iterations, most recently taught Spring 2019)
Performing Life (fifth iteration, most recently taught on Zoom, Spring 2021)

These classes follow directly from my own research projects and/or respond to perceived curricular needs—e.g. I started teaching Performing Life because so many students were working in performance but there wasn't a seminar-level course to consider its history or discourse. The Contemporary Exhibition proved to be a helpful "crash course" in the history, theory, and practice of exhibition making for many students who went on to explore curatorial practice or start artist-run spaces.

I think of all of these classes as a way of teaching art history, though not necessarily in a chronological order. With Pauline Oliveros for Artists, I deliberately placed the composer, musician, and educator Pauline Oliveros as a central figure in a consideration of art history—one that was distinctly feminist and queer, and deliberately emphasized sound over vision. This semester I have been teaching Routine Pleasures for the second time, substantially reworking a syllabus first developed ten years ago and subsequently developed as an exhibition and publication. All of these classes change with repetition, shaped in large part by the experience of actually manifesting a syllabus as a class and engaging in a collaborative process with my students. They are shaped by my own research and new scholarship in the field.

341

Dear Michael,

Sorry for my leisurely response. This is because I found myself in the midst of cleaning up/revising my "short" DLB history, including adding the end stage of DLB after David Gamper passed away. After that shock, DLB had a few concerts, taking it to its twenty-fifth year in 2013 (and a repeat concert in 2014).

I thought I would have this done before I answered your email but, of course, it was a little more of a project than I thought it would be (surprise, surprise). To cut to the chase, let's go with your plan of meeting in mid-January '23 that works with your proposal, in Seattle on ca. 18 Jan or whatever can work. If you need it to be on 17th it would have to be late–say 3:00 pm?–Then you could go to centrum in aft/eve. Maybe 18 Jan is better because I have more flex time–would that work and not get you too late to arrive at Centrum?

As for visiting CENTRUM, I hope you are in contact with Gregg Miller who is (was?) program manager. He had a notion to make for better access to the cistern. Maybe that happened or maybe not. For several years now it has not provided access to the cistern; maybe that has changed?

Anyway, time to get this to you before yet another distraction! All the best and, hopefully, more relatively soon!

Stuart

342

Remember to ask Stuart about David Gamper. Among the DLB members, his story is the least well-known.

I should also ask about Panaiotis and his departure from the band. "Creative differences"? Just like a real band.

343

Yesterday's trip to CalArts was accompanied by Rhys Chatham's *Two Gongs*, played (mostly) at a high volume. I haven't listened to this epic oceanic roar in a long time, but the cascading sixty-one minutes of its ebb and (mostly) flow matched my tempestuous mood on the third straight day of this crushing commute and ended as if on cue as I landed in the CalArts parking lot.

Rumble . . .

Shimmer . . .

Timbre

This sensory overload was followed by the final edition of the Routine Pleasures class in which the students' presentations broke our unusual six-hour threshold and clocked in around seven hours and forty minutes. The rest of the evening was off-gassing.

Two Gongs, composed by Chatham in 1971, was performed in 1989 by a duo comprised of the composer and Yoshi Wada—a unit of two they called Eat Fuck Kill—and released on Table of the Elements in 2002. A review on *Pitchfork*, quoted on the back of the CD, observes that "the resulting investigation of these gongs sounds not so much like an idealized Music of the Spheres as it is a 'Music of Two Enormous Fucking Ball Bearings the Size of Jupiter Grinding Together Like Electric Teenagers.'" Ah, (it's almost) the end of a semester.

8. Which aspects of your teaching have been most effective?

A student in the Routine Pleasures class read the course description and remarked that they didn't know "any of this stuff." That's a big reason why I teach what I teach: I want to share my own excitement about worthy but lesser-known artists; I want to bring new scholarship onto syllabi and into the classroom.

I also try to create space for students to bring in their own interests and enthusiasms—to meet the class "rubrics" halfway. Individualized research projects and student presentations are an important part of most of my classes. While this is hardly unique, I think it helps students better articulate and more coherently share their ideas and interests.

I think I do a pretty good job at getting students enthused about looking (and listening), at talking about art, and thinking about the many roles or positions an artist can occupy in the world.

I emphasize and prioritize duration and extended engagement with whatever subject is at hand.

I think I've also prioritized some preparation for students' lives after CalArts—foregrounding visiting professionals from different parts of the field, leading field trips to a variety of exhibition spaces from big museums to tiny artist-run galleries, focusing on noteworthy (and not necessarily famous) alumni as examples, etc.

I try to get students to get off the island on a regular basis, to engage the (art) world.

9. Which aspects of your teaching have been least effective?

I have a hard time getting quiet students to contribute on a regular basis.

I'm not very disciplined at keeping attendance or grading assignments.

345

Some back and forth with Stuart Dempster has been one of the joys of a hectic week. It's remarkable how quickly formality can give way to familiarity, and we've arrived at an amenable date and time for a mid-January conversation in Seattle, a day ahead of my Centrum residency. He asked me to shoot him a list of DLB recordings I have access to. Sheepishly, I sent him a picture I had taken of all (?) fourteen albums (three records, eleven CDs) arranged on the floor of my office. Stuart has described himself as a "sound gatherer," which is an enviable job description. Will he think I'm a *sound stalker*?

346

As my third of eight scheduled meetings at CalArts today, I had tea with Celia Hollander who has returned to the mothership to teach a class on acoustics. Among other topics, which slid more or less frictionlessly from one to the next, we discussed: our previous brief lives in the architecture field; the strange labyrinth that is the CalArts building, designed by Thornton Ladd, who eventually abandoned architecture to write a concordance of Jungian psychology; Jungian psychology, which to my surprise Celia had been studying, at least in some casual sense; autodidacticism and what it means to be "trained" in music or anything else. Celia mentioned an essay by Laurie Spiegel that discusses synth music as a new kind of folk (or possibly primitivism or populism). I asked her to send the essay, if she could. She mentioned it in relation to my daily Oliveros performance, which I told her about, and my assertion that I was performing *Sonic Mediation XXI* in an amateur or untrained way, which she gently pushed back on. Celia occasionally sat in on my Pauline Oliveros for Artists class while in the MFA Experimental Composition program. We had several independent meetings during that time, and then Celia invited me to join the composer Michael Pisaro, her faculty mentor, for her final review. It was the only time I've participated in a review in the School of Music. Tonight, after my eighth meeting and before heading home, I went to Whole Foods for groceries and ran into Michael Pisaro, who I hadn't seen at CalArts all semester. He was examining the underwhelming Brussels sprouts while I was picking through the wilted cilantro. I told him I had seen Celia earlier in the day; he mentioned her class on acoustics. We exchanged pleasantries and exit strategies for the fall semester.

347

I think I found the essay by Laurie Spiegel titled "Should Music-Making Be Reserved for an Elite?" and published in *Computer Music Journal* in 1998. Here's some of it:

It is important to place within a larger perspective the relatively recent (a few hundred years) mainly Indo-European sociomusical model in which music is assumed to consist of individual complete unique works actively created and performed by a small number of elite experts for a large passive listening audience.

The 20th century's addition of both recorded and broadcast media to the previously-dominant medium of the concert hall had skewed even further an already much distorted ratio of passive listeners to active music. But more recently, countertrends have shown up: Music is increasingly often being defined in terms of process instead of as specific sounds, in part due to how it is used, and as part of our century's paradigm shift from conceptualizing as entities and categories to thinking in terms systems and their components and dynamics. Recording has made all sound replicable to a degree far surpassing the only previous sound replication technique (written notated music). And a greatly expanded variety of technologies for sound capture, manipulation, and dissemination are cheaply available to all.

This is not new. It is a return. Long before concert halls, famous virtuosi, classic instrumental scores, publishers, recordings, and broadcasts—globally and for our entire human past—music was almost certainly something that most people did actively. In many cultures it still is, and much of this music is conceptually quite remote in purpose, concept, and form from the finite-length fixed-form single-author masterworks that many here view as both norm and ideal.

Though relatively low in numbers in our own highly specialized and data drenched culture, many non-musicians do still enjoy the process (per se) of making music themselves, whether alone or with family or friends, at home or in other grassroots venues such as churches, clubs or schools, whether the music is vocal, instrumental or electroacoustic, whether solo or group, established repertoire such as chamber or folk music or more open ended improvisational forms such as are found in jazz or rock.

Unfortunately, for various reasons—technical, educational, economic, physical, psychological, competitive, and other—far more people in our current culture would love to make music than are able to do so. At this stage, computers can and do help them to in ways not widely possible a mere two decades ago. Seeing this happen has been one of the greatest gratifications of my own work . . . To the extent that the making of music is a process restricted to very few, music's benefit, value, and pleasure for the human community overall are being very sadly curtailed.

348

What Are You Doing the Rest of Your Life?—a playlist:

Bill Evans
Morning Glory: The 1973 Concert at The Teatro Gran Rex, Buenos Aires
Resonance Records, 2022

Bill Dixon
November 1981
Soul Note, 1982

Dave Douglas
A Thousand Evenings
BMG Classics / RCA Victor, 2000

Eric Dolphy
Last Date
Limelight, 1965

349

Completion/Depletion—a playlist:

Sarah Davachi
Pale Bloom
W.25th, 2019

Harold Budd
Luxa
All Saints Records, 1996

350

Today I am trying to catch up, after four very full days at the end of a very full semester at CalArts. Part of catching up is also trying to assess what catching up even means at this exact moment. It was my last day on campus until September, unless I have a need or desire to return sooner. I tried to take all the books I could imagine needing. (These included John Dewey's *Art as Experience* because I've been wanting to spend some time thinking about Oliveros's contribution to pedagogy, and also Heidegger's *Basic Writings*—an absurd title, really—and Hegel's *The Essential Writings*. These last two seem ridiculously aspirational, but a pile of books is usually aspirational, to paraphrase Benjamin.) After a morning Zoom meeting, a first pass at tidying my office, and two loads of laundry, I am doing much of this work supine, on the couch. In addition to school and the holidays, there are myriad other deadlines and obligations that arrive this time of year—letters of recommendation, grant jurying, a long-delayed commissioned essay, preparation for tomorrow's public conversation with James Benning and Sharon Lockhart about their new book. My inbox is a hot mess—and has been a mess all semester. There are too many open tabs on my laptop, which I try to keep quarantined into separate windows for distinct categories or areas: general email and calendar and drive stuff; CalArts—including various docs and spreadsheets; travel planning; music; *New York Times* articles I want to read but don't have time for; and so on. (I bookmark endlessly, but keeping a tab open is a more optimistic form of purgatory.) The distinction between these areas invariably breaks down, and I have to reshuffle my tabs whenever things become total chaos. The music window usually includes the present Google Doc, which has been open in perpetuity most of the year, and a parallel Google Doc with my Deep Listening Band discography and related notes.

These are typically accompanied by some combination of tabs for Discogs, Bandcamp, various record companies, Wikipedia entries on composers or unfamiliar instruments, blogs, and other things that are part of my current and ongoing research. Today I am considering buying a decent audio recorder (inspired in part by a field recording Celia Hollander shared with me) that I can take to Centrum and am sorting through some affordable possibilities. A few days ago, I was shopping for giant clipboards (inspired by one my student Lisa Banta brought to the Routine Pleasures class) and contemplated making some drawings or maps during the residency. Maybe I'll do both, or neither. Each tab is a new labyrinth. For now, meaning the next two weeks, I'm trying to zero out. At the end of the year and at the end of this "performance in writing," I am hoping to close most of the tabs and windows, at least for an elongated moment.

351

What constitutes your musical universe?

As I get further and further into this meditation, and as I near its intended conclusion after one year, inevitable questions arise about my intentions for it. "Sounds like a book," people say when I tell them what I've been doing. "I'm not sure who would really want to read it," is my usual response, which is true. People claim to want to read it, which is flattering, and those people are called friends for a reason. I am writing for myself, first and foremost, but of course when one writes one tends to imagine an audience, however big or small. My daily log was written for an audience of exactly one—me. But this text is different: I will happily share it when it's done. I've already shared a few excerpts with a small number of people (and in my residency applications). But thinking too much about the outcome tends to change the nature of the meditation. It's the "observer effect." Even now, two weeks from the finish line, I am wondering about what I've accomplished, if that's even the right word. I'm also aware of how much I didn't attend to, and will likely not attend to, in relation to Pauline Oliveros specifically or my musical universe more expansively. But I think I've already come to terms with my inability to get it all said.

I've been reflecting on my one year (2013) without buying books, but also thinking about what came *after* that year-long act of self-deprivation. Most importantly, it was the beginning of my boycott of Amazon—which simply began as a side effect of not buying books. In any event, the ten-year anniversary of that boycott will nearly coincide with the conclusion of writing this text. (Is a boycott a performance? A "piece"? Thoughts inevitably turn to Lee Lozano, who turned the boycott into a fine art.) The reality is that my musical universe keeps evolving and expanding, much like the actual universe. What constitutes it changes every day. And presumably I change along with it, even if imperceptibly.

352

The Sound of Music.

353

When I tell people I'm writing this daily text, one of the frequent questions is, "Do you edit it?" The answer—and reality—is that I barely have time to *write* it, let alone read it, and therefore don't have time to go back to rework what I've written. And that's certainly true on a macro scale. I do sometimes go back into a thought that's relatively fresh or fix an error of fact (especially spelling or grammar or a date) when I encounter it, but the general shape of things stays unchanged in deference to the present. I suppose the text is an ongoing record of an Eternal Now, meted out in day-long units. Sometimes I use the "find" function to see when I wrote about (or listened to) someone or something. Returning to the depths of the text is a little like stepping into a labyrinth of my own making. And when I do step into that labyrinth, I hate certain things about it and myself when I read it. Lol. Meanwhile, in the fleeting present, I keep on listening and observing my musical universe. This morning I'm listening to *Archie Shepp—Bill Dixon Quartet* (1962), ramblin' through their cover of Ornette Coleman's "Peace," prompted by my recent purchase of a book called *Free Jazz Communism: Archie Shepp—Bill Dixon Quartet at the 8th World Festival of Youth and Students in Helsinki 1962*. (The appealing yellow and black cover of this third edition pairs so nicely with *The Cricket: Black Music in Evolution, 1968–69*, also featuring Shepp, whose *Three for a Quarter, One for a Dime* gets roughed up by Mwanafunzi Katibu. Ouch.) Now to find time to actually read the book.

354

Today my ears were restless. I wanted to listen to too many things all at once, but then couldn't commit to any of them. Or most. I went to Kenneth Hahn for some overdue exercise and to clear my head. I started listening to a handful of albums I've hearted on Spotify before finally settling on Andrew Hill's *Point of Departure* (1965), which I've heard dozens of times over the years but not for a long time. I listened to it all the way through as I ambled about the park. (Three miles and thirty flights is my usual goal, which usually coincides with the length of an LP). Later, when I got home, I listened to Nels Cline's Andrew Hill tribute album, *New Monastery*. The album cover features a close-up of Hill's right eye, covered by the lens of his sunglasses. It's a detail of the photo taken by Reid Miles that was originally used on the classic Blue Note cover of *Point of Departure*. I love how Cline gets at the rhythmic and timbral interplay of Hill's music through very different instrumentation—eschewing piano for guitar and accordion, for example. I also listened to it all the way through. In between there were a half-dozen partial listens and false starts, and much more after, flitting about from one to the next after a song or two, from Andrea Parkins to Cecil Taylor to Andrew Hill to Mal Waldron to *Lost in the Stars: The Music of Kurt Weill* (1985; another tribute album, very eclectic) then back to Mal Waldron, then to Mal Waldron with Steve Lacy, then to Steve Lacy with Mal Waldron to Anthony Braxton (*Six Monk's Compositions* [1987], also with Mal Waldron), which led to the discovery of an album of bagpipe performances of Braxton's music that I didn't have the patience for in the aftermath of dinner, then to John McCowen, and then to Kali Malone. Now I'm listening to Charlie Morrow. There's a thread that connects some of these, and there are surely some invisible threads too.

355

Focus on Scott LaFaro—a playlist:

Bill Evans
The Complete Village Vanguard Recordings, 1961
Riverside, 2005

Ornette Coleman Double Quartet
Free Jazz: A Collective Improvisation
Atlantic, 1961

356

It's been many years since I've listened to Ornette Coleman's *Free Jazz* (1961), a canonical work in the field described and immediately defined by its title and an album that was part of my own (free) jazz initiation over thirty years ago. I jumped pretty quickly from "jazz" into "free jazz"—according to my Spotify Wrapped I remain a fan of both kinds. Actually, freedom in jazz is relative, and even Coleman's *Free Jazz* has some preordained structure, some moments of collective congruence. It's also the first album-length improvisation, with one take split over two sides of the LP. (The eventual CD stitches them back together and is accompanied by the shorter "First Take," which was a preemptive attempt at "Free Jazz.") I can't really recall my first take on it, though I recall having the CD of it in college and was compelled by the Jackson Pollock painting on the cover. I was also a fan of Coleman's *The Shape of Jazz to Come* (1959), and might have sought that out because of John Zorn's cover of *Lonely Woman* (1959) on the first *Naked City* (1990) album. This all happened in a blip. I was first listening to Zorn's *Spy vs. Spy: The Music of Ornette Coleman* (1989) around the same time I was listening to Ornette Coleman. Both were revelations to me, circa 1992, even if I was receiving them ahistorically. Zorn was an important "gateway drug" for so many things in my musical universe, like Sonic Youth before him.

But yesterday I decided to listen to *Free Jazz* again because I've been on a Scott LaFaro tear—enjoying listening to him and the way he takes a concept or a texture or a technique and just totally burrows into it, simultaneously nudging the bass into the foreground. *Free Jazz* is one of the handful of Ornette Coleman albums that LaFaro plays on when he temporarily took over bass-playing duties for Charlie Haden in Coleman's quartet.

As a pure coincidence, yesterday was exactly the sixty-second anniversary of the recording date for *Free Jazz*. LaFaro died in a car accident the following year, on July 6, 1961, a few days after recording a monster set at the Village Vanguard as part of the Bills Evans Trio. *Free Jazz* features a double quartet, which is an odd configuration, in 1960 or today. One occasionally (I mean quite rarely) sees an octet, but the double quartet was a way of taking the quartet structure, which Coleman employed on his earlier records, and expanding it. Doubling it somehow increases the complexity exponentially. He also used the doubling to structure the stereo recording, with one quartet in each speaker channel. When I first listened to it, some of the names of the players—Eric Dolphy, Don Cherry, Freddie Hubbard among the eight—were still quite new to me, and I could not immediately identify their "signatures" the way I can now. Compared to the howling frenzy of John Coltrane's eleven-man—*undectet*!—collective improvisation *Ascension* (recorded in 1965) which I also first heard around the same time, *Free Jazz* is a relatively orderly, if still frenetic affair. (Freddie Hubbard appears on both album-length jams, fwiw.) It's kind of like a Noah's Ark concept, with two of everything. One of the things I love about *Free Jazz*, from the perspective of the present, is the way this double quartet structure induces dialogue between pairs of instrumentalists on a single instrument—Ed Blackwell and Billy Higgins on drums; Hubbard and Cherry on trumpet/pocket trumpet; LaFaro and Haden on bass. Coleman and Dolphy pair up differently: Dolphy's bass clarinet always stands out in a crowd (he takes the first solo here), as does Coleman's plastic alto saxophone, and the two are well matched as they explore their differences. I wonder if there was any consideration of Dolphy playing alto sax, too, which might have been weirder. But there's nothing remotely conventional about this double quartet beyond the idea of a quartet. The pairing of LaFaro (bowing, often) and Haden (plucking, mostly) is the most compelling thread for me, at least at the moment, and inaugurates a tradition in (free) jazz of using two bassists to open up space and expand time. Coleman took up this idea later, as did Cherry and Coltrane, and then Pharoah Sanders, Albert Ayler, Andrew Hill, Cecil Taylor, Muhal Richard Abrams, Roscoe Mitchell, Horace Tapscott . . . Several of Bill Dixon's records feature two bassists—*Thoughts* (recorded 1985) has three!

357

Two Bass Minimum—a playlist:

Andrew Hill
(Richard Davis and Eddie Khan, bass)
Smoke Stack
Blue Note, 1966

James Ilgenfritz
(James Ilgenfritz and Dominic Lash, contrabass)
Floorplan I
Infrequent Seams, 2014

Bill Dixon
(Peter Kowald, double bass; Mario Pavone and William Parker, bass)
Thoughts
Soul Note, 1987

Joëlle Leándre and William Parker
Live at Dunois
Leo Records, 2009

Roscoe Mitchell and the Note Factory
(William Parker, bass and percussion; Jaribu Shahid, bass)
This Dance Is for Steve McCall
Black Saint, 1993

Cecil Taylor
(Alan Silva and Henry Grimes, double bass)
Conquistador!
Blue Note, 1968 (recorded in 1966)

358

Today, just in the nick of time, I finished putting together a holiday playlist on Spotify. I had started it around Thanksgiving, then got busy with other things and set it aside. Sometimes it helps to come back to things. The playlist pulls together bits and pieces and odds and ends of music discovered or recovered over the course of the year. Old favorites include Sun Ra, Bitchin Bajas, Jeff Parker, Pharoah Sanders, Nels Cline . . . New finds include Cheri Knight ("Tips on Filmmaking" [2022]), Wei Zhongle (very 80s prog-sounding band, high on Adrian Belew, featuring my new favorite avant-garde contrabass clarinetist John McCowen), Mitski (the utterly catchy "Glide" from the intriguing A.I. film *After Yang* [2021]), Ethiopian keyboardist Hailu Mergia, Pamela Z (who I had heard of, but not yet heard), and the Oakland Elementary School Arkestra (which brings together Sun Ra and Terry Riley—finally!). This Arkestra's cover of Sun Ra's "We Travel the Space Ways" (1967) provides the title for the whole playlist. It's actually a lot of work putting these together, but fun, when there's time to play, explore, and edit. Inevitably I uncovered more than I could reasonably fit into this context. The playlist is exactly two hours and wildly eclectic—at least by my own standards. Unlike most of the playlists I've made for myself in the past year, many of which are documented in this text, the holiday playlist is about song form (nothing over about ten minutes), clever transitions, and a few kooky juxtapositions. There are even a few actual Christmas songs: Bill Evans's "Santa Claus is Coming to Town" from *Trio 64* (1964), and Low's "The Coming of Jah," an unexpected reggae song from the band's EP *Santa's Coming Over* (2008). The band has an earlier album titled *Christmas* (1999) which is excellent and melancholy.

R.I.P. Low drummer Mimi Parker, who died of ovarian cancer on November 5.

I haven't listened to Low much this past year, though they were in heavy rotation during the early part of COVID, their dirge-like songs a fitting soundtrack for the slow drip of my days. I hadn't heard "The Coming of Jah" until putting this together. It's almost humorous, which is unusual but not unprecedented for a band that once played a Misfits style version of their sublime "Over the Ocean." Some levity seemed in order here. This is the fourth year I've made a holiday playlist on Spotify—one each year I've subscribed to the platform—and it's fun to share them with a small group of friends and loved ones, but probably most fun for the person making it. Ho ho ho, he he he.

359

9 hours and 16 seconds

An email from Celia Hollander included links to two different websites. One features a nine-hour field recording of a twenty-mile walk she took across Los Angeles from Highland Park to Venice, made using binaural, in-ear microphones.

I have embarked on numerous walks of this nature and consider them as a type of musical act: the route is a score, with room for improvisation, the walk is the performance, whether solo or accompanied, and the recording is documentation.

I hope to listen to it at some point, not necessarily replicating the walk, but at least as a counterpoint to nine continuous hours of my own day. The other link details a sixteen-second recording found on a digital recorder, of her and a group of fellow musicians realizing they had neglected to capture a performance. Collectively, the group laughs at their loss.

I imagine us improvising for around twenty minutes, ending naturally at the perfect time and patiently letting all of the instruments ring out, only to discover that none of it was documented, all of it lost. As this dawns on us collectively, you can hear about four people total (including me) laugh. I don't have enough context to identify everyone, where we were, when this was or why we were together. I'll never know what music we didn't record.

Playing music with others is sharing a present moment: it's intimate, dynamic, and leaves no trace. Recording music is an act of listening towards the future: projecting how others will eavesdrop on the moment, a process of documentation. The producing process exists outside of time wherein the audio can be edited, processed, crafted, and rearranged—evading physical constraints of acoustics or human capacity . . .

The idea of "losing" music, for most of humanity, would have been inconceivable. The idea of owning music in the way we do today only lasts as long as the history of recording technology and the subsequent commodification of audio with records, tapes, and CDs. This has already been disrupted with digital audio, pirating, and now, the streaming economy—where people rent the opportunity to unburden themselves from ownership. NFTs are another cultural development, introducing a method for owning digital media, with the caveats of market speculation and the risk of losing your private digital keys. As a digital audio composer, it's refreshing to remember that music, and most things I value in life are inherently unownable, undocumentable, continuously changing, and ephemeral. Whatever music we made that day was in a shared moment of listening, collaboration, play, and presence.

Nothing was lost.

Perhaps inevitably, I read this account of loss and acceptance of that loss in relation to my own ongoing performance, using writing as a tool to record a year of contemplating my musical universe. Of course this tool is imperfect—most tools are situational and not perfect for every occasion. Writing, as a tool for recording or capturing, is so common, so pervasive, it often goes unseen, unexamined. For thousands of years, writing, along with drawing or painting, was the only means of recording human activity, beliefs, and aspirations. Before writing, there was oral transmission, storytelling. There were no other recording devices.

In my daily missives, I am acutely aware of how little I actually manage to capture about my musical universe but especially about the exponentially larger and practically unfathomable universe that contains it. I've said (written) it many times before: *essaying* means to try. And this essay (or collection of little essays) is an attempt to capture my own relationship to something inherently ephemeral, fleeting. There is pleasure—and struggle—in that constant attempting. In the end, *that* is perhaps all I can document.

360

At Kenneth Hahn today, attempting to walk off some of the excesses of the holiday, I listened to ELUCID's twenty-nine-minute DJ mix *BRB Gotta Charge My Toothbrush* (2022) for the second time in recent days. I had found it while putting together my Christmas playlist, but it was too long for that purpose. Nevertheless, it provided an enjoyable soundtrack for my walk. It's chock-full of samples: Art Ensemble of Chicago ("Certain Blacks"), Werner Herzog (*Herdsmen of the Sun* [1989]), June Tyson/Sun Ra, and Pharoah Sanders (the doubled bassline for "Love is Everywhere" [1974]) are among those I recognized. Toward the end, there's an intriguing passage of spoken text, slowed down and layered over some quietly chiming marimbas—or is that a mbira?

The following is a notation—a way of marking down things heard, felt, sensed.

There is said to be a universal hum. An imperceptible vibration producing a sound ten thousand times lower than can be registered by the human ear. It can be measured on the ocean's floor, but its source is not exactly known: perhaps the hush of oceanic waves, perhaps the turbulence in the atmosphere, or the far bluster of planetary storms.

It is not seen, it is not felt. Its repercussions are unknown.

There is said to be another hum. Some can hear it, indeed are hounded by it. For many years dismissed, its existence is now acknowledged. It is called the "worldwide hum" or "earth audio resonance."

I thought this could be Sun Ra, or perhaps Carl Sagan (both poets of the cosmos), but it didn't sound like the voice of either person, even as distorted as it is. When I got home, I searched the opening of the quote—thank you Google—which led me to an article by Sharifa Rhodes-Pitts titled "The Music of the Spheres" from *e-flux Journal* #105 (2019). I couldn't find a reading of it by the author, which makes me think what I heard on *BRB* was EUCLID's recitation, rather than a sample. But either way, I'm happy to discover the article. The hum Rhodes-Pitts describes moves decisively and somewhat unexpectedly along a chain of thought from the cosmos and a philosophical tussle between Aristotle and Pythagoras over the whether or not the heavens made a sound, to Hannah Arendt who reminds us of the astrological origins of the term "revolution," to the assassination of Black Panther Sam Napier, circulation manager of the party's newspaper, and two girls who were tied up and told to hum as Napier was shot dead. "There is a nonuniversal hum," remarks Rhodes-Pitts. "It is a hum that has gone unheard, barely noted."

What constitutes your musical universe?

361

Dear Stuart,

Hope the holiday season is treating you well.

Since our last exchange I've finalized my travel plans and should be landing at Sea-Tac a few hours ahead of our 3 p.m. meeting on January 17. And I've booked a room at the Silver Cloud near the university. Thank you for that recommendation.

I'm attaching a PDF of my working discography for Deep Listening Band, with all of the recordings I've located, as well as a list of precedents for DLB and adjacencies to DLB. Most of these include you and/or Pauline, though I've also added a few other things by Joe McPhee, Fritz Hauser, Alvin Curran, etc. that seem directly or obliquely relevant in relation to DLB. There are a few items that I've highlighted in yellow that I have yet to track down or would otherwise like to know more about. The only adjacent recording I haven't been able to track down is the Triple Point recording you're a guest on—*Sound Shadows* (Deep Listening, 2009)—which is on the list.

Of course we can talk about any and all of that when we get together, which I'm greatly looking forward to.

Best wishes for a happy new year.

Michael

362

All of these Sonic Meditations are intended to begin with observation of the breath cycle.

I am reminded of this prefatory note as I near the end of the year-long meditation. Have I been paying attention to my breath? Likely not enough. I have been aware of breathing from time to time, especially when losing breath while climbing hills at Kenneth Hahn (though most days I have not necessarily focused my attention on it, which is, well, if not a failure, then certainly an area for growth). What exactly have I learned this year? That learning is often re-learning, among other lessons. And that part of what makes these *Sonic Meditations* valuable is the way they focus and re-focus attention on the common, even involuntary stuff of every day. They also occasionally open up contemplation of the sublime. Like the hum described by Sharifa Rhodes-Pitts, a thought can be earthbound and cosmic at the same time.

The holiday period is strangely unlike the rest of the year. Along with the actual, sometimes festive, sometimes trying obligations of the holiday, it's a time for tying up loose ends while also preparing for what comes next. Unlike the yawning stretch of summer, which you won't find me complaining about given the privilege of my academic position, the holiday break is all-too-concise but nevertheless offers an opportunity for a reset of sorts. In fact, given its relationship to the Christian calendar, it practically demands a reset. Provided one isn't stuck in an airport or digging themselves out of a snowbank, one might even locate some time for reflection—or projection into the future. Ideally every day would be like this, with more time to attend to breathing, but of course it couldn't be.

Today I continued to catch up on answering long-neglected emails, many of which hit my inbox inopportunely in the final throes of the semester, and attended to other rainy-day tasks, a day after the rain. Tidying up my desktop (the digital one at least), organizing the folders on my Google Drive, backing up my files. Listening to music—Stuart Dempster and Bill Dixon—along with my neighbor playing basketball and the lumbering city trucks collecting the garbage, yard waste, and recyclables. Eating Christmas cookies from my mom. Putting books on shelves. And breathing.

BREATHE IN / BREATHE OUT

Begin by listening to your own breathing. Amplify the sound of your breath by placing palms of your hands over your ears. Listen as the sound of your breath turns into the sound of wind. It might be a gentle wind, a gusty wind, a howling wind, or some other kind of wind. Make the wind sounds audible.

Open your ears gradually as your wind sounds join others' wind sounds until one prevailing beneficial wind sounds. Afterwards, listen for the calm.

for Ingrid Sertso
January 1982

363

In recent days I've turned attention to several new performances of Oliveros compositions, including Oliveros and James Ilgenfritz's *Altamirage* (2022), which was released a few months ago. Oliveros appears on the album, in a MIDI accordion-contrabass duet with Ilgenfritz on the four numbered movements of the title composition. Or improvisation? I don't know exactly when this was recorded, but I'm guessing it was among the last things Oliveros recorded. She was prolific until death, and maybe even more since! (We apostles can only hope.) The other works included here are early Oliveros compositions, *Outline for Flute, Percussion, and String Bass* (1963) and *Trio for Trumpet, Accordion, and String Bass* (1961), performed by Ilgenfritz and the Anagram Ensemble. Both represent some of her earliest efforts to bring collective improvisation into composition, or rather, to use composition as a means for instigating and fostering collective improvisation while using staff notation and maintaining a foothold in her Western classical training. This impulse would manifest more radically in *Sonic Mediations* a decade later with her (near total) abandonment of staff notation in favor of text scores and various versions of the mandala diagram, both of which allow—and in fact demand—considerable interpretation from the performers or participants. It is perhaps ironic that these new interpretations of relatively formative compositions would implicate Oliveros in the stuffy, patriarchal conservatory she took considerable pains to unravel (pun acknowledged) and throw overboard. In her album notes, sound artist and Oliveros associate Maria Chavez refers to the new interpretations of early compositions as a "rare glimpse" into the composer—one with specific gender implications. "This collection of recordings serves as a rare marker in time, showing us the early stage of Pauline and her compositional practice, through the lens of contemporary performers who worked with her and knew her well," notes Chavez.

This direct link provides us with this rare glimpse into the early thought process of Pauline. One that I'm learning more about as I listen to her past works. I keep finding humor and this quiet edginess about these pieces, or as I like to refer to her, as a quiet revolutionary. But I also wonder if maybe it wasn't that she approached things quietly, but rather, was ignored due to being too contemporary in a time where long durational works were being made by individuals that identified as male.

Beyond that, is it possible to interpret these early Oliveros works without considering her more radical approaches to composition that would follow and her own accumulated archive of improvisational archive, solo and collectively? I can only imagine that Ilgenfritz, who jammed with the *maestra* herself, would probably acknowledge such a conceptual, temporal leap. Oliveros did eventually make works of longer duration, beginning with electronic works that followed in the 1960s, often lasting a half hour, which is the full length of a reel of magnetic tape. In the 1970s she made a series of solo performances for accordion and voice (her own) with an evolving title—*Rose Mountain Slow Runner*, *Horse Sings from Cloud*, *The Pathways of the Grandmothers*—with the last of these clocking an hour and a half. ("The title itself is a meditation.") While occupying space is often understood as a political tactic, occupying time is certainly every bit as meaningful.

364

I've been listening to Ghost Ensemble's *Mountain Air*, released on CD last year. They had performed it at REDCAT in March 2020, and I managed to miss it for reasons that I can't quite remember, though the timing was bad—the pandemic landed hard and shut down CalArts and much of Los Angeles a week later. I had a brief email exchange with ensemble leader and accordionist Ben Richter a few months earlier. In fall of 2019, Ben was teaching a class called The Art of Listening in the School of Music, while I was teaching Pauline Oliveros for Artists in the School of Art. We had a mutual student who introduced us by email. Ben mentioned the upcoming performance at REDCAT. And then I missed it.

Mountain Air is a performance and renaming of Oliveros's composition *Arctic Air (for Orchestra)*, composed for the Fairbanks Symphony Orchestra in 1992. "Depending on the geographical location the piece takes on different titles," Oliveros notes at the end of the composition, and subsequent versions were named *Desert Air*, *Tropical Air*, *Canadian Art*, and *Ohio Air*. The Ghost Ensemble version was recorded at (the appropriately named) Wind River in the Santa Cruz Mountains. (Not coincidentally, James Ilgenfritz is also a member of Ghost Ensemble.) The composition considers the relationship and difference between sounding just *inside* the ear and sounding just *outside* the ear. Air quality is a consideration. To say the least, a performance of the composition requires utmost and subtle attention. "Sound levels of the players are to be extremely soft—at threshold, almost sounding, almost not sounding," as the composer indicates. "All the options are performed at a very soft dynamic. This requires concentrated listening and musical bravery." As is so often the case with Oliveros, performance is directly tied to active listening and hence the perceptual-physiological reality of each performer, and then of course the way the ensemble assembles those realities collectively.

Alongside this collective, instrumental performance, Oliveros's text "The Earthworm Also Sings" "is to be read in a slow pace by a speaker/singer." The text, subtitled "A Composer's Guide to Deep Listening," is among my favorite of her writings. First delivered by Oliveros at the Glenn Gould Conference on Music and Technology on September 24, 1992, the text is dedicated to her friend John Cage who had died the month prior. I have assigned the text to my Foundation students and my recent Routine Pleasures class (but not to my Oliveros class for some reason—next time). It recalls moments of earlier texts, like "Some Sound Observations" and "Rags and Patches," that at moments intimate the sublime. This one does that throughout.

Rocks are her ears recording all of her events from the beginning
My earth body returns to hers
where the earthworm also sings
Inside/outside vibrations
My bones resonate
My stomach, spleen, liver, kidneys, lungs and heart resonate
These organs are sound
contain sound

The rhythms of my bodily life
encoded in the theater of my mother's womb
I listened from the beginning . . .

This should be required reading on every occasion of a new year—for me at least.

365

The last day of the year ends softly with the unusually quiet morning gently accompanied by the drizzle of rain, the occasional splash of cars racing down Arlington, and chirps of birds who arrange themselves like whole notes on the staff lines of electrical cable stretched over the backyard. The hum of the fridge holds it all in place. Leslie is sleeping in on her birthday.

The last day of this text ends softly, too, not with a bang—hopefully the rain dampens the usual holiday fireworks barrage tonight—but a whisper. I will try to resist any urge to conclude with some *grand summa* and let the accumulated pile of days speak for itself. I could continue with this document, but won't, in favor of other projects that need and deserve my time. (In many ways, this text has been a rehearsal for whatever comes next.)

The music won't stop, of course, and I will keep listening. Likewise, Pauline Oliveros's prompt will continue to resonate as I fluctuate between hazy awareness and sharp attention, moment by moment, day by day. I have put myself at the center of Oliveros's mandala for a year. Has it made me more attuned to the world or only to myself? Both probably. But perhaps it's too soon to answer. There are some questions that need to be answered without adherence to a clock or a calendar.

NOTES

This book was written from January 1 to December 31, 2022, as a daily performance of Pauline Oliveros's *Sonic Meditation XXI*. I understand the text as a kind of embodied scholarship on and around Oliveros—a daily record of listening, thinking, reading about music and sound, and of "being in the moment," with thoughts accruing and changing over time. Editing was kept to a minimum to maintain the feel of the text as written. A few additional corrections were made for this second edition. Some ideas are hunches, and I've tried to be clear about the difference between fact and speculation. For several works by Pauline Oliveros, the date and title provided are based on contradictory evidence. In some cases, the title of a work changed over time, and the date may refer to when the score was written, an initial performance, or the release of a recording or published score. I have tried to account for these differences and developments as much as possible. The citations that appear in the text and follow it have been added to provide the reader further information or clarity; in a few cases original sources have proven impossible to retrieve. Reference numbers that follow refer to the 365 sections of the book, rather than page numbers.

1 Pauline Oliveros, *Sonic Meditations* (Smith Publications, 1974). Oliveros wrote *Sonic Meditations I–XII* in 1971; *Sonic Meditations XIII–XXV* were written in 1973. Prior to the publication of the full set of 25 by Smith Publications, they were distributed by Oliveros in handwritten or typed and reproduced form to her friends and students, including the ♀ Ensemble, who performed many of these scores for the first time. Some appeared in various publications. Most references throughout refer to the *Sonic Meditations* as written and published in 1974.

2 Oliveros, *Sonic Meditations.*

3 Pauline Oliveros, "Some Sound Observations," *Source: Music of the Avant-Garde*, v. 3, 1968. Reprinted in *Software for the People: Collected Writings 1963–1980* (Smith Publications, 1984).

5 James Tenney's *Postal Pieces* are in fact a set of postcards, produced over time at the California Institute of the Arts, and collectively dated 1954–1971. Each "Scorecard" is numbered and gives an individual composition date. *Swell Piece #2* and *#3* are grouped on one card and dated March 1971. One additional postcard, *Scorecard No. 11: Valentine/Manifesto*, dated 1/8/73, was published posthumously, produced by Tashi Wada for the James Tenney Estate in February 2017.

Oliveros, *Sonic Meditations.*

6 Pauline Oliveros, *Deep Listening: A Composer's Sound Practice* (New York: Deep Listening Publications, 2005), xxiii.

8 Oliveros, *Sonic Meditations.*

9 Pauline Oliveros, "Rags and Patches" was originally written for the journal *Numus West* in 1974, but was not published. It appeared in Pauline Oliveros, *Software for the People: Collected Writings 1963–1980* (Smith Publications, 1984), 113.

14 Oliveros, "Rags and Patches," 113.

15 Oliveros, *Sonic Meditations.*

16 Christoph Cox, "Correspondences," in *steve roden. some reconstructions of wanderings and inner space* (Santa Barbara Contemporary Arts Forum, 2022). I mistakenly remembered Steve's green colored pencil lines as marker lines.

17 Richard Kostelanetz, *Conversing with John Cage* (New York City: Routledge, 2003), 70.

23 Album notes for Simone Forti, *Al Di Là* (Saltern, 2018). Compact disc with booklet.

25 Album notes for Golden Offence Orchestra, *Ode to Pauline Oliveros* (XKathedral, 2017). Cassette.

26 Oliveros, *Sonic Meditation V*.

29 Barbara T. Smith and Kate Johnson, *The inner landscape: performances by Barbara T. Smith*, 1969–2001 (West Hollywood: EZTV, 2004). Video.

Oliveros, *Horse Sings from Cloud* (1975).

31 Nancy Buchanan, email to the author, January 30, 2022.

32 Oliveros, *Horse Sings from Cloud*.

"All Music Can Be Understood: Music with Roots in the Aether," in Robert Ashley, *Outside of Time: Ideas about Music* (Cologne: Edition MusikTexte, 2009), 212.

33 Dialogue from Pauline Oliveros and Robert Ashley, "Unnatural Acts Between Consenting Adults" in Ashley's *Music with Roots in the Aether* (1975–1976), video. This dialogue is transcribed with a few changes in bookform in Ashley, *Music with Roots in the Aether: Interviews with and Essays about Seven American Composers* (Cologne: Edition MusikTexte, 2000)

35 Oliveros and Ashley, "Unnatural Acts Between Consenting Adults."

36 Elizabeth Freeman, *Time Binds: Queer Temporalities, Queer Histories* (Durham and London: Duke University Press, 2010), 62.

Dialogue from Oliveros and Ashley.

39 Linda Montano, *Art in Everyday Life* (Los Angeles: Astro Artz and Barrytown: Station Hill Press, 1981).

40 This text previously appeared on lindamarymontano.blogspot.com.

Oliveros, *Sonic Meditations*.

44 Rick Rojas, "Curling's Scottish Soundtrack, Delivered by Bagpipers from Beijing," *New York Times*, February 12, 2022. Accessed online May 23, 2024.

Tom Johnson, album notes for Yoshi Wada, *Off the Wall* (FMP, 1985).

75 Éliane Radigue interviewed by Stephen O'Malley, 2008. This text previously appeared on the Ideologic Organ blog.

87 From a prospectus for California Institute of the Arts, either 1968 or 1971, with design by David Mekelburg and Christian Hedberg.

88 Stuart Dempster interviewed by Jason M. Miller, *Tones & Drones*, December 14, 2020. *Tones & Drones* is a podcast is produced in the studios of 91.3 FM KVLU Public Radio, Beaumont, Texas.

90 Album notes for Hinnerick Bröskamp, *Vor der Flut (Hommage an einen Wasserspeicher)* (Eigelstein, 1985).

92 Pauline Oliveros, "Space for Listening and Listening to Space: A Musician's Way of 'Looking'," in *Sounding the Margins: Collected Writings 1992–2009* (Kingston, NY: Deep Listening Publications, 2010).

97 Stuart Dempster, *The Modern Trombone: A Definition of Its Idioms* (Berkeley: University of California Press, 1979), 1–2.

101 Dempster, *The Modern Trombone*, 73–74.

105 This version of the score comes from a postcard issued by Pauline Oliveros Publications, though a note on the card states "From Sonic Meditations." The closest equivalent in substance is *Sonic Meditation XVI*, though the idea also seems to follow from and simplify *Sonic Meditation III (Telepathic Improvisation).*

106 It turns out that the Big Jewish Band of San Diego was in fact bigger than two people. Ronald Robboy formed the New Kabbalah Blues Band in 1971—with Oliveros as Dr. Pinkus Olinsky on accordion—to accompany a poem by Jerome Rothenberg. New Kabbalah Blues Band later became A Big Jewish Band, and then The Big Jewish Band. The most thorough account I've found of this evolving band, albeit still brief, is found in Bill Perrine's *Alien Territory: Radical, Experimental, & Irrelevant Music in 1970s San Diego* (San Diego: Termite House, 2023).

108 Pauline Oliveros, album notes for *In Memorium, Mr. Whitney / St. George and the Dragon* (Mode, 1994). Compact disc.

113 Marcus J. Moore and Giovanni Russonello, "The Multifaceted Mingus," *New York Times*, April 21, 2022. Online edition.

119 Heidi Von Gunden, *The Music of Pauline Oliveros* (Metuchen and London: The Scarecrow Press, 1983), 26–28.

Pauline Oliveros, "Memoir of a Community Enterprise," in David W. Bernstein, ed., *The San Francisco Tape Music Center: 1960s Counterculture and the Avant-Garde* (Berkeley: University of California Press, 2008), 88.

120 Oliveros, "Memoir of a Community Enterprise," 109.

121 Oliveros, *Sonic Meditations.*

122 Von Gunden, *The Music of Pauline Oliveros*, 147.

Oliveros, "Memoir of a Community Enterprise," 80–81.

123 Tara Rodgers, *Pink Noises: Women on Electronic Music and Sound* (Durham: Duke University Press, 2010), 29.

124 Oliveros, "Memoir of a Community Enterprise," 91.

125 Rodgers, *Pink Noises*, 28.

128 Von Guden, *The Music of Pauline Oliveros*, 65.

Rodgers, *Pink Noises*, 29.

129 Dennis Overbye, "Hear the Weird Sounds of a Black Hole Singing," *New York Times*, May 7, 2022. Online edition.

137 Raven Chacon, program notes for *The Journey of the Horizontal People* (2016), for Kronos Quartet, *50 For The Future: The Kronos Learning Repertoire*. Accessed May 28, 2024. https://50ftf.kronosquartet.org/composers/raven-chacon

Anthony Huberman, "On Raven Chacon." Accessed May 28, 2024. https://wattis.org/browse-the-library/911/essays-about-exhibitions/i-on-raven-chacon-i-by-anthony-huberman

141 "Charlie Morrow, by Tim Page – A Portrait." Accessed May 28, 2024. https://www.charliemorrow.com/portrait.html

144 In 2024 LAXART relocated and changed its name to The Brick. Online announcement for Wadada Leo Smith's *Redkoral Quartet: Dark Lady of the Sonnets*. Accessed May 29, 2024. https://the-brick.org/smith-performance

155 Oliveros, *Horse Sings from Cloud.*

160 Bitchin Bajas, "Demeter," Bandcamp. https://bitchinbajas.bandcamp.com/track/demeter

161 Liner notes for Deep Listening Band & the Long String Instrument [Ellen Fullman], *Suspended Music* (1994). Compact disc.

165 Judith Hamann, *Peaks*, Bandcamp. https://blacktruffle.bandcamp.com/album/peaks

172 Aki Onda, *Nam June's Spirit Was Speaking to Me* (Recital, 2020).

174 Oliveros, "Memoir of a Community Enterprise," 80–81.

180 Pauline Oliveros and Panaiotis, "The Expanded Instrument System (EIS)," an undated, four-page paper in the Oliveros Papers at Olin Library, Mills College. Seemingly written in 1990 or 1991, this is perhaps the first conceptual and technical treatise on the EIS, with subsequent adaptions and revisions to the Expanded Instrument System and its conceptual framework by Oliveros and David Gamper, following the exit of Panaiotis from Deep Listening Band in 1993. Evidence suggests that some of the earliest uses of the EIS happened in DLB concert settings in 1990 and 1991, and later joined the band in the recording studio.

181 Rodgers, *Pink Noises*, 29.

182 This remains inconclusive, but I'm willing (and happy, at least on this count) to be proven wrong. I am unable to locate the interview I remember in which she describes her paternal heritage as Spanish. Composer and Oliveros friend Maria Chavez, who was born in Peru and raised in Texas, has referred to Oliveros as "Tejana." See Sara Skolnick, "A Tribute to Pauline Oliveros, the Queer Tejana who Revolutionized Experimental Music," *Remezcla*, December 6, 2016 (https://remezcla.com/features/music/pauline-oliveros-maria-chavez-interview/). David Evans Frantz, co-curator of *Axis Mundo*, made a similar case to me when I asked him about it, but I have yet to find any direct evidence of Oliveros's ethnicity either way. In any event, she did not foreground it, as she did with her identity as a feminist and, to a lesser extent, as a lesbian.

182 Pauline Oliveros, flyer for *Cheap Commissions* (1986).

187 The score for *Ten Grand Hosery* (1972) appears in Dempster, *The Modern Trombone*.

Dempster, *The Modern Trombone*, 70–71.

190 Press release for Dave Muller, *Sunset, Sunrise (repeat) b/w The Record Pavilion*, July 9–August 13, 2022, Blum & Poe, Los Angeles.

194 Derek Bailey, *Improvisation: Its Nature and Practice in Music* (Da Capo, 1993), 8, 83, 141.

195 Phil Freeman, interview with Derek Bailey, *Jazziz*, March 2002. (https://web.archive.org/web/20060113133830/http://www.bagatellen.com/archives/frontpage/001106.html) I first used this quote in an essay on Ricky Swallow in 2009.

Roland Barthes, *By Roland Barthes*, translated by Richard Howard (Farrar, Straus and Giroux, Inc., 1977), 136.

201 Pauline Oliveros, *Anthology of Text Scores*, edited by Samuel Golter and Lawton Hall (Deep Listening Publications, 2013), 60.

Montano, *Art in Everyday Life.*

207 Pauline Oliveros, Alien Bog/Beautiful Soop, Pogus Productions, 1997. Compact disc.

208 Unless otherwise cited, quotes in sections 208–217 are referenced from material in the Pauline Oliveros Papers, Special Collections, F. W. Olin Library, Mills College at Northeastern University, Oakland.

212 Oliveros, *Sonic Meditations.*

214 Pauline Oliveros, "Listening Questions," in *Deep Listening: A Composer's Sound Practice* (Deep Listening Publications, 2005), 55.

224 Susan Mahr, "Cicadas," University of Wisconsin-Madison, Wisconsin Horticulture, Division of Extention. https://hort.extension.wisc.edu/articles/cicadas/

230 Allie Townsend, "Top Ten Toys," *Time*, Dec. 9, 2010. https://content.time.com/time/specials/packages/article/0,28804,2035319_2034286_2034245,00.html

232 Willie Nelson, "Funny How Time Slips Away" (1962).

234 From the 1949 song "M.T.A" by Jacqueline Steiner and Bess Lomax Hawes, as a campaign anthem for Progressive candidate Walter A. O'Brien, a fare jumper who was running for mayor of Boston. The song, sometimes called "The MTA Song" or "Charlie on the MTA," was later popularized by the Kingston Trio. The 1949 "original" was adapted from Henry Clay Work's "The Ship That Never Returned" (1865) which later begat Vernon Dalhart's "Wreck of the Old 97" (1924). The "Bullshit!" refrain in the version I heard on my eighteenth birthday was apparently an audience amendment.

246 Deborah A. Miranda, "Teaching on Stolen Ground," in Jennifer Sinor and Rona Kaufman, eds., *Placing the Academy: Essays on Landscape, Work, and Identity* (Utah State University Press, 2007), 178.

263 https://www.discogs.com/genre/non-music

https://www.discogs.com/style/leftfield

265 *freq_wave (Pacific; Los Angeles)*, co-curated by CM von Hausswolff and Robert Takahashi Crouch, for Fulcrum Arts, at the Mt. Wilson Observatory, September 23–25, 2022.
See: https://www.fulcrumarts.org/freq_wave/

265 Von Hausswolff and Crouch, *freq_wave (Pacific; Los Angeles).*

265 Roland Barthes, *The Rustle of Language*, translated by Richard Howard, (Berkeley and Los Angeles: University of California Press, 1989), 77.

287 Vanessa Harding, exhibition notes for *Transpose? I Suppose!*, L-Shape Gallery, California Institute of the Arts, October 10–15, 2022.

294 Aquarium Drunkard, "Dead Notes #12: June 8,1974 – Oakland, CA," March 10, 2016. https://aquariumdrunkard.com/2016/03/10/dead-notes-12-june-81974-buffalo-ny/

302 Steve Roden's email signature, borrowed from Josef Albers.

306 *American Heritage Dictionary, Second College Edition* (Boston: Houghton Mifflin Company, 1985).

332 Alvin Curran and David W. Bernstein, "An American in Rome," *Alvin Curran: Live in Roma* (Die Schachtel, 2010).

333 Curran and Bernstein, "An American in Rome."

343 Rhys Chatham, *Two Gongs (1971)* (Table of the Elements, 2006). Compact disc.

359 See: https://www.fulcrumarts.org/sequencing/la-interval/ and https://interludedocs.com/2022/05/doc-063-celia-hollander/

362 Oliveros, *Anthology of Text Scores.*

363 Pauline Oliveros & James Ilgenfritz with Anagram Ensemble, *Altamirage* (Infrequent Seams, 2022).

364 Oliveros, *Anthology of Text Scores.*

CREDITS

Cover image: Photograph of Pauline Oliveros by Bruce Whyte, from Pauline Oliveros Papers, Special Collections, F. W. Olin Library, Mills College at Northeastern University, Oakland, California. Used by permission of The Pauline Oliveros Trust.

Sonic Meditations by Pauline Oliveros. Used by permission of Smith Publications, Sharon, Vermont.

Software for People: Collected Writings 1963–1980 by Pauline Oliveros. Used by permission of Smith Publications, Sharon, Vermont.

Cited materials from Pauline Oliveros Papers, Special Collections, F. W. Olin Library, Mills College at Northeastern University, Oakland, California. Used by permission of The Pauline Oliveros Trust.

ACKNOWLEDGEMENTS

To all of the musicians, artists, and composers—friends and strangers, living and dead—who became the unwitting subjects in these pages, I appreciate you and the work you do.

Of course no subject has received more attention in these pages than Pauline Oliveros, and I could have hardly imagined this one-year project and my continued investment in her work when she gave me an hour of her time at EMPAC in 2015. Hopefully this book serves as evidence of my gratitude for that meeting, as well as for her music, ideas, and writing—all gifts that keep on giving. And I am forever beholden to Vic Brooks, who arranged that seemingly chance encounter with nimble urgency, and to Jennifer West, who invited me to collaborate with her at EMPAC in the first place.

Stuart Dempster, who I met just a few weeks after writing this book, has responded to my many queries with just as many helpful replies, not to mention hospitality, good humor, and mischievous word play, bringing me ever closer to Pauline and Deep Listening Band.

When I met Pauline, she sent me to her papers in the Special Collections at the F. W. Olin Library at Mills College. I went, almost immediately, and Janice Braun and Rebecca Leung have been exceedingly helpful guides who facilitated my research there over multiple visits. My esteem also goes to IONE and The Pauline Oliveros Trust in sharing these materials.

I am also indebted to so much of the existing scholarship on Oliveros, especially the book-length studies of the composer by Heidi Von Gunden and Martha Mockus, as well as David W. Bernstein's important history of the Tape Music Center. These remain indispensable introductions to Oliveros's work and life.

And Discogs, where would I be without you?

My comrades in the Varese Group were among the earliest audience for my Oliveros soundings, and their welcoming response was heartening.

My colleagues and students at CalArts are a constant source of support and inspiration—especially the participants in my Pauline Oliveros for Artists seminar, who first performed *Sonic Meditation XXI* with me in Fall 2019, and those in my Routine Pleasures class in Fall 2022 whose fortnightly meetings overlapped with the writing of this text. I was also fortunate to receive the support of several faculty development grants from the CalArts Provost's Office that have helped further this research.

The Headlands Center for the Arts, Centrum, and Labyrinth all provided residency opportunities in the immediate wake of writing this book, allowing my work on Oliveros to continue and expand. Stay tuned!

I can't imagine a more thoughtful intermediary for this project than Vivian Sming, who took on the challenge of putting (my) *Sonic Meditation XXI* into the world, and in the process figured out how to transform an unwieldy four-hundred-page Google doc into such an appealing book. I am thankful to have her as my text's first and most attentive audience. Kathryn Cua has also been a careful proofreading accomplice. Thank you.

To my friend Greg Pilon, who always egged me on, I am so sad you aren't around to read this.

To my friend and occasional collaborator Steve Roden, your example inspired this project as much as anyone. You are missed.

To Leslie, who has listened along with me the most, I am truly grateful for your remarkable patience, enthusiasm, and boundless encouragement.

AUTHOR

Michael Ned Holte is a writer, curator, and faculty member in the art program at CalArts. His exhibition, *how we are in time and space: Nancy Buchanan, Marcia Hafif, Barbara T. Smith*, at the Armory Center for the Arts, Pasadena, was named by *Hyperallergic* as one of the top 50 exhibitions of 2022. His writing on art and culture has appeared in *Afterall*, *Artforum*, *East of Borneo*, *Poetry*, and *X-TRA*, among many other publications. He is the author of *Bog Time*, a pamphlet on the early tape and electronic music of Pauline Oliveros.

Michael Ned Holte
Good Listener: Meditations on Music and Pauline Oliveros

PROOFREADERS
Kathryn Cua
Vivian Sming

DESIGN
Sming Sming Books

PUBLISHER
Sming Sming Books
Saratoga, CA
smingsming.com

PRINTER
Bookmobile
Minneapolis, MN

Second Edition

ISBN 978-1-953189-22-6